Hewitt On Hockey....

Garden City Hockey Heroes

A HISTORY OF
JUNIOR A HOCKEY IN ST. CATHARINES, ONTARIO

Written by

John Charles Hewitt

Design & Layout

Sheila A. Kennedy

Copyright © 2008 Hewitt on Hockey ... Garden City Hockey Heroes

All rights reserved. No part of this publication may be reproduced in any form without the written permission from the publisher.

St. Catharines Museum photos and collections are the property of the St. Catharines Museum.

Printed in Canada

Lincoln Graphics Inc., St. Catharines, Ontario

ISBN #

978-0-9811415-0-3

Written by

John Charles Hewitt

Editors

John Hewitt and Candy Hillier

Design, Pre-Press Production

Sheila A. Kennedy

Kennedy Graphics, Thorold, Ontario, kennedygraphics@sympatico.ca

Published and Distributed by

Mr. BOOKS, St. Catharines, Ontario, www.mrbooks.ca

Cover Photo: 1954 Teepees Memorial Cup Victory, May 16, 1954

St. Catharines Museum - *Higgins Collection N 10,023*

THIS BOOK IS DEDICATED TO

Jack Gatecliff

the former *St. Catharines Standard* sports editor who was with the paper from 1947 to 2000.

Photo courtesy of Alice Gatecliff

In 1995 Jack was the only recipient of the Elmer Ferguson Award. This led to his induction into the print journalists' section of the Hockey Hall of Fame.

One year later, Garden City Arena in St. Catharines was renamed in Gatecliff's honour. It became part of the Jack Gatecliff/Rex Stimers Garden City Arena Complex.

In the fall of 2001, Arden Phair, Curator of Collections at the St. Catharines Museum, asked me if I would help to index Jack's *Through the Sports Gate* columns, which he had saved in several scrapbooks and donated to the Museum before he passed away on September 5, 2000.

After going through his estimated 10,000 columns a few times, I have really come to appreciate Jack's contributions to the local and regional sports scene.

His writings also made me realize that there was no organized history of Junior A hockey in St. Catharines and no team here since 1977. I thought it was something that had to be written before this part of St. Catharines sports history faded out of sight.

Jack Gatecliff's coverage of the Junior A Falcons, Teepees, Black Hawks, and Fincups, provided the foundation upon which this book was written. It wouldn't have been possible without him.

SPONSORS

This project was made possible in part by the generous financial support of the following sponsors:

BOB GALE
GALES GAS BARS LIMITED

Brox Company Limited

TRW Canada Limited

Molson Canada

Janine Muller

George Darte Funeral Chapel Inc.

Brian Cullen Motors

Tom and Elizabeth Rankin

Bob Cornelius

Dairy Queen, 415 Merritt St., St. Catharines

Al McDonough

TABLE OF CONTENTS

Dedication 3

Sponsors 4

Foreword *by Marcel Dionne* 7

Introduction 9

St. Catharines Junior A Hockey Memorabilia Photos 10

Rudy Pilous *The Driving Force Behind Junior Hockey In The Garden City* 13

The St. Catharines Falcons 1943-1947

    Junior Hockey Finds A Home In The Garden City 15

    1943-1944 The Falcons Get Off The Ground 17

    1944-1945 Doug McMurdy Wins First Red Tilson Trophy 21

    1945-1946 Laurie Peterson Leads Falcons In Scoring For Second Straight Year 25

Jack Gatecliff 28

    1946-1947 Falcons Struggle On And Off The Ice In Last Year 29

Vic Teal 32

George Stauffer *The Saviour Of Junior Hockey In St. Catharines* 33

The St. Catharines Teepees 1947-1962 35

    1947-1948 The Teepees Put St. Catharines On The Hockey Map 36

Rex Stimers 42

Tommy Garriock 43

    1948-1949 Teepees Set New Attendance Records 45

    1949-1950 Stauffer Cuts Ties With Boston Bruins 49

    1950-1951 Rudy Pilous New Teepees Bench Boss 53

    1951-1952 Teepees Reach OHA Finals For First Time In Nine Years 59

    1952-1953 The Teepees Build For The Future 63

    1953-1954 The Road To The Memorial Cup 67

Terry O'Malley 71

    1954-1955 Hank Ciesla Ends Junior A Career With The Red Tilson Trophy 75

    1955-1956 Bobby Hull Joins The Teepees 79

    1956-1957 Rudy Pilous Signs 16-Year-Old Stan Mikita 83

    1957-1958 Teepees Finish First For The Fourth Time In Five Years 89

    1958-1959 Mikita Wins Scoring Title And Red Tilson Trophy 95

    1959-1960 Max Kaminsky leads Teepees To A Second Memorial Cup 99

    1960-1961 Former NHLer Gus Bodnar Steps Behind The Teepees Bench 105

    1961-1962 The Teepees Last Season 109

The St. Catharines Black Hawks 1962-1976 115

Fred Muller *The Second Man To Save Junior Hockey in St. Catharines* 116

    1962-1963 First Black Hawks Team Misses The Playoffs 119

    1963-1964 Hawks Top Scorer Fred Stanfield Wins The Max Kaminsky Trophy 123

TABLE OF CONTENTS

1964-1965 Fred Muller – The Hawks New President 127
1965-1966 Brenchley Out And O'Flaherty In As Hawks Coach 131
1966-1967 Goalie Peter McDuffe Is League's Top Netminder 137
1967-1968 Fred Muller Replaces Ken Campbell as GM 141
1968-1969 New Coach Brian Shaw Lays Down The Law 145
1969-1970 The Black Hawks Get Bigger And Stronger 151
1970-1971 Hawks Win Third OHA Title 155
1971-1972 Goaltending Problems And Injuries Weaken The Hawks 161
1972-1973 Hap Emms Buys The Black Hawks 165
1973-1974 Hawks Capture Fourth OHA Title 167
Hap Emms – *He Knew How To Win* 172
1974-1975 St. Catharines Fans Lose Interest In The Black Hawks 173
1975-1976 The Hawks Fly Away 177
Archie Katzman 182

The St. Catharines Fincups 1976-1977
1976-1977 Hamilton Fincups Find A Home In St. Catharines 183

Epilogue 192
Niagara IceDogs 194
Memorial Cup Championship – 50th Anniversary Celebration & Homecoming Photos 196
Honour Roll 201

Appendix
Ontario Hockey League - OHL 202
Junior A Trophies 203
St. Catharines Junior A Hockey
Records and Statistics 205
Firsts and Lasts 211
Trivia 215

Errors and Omissions 219
Thank You 220
Index 222

FOREWORD

Coming from Drummondville, Quebec, to St. Catharines at 17 years of age in 1968 was the ultimate move for me. Playing for the St. Catharines Black Hawks for three years prepared me for not only my NHL career, but for my life as well.

Living in a new city and experiencing a new culture had a huge impact upon my life. I spoke very little English when I arrived and learned the language by watching television and reading papers. Attending a French school in Welland really helped me. I came into contact with many different ethnic groups in the Niagara region and I benefited from the experience. I made friendships that have lasted a lifetime.

When I first stepped into Garden City Arena in the fall of 1968, I saw the large framed pictures of former St. Catharines Teepees and Black Hawks who had made it to the NHL. I was in awe of these players whom I had seen playing on television: Brian Cullen, Stan Mikita, Bobby Hull, Pierre Pilote, Phil Esposito, and many others. These men were my heroes. I didn't know them then, but I wish I had. What stories they would have been able to tell.

I soon realized there was a lot of history here and I paid attention, especially to tales about characters like legendary sports broadcaster Rex Stimers who had died two years before I joined the team. Were all those stories about Rex true? Unbelievable!

One of the men I got to know and respect was *St. Catharines Standard* sports editor Jack Gatecliff. Jack meant so much to all of us. He kept in touch with us even after we left the city, and he let his readers know what we were doing. We all miss Jack.

And who could forget CKTB sports announcer Tommy Garriock? I remember driving home one night listening to Tommy giving the exact – and I mean exact – time of each goal that was scored in each of his hockey game summaries. He was amazing.

Playing for the Black Hawks from 1968 to 1971 was a very lucky time for me. I had the support and encouragement of scout John Choyce, Chicago Black Hawk director of player personnel Ken Campbell, coaches Brian Shaw and Frank Milne, and of course, team owner Fred Muller who brought me to the Garden City. Fred was the key guy for all of us. He treated us so well.

In each of the three years I played in St. Catharines we had strong teams that stuck together through good and bad times. We never had trouble with anybody. There was never a problem in the dressing room. We had a lot of guys who went on to play in the NHL and other pro leagues. Some had better careers than others, but

FOREWORD

nevertheless they went up. After I made it to the NHL, I played against many of my ex-teammates like Dick Redmond, Dennis O'Brien, Bobby Sheehan, Dave Burrows, Rick Dudley, and Bob MacMillan.

When I first played in the OHA Junior A League, there were some critics who said I was too small to succeed, but I proved they were wrong. I scored 100 points in my rookie year and finished second to Rejean Houle for the OHA scoring championship, which I won in the next two seasons. One of the highlights of my career was playing against great junior players who became NHL stars like Gilbert Perreault, Darryl Sittler, Billy Harris, Steve Shutt, and Guy Lafleur.

In my rookie year, we met the Montreal Junior Canadiens in the 1969 OHA finals. I'll never forget the thrill of playing in front of 20,000 fans in the Montreal Forum. Montreal captured the OHA title that spring, but our day would come two years later.

In 1971 we eliminated the Canadiens in the second round of the playoffs, and went on to eliminate the Toronto Marlies in four straight games to win the league title. As captain, I was fortunate to be presented with the J. Ross Robertson Cup. That's what it was all about!

The dark side of my junior career was the Eastern Canada final series with the Quebec Remparts after we won the OHA championship. You look back and it left us with a black eye. I know Fred Muller was trying to protect the welfare of everybody, but at the end of the day, if you lose, you lose. Being from Quebec, I was under terrific pressure in that series and so was Pierre Guite.

The ultimate game to me was game five in Toronto and we beat the Remparts 6-3, narrowing their series lead to 3-2 in the best-of-seven-series. We could see that we were there. We just got caught off guard in Quebec and were not prepared. The Remparts goalie Michel Deguise was outstanding.

Looking back now, I realize that playing junior hockey in St. Catharines represented the best years of my life. Those were the fun days. We were innocent young men, playing without the pressure we would soon experience when we entered the world of professional hockey.

Opening up Garden City Hockey Heroes written by John Hewitt, reading the stories, and looking at the hundreds of photos, has brought back a flood of memories for me. I'm sure it will do the same thing for everyone who has ever had the privilege of playing Junior A hockey in St. Catharines. It's a book of interest for everybody, especially hockey fans who saw any of the junior teams in action from the Falcons in 1943 to the Fincups in 1977.

"J'espère que vous aimerer se livre."

Marcel Dionne
Niagara Falls, Ontario

INTRODUCTION

St. Catharines Museum - *Dan Meighan Collection 1987.171.5*

In 1938 the city of St. Catharines had no covered hockey arena and no artifical ice surface. Local hockey players often traveled to Grimsby or Niagara Falls to play. Thorold built an arena in 1936, but it had natural ice.

Everything changed on December 20, 1938. That's when the new Garden City Arena was opened to the public. Built for around $105,000, the building had gone over budget leaving no money to pay for the seats. To raise the revenue, Conn Smythe, owner-manager of the Toronto Maple Leafs, brought his team to the new arena and played one period against each of the three area senior teams from St. Catharines, Niagara Falls, and Port Colborne. The game attracted 3,500 fans. Adults paid a dollar and children got in for fifty cents, taking their choice of seats.

Winnipeg native Rudy Pilous was one of the players on the St. Catharines senior team, the Chiefs, which played against the Toronto Maple Leafs. Five years later Pilous and his friend Jay MacDonald introduced junior A hockey to the Garden City, and over the next 34 years the Falcons, then the Teepees, Black Hawks, and finally the Fincups, dominated the local sports scene.

This is the story of 34 years of junior A hockey in the Garden City. It's a glimpse into the highs and lows of each of those teams with regular-season, playoff and attendance records.

As you flip through the pages, you will be introduced – or for many former St. Catharines Junior A fans – reintroduced to the players, coaches, executives, trainers and media personalities associated with those clubs. Throughout the book there are bios for each of the 124 St. Catharines Junior A players who made it to the NHL, as well as for many other noted personalities.

The time has come to recognize the teams and individuals who put St. Catharines on the hockey map and left many of us with memories which will last a lifetime.

ST. CATHARINES JUNIOR A HOCKEY MEMORABILIA

St. Catharines Teepees 1953-54 Memorial Cup Champions
St. Catharines Museum – McSloy Estate Collection 1971.682

St. Catharines Teepees jacket worn by Marv Edwards
St. Catharines Museum – Marv Edwards Collection 2003.172.6

Teepee letterhead used to write notes inserted into home game programs
St. Catharines Museum – Monica Smith Collection 1998.79

Crest from 1959-60 Teepees sweater
St. Catharines Museum Collection – Bill Argent Collection 2004.95.1

Scale model of an Indian teepee made of birch bark
St. Catharines Museum – Marv Edwards Collection 2003.172

10

ST. CATHARINES JUNIOR A HOCKEY MEMORABILIA

St. Catharines Black Hawk Crest - Courtesy of Frank Milne

St. Catharines Black Hawks jacket worn by George Hulme
St. Catharines Museum
— George Hulme Collection 2004.72.1

1965-66 program
St. Catharines Museum
— Bonnie Saveall Collection 2004.88.6

1969-70 program
St. Catharines Museum

Skates worn by ex-Teepee Frank Martin with the Chicago Black Hawks
St. Catharines Museum — Frank Martin Collection 1997.82

Goalie stick used by former Teepee Marv Edwards with the California Golden Seals
St. Catharines Museum — Marv Edwards Collection 2003.179.4

Fedora worn by ex-Teepee Pat Kelly in the 1950s
St. Catharines Museum — Pat Kelly Collection 2005.95

RUDY PILOUS

THE DRIVING FORCE BEHIND JUNIOR HOCKEY IN THE GARDEN CITY

St. Catharines Standard photo

Rudy Pilous and his wife Margaret with children RoseMarie (left) and Mary Lou pose with the Memorial Cup in 1954.

St. Catharines Museum - Jack Higgins Ref. File, 2004

For a boy who left school in Winnipeg in the ninth grade and started his work career exercising horses for the Alf Tarn and Sleepy Armstrong Stables, Winnipeg native Rudy Pilous had quite a hockey career.

Pilous' involvement with hockey began as a junior A player in Portage La Prairie and then in his hometown of Winnipeg, Manitoba. He moved on to senior A in Selkirk, Manitoba and Nelson, British Columbia, before he spent 1936-37 playing with the Richmond Hawks in England. In 1937 he joined the New York Rovers, a New York Rangers farm club, but by then he realized he wasn't going to make it to the NHL. "You're not a quick enough skater," Rovers coach Frank Boucher told him.

In 1938 he found an opportunity to play senior A hockey in St. Catharines, Ontario – he didn't even know where the city was located – and it changed his life. He in turn changed the sports scene in the Garden City, like it had never been changed before.

The 6-foot, 172-pound left winger played three seasons for the Senior A St. Catharines Chiefs (renamed Saints in 1939) and settled down in the city, working at McKinnon Industries, where he eventually became a foreman of receiving.

In 1943, Pilous and his friend Jay MacDonald founded the St. Catharines Falcons, the first Junior A hockey club in the city. Pilous talked six businessmen into financing the team; then he recruited the players and coached the team in its inaugural season.

After two successful years he turned the coaching duties over to Red Reynolds, but returned behind the bench in January, 1946, when it looked like the team wouldn't make the playoffs. The team did – after he took over.

In the summer of 1946, he quit his job and joined the Buffalo Bisons, acting as a scout and becoming involved with sales and promotions for the organization. From 1947 to 1950 he managed the Bisons minor league team in Houston, and then coached in San Diego and Louisville, winning championships with Houston in 1948 and San Diego in 1949. Former Montreal Canadiens NHL star and coach, Toe Blake, was behind the Houston bench in 1947-48.

In 1950 George Stauffer, president/GM of Thompson Products in St. Catharines, persuaded Pilous to return to the Garden City and become coach/manager of the Junior A team now renamed the Teepees. His appointment marked the beginning of the golden era of hockey in St. Catharines. For 7½ seasons, Pilous was the most successful coach in the OHA Junior A League. From 1950 to 1959 the Teepees finished first five times, capturing a Memorial Cup in 1954. He was selected by the *Hockey News* as hockey's outstanding executive for 1955-56. It was the first time an executive had been selected from amateur hockey.

"He was the greatest motivator I ever played for," said ex-Teepee goalie, Norm Defelice.

On January 1, 1958, he became the bench boss of the Chicago Black Hawks*, signing for $8,000, less than he was making with the Teepees. He remained the GM of the Teepees who won a second Memorial Cup in 1960. In 1959 he had purchased the club from Thompson Products

Rudy Pilous in a New York Rovers uniform in the 1937-38 season

Ernie Fitzsimmons Collection

President George Stauffer for $1, but he gave up ownership in 1961.

In 1961 the Winnipeg native coached the Hawks to their first Stanley Cup in 23 years. Despite his success he was fired in 1963 in a letter with no explanation. The job of coaching in Chicago was a cinch, he told his successor Billy Reay: "All you have to do is win."

He spent the next two years coaching Toronto Maple Leafs farm clubs in the Western Hockey League, first with Denver, the 1964 league champions, and then in Victoria, British Columbia.

"I think the other [NHL] teams must have blackballed him because he was a great coach," former Teepees owner George Stauffer told ex-*St. Catharines Standard* sports editor Jack Gatecliff, in 1997.

Following their successful three-night stand with the McKinnon entertainers in presenting the 4th annual minstrel and variety show, the lads of department 42 presented their talented colleagues, Ollie Purdy and Rudy Pilous, with beautiful floral bouquets of potted dandelions. Rudy and Ollie, being colour blind, thought they were orchids. As yet, nobody has divulged this fact to them.

Photo courtesy of McKinnon Doings April, 1943

In 1965-66 after a disagreement with Maple Leafs management, he made a one-year return to junior hockey as coach/manager of the Hamilton Red Wings.

In 1966 he signed a four-year deal to put together an NHL expansion team in Oakland, California, but before the team made its debut, he was squeezed out of the organization. He was paid the balance of his contract, but he never got another chance in the NHL, despite his winning record.

After spending 1968 to 1970 as coach/GM with the WHL Denver Spurs, he sold his St. Catharines home and moved to Brandon, Manitoba, where he became part owner, manager and coach of the Western Junior Hockey League Brandon Wheat Kings. That lasted until 1974 when he was hired by the WHA Winnipeg Jets, coached at that time by Pilous' former Chicago Black Hawks star, Bobby Hull. Pilous was GM when the Jets won Avco Cups in 1976 and 1978.

"That was the most entertaining pro team I was ever connected with," Pilous told Gatecliff in 1985.

After losing his GM job to former NHL tough-guy John Ferguson in 1979, Pilous scouted for the Detroit Red Wings for one year and then the Los Angeles Kings from 1980 to 1982. In 1982, the Toronto Maple Leafs hired him as director of operations for their AHL farm club, the St. Catharines Saints. When the Saints left the city in 1986 Pilous' hockey career was over, but Toronto Maple Leafs owner, Harold Ballard, made him manager of his Hamilton Tiger-Cats concession business.

Pilous enjoyed success off the ice as well. During his career he became a popular after-dinner speaker, entertaining audiences with his ethnic stories and skillful mimicking of different dialects. He started to use dialects when he mimicked co-workers while working as a railroad water boy in Winnipeg and added to his repetoire when he played hockey in England.

He was elected to the Hockey Hall of Fame and the Manitoba Hockey Hall of Fame in 1985 and the St. Catharines Sports Hall of Fame in 1990.

Pilous, who claimed he had coached at least 75 players to the NHL, died at his St. Catharines home at age 80 in December, 1994. Today he is survived by daughters RoseMarie and Mary Lou and two grandsons.

Player, coach, scout, manager and owner, Rudy Pilous did it all. ■

* *The Chicago Black Hawks were re-named the Chicago Blackhawks in 1986.*

Plaque hanging in the Manitoba Hockey Hall of Fame

Photo courtesy A.Phair

FALCONS 1943-1947

JUNIOR HOCKEY FINDS A HOME IN THE GARDEN CITY
THE ST. CATHARINES FALCONS 1943 - 1947

It was just another hockey game in May of 1943. At least that's what Winnipeg native Rudy Pilous thought when his friend Paul Mundrick invited him to attend a Memorial Cup hockey game in Maple Leaf Gardens. Mundrick, a former teammate of Pilous with the St. Catharines Senior A Saints, wanted to see his brother George play for the Winnipeg Rangers, who were battling Oshawa Generals for junior hockey's most coveted trophy.

When Pilous and his friend Jay MacDonald sat down to watch the game, it wasn't the action on the ice that caught their attention. It was the size of the crowd in the Gardens. The series averaged more than 12,000 fans a game and 14,485 watched Winnipeg win the Memorial Cup in game six.

"When I saw that huge crowd I thought that St. Catharines...a real sports city...was missing a real bet by not getting in on this big time amateur league," Pilous told *St. Catharines Standard* sports editor Jack Gatecliff in 1955.

By the time 28 year-old Pilous and MacDonald returned home, they had formulated a plan to bring junior A hockey to St. Catharines. Pilous would have been coach/general manager, but Ted Graves actually became the manager because of an OHA rule at the time. MacDonald would become the team's secretary.

Pilous asked W. A. Hewitt, then Secretary of the OHA, if a junior A franchise for St. Catharines would be approved. "Yes, just as long as the team is a respectable group of players," the father of broadcaster Foster Hewitt said.

What they needed next were money and players. Pilous knew where he could get the money. "I came back home really enthused and in the next week talked the late Pete Grammar, Ted and Os Graves, Jack Leach, Cal Wilson, and Tom Heit into tossing $500 each into the pot to get the show on the road," Pilous said.

Courtesy of Blake Bellinger

Pilous also knew exactly where to go to get the players.

"... With the magnificent sum of $200 and a return ticket, I hit out for the West. Have to admit that I got my money's worth too... Doug McMurdy, Harvey Jessiman, Laurie Peterson, Bing Juckes, and Stan Warecki from the Winnipeg district, and Dutch Delmonte from Timmins. That was the heart of the first club....I only had to guarantee them $10 a week."

There was, however, a major problem facing Pilous after he paid the $10 franchise fee to the Ontario Hockey Association. He had signed seven players outside the OHA, but the league allowed only two branch-to-branch transfers. Never at a loss for words, Pilous did some fast talking at the OHA meeting and told the other junior teams that his club had to have the imports to complete the season. The president of the OHA at that time was Port Colborne native Francis W. (Dinty) Moore. He backed Pilous and said the Falcons needed all the help they could get. With the season about to start in a few weeks, Pilous got his way.

To succeed with a junior A club in St. Catharines, Pilous was facing several challenges. In 1943 World War II was still on; many hockey players had joined the Canadian Armed Forces and others expected to be conscripted at any time. In addition, Pilous would have to convince St. Catharines fans that they should follow the junior club, despite the fact that the local Saints Senior A team was drawing capacity crowds to Garden City Arena, which was considered to be second only to Maple Leaf Gardens.

To begin operations, the junior team needed a name. A contest, which was open to children under 16 years of age, was advertised in the *St. Catharines Standard* and then-*Standard* sports editor Clayton Browne outlined the criteria for the new name: "The ultimate finding will be considered for its brevity, punch and meaning."

The winner of the contest was nine-year-old Jimmy Stirrett of Port Dalhousie. "I was interested in birds," Stirrett, a real estate agent, said 60 years

St. Catharines Standard photo

PAUL MUNDRICK

Like his friend Rudy Pilous, Winnipeg native Paul Mundrick came to the Garden City to play senior A hockey. He turned pro with the AHL Buffalo Bisons in 1944 and spent four seasons in the Queen City. The right winger also saw action in four other leagues before his career ended in 1950. He passed away in Kenmore, New York, in 1987.

JAY MacDONALD

St. Catharines Standard photo

James Augustyn MacDonald was no stranger to sport in the Garden City by 1943. In 1933 he helped bring the first juvenile box lacrosse title to St. Catharines. In 1938 he won a Mann Cup ring as property man for the St. Cath-arines Athletics and after his playing career was over, he was a lacrosse referee.

When Rudy Pilous and he formed the first junior A team in the city, MacDonald was the club's secretary and retained that position for several years. While with the Falcons, MacDonald accepted a job as publicity director for the AHL Buffalo Bisons and that led to a similar position with the Buffalo Bills football team.

In 1949 he was working at the Stamford racetrack and still had time to organize and manage the St. Catharines Stags, one of the top baseball teams in Niagara.

By 1951 he was made a director and secretary-treasurer for the Stamford track.

After the Ontario Jockey Club bought the racetrack, he managed the Niagara Falls Arena during the winter. In the 1960s he worked in the money room for the Ontario Jockey Club's three racetracks.

When the Falcons became the Teepees, he had an office under the stands in Garden City Arena named the "dugout" where he entertained the media and visiting hockey personalities.

He passed away in St. Catharines in November, 1985.

FALCONS 1943-1947

FALCONS OWNERS

St. Catharines Museum
- Gatecliff Collection
1998.20

E.J. (Ted) Graves

In addition to being one of the six original owners of the St. Catharines Falcons, Ted Graves was the club's vice-president and became the manager to fill OHA requirements in 1943. He was with the insurance firm of Kernahan and Graves for 25 years before he went into the hotel business in Thorold in 1958.

On September 14, 1966, the 58-year-old businessman suffered a heart attack and died in a traffic accident on Highway 406. His death came three years to the day after his brother Oswin drowned in Lake Ontario. Thirty years earlier, his father had died in a car crash near Buffalo, New York.

St. Catharines Standard
photo

Oswin T. Graves

St. Catharines native Os Graves was the president and general manager of Kernahan and Graves. He was a member of the St. Catharines Yacht Club, the Lions Club, and the local Canadian Legion. On September 14, 1963, the 60-year-old drowned when he fell from his cabin cruiser while apparently trying to lower the anchor into Lake Ontario.

St. Catharines Standard
photo

Jack Leach

Jack Leach was the secretary-treasurer of the first junior A team in the Garden City. In his younger days, he was an excellent golfer and badminton player. He was very involved in community activities outside sport such as the Rotary Club, General Hospital Board, and the Red Cross. For 35 years, he was the secretary-treasurer of Thompson Products. He passed away in October, 1976.

Courtesy of Marcella Heit

Thomas Heit

Tommy Heit was born in Toronto, but spent some of his youth in Chicago. He spent many hours on the road transporting players to out-of-town games. For a time, he owned a retail business in the city before selling stocks and bonds for local brokerage houses. "He was a good man and he had a wonderful sense of humour," Marcella, his wife, said in July, 2004. "He was a true giver."

Heit passed away in 1985 at age 69.

Courtesy of Nick Grammar

Pete Grammar

Pete Grammar was born in Greece and came to Hamilton, Ontario, when he was 11 years old. After working in a Hamilton restaurant, in 1921 he moved to St. Catharines where he opened up Diana Sweets. This became one of the city's favourite dining spots, especially for students. In 1941, he bought the building and the adjacent Woolworth store.

"The Di was the place to be for all the kids and I worked there after school in the 1930s and '40s," Jack Grammar, Pete Grammar's son told Jack Gatecliff in 1993.

"He liked people," Jack said. "It was a hangout," he recalled in 2004.

Pete Grammar was very civic-minded as he helped to sponsor sports teams. He served two terms on city council, as did his son Jack several years later.

Pete Grammar died of a heart attack in 1952 at age 53. Diana Sweets was sold in 1963 and if you look for it on St. Paul Street today, you will notice that it's no longer there. One more piece of the city's history, gone forever.

St. Catharines Museum
- Stauffer Collection,
TP Friendly Forum June 30, 1954

J.C. (Cal) Wilson

Cal Wilson was the vice-president of sales and advertising for Thompson Products. He was responsible for spreading the TP gospel for more than 20 years. He was a native of Weyburn, Saskatchewan, where his father was a Presbyterian church minister. Wilson resigned from TP in 1956.

Continued from page 15

later from his St. Catharines home. One of the birds that impressed him was a falcon, so he submitted the name. The youngster received a war savings certificate and two tickets to all Falcons home games. "I had my picture taken with Rudy Pilous," Stirrett recalled.

On the left, nine-year-old Jimmy Stirrett, winner of name-the-team contest in 1943, poses with J. C. (Cal) Wilson, one of the Falcons owners.
St. Catharines Standard photo

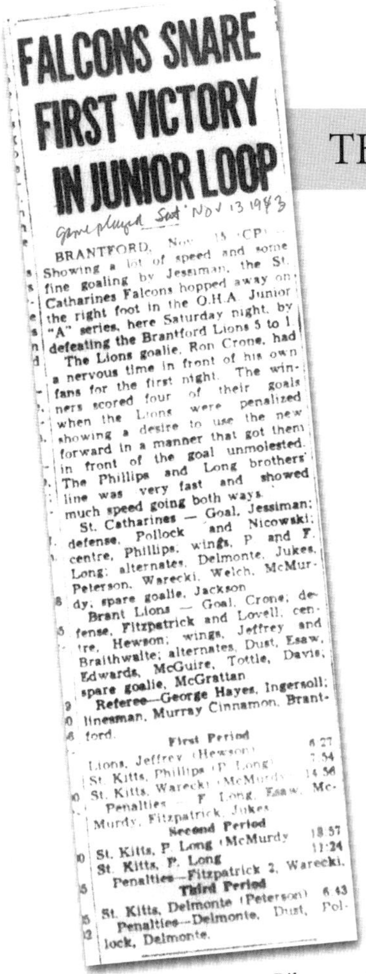

FALCONS SNARE FIRST VICTORY IN JUNIOR LOOP

Game played Sat Nov 13 1943

BRANTFORD, Nov. 15 (CP) — Showing a lot of speed and some fine goaling by Jessiman, the St. Catharines Falcons hopped away on the right foot in the O.H.A. Junior "A" series, here Saturday night, by defeating the Brantford Lions 5 to 1.

The Lions goalie, Ron Crone, had a nervous time in front of his own fans for the first night. The winners scored four of their goals when the Lions were penalized showing a desire to use the new forward in a manner that got them in front of the goal unmolested. The Phillips and Long brothers line was very fast and showed much speed going both ways.

St. Catharines — Goal, Jessiman; defense, Pollock and Nicowski; centre, Phillips; wings, P. and F. Long; alternates, Delmonte, Jukes, Peterson, Warecki, Welch, McMurdy; spare goalie, Jackson.

Brant Lions — Goal, Crone; defense, Fitzpatrick and Lovell; centre, Hewson; wings, Jeffrey and Braithwaite; alternates, Dust, Esaw, Edwards, McGuire, Tottle, Davis; spare goalie, McGrattan.

Referee—George Hayes, Ingersoll; linesman, Murray Cinnamon, Brantford.

First Period

Lions, Jeffrey (Hewson)	6:27
St. Kitts, Phillips (P. Long)	7:54
St. Kitts, Warecki (McMurdy)	14:56

Penalties — F. Long, Esaw, McMurdy, Fitzpatrick, Jukes.

Second Period

St. Kitts, P. Long (McMurdy)	18:57
St. Kitts, P. Long	11:24

Penalties—Fitzpatrick 2, Warecki.

Third Period

St. Kitts, Delmonte (Peterson)	6:43

Penalties—Delmonte, Dust, Pollock, Delmonte.

THE FALCONS GET OFF THE GROUND

In their inaugural season, the St. Catharines Falcons played in the OHA Junior A League which had ten teams divided into two groups. Group 1 was made up of the Oshawa Generals, Toronto Marlboros, St. Michael's College Majors, Toronto Young Rangers, and Hamilton Whizzers. Group 2 consisted of the Brantford Lions, Stratford Kroehlers, Galt Canadians, St. Catharines Falcons, and Port Colborne Recs. There was an interlocking home and home schedule and each club, which could dress 12 players, would play 26 games.

The Falcons played their first regular-season game of junior A hockey in Brantford on Saturday, November 13, 1943.

"Showing a lot of speed and some fine goaltending by Jessiman, the St. Catharines Falcons hopped away on the right foot... by defeating the Brantford Lions 5-1," the *St. Catharines Standard* reported. Nick Phillips of Niagara Falls scored the first-ever goal by a St. Catharines Junior A player.

The first home game for the Falcons took place on Friday, November 19, 1943.

Pilous and MacDonald thought everything was ready for the game, but just before the puck was dropped, MacDonald discovered that nobody had thought of lining up a timekeeper. Rushing into the stands, he ran into local public school principal, Ashton Morrison.

Morrison recalled the meeting for Jack Gatecliff in February, 1955. "I was in the lobby waiting for the junior game to start when Jay MacDonald rushed by in a dither saying he had forgotten to get anyone to work on the penalty bench. I told him that I'd do it if he was stuck, but he replied that they had to have someone with experience. Arena manager Lee Blank assured him that I was capable and I've been there ever since."

For most of the season, Morrison, who came to Alexandra School in 1924, paid his own way into the arena, until one of the Falcons directors saw him purchasing a ticket. From that moment on, he got in free of charge.

The game and penalty timekeeping job lasted for more than twenty years. It's estimated that Morrison watched the clock for 800 games. His only regret was that he didn't have a padded seat in the penalty box.

Morrison and Dr. Leon Hipwell of Toronto had formed the Ontario Minor Hockey Association in 1940 and

Continued on page 19

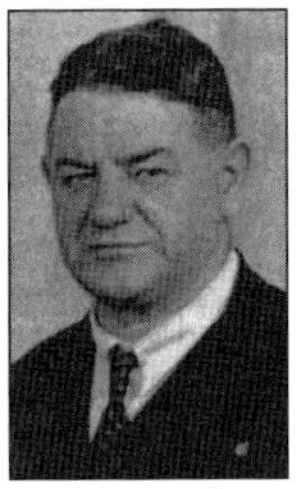

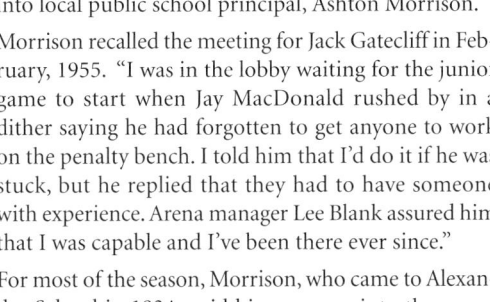

Trainer Jimmy Joy

St. Catharines Museum - *Frank Martin Ref. File, Jan. 13, 2004*

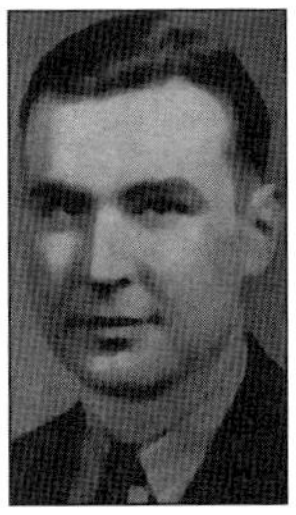

Coach Rudy Pilous

St. Catharines Standard photo

ATTENDANCE FIGURES

Average per regular-season game: 884
Season's largest crowd: 2,760
Season's smallest crowd: 439

PLAYOFF ROUNDS:

1 - Eliminated by Oshawa 4-2

1943-1944

GAMES PLAYED	WON	LOST	TIED	FOR	AGAINST	POINTS	FINISH
26	15	9	2	125	103	32	1/5

Leading Scorers (Unofficial)

PLAYER	GOALS	ASSISTS	POINTS
Stan Warecki	19	14	33
Nick Phillips	17	12	29
Pete Long	14	15	29
Bobby Thorpe	17	9	26
Doug McMurdy	7	13	20

Leading Goaltenders (Unofficial)

PLAYER	GP	GA	SO	GAA
Harvey Jessiman	24	94	2	3.91
Neal Jackson	2	9	0	4.50

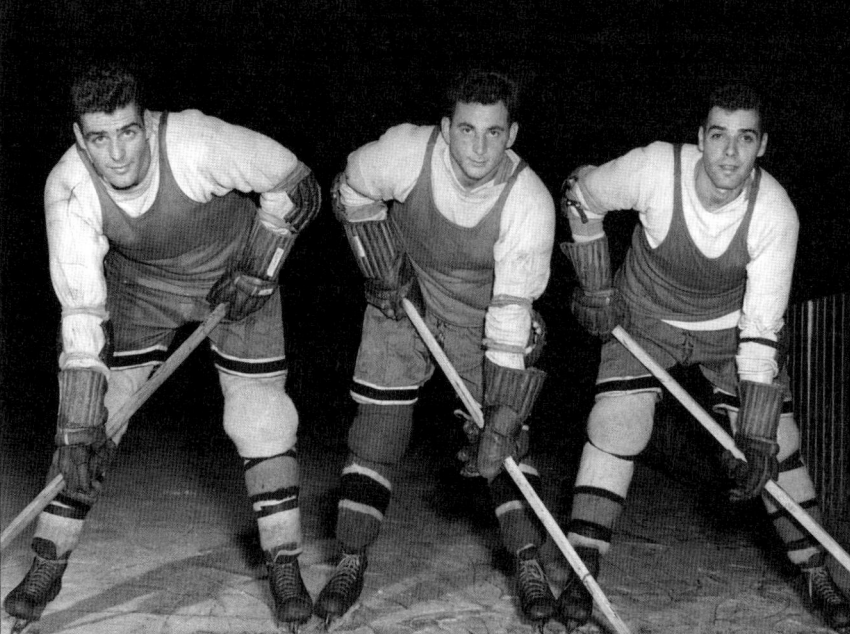

The Falcons line, from left to right, Pete Long, Nick Phillips, and Frank Long

St. Catharines Museum - *Frank Long Collection, C10,60*

FALCONS 1943-1944

ST. CATHARINES FALCONS LINEUP* – *First Junior A Game*

St. Catharines Standard photo

Harvey Jessiman
Captain
#1 - Goal

Harv hails from Winnipeg. He's 18 years old, 5'10" and weighs 150 lbs. He started playing junior at 15 with Winnipeg Monarchs. Last year he played left wing with the Monarchs.

St. Catharines Standard photo

Tom Pollock
#3 - Defence

Born in Hamiota, Manitoba, Tom is 18, stands 5' 10" and weighs 168 lbs. Last year he was with Portage La Prairie Juniors.

Courtesy of Henry Nicowski

Henry Nicowski
#2 - Defence

A graduate of local minor hockey circles, Henry is 19, stands 5'11" and weighs 170 lbs. Last year he played with the Niagara Falls Jr. B squad.

Courtesy of Nick Phillips

Nick Phillips
#8 - Centre

A brother of Sammy Phillips, who performed with the senior Saints, Nickie, 19, is 5'8" and weighs 155 lbs. The Niagara Falls native played all his hockey in the Roar City.

Alternates:

Pete Long
#9 - Right Wing

Last year Pete was with the Niagara Falls Jr. B team. He was born in the Falls and is 19 years old, 5'9" and weighs 155 lbs.

St. Catharines Standard photo

St. Catharines Standard photo

Frank Long
#7 - Left Wing

Niagara Falls native Frank Long, brother of Pete, is 18, 5'11" and weighs 165 lbs. He also played with the Falls Jr. B team last year.

St. Catharines Standard photo

Armand Delmonte (Dutch)
#12 - Right Wing

A brother of Joe of the senior Saints, Dutch is the youngest player on the team at 16. He is 5' 9" and weighs 145 lbs. Born in Timmins, he played Junior B last year and his team lost out to Port Colborne.

Courtesy of Shirley Angood

Winston Juckes (Bing)
#10 - Right Wing

Bing was born in Hamiota, Manitoba, a town just outside Winnipeg. Last year he played with the Manitoba Juvenile Champions, the Winnipeg St. James Canadians. Bing is 17, 5'9" and weighs 152 lbs.

St. Catharines Standard photo

Laurie Peterson
 # 11 - Centre

Laurie was born in Selkirk, Manitoba in 1926. Last year he was with the Wolsey Flyers and the year before with the St. James Canadians in juvenile ranks. He is 17, 5'10" and weighs 155 lbs.

St. Catharines Standard photo

Stan Warecki
 # 4 - Left Wing

Winnipeger Stan Warecki won the Memorial Cup In 1943 with the Winnipeg Rangers. He is 18, 5'10" and weighs 165 lbs.

St. Catharines Standard photo

Stan Welsh
 # 5 - Centre

St. Catharines native Stan Welsh played the last two seasons with the local juvenile Lions. He is 18, stands 5'9" and weighs 155 lbs.

Courtesy of J.K. Jouppien

Doug McMurdy
 # 13 - Defence

Another Winnipeg boy, McMurdy, 17, is 5'11" and weighs 170 lbs. Last year he was with the St. James Canadians who were eliminated by the champion Winnipeg Rangers.

Courtesy of Neal Jackson

Neal Jackson
#15 - Backup Goalie

Neal is a St. Catharines boy who played the last two years with Vic Teal's Juvenile Lions and along with Stan Welsh helped capture the OHA championship and the Syl Apps Trophy in 1943. He is 18, 5'10" and weighs 145 lbs.

Not Included in the first game lineup were:

Courtesy of Jimmy Thorpe

Bobby Thorpe #6

A Port Dalhousie boy, Thorpe was stationed with the Canadian Army in Brampton and played when conditions permitted. The right winger was 19, 5'10" and weighed 155 lbs.

Courtesy of Eddie Barber

Eddie Barber #16

Nineteen-year-old Eddie Barber was the first person from the village of Thorold South to play junior A hockey. The left winger was 5'6"and weighed 175 lbs.

St. Catharines Standard photo

Dean McBride

Dean McBride was a 6'1" defenceman who was called up to the Falcons from the St. Catharines Lions juvenile team in the 1944 playoffs against the Oshawa Generals.

St. Catharines Standard photo

Bob Hookings

St. Catharines native Bob Hookings was a 17-year-old Lions juvenile defenceman who saw action with the Falcons in the 1944 playoffs.

*Player information came from the 1943-44 Falcons Program.
St. Catharines Museum - Doug McMurdy Collection 2004 110.2

Continued from page 17

Morrison was president of the OMHA from 1940 to 1943.

In 1975, "The Keeper of the Clock" was presented with the Golden Stick Award from the OHA for his dedication and hard work for minor hockey.

Morrison receiving OHA Gold Stick Award October 20, 1975

St. Catharines Standard photo

Before the game against the Stratford Kroehlers, each of the players was introduced over the arena P. A. system. The players formed into a "V" on the ice that predicted victory. Music by the Lincoln-Welland Regiment band livened up the evening.

And then it was time for the action. At 8:30 p.m. sharp, Mayor Dr. W.J. Macdonald dropped the puck for the first junior A contest in the Garden City. A crowd of 1,050 who had paid 50 or 75 cents for a seat, sat back and watched the Falcons, dressed in near-replicas of the Boston Bruins uniforms, hammer the Kroehlers 11-4.

At the end of the 26-game schedule, the Falcons finished first in Group 2 with 32 points consisting of 15 wins, 9 losses, and 2 ties. The team actually played 27 games because one game was replayed due to a protest against Brantford for using an illegal player on January 15, 1944. Spare goaltender Neal Jackson was in the net for both tie games.

A perusal of game summaries showed that Winnipeg native Stan Warecki led the team in scoring with 33 points, followed by Niagara Falls natives, Nick Phillips and Pete Long, with 29 points each.

The fine play of the new team attracted 18,613 fans to 13 regular-season games and three playoff games at Garden City Arena. Most of the games were played on Tuesday and Friday evenings.

In the playoffs, the Falcons met the leader of Group 1, the powerful Oshawa Generals. The all-Niagara Falls line of Nick Phillips and Frank and Pete Long scored 13 goals in the series, and led the club to a 2-1 series lead, but Oshawa, led by future NHLers, Bill Ezinicki and Floyd Curry, eliminated the Falcons in six games.

The Falcons, who lost the sixth game 3-2 after leading 2-0 for two periods, put up a valiant fight and gave the Generals, who went on to win the Memorial Cup, all they could handle. Ezinicki, who scored the winning goal for the Generals, called it: "My greatest moment in hockey." ∎

STAN WARECKI

Courtesy of Wanda Swan

In the spring of 1943, 17-year-old Winnipeg native Stan Warecki won a Memorial Cup with the Winnipeg Rangers, who were inducted into the Manitoba Sports Hall of Fame in 2002.

In 1943-44, the Falcons left winger was a standout, leading the team in scoring with 19 goals and 33 points in 26 games. He added seven points in six playoff games. After the Falcons were eliminated by the Oshawa Generals, Eddie Shore, coach/GM of the AHL Buffalo Bisons, came calling and Warecki joined the club for three games as the Bisons won the American League championship.

After a stint in the Canadian Army, Warecki resumed his hockey career on the West coast, first with the Pacific Coast Hockey League Seattle Ironmen, and then the San Diego Skyhawks, where he won the league championship with his former junior coach Rudy Pilous in 1949.

St. Catharines Museum - Gatecliff Collection 1988.20

BOBBY THORPE

St. Catharines Standard photo

Port Dalhousie native Bobby Thorpe, a private in the Canadian Army who played whenever he could leave his base at Brampton, led the club to its first-ever home victory with three goals. Thorpe didn't get on the ice until the second period and scored his first goal when the Falcons were two men short. In only nine games, the right winger scored 17 goals and 26 points.

In 1944 he won a Mann Cup with the St. Catharines Athletics and an Ontario lacrosse championship in 1945.

After leaving the army, Thorpe played minor pro hockey in several cities and had a very successful lacrosse career in Peterborough, winning four consecutive Mann Cups, 1951 to 1954. He was inducted into both the Canadian (1986) and Ontario Lacrosse Halls of Fame. In 1993 he was inducted into the St. Catharines Sports Hall of Fame. Thorpe died in 2002 in St. Catharines.

WINSTON (BING) JUCKES

Courtesy of Shirley Angood

Bing Juckes was the second St. Catharines Junior A player to see action in the NHL.

After playing one year with the Falcons, the left winger played junior and senior hockey in Manitoba until 1947. While with the AHL New Haven Ramblers in 1947-48, he saw action with the New York Rangers in two games. From 1949 to 1954 he toiled in the minors and was a First Team All-Star with the United States Hockey League St. Paul Saints in 1949. In 1949-50, he got a second shot with the Rangers and this time dressed for 14 games and scored two goals. He played senior hockey in Western Canada before retiring in 1955.

The Hamiota Manitoba native coached for a number of years and was involved in several business ventures, eventually settling in West Point, Mississippi, where he established the Limeco Lime Plant in 1978. He died in 1990.

Warecki eventually found a home in the Eastern Hockey League with the Washington Lions and Charlotte Clippers with whom he won an EHL championship in 1957.

After his hockey career ended, he lived in San Diego, California. He passed away in 1986 in Winnipeg at age 60.

MA DEARING

After coach Rudy Pilous brought in hockey players from the West in 1943, he started looking for boarding houses for them in the Garden City. One of the ladies he asked to take in hockey players was Rhoda Dearing. The players who stayed with her called her Ma Dearing.

In 1943-44 she took in Harvey Jessiman, Laurie Peterson, and Bing Juckes. The players received regular meals and soon learned that Ma was the boss. "My mother never cooked special for any of us," said Ma's daughter, Marian Romanowsky. "Mother made sure they did what they were supposed to do."

Harvey Jessiman irked Mrs. Dearing because he had to have Heinz ketchup on everything he ate. Ma Dearing couldn't understand how he could appreciate her meals if they were covered with the red stuff. When Harvey got married years later, she presented him with a case of ketchup as a wedding present.

Marian was living at home when her mother started taking in boarders. She was a little older than the players and considered them to be her brothers.

"I never missed a game," she said from her Ontario Street home in the fall of 2004. She even went on the bus to some of the road games. The family album has plenty of pictures taken of Falcons players at the Dearings' home on 39 Louisa Street.

Laurie Peterson, Marian Dearing, Bing Juckes
Courtesy of Marian Romanowsky

Ma Dearing and Tom Pollock
Courtesy of Marian Romanowsky

St. Catharines Standard photo

October 15, 1996.

Members of two St. Catharines hockey teams took part in a reunion Friday night. Members of the 1943-44 Falcons, the first Junior A hockey team in St. Catharines, were (front row) Bob Thorpe, Dean McBride, Nick Phillips, Frank Long, Stan Welsh, and Harvey Jessiman. Members of the 1939 midgets, which was the first St. Catharines team to win an Ontario minor hockey championship, were (back row) Harold Crooker, John Kuzmaski, Jack Rodgers, Henry Nicowski, Bert Rolston, Mike O'Toole, and Ray Smith.

FALCONS 1944-1945

DOUG McMURDY WINS FIRST RED TILSON TROPHY

When the Falcons second season started, the league had a different look. There were seven teams in one group, as Hamilton had dropped out just before the schedule started. On December 12, 1944, Port Colborne Recs folded, leaving six teams to finish the year. The management of the club was basically the same, except that J.C. (Cal) Wilson was replaced as president by Ted Graves who continued to be the team's manager.

In 1944-45, the Falcons added several St. Catharines players to the team, including defencemen Dean McBride and Bob Hookings, who had seen some action in the first season. Others who made the club were Eric Unger, Dennis White, Jim Dawdy, and Jack Gatecliff. White, Dawdy and Gatecliff spent part of the season on the same line. Unger and McBride had attended the Toronto Maple Leafs training camp before joining the Falcons.

Two other local boys made an immediate impression in their rookie season.

"... Standing out like a sore thumb was a brace of Garden City boys in the Smelle twins, Carl and Tom. In their initial year in junior A, they loomed as strong and starry as any on the Pilous team," the *Standard* reported. Carl, a bruising defenceman, and Tom, a high-scoring left winger, spent two years with the Falcons before playing senior A hockey in Hamilton, New Brunswick, Quebec and Sault Ste. Marie.

"We more than hated to lose," Tom Smelle said from his St. Catharines home in the fall of 2003.

Carl died in 1986. The Smelle twins were inducted into the St. Catharines Sports Hall of Fame in 2004.

Eric Unger *Dennis White*

Jack Gatecliff *Jim Dawdy*
St. Catharines Museum - *Gatecliff Collection*
1998.20

Tom Smelle
Courtesy of Tom Smelle

Carl Smelle
Courtesy of Tom Smelle

ATTENDANCE FIGURES
Average per regular-season game: 1,659
Season's largest crowd: 3,797
Season's smallest crowd: 674

PLAYOFF ROUNDS:
1 - Eliminated by St. Mike's 4-1

1944-1945

GAMES PLAYED	WON	LOST	TIED	FOR	AGAINST	POINTS	FINISH
22	14	8	0	115	98	28	2/6

Leading Scorers (Unofficial)

PLAYER	GOALS	ASSISTS	POINTS
Laurie Peterson	18	21	39
Doug McMurdy	11	25	36
Dutch Delmonte	17	14	31
Tom Smelle	14	7	21
Eric Unger	8	10	18

Leading Goaltenders (Unofficial)

PLAYER	GP	GA	SO	GAA
Harvey Jessiman	22	98	0	4.36

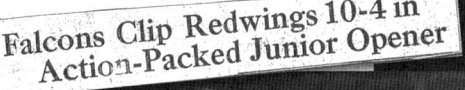

Falcon forward Tom Smelle (12) tests Galt goalie Bruce Philby in the Nov. 21, 1944 home opener.

St. Catharines Standard, November 21, 1944

FALCONS 1944-1945

CLAYTON E. BROWNE

When the St. Catharines Falcons started playing in 1943, St. Catharines Standard sports editor Clayton Browne was there to follow the team. Browne was named the Standard's first sports editor in 1929 and stayed on the job until 1956. It is estimated that he wrote 8,500 columns and thousands of sports reports without a byline. He covered virtually every sport known to North America and was present when the St. Catharines Teepees won their first Memorial Cup in 1954.

St. Catharines Standard photo

Browne did not hesitate to give his opinion about players, teams and officials in his columns and some people appreciated his thoughts. "I always found his criticism to be both fair and constructive," former Alexander School Principal J. Stanley Elliott told Jack Gatecliff. "I know he helped me correct many mistakes my teams had been making." Browne died in St. Catharines in December, 1968.

Laurie Peterson, the Falcons top scorer in 1944-45
St. Catharines Standard photo

Jack Gatecliff
St. Catharines Standard photo

Jack Gatecliff, who was a member of the 1944 Mann Cup champion St. Catharines Athletics, left the team in the second part of the season and joined the Canadian Infantry Corps.

Standard sports editor Clayton Browne, who criticized Gatecliff for being non-aggressive on the ice, thought the army might help the Russell Avenue resident to be a better player. "If by any chance 'Gate' is aligned with Army Air Corps and they teach him 'the old college try and one punch,' he'll make a grand Senior Saint after the war," Browne wrote.

It never happened. Gatecliff spent only six months at Camp Borden and then was given a medical discharge because he dislocated his shoulder. In 1946-47 he played hockey for one year in Scotland for the Paisley Pirates, and then came back to apply for a reporting job in the *St. Catharines Standard* sports department. He was hired and stayed with the *Standard* for 53 years, replacing Browne as sports editor in 1955.

The Falcons, now known as the Gold and White, started the season on a strong note, whipping the Galt Red Wings (who arrived 30 minutes late for the game with tire trouble) 10-4 before a crowd of 1,489 at Garden City Arena. Laurie Peterson scored four goals and Doug McMurdy added four assists. The team won six of its first seven games.

On December 5, 1944, the Falcons played a game for a cause that would seem very odd by today's standards. St. Catharines fans turned out and donated 2,472 cigarettes to the Red Cross for hospitalized armed servicemen overseas. Vice-President Jack Leach promoted the idea. How times have changed!

Most of the teams transported their players on road games by car and sometimes that led to big problems.

Falcons to Aid Armed Forces in Hospitals

St. Catharines Falcons are starting the ball rolling to give the Garden City some noteworthy publicity that could reach national proportions, if similarly adopted by other junior, senior or even professional hockey clubs. Acting on a quick suggestion that the scarcity of cigarets is proving a terrific hardship to hospitalized members of the Allied forces, Pres.-Mgr. E. J. (Ted) Graves last night announced that, commencing with tonight's OHA junior A game with Port Colborne Recs at St. Catharines Falcons, the city club will send cigarets twice in number to the paid attendance at all games at the Garden City arena during the entire 1944-45 schedule to the Canadian Red Cross for their distribution.

The text of the wire sent from St. Catharines to columnist Jim Coleman of the Toronto Globe-Mail, who originated the idea, is as follows:

"We believe the suggestion in your column regarding cigaret shortages overseas is a good one. Although we may not be considered the No. 1 team in OHA junior hockey, we wish at least to be the first to assist with the suggestion. It is our intention to send cigarets equal in number to twice the attendance at each home game of St. Catharines junior Falcons for the balance of our schedule, beginning Tuesday, Dec. 5, when Port Colborne visits St. Catharines. These cigarets will be sent to hospital patients, care of the Red Cross overseas."

Thus, if tonight's attendance is 2000 for Falcons-Recs, the Canadian Red Cross will receive double that or 4000 cigarets for hospitalized members of the armed forces. The Falcons' executive is to be congratulated on its initiative in this matter, a courtesy which will be appreciated to the utmost by wounded or ill active service members.

St. Catharines Standard

Ed Wiley, coach of the Toronto Young Rangers, missed a 6-4 loss to the Falcons because there was no room for him in the club's two cars!

On the way to a game in Oshawa on January 6, 1945, the Falcons equipment and four players were delayed when their car motor "froze up." The Falcons played the first period with only eight players. "In addition they went on without skates for the octet, using borrowed supplies from the Generals, also without a set of goal pads for Capt. Harv Jessiman," the *Standard* reported.

After taking a first period lead 1-0, defenceman Doug McMurdy recalled that Generals coach, ex-Toronto Maple Leaf star Charlie Conacher, stormed into the Falcons dressing room and demanded that the borrowed equipment be returned immediately! With the addition of the missing players and equipment for the second period, the Falcons prevailed 4-2. McMurdy played the whole game.

On February 21, 1945, Doug McMurdy, Harvey Jessiman, Tom and Carl Smelle, Dean McBride, Dutch Delmonte, and Laurie Peterson were invited to play for an OHA Junior A All-Star team in Maple Leaf Gardens against a team of former NHL stars, including Charlie and Lionel Conacher, Eddie Shore, Red Horner, and Bobby Bauer.

The game was played in three 15-minute periods and the bluelines were eliminated. Proceeds of the game went to help the Royal Canadian Navy.

During the regular season, the Falcons had the distinction of being the only team in the league to defeat the St. Michael's College Majors (in Maple Leaf Gardens) 8-6.

At the end of their second regular season, the Falcons finished the 22-game schedule in second place with 28 points and faced St. Michael's in the playoffs. Laurie Peterson was the club's top scorer in the regular season with 39 points (46 according to one source).

The Majors, who out-scored the Falcons 39-10 and eliminated

them from the playoffs in five games, went on to capture the Memorial Cup. The high-scoring team had future NHLers Tod Sloan, Jim Thomson, Gus Mortson, and Red Kelly in its lineup.

It's interesting to note that playoff game two in St. Catharines drew 3,469 fans to see the Falcons defeat the Majors 4-2. Jessiman blanked St. Mike's for the first 42 minutes of the game and drew rave reviews. "He was super-sensational. He blocked, cleared, dived and grabbed them from solos to three-man plays and is the inspiration for the rest of the team," the *Standard* reported.

Game four drew 3,797 fans to Garden City Arena – the season's largest crowd – and although Jessiman was outstanding, St. Mike's prevailed 9-2.

The total attendance for year two rose to 25,510, an increase of 6,897 from the Falcons first year of operations, despite playing three fewer games. It looked like junior A hockey had a bright future in St. Catharines, especially after the St. Catharines Saints, the city's Senior A team since 1938, folded in 1945. ■

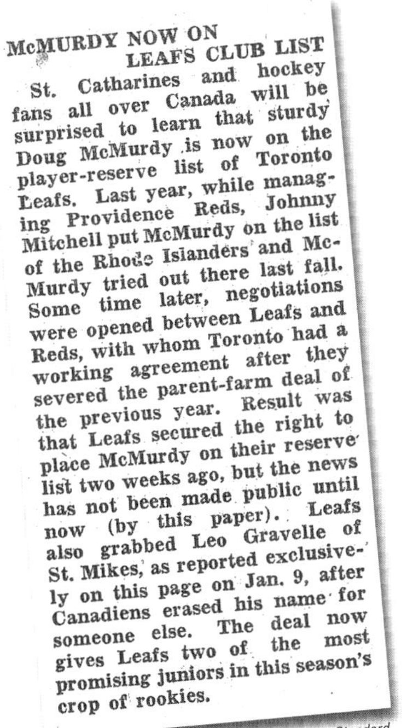

McMURDY NOW ON LEAFS CLUB LIST

St. Catharines and hockey fans all over Canada will be surprised to learn that sturdy Doug McMurdy is now on the player-reserve list of Toronto Leafs. Last year, while managing Providence Reds, Johnny Mitchell put McMurdy on the list of the Rhode Islanders and McMurdy tried out there last fall. Some time later, negotiations were opened between Leafs and Reds, with whom Toronto had a working agreement after they severed the parent-farm deal of the previous year. Result was that Leafs secured the right to place McMurdy on their reserve list two weeks ago, but the news has not been made public until now (by this paper). Leafs also grabbed Leo Gravelle of St. Mikes, as reported exclusively on this page on Jan. 9, after Canadiens erased his name for someone else. The deal now gives Leafs two of the most promising juniors in this season's crop of rookies.

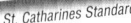

St. Catharines Standard

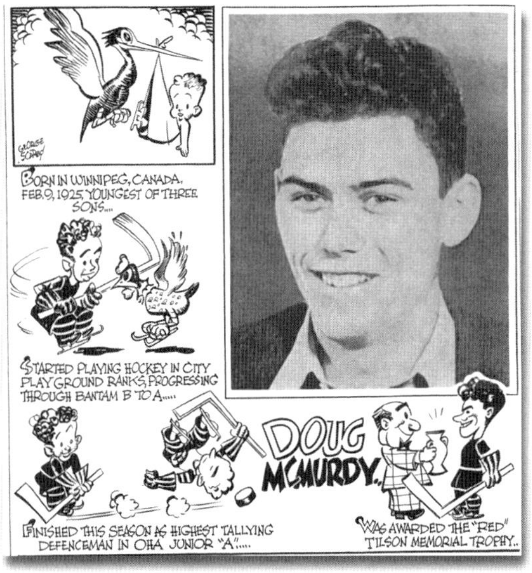

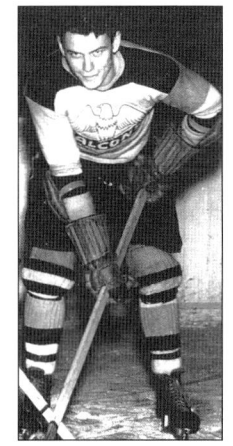

St. Catharines Museum - *Thompson Products Collection, Friendly Forum 1999.76.1*

Courtesy of Tom Smelle

DOUG McMURDY

Rudy Pilous coached many junior hockey players during his career, but Winnipeg native Doug McMurdy was his favourite.

"He was the best junior player I ever had," Pilous said on numerous occasions.

At the end of the 1944-45 season, McMurdy was the highest scoring rearguard in the OHA Junior A League and became the first player to receive the Red Tilson Memorial Trophy. The trophy, named in honour of former Oshawa Generals player Albert (Red) Tilson, who was killed in World War II, is now the Ontario Hockey League's most prestigious award. At the time, it was presented annually to the OHA Junior A player voted the most outstanding and gentlemanly during the regular season. Today it is awarded to the OHL's best player, with a separate trophy for the most sportsmanlike player.

Four more St. Catharines juniors, Brian Cullen, Hank Ciesla, Stan Mikita, and Dale McCourt, would win this coveted award over the next 32 years.

McMurdy turned pro with the Toronto Maple Leafs who converted him from a defenceman to a centre. He still wonders why it happened, but in those days you didn't ask questions. After three years with Leafs farm clubs in Pittsburgh and Tulsa, he was sold to Eddie Shore, owner of the AHL Springfield Indians. Over the years several teams came calling for the talented player, but Shore refused to let him go.

After a distinguished career in the minors that included a short coaching stint, McMurdy was inducted into the Springfield Hockey Hall of Fame in 2000. In 664 regular-season pro games, he earned 592 points, including 201 goals. He now lives in West Brookfield, Massachusetts.

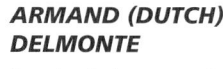

Courtesy of Tom Smelle

ARMAND (DUTCH) DELMONTE

Dutch Delmonte played two seasons (1943 to 1945) in St. Catharines, scoring 25 goals and earning 43 points in 44 games. In 1945-46 the Timmins native played for the Boston Olympics of the Eastern Amateur Hockey League, a Boston Bruins farm team.

The Bruins called him up for one game during the season, making the 18-year-old the first St. Catharines Junior A player to see action in the NHL.

From 1946 to 1954, the right winger played in the minors, enjoying his most productive years with St. Paul Saints of the United States Hockey League, winning the league championship in 1949. In 1953 he won a Calder Cup with the AHL Cleveland Barons. After retiring at age 26, he opened Dutch Delmonte's restaurant/bar in St. Paul, Minnesota, in 1962. He died in 1981.

St. Catharines Museum - *McBride Collection N 10,452*

DEAN McBRIDE

St. Catharines native Dean McBride played defence for the St. Catharines Falcons for a few games the first season and all of 1944-45. In 1945 he was traded to the Junior A Galt Red Wings and stayed with the team for two seasons. In his second year he played in front of future NHL Hall of Fame netminder, Terry Sawchuk.

In 1944, 1947 and 1948, the 6-foot-1, 180-pound rearguard attended the

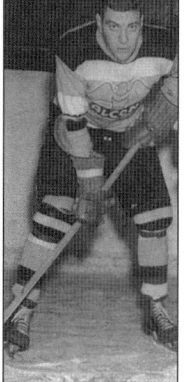

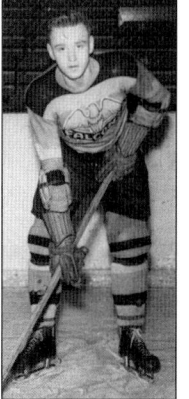

Toronto Maple Leafs training camps and rubbed shoulders with some of the legends of hockey, including Syl Apps, Howie Meeker, Max Bentley, and Turk Broda. In 1947-48 he played for the Toronto Marlboros Senior A team and was named to the OHA All-Star Team. In the fall of 1948, he was signed by Punch Imlach who was player/coach of the Quebec Aces of the Quebec Senior Hockey League.

While with the Aces from 1948 to 1950, McBride played with Herb Carnegie, an outstanding player whom many think was kept out of the NHL because he was black. After two years in Quebec, he was traded to the Sydney Millionaires, a Senior A club in the Maritime Senior Hockey League. In 1951 the Millionaires won the league championship. Sydney traded him to the Glace Bay Miners and from 1952 to 1955, McBride played with the Senior A Soo Indians of the Northern Ontario Hockey Association. In 1955 he suited up with the International Hockey League Fort Wayne Komets and stayed until he retired in December, 1958, at age 31. McBride passed away in St. Catharines on January 5, 2004.

HARVEY JESSIMAN

At 15 Jessiman was the goaltender for the Junior A Winnipeg Monarchs, but the next year he decided to suit up as a forward, playing centre or left wing. Rudy Pilous signed the teenager who had been the property of the Detroit Red Wings since he was 14.

In his first season, Jessiman, the team's captain, backstopped the club to a record of 15 wins in 26 regular-season games. He had a goals-against average of 3.91 and two shutouts. The Falcons finished second in 1944-45, with Jessiman once again playing a leading role. In the fall of 1945 he turned pro with the Red Wings, who assigned him to the United States Hockey League Omaha Knights. One of his roommates that season was a teenager named Gordie Howe.

In each of his two years in Omaha, Jessiman made the league all-star team and won the Charles Gardiner Trophy, awarded to the USHL's best goaltender. Despite his success in Omaha, Detroit Red Wings sold him to the AHL Philadelphia Rockets in 1947.

After spending the 1949-50 season with the USHL Louisville Blades, where he was reunited with ex-Falcons coach Rudy Pilous, he retired at age 24.

He returned to St. Catharines and in 1950 landed a sales job with Toledo Steel Products, a subsidiary of Thompson Products. For the last several years he has lived in Burlington, Ontario.

Harvey Jessiman — *St. Catharines Standard photo*

High-scoring Falcons line of Dutch Delmonte, Laurie Peterson, and Tom Smelle
St. Catharines Museum -Tom Smelle Collection, C10,856

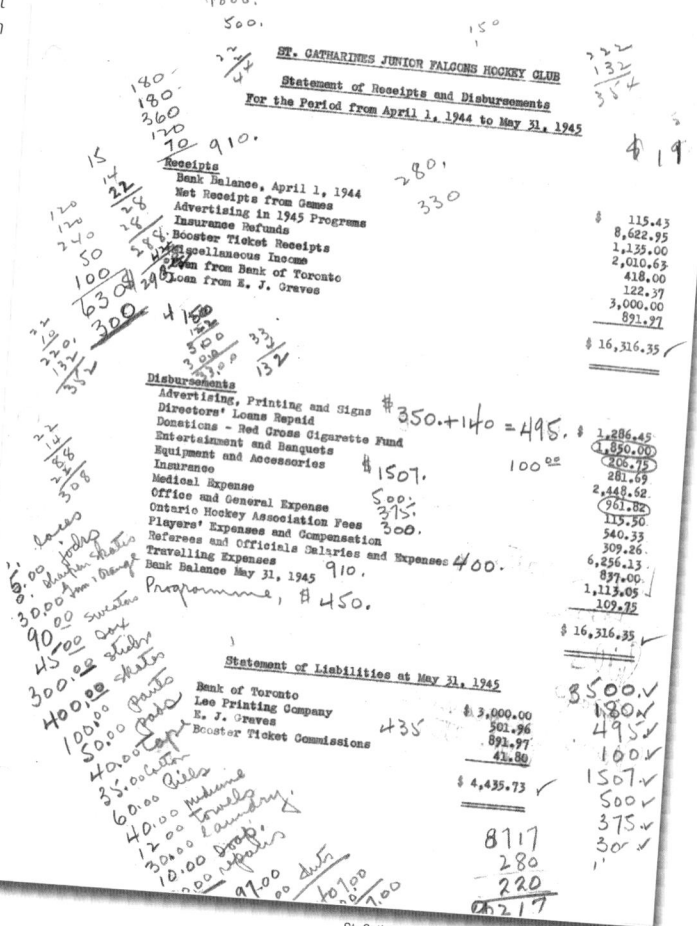
St. Catharines Museum - Gatecliff Collection 2003.165

FALCONS 1945-1946

LAURIE PETERSON LEADS FALCONS IN SCORING FOR SECOND STRAIGHT YEAR

ATTENDANCE FIGURES
Average per regular-season game: 2,194
Season's largest crowd: 4,244
Season's smallest crowd: 658

PLAYOFF ROUNDS:
1 - Eliminated by Oshawa 3-1

Pilous Shuffles Off To Buffalo

In their third season, the Falcons were joined by teams from Hamilton and Barrie, making it an eight-team league.

On November 13, 1945, the Falcons opened the season on the road with a 6-3 victory over Galt Red Wings. Former St. Catharines Senior A player Red Reynolds was behind the Falcons bench, replacing Rudy Pilous who was working with the Buffalo Bisons in the Aud.

The Falcons opened the season at home November 16, wearing the white and blue uniforms of the St. Catharines Saints who had ceased operations in 1945. A shortage of woolen togs at the time may have been the reason for the switch. The team walloped the Hamilton Lloyds 19-0 and everyone on the team figured in the scoring except the goaltender. It turned out to be the most lopsided victory in the team's history.

On February 16, 1946, the club switched to lemon-coloured uniforms which had the player's number on the front and back. Today only two known original Falcons sweaters are in the St. Catharines Museum; they were donated by the family of former Falcon Dean McBride. The woolen sweaters, numbers 2 and 16, have been restored – they were full of holes – and one was featured at the September 25, 2004, St. Catharines Junior A hockey display at the Museum.

After stumbling at the start of the season, Galt went 18 straight games without a defeat. Former Falcons, Dean McBride and Tom Pollock, patrolled the blueline for the Red Wings. Pollock had been released from the Falcons in 1944 because he was unable to make the team through failure to get and keep in condition, the *Standard* reported.

The Smelle twins, Carl and Tom, were back for their second season after trying out with the AHL Pittsburgh Hornets.

Centre Laurie Peterson, the only Falcon to wear a leather helmet, was the new captain, replacing Jessiman who had signed a pro contract with the Omaha Knights of the United States Hockey League.

1945-1946

GAMES PLAYED	WON	LOST	TIED	FOR	AGAINST	POINTS	FINISH
28	14	14	0	134	123	28	4/8

Leading Scorers (Official)

PLAYER	GOALS	ASSISTS	POINTS
Laurie Peterson	23	24	47
Tom Smelle	23	17	40
Chick Zamick	18	21	39
Vic Auger	18	11	29
Jim Dawdy	13	14	27

Leading Goaltenders (Official)

PLAYER	GP	GA	SO	GAA
Max Haunn	25	104	2	4.16
Don O'Hearn	3	19	0	6.33

St. Catharines Standard photo

St. Catharines Mayor W.J. Macdonald (left) drops the puck between Falcon Laurie Peterson, wearing a St. Kitts sweater, and Hamilton Lloyds captain, Ron Kemp at the Falcons home opener on November 16, 1945. The Falcons won 19-0.

St. Catharines Museum - McBride Collection 1998.388

RED REYNOLDS
Red Reynolds was a well-travelled junior and senior hockey player who played for the St Catharines Senior A Chiefs and then Saints from 1939 to 1944. In 1943-44, he was the team captain. He coached the Falcons for the first part of the 1945-4 season.

St. Catharines Standard photo

FALCONS 1945-1946

DON (NIP) O'HEARN

Nip O'Hearn with the American Hockey League Springfield Indians.
Standard photo courtesy of Nip O'Hearn

During the season, St. Catharines native Don (Nip) O'Hearn made his debut in the net for the Falcons. After playing only a few games, O'Hearn started out on a hockey journey that took him across North America.

O'Hearn started his pro career at an early age. "I kind'a lucked into turning pro when I was 14, but I did come back and play a few other winters in St. Catharines," O'Hearn told Jack Gatecliff in 1985. He faced his first pro shots in 1943 in a practice with the AHL Buffalo Bisons who sent him to their Dallas farm club. After moving back and forth between amateur and pro teams, he began a hockey journey – mainly with teams owned by Eddie Shore – which took him to at least seven leagues and 18 different teams from 1947 to 1963.

O'Hearn was also an accomplished lacrosse player winning five Mann Cups with Peterborough, St. Catharines, and Victoria. He was inducted into the Ontario Lacrosse Hall of Fame in 1997 and the Canadian Lacrosse Hall of Fame in 1998.

O'Hearn, who lives in Port Dalhousie, became a member of the St. Catharines Sports Hall of Fame in 2004.

When the team began to falter early in 1946, Pilous replaced Reynolds behind the bench on January 18, and the club responded, winning that night 7-4 against the Toronto Young Rangers. The club finished the 28-game schedule in fourth place in the league with 14 wins and 28 points. Once again, Laurie Peterson was the team's points leader with 47 points.

Attendance increased for the second straight year with 36,103 fans paying to see the Falcons in 14 regular-season and two playoff contests. The 1945-46 team drew a record crowd of 4,244 to its February 1, 1946 game with St. Michael's College.

For the second time in three years, the team faced the Oshawa Generals in the playoffs, but the result was the same, as the Generals won the best-of-five-series, 3-1. Oshawa outscored the Falcons 25-11 and in one game the Generals Ike Hildebrand scored six goals. "The ex-Adanac has been just poison to our side," *Standard* sports editor Browne said.

Cover courtesy of Val DeLory

Prices for seats in the playoffs were increased because the OHA was taking 7½% from the gross gate in the semi-finals. Blues were 75 cents, corners 50 cents, and side reds were $1.00.

During the fourth and last playoff game in St. Catharines, an electrical storm cut the power off in the arena for more than 15 minutes. There was so much smoking in the arena that when the game resumed, the air was hazy blue.

For some reason, Falcon star Jim Dawdy didn't play in the last game. "He was about the best two-way player Falcons had during the playoffs, anyway, if not during the season," Browne wrote. ■

VICTOR (CHICK) ZAMICK

Courtesy of Val DeLory

One of the Falcons stars in 1945-46 was Chick Zamick, a little guy who was a wizard with the puck, according to former teammate Doug Davidson who spoke from Niagara-on-the-Lake in May, 2004. Davidson played one year for the Falcons and later played on a Mann Cup lacrosse championship team in Hamilton.

Zamick, who came to St. Catharines from the St. Boniface Manitoba Juniors, was the third leading scorer that season with 18 goals and 39 points in 28 games.

"He is smooth, tricky, clean and faster than expected," a Standard reporter wrote at the time.

After leaving the Falcons, Zamick had a short stint in the army followed by an attempt to make a living as a flyweight boxer. In 1947, he was recruited

Falcon forward Bob Twaddle (9) scores against St. Mike's goalie Pat Boehmer in a 11-2 loss February 1, 1946.
St. Catharines Standard photo

Falcons Laurie Peterson (6) and Jim Dawdy (15) storm the Oshawa Generals net in a 7-2 loss February 25, 1946.
St. Catharines Standard photo

26

FALCONS 1945-1946

to play hockey for the Nottingham Panthers in the English National League for 15 pounds a week and his hockey career took off.

In his first season, he won the league scoring championship and repeated the feat five more times in his career. In 11 seasons with Nottingham, he scored 778 goals and 1,423 points in 624 games. In 1954-55, he had a high of 112 goals and 281 points. He was on nine consecutive all-star teams and twice was voted sportsman of the year. Later Zamick coached in Switzerland for three years before returning to Nottingham where he became a successful businessman. He still resides in his adopted city today. He is now a member of the Manitoba Hockey Hall of Fame and the British Ice Hockey Hall of Fame.

LAURIE PETERSON

Courtesy of Val DeLory

St. Catharines Falcon Laurie Peterson was a way ahead of his time. The centreman was the only player on the team who wore a helmet. The Selkirk Manitoba native was the team's scoring leader with 47 points in his third junior season.

Two years after turning pro in 1946 with Dallas, he was playing with San Diego of the Pacific Coast Hockey League and Houston of the USHL. Later that season, he was sold by Buffalo to the PCHL Fresno Falcons where he joined his brother Joe until 1950. In 1950-51, he played with North Sydney in the Maritime Major Hockey League and lost the scoring championship on the last day of the season. In 1952 he was with the Northern Ontario Hockey League Sault Ste. Marie (U.S.A.) Indians, and during his five-year stay with the club he won the league scoring championship in 1956-57 with 82 points, including 36 goals. After the Soo Indians folded in 1957, he suited up with the IHL Louisville Rebels and had a good year with 70 points in 61 games; however, he decided to return to Sault Ste. Marie, Ontario, where he joined the staff of the Sault Daily Star circulation department.

He ended his hockey career at 32 with the Soo (Ontario) Greyhounds in 1959. In 1984 at 57, he joined the Old Greyhounds team and accompanied it to Italy where the club played seven exhibition games on outdoor rinks. Peterson has been retired since 1991 and resides in Sault Ste. Marie.

VAL DeLORY

Courtesy of Val DeLory

Toronto native Valentine (Val) DeLory joined the Falcons for the 1945-46 season and had 22 points in 23 games. The next year the left-winger played with the Hamilton Szabos before moving to the Eastern Amateur Hockey League New York Rovers. In his second year with the Rovers, he was called up to the New York Rangers for one game.

In 1949-50 he was a First Team All-Star and the leading scorer in the EAHL with 73 points, including 36 goals. Today he is a member of the New York Rovers Hall of Fame.

After his hockey career ended in 1953, he joined the North York Fire Department and stayed for 30 years. He now resides in Parry Sound, Ontario.

Val's grandson James, a 6-foot-5, 237-pound Oshawa General defenceman, was selected by the San Jose Sharks in the 2006 NHL draft.

VIC AUGER

ED BURY

JIM DAWDY

MAX HAUNN

BOBBY ROBERTSON

CARL SMELLE

TOM SMELLE

The above photos courtesy of Val DeLory

St. Catharines Standard *sports editor Jack Gatecliff gets a lift from NHL stars Stan Mikita, (left) and Marcel Dionne at "Gate's" testimonial dinner on June 8, 1987. Sharing in the fun are dinner chairman Archie Katzman (extreme left) NHL star Dennis Hull and* Standard *publisher Henry Burgoyne.*

St. Catharines Standard photo

Gate at the typewriter
St. Catharines Standard photo

JACK GATECLIFF

In the spring of 1947, St. Catharines native Jack Gatecliff was hired as a sports writer for the *St. Catharines Standard*. It was his first and only job, and the beginning of a distinguished writing career that spanned seven decades. Starting as the number two man in the sports department, Gatecliff began writing a column entitled *Across Minor Sports "Gate"* on July 9, 1947. In 1951, the column's heading was changed to *Through the Sports Gate* and it appeared as a regular feature in the *Standard* until the summer of 2000.

During his career Gatecliff covered the ups and downs of the Junior A Teepees, Black Hawks, and Fincups from 1947 to 1977.

In 1955 he was promoted to sports editor and stayed on the job until 1991 when he retired. But he didn't stop writing. His column and special feature stories continued until just before his death on September 5, 2000.

During his career Gatecliff received numerous honours, including 17 Western Ontario Newspaper Association awards. The man who loved sports and played with the Mann Cup champions, the St. Catharines Athletics in 1944, was inducted into the Ontario and Canadian Lacrosse Halls of Fame. He also played for the 1944-45 St. Catharines Falcons, the Garden City's first Junior A hockey team.

In 1984 he was named the best American Hockey League writer, and in 1990 he entered the St. Catharines Sports Hall of Fame. Five years later he was inducted into the Hockey Hall of Fame in the Media Division. In 1998 he became a member of the Buffalo Sabres Hall of Fame. The list goes on.

Former *Standard* Managing Editor, Murray Thompson, summed up what many readers thought of Gatecliff: "His writing is perceptive, interesting, honest and kind – just like Jack."

"…Sports writing was a rare combination of a vocation and avocation rolled into one – a regular weekly cheque for a continuing hobby," said Gatecliff in 1996.

Gate's columns continue to be used as a source of sports knowledge from the past and although he may have never realized it, he was a historian who gave us a picture of the society in which he lived.

FALCONS 1946-1947

FALCONS STRUGGLE ON AND OFF THE ICE IN LAST YEAR

ATTENDANCE FIGURES
Average per regular-season game: 1,186
Season's largest crowd: 1,649
Season's smallest crowd: 732

PLAYOFF ROUNDS: 0

In 1946-47 the OHA Junior A League consisted of ten teams, as Stratford returned and Windsor made its debut. Seven of the clubs, including St. Catharines, were assigned a double schedule of 30 games (six games were four-pointers). Three teams, Windsor, Toronto Marlboros, and Toronto Young Rangers were to play a single schedule of 18, four-point games. The final standings posted in the *Globe and Mail* showed each team as having played 36 games, but that was because some were four-point games.

Under new coach Vic Teal, who had an outstanding minor hockey coaching record in St. Catharines, season number four was not successful and the club struggled to rebuild with several young players. According to then-*Standard* sports editor, Clayton Browne, the team was almost native-born, or had come up through the city's minor hockey system with nine juveniles making the jump to junior A. Included among that group were Bill (Whitey) Frick, Ken (Chic) Mann, Bill Buschlen, and Bob Twaddle.

The team's effort at rebuilding showed on the scoreboard and in the standings.

The Falcons lost their first game, a four-pointer, to Toronto Young Rangers 8-7, on November 2, 1946. It was an omen for the rest of the schedule.

Even the introduction of brand new Art Ross nets in Garden City Arena on November 30, 1946, didn't help. Connie Smythe, Toronto Maple Leafs GM, bought the nets after the Leafs had trained at Garden City Arena that fall.

The club didn't get its first victory until December 7, 1946, a 6-3 home win over Hamilton Szabos. Ironically, it came after captain Eric Unger left the team to turn pro with the Philadelphia Rockets at the end of November.

On December 11, 1946, Falcons forward Whitey Frick was hit in the right eye with a flying puck in a game against the Stratford Kroehlers. Doctors advised him not to play for the rest of the season, ending his junior career. Later, the Peterborough native, who won Mann Cups with St. Catharines Athletics in 1944 and 1946, played in Scotland. He would go on to a career as a pattern maker in General Motors and officiate for many years at OHA hockey and OLA lacrosse games in his spare time. Today Frick, who was St. Catharines Sportsman of the year in 1985 and has been a member of the St. Catharines Sports Hall of Fame since 1995, lives in the Garden City.

On January 4, 1947, the Galt Red Wings shellacked the Falcons 18-1. "Goalie Maxie Haunn saw more rubber here Saturday than ever before in 60 minutes," the *Canadian Press* reported. It was the worst defeat ever suffered by a St. Catharines junior A club.

On Saturday, January 18, 1947, 1,500 fans at Garden City Arena witnessed a free-for-all and then a near riot in the dying seconds of a game with the Barrie Flyers. It started with a fight between Fiery Goegan and Bruno Favero of Barrie. "Goegan and Favero were down like a pair of terriers," the *Standard* reported. When the two players dropped their sticks, six youngsters jumped over the boards to grab them. This led to the clearing of each team bench followed by hundreds of fans who took to the ice. There wasn't a policeman in sight. It

1946-1947

GAMES PLAYED	WON	LOST	TIED	FOR	AGAINST	POINTS	FINISH
36	7	25	4	101	219	18	8/10

Leading Scorers (Unofficial)

PLAYER	GOALS	ASSISTS	POINTS
Bob Twaddle	16	13	29
Fiori Goegan	9	12	21
Francis MacDonald	18	3	21
Bob Woods	7	12	19
C. Currie	9	7	16

Leading Goaltenders (Unofficial)

PLAYER	GP	GA	SO	GAA
Max Haunn	28	204	0	7.29
Don O'Hearn	2	14	0	7

Galt Red Wings Wallop Falcons, 18-1

Galt, Jan. 5 (CP).—Maxie Haunn, net-minder for St. Catharines Falcons, saw more rubber here Saturday night than ever before in 60 minutes as Galt Red Wings administered a severe drubbing to the Falcons to take an 18-1 victory. Besides sending St. Catharines into an unpleasant tizzy, the Red Wings set a few season records for OHA junior "A" hockey.

They scored eight goals in the second period, two better than they did in the first, and four in the final frame.

St. Catharines—Goal, Haunn; defense, Kafun, Goegan; centre, Mann; wings, Twaddle, Moy; alternates, Kodatsky, Biddie, Aitken, Thomson, Currie.
Galt—Goal, Sawchuk; defense, Robertson, McBride; centre, Anderson; wings, Giesbrecht, Wiseman, Pavelich, Scott, Glover, Unlac; alternates, Tkatchuk, Bert Cooney, Hnatuk.
Officials—J. McEachern, N. Kenney.

First Period
1—Galt, McBride (Unlac) .... :32
2—Galt, Pavelich
(Giesbrecht, McBride) ....
3—Galt, Wiseman 3:31
(Tkatchuk, Pavelich)
4—Galt, Wiseman 5:38
5—Galt, Pavelich 10:34
6—Galt, Wiseman (Giesbrecht) . 11:09
Penalties—Biddle (2), McBride, Tkatchuk 2, Robertson.

Second Period
7—Galt, Hnatuk (Tkatchuk) 2:31
8—Galt, Unlac (Glover) 5:49
9—Galt, Pavelich
(Wiseman, Giesbrecht) ....
10—Galt, Pavelich (McBride) 9:02
11—Galt, Hnatuk (Scott, Tkatchuk) 10:44
12—Galt, Anderson (Glover) 14:31
13—Galt, Glover 14:52
(McBride, Anderson)
14—Galt, Giesbrecht 16:39
(Pavelich, Wiseman)
Penalties—None. 19:29

Third Period
15—Galt, Anderson (Unlac, Glover) 4:22
16—Galt, Glover (Anderson) 5:29
17—Galt, Anderson (Glover, Unlac) 5:53
18—Galt, Glover (Anderson) ....
19—St. Catharines, Currie
(Kodatsky) 13:27
Penalties—Twaddle.

Article from CP and photo of Max Haunn courtesy of the St. Catharines Standard

FALCONS 1946-1947

George Stauffer and Rex Stimers at a hockey game in 1946
St. Catharines Museum
- Thompson Products Collection N 5766

Bob Twaddle (4) Bill McOustra (14) and Andy Thomson made up one of the Falcons three forward lines in the 1946-47 season. Twaddle ended the regular season as the team's leading scorer.
St. Catharines Standard photo

BOB TWADDLE

Bob Twaddle ended the 1946-47 season as the team's leading scorer with 29 points, including 16 goals. He was the first St. Catharines native to lead a St.Catharines Junior A club in scoring.

When Twaddle wasn't playing hockey, he was a baseball pitcher who made a name for himself one season in the city midget league. He averaged 12 strikeouts a game and held the city and district record with a mark of 22 strikeouts in one nine-inning game. His baseball talent didn't go unnoticed. The Brooklyn Dodgers invited him to their baseball training camp in Thomasville, North Carolina, and for the next three years he played in the Dodgers farm system. In 1946 he pitched for the Cambridge Maryland Dodgers of the Eastern Shore League and in 1947 for the Sheboygan Wisconsin Indians, a club that broke at least six records in the Wisconsin State League. In 1948 he was on the roster of the Johnston Johnnies in Johnston, Pennsylvania.

Twaddle was shocked by the Jim Crow Laws that segregated whites and blacks in the South at the time. He soon learned that it was dangerous to speak out against the system.

Today he lives in St. Catharines.

St. Catharines Standard photo

Whitey Frick
Courtesy of Whitey Frick

took several minutes to sort things out and some remembered that the game ended in a 5-5 draw.

For the first time in four years, the Falcons missed the playoffs, finishing eighth in the league with only seven wins and 18 points in 36 games. Some of those points came from four-point contests. The one piece of good news was that Bob Twaddle became the first St. Catharines native to lead the club in scoring during the regular season with 29 points, including 16 goals. Despite being walloped in their last home game against the Oshawa Generals 14-3, a crowd of 1,589 showed up to support the team.

Total attendance for the season was disappointing. Only 17,786, showed up for 15 home games, compared to 30,714 for 14 home games in 1945-46. After only four years, it looked like the Falcons might declare bankruptcy and drop out of the league. ■

30

FALCONS 1946-1947

Eric Unger playing for Canada in 1954 World Tournament
St. Catharines Museum - Eric Unger Collection, C10,834

St. Catharines Museum - Eric Unger Collection, C10,848

ERIC UNGER

The captain of the 1946-47 Falcons, Saskatchewan native Eric Unger, decided to leave the team at the end of November and signed a pro contract with the AHL Philadelphia Rockets. He received a signing bonus of $1,000 and then headed down to Crew Motors on Ontario Street in St. Catharines to buy a new car for a price slightly higher than his bonus.

After a pro career that included stops in Springfield, Fort Worth, Vancouver and Halifax, Unger played Senior A hockey in Chatham and was added to the Canadian National team, the East York Lyndhursts in the 1954 World Hockey Tournament. The centreman was the third-leading scorer in the tournament and Canada brought home a silver medal after losing to the Moscow Dynamos.

Today he is retired and living the good life in the Rose City. He was inducted into the Welland Sports Wall of Fame in 1996.

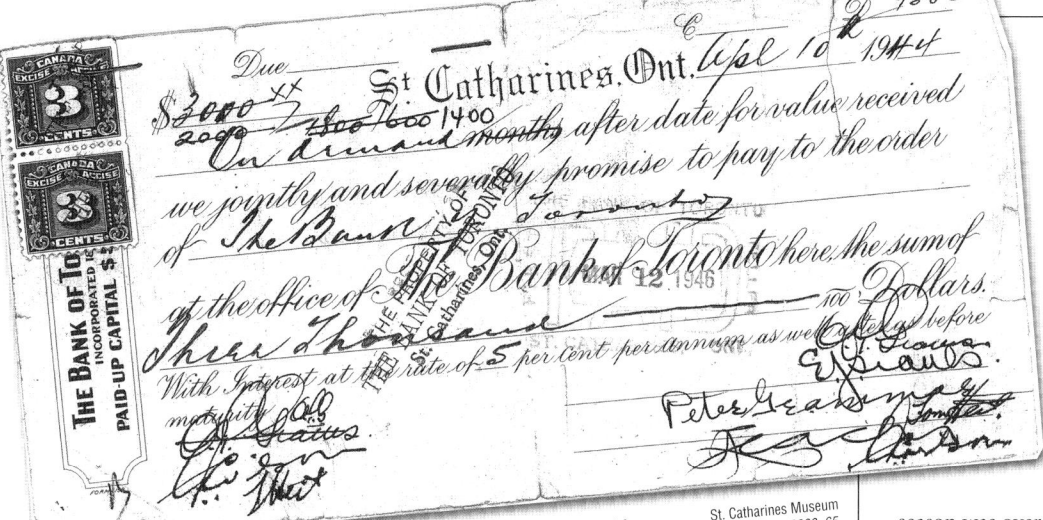

Loan from the Bank of Toronto to Falcon owners for $3,000. in April, 1944
St. Catharines Museum - Gatecliff Collection 2003. 65

FINANCIAL SHORTCOMINGS

Rudy Pilous, who had founded the club and guided it over most of the first three seasons, was no longer in the picture as he had decided to stay with the American Hockey League Buffalo Bisons organization in 1946.

The big problem was financing the club. In 1944-45 the Falcons had revenues of approximately $12,000 but the expenses totaled over $16,000. The deficit forced the owners to borrow $3,000 from the bank and one owner, Ted Graves, gave a personal loan of almost $900.

In 1945-46 the receipts rose to $17,795.57, but the deficit was $5,227. At the start of the season the six directors had given $4,200 to the club, but when the season was over there was still $1,027 owing.

In 1946-47 there was no relief in sight. Bailing the club out financially could only last so long, and when it appeared the club might fold the president of a St. Catharines business rescued the team.

31

VIC TEAL

The snowstorm that collapsed the Fort Erie Arena in 1938 changed Vic Teal's life. Teal, a former minor pro hockey player, was the arena's engineer, but when the arena was destroyed the Fort Erie native applied for and got the stationary engineer's job at the new Garden City Arena in St. Catharines in 1938.

After starting his job he began teaching hockey skills, dedication and good citizenship to youngsters, many of whom had never played on artificial ice.

Teal helped to found the first citywide minor hockey association, and three months after the arena opened he coached the St. Catharines Midget Lions team to an Ontario Minor Hockey Association championship. It was the beginning of a coaching career record that is probably unmatched in minor hockey history.

He coached St. Catharines juvenile teams to 13 consecutive Southern Ontario championships from 1942-43 to 1954-55. In 17 years he won 15 juvenile titles.

For many years he coached St. Catharines bantam, midget and juvenile teams, conducting pre-school practices from 6 a.m. to 8:30 a.m. At the time, there was one classification for all teams, no A, AA, or AAA divisions in the province. Overall, Teal's teams won 26 OMHA championships. Many of those teams went on to win all-Ontario titles.

Several of Teal's players made it to the NHL, including Frank Martin, Hank Ciesla, Elmer Vasko, Stan Mikita, and Gerry Cheevers. Several others had successful junior A and/or minor pro careers such as Obie O'Brien, Dean McBride, Tom and Carl Smelle, and Connie Switzer.

In 1946-47 Teal coached the Junior A Falcons. Two of his sons, Allan (Skip) and Vic Jr. (Skeeter), had successful junior A careers; Skip won a Memorial Cup with Barrie Flyers in 1953 and Skeeter was the captain of the 1968-69 Black Hawks.

Teal died in 1977 and that year, to honour his contributions to St. Catharines minor hockey, the Vic Teal Memorial Tournament was held in the Garden City, drawing teams from Canada and the United States. It continues to be held every year at Bill Burgoyne Arena in St. Catharines. In 1991, Teal was inducted into the St. Catharines Sports Hall of Fame.

Vic Teal — St. Catharines Museum - Garden City Arena Collection N 5684

Teal with young hockey player — St. Catharines Museum - Skeeter Teal Collection, C10,970

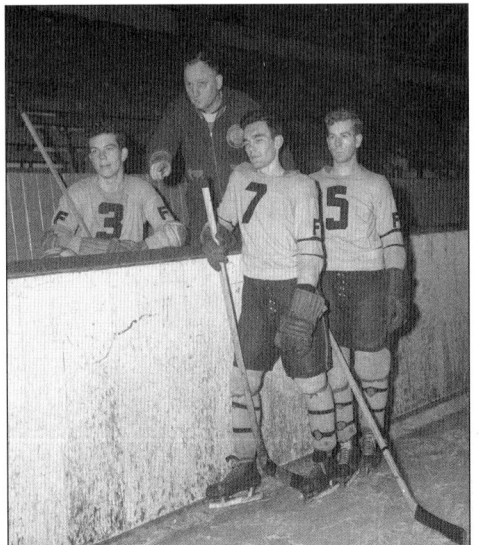

St. Catharines Standard photo

Some of St. Kitts Falcons Who'll Play Here

Coach Vic Teal gives a few final pointers to his St. Catharines Falcons — Les Biddie (3), Ken Mann (7), and Bud Aiken (5). Biddie is a tall, rangy defenceman. Mann, Falcons ace puck ragger, was brought up this year from St. Catharines Lions, last year's O.M.H.A. juvenile champs, and plays centre.

GEORGE STAUFFER
THE SAVIOUR OF JUNIOR HOCKEY IN ST. CATHARINES

St. Catharines Museum - *Wendy Hyndman Collection 2004.127.11*

Ottawa Ohio native George Stauffer was the white knight who rode into St. Catharines, Ontario, during the depression. He rescued a business – and then a hockey team.

Stauffer, a graduate of the United States Military Academy at West Point, was a Thompson Products trouble-shooter who was sent to the company's Garden City plant in 1937. When he arrived, TP was losing money and his mandate from head office in Cleveland was to show a profit or close the plant, which at that time had about 150 employees and sales of $260,000.

Stauffer took charge of the situation immediately and gave every worker an automatic 5% raise. Using a non-confrontational approach, he made the company a profitable operation by 1938.

After World War II began in 1939, the company started making anti-aircraft artillery and metal-piercing shells. Soon 1,600 employees were working three shifts in the plant, seven days a week.

One of his proudest achievements was keeping labour peace at TP with no certified union. In 1938 he established the Old Guard Association, the Employee Association, and then the Friendly Forum, an in-house magazine that kept employees up to date on what was happening inside and outside the company.

Stauffer soon won the respect and confidence of top Canadian industrialists as the company diversified its product line and expanded.

He showed leadership in the community as well, heading the building committee of the Hotel Dieu Hospital and helping to raise money for the General Hospital and a lab at Ridley College. He also was involved with other projects, including the city's new rink, Garden City Arena, which opened in 1938.

For years Thompson Products, under Stauffer's leadership, sponsored many teams in a variety of sports, and even built a baseball diamond with night lights on land near the plant. The plant slogan was: "Good sportsmanship and good fellowship make good citizenship."

The former West Point halfback knew little about hockey, but in 1947 he saw that the St. Catharines Junior A Falcons hockey club was going to go under and he wasn't about to let that happen. "We couldn't sit back and see a great St. Catharines institution go down the drain," Staufffer said in 1988. He bought the club for $2,500 and renamed the team the Tee Pees, after Thompson Products.

For many years, Teepee hockey players found employment with TP and several, including Al Kellogg, George (Porky) Douglas, Bob Twaddle, and Bill Buschlen, ended up with permanent jobs. "George Stauffer was great to hockey players," former Teepee netminder Don Campbell said.

St. Catharines Sportscaster Rex Stimers used to end his early evening reports on radio station CKTB with the statement: "Thompson Products: A good place to work."

Former NHL star Art Jackson, a TP employee, was appointed coach of the first Teepees team in 1947 and lasted for three seasons. "Art was a good player, but he wasn't a great coach, so I contacted Buffalo Bisons who Rudy [Pilous] was working for in 1950 and asked if we could have him back," Stauffer told ex-*St. Catharines Standard* sports editor Jack Gatecliff in 1997. Stauffer got his man.

Rudy Pilous returned as Teepees coach/manager in 1950, and for the next decade, the team was a

FALCON FRANCHISE GOES TO T-P PLANT

George A. Stauffer, president and general manager of Thompson Products, Ltd., announced late yesterday afternoon the conclusion of negotiations that saw the T-P Company acquire the hockey franchise of St. Catharines Falcons of O.H.A. Junior A. The transfer of the club franchise will become effective at the end of the current hockey season. It was revealed that negotiations had been underway for the past three months, with the current Falcon directors, who are J. Cal Wilson, Jack R. Leach, E. J. Graves, O. T. Graves, Peter Grammar and Thomas Helt.

G. A. Stauffer will be president of the club and chairman of the board of directors of the newly-acquired T-P juniors, while J. Cal Wilson, sales manager of Thompson Products and vice-president of Falcons, will likely continue in the same capacity for T-P's. J. R. Leach, secy.-treasurer of Thompson Products, Ltd., and also holding the same office in the present Falcons' directorate, will continue in the financial office for the T-P hockey club. The franchise transfer will be hailed with much delight by the hockey fraternity of this city and the entire province.

St. Catharines Standard, January 18, 1947

GEORGE STAUFFER

powerhouse in the OHA. In the 15 years of its existence the Teepees finished first five times, winning Memorial Cups in 1954 and 1960 – and they never missed the playoffs. Many of the Teepees, including Pierre Pilote, Jerry Toppazzini, Red Sullivan, Brian Cullen, Stan Mikita, Bobby Hull, Chico Maki, Pat Stapleton, Phil Esposito, and Roger Crozier went on to star in the NHL.

Attending Teepees games became a social occasion in the city, as the team was a success on and off the ice. Although the team, renamed the Black Hawks in 1962, would see success under owner Fred Muller, the glory days of the Teepees were never duplicated.

In 1959 Stauffer sold the Teepees to Rudy Pilous for $1, but he remained as a director of the club. Although he put a great deal of money and countless hours into the hockey club, he never took a nickel out. He retired as chairman of the board of Thompson Products in 1960 and faded out of the hockey scene.

What many people don't know is that Stauffer was bothered by the treatment of junior hockey players who signed C forms and became the property of pro clubs. "The youngsters' signatures on C forms and their subsequent confinement in trading or selling, to me seemed like white slavery," he wrote to Jack Gatecliff in 1997. He talked friends into inviting the Cornell University hockey coach to come to St. Catharines. After his visit, Cornell's director of athletics set up a pipeline for scholarships for eligible youngsters of high school age at Cornell and other Eastern universities. Over the years, many hockey players in the region turned down junior A hockey opportunities to get an education on hockey scholarships south of the border and went on to enjoy successful off-ice careers. St. Catharines natives, Terry O'Malley, Bill Oliver, and Jerry Kostandoff, were some of the first to take advantage of these opportunities.

In 1988 Stauffer was honoured at a testimonial dinner in recognition of his industrial, sports and community work, which covered more than 50 years. At his request, all proceeds went to the Leonard B. Herzog Foundation to aid St. Catharines hospitals.

"The local plant is still profitable with 1,000 workers," he said in 1997, the year he was inducted into the St. Catharines Sports Hall of Fame.

"George was born in Ottawa, Ohio, but he has become the most loyal Canadian I've ever met," said St. Catharines lawyer and long-time friend Ross Wilson in 1988.

Stauffer died on January 1, 2000, at age 93, leaving behind sons Tom and Peter and a legacy of goodwill to the community that he came to love. ■

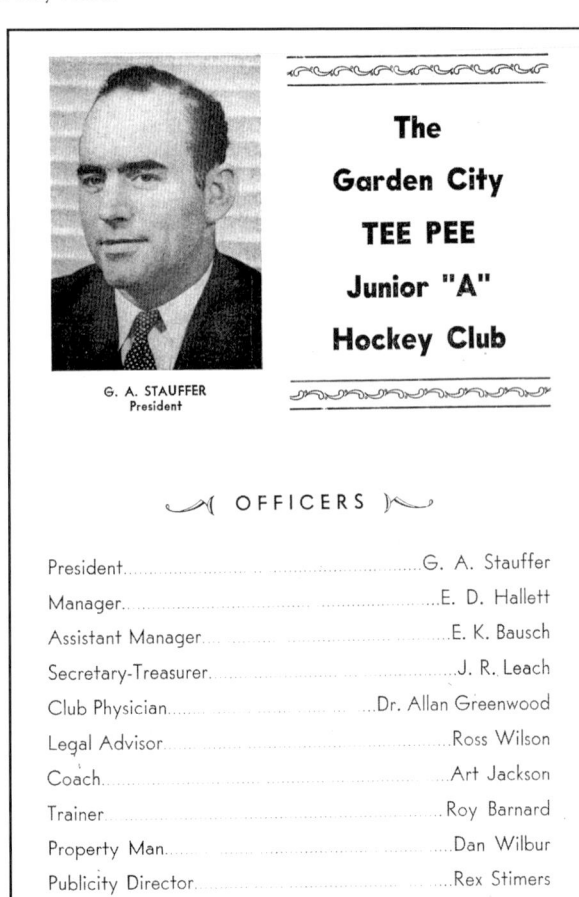

1947-48 Program St. Catharines Museum - *Buschlen Collection 2004.40.10*

Jack Higgins, Marv Edwards and George Stauffer pose with the Memorial Cup.

Courtesy of Jack Higgins

1947-1948 TEEPEES

Back row: Dan Wilbur, Stan Stocker, Tom Buck, Bill Davidson, Zellio Toppazzini, Doug Mullens, Bill Kodatsky, Doug Houston, Jim Maxwell. Front row: Art Jackson, Fiori Goegan, Jack McIntyre, George (Red) Sullivan, Ivan McClelland, Cecil Gruhl, Joe Krahulec, Fred Hildebrand. Absent: Wayne Service, Walter (Buddy) Evans, Bill Buschlen

St. Catharines Museum - *Wendy Hyndman Collection 2004.127.9*

TEEPEES 1947-1948

THE TEEPEES PUT ST. CATHARINES ON THE HOCKEY MAP

Former NHL Star Art Jackson Is The First Coach Of The Teepees

Thompson Products President and GM George Stauffer, an engineering graduate of West Point, announced on Friday, January 17, 1947, that the Falcons had been purchased by his company for $2,500 – and the club's books were balanced.

The team was renamed the Tee Pees and the hockey club went under the name of Garden City Tee Pee Junior "A" Hockey Club Inc. Art Jackson, who worked in the TP's personnel department, was the new coach.

Art Jackson
St. Catharines Museum
- Hyndman Collection 2004.127.23

The Toronto native was a former St. Michael's College star who was with the team when it went through the entire 1933-34 season without losing a game en route to the Memorial Cup. He went on to play in the NHL, winning Stanley Cups with Boston Bruins in 1941 and Toronto Maple Leafs in 1945. He passed away in St. Catharines in 1971.

An agreement was reached with Art Ross, GM of the Boston Bruins, whereby the Bruins would place for selection in St. Catharines all the players of junior age on their reserve list. This agreement would last for only three years.

At the start of the season, the *St. Catharines Standard* referred to the team as the St. Catharines Teepees Bruins. Forty-five players showed up for the Teepees first training camp, but at the end only 15 remained, and most of them were on the Boston Bruins reserve list.

The first-ever game played by the Teepees took place in Oshawa before a crowd of 4,000. Little was expected from the league's new team as it had lost its three pre-season games. During the game the Generals built up a 4-0 lead, but the Teepees scored a moral victory by fighting back and losing only 5-4. Thirty-five penalties were called during the game, including 14 misconducts. The new kids on the block were given a fine ovation from the Oshawa fans at the end of the game. The Teepee era was under way.

The first home game for the Teepees was against the Toronto Marlboros on Friday, October 31, 1947, and the Teepees prevailed 4-2 before 2,235 fans.

The first-ever Teepees goal in Garden City Arena was scored by left winger Doug Mullens and assisted by Port Credit native Andy Milne. "They are going to be popular here for no other reason than that they hit the enemy with all they have," *Standard* sports editor Clayton Browne predicted.

Players with the team who came through the St. Catharines minor hockey system were Bill Buschlen, Jim Maxwell, Tom Buck, Stan Stocker, and George Whelan.

In its first season under the sponsorship of Thompson Products, the team finished sixth in the ten-team league with 38 points in 36 games. One of the problems during the season was a lack of scoring. In 36 games the club had scored only 137 goals, but allowed 155, which was the third highest in the league.

Netminder Cec Gruhl played in most of the Teepees games. He died in Port Colborne in 1995 at age 67.

Continued on page 40

Clayton Browne, former St. Catharines Standard sports editor, December 30, 1943

ATTENDANCE FIGURES
Average per regular-season game: 2,458
Season's largest crowd: 3,744
Season's smallest crowd: 1,175

PLAYOFF ROUNDS:
1 - Galt won 2-1

1947-1948

GAMES PLAYED	WON	LOST	TIED	FOR	AGAINST	POINTS	FINISH
36	19	17	0	137	155	38	6/10

Leading Scorers

PLAYER	GOALS	ASSISTS	POINTS
Zellio Toppazzini	26	19	45
Fred Hildebrand	15	20	35
Bill Buschlen	17	16	33
Fiori Goegan	14	15	29
Wayne Service	13	10	23

Leading Goaltenders

PLAYER	GP	GA	SO	GAA
Cec Gruhl	34.5	144	0	4.17
Ivan McLelland	1.5	11	0	7.30

St. Catharines Standard photo

TEEPEES 1947-1948

OPENING GAME LINEUP
FIRST TEEPEE GAME - OCTOBER 31, 1947

1947-48 photos are from St. Catharines Museum - Wendy Hyndman Collection 2004.127. *Players information: St. Catharines Standard: Your Teepees!*

Cecil Gruhl - Goal
19, born in Welland and raised in Port Colborne. Spent last year with Dallas in Buffalo Bisons Organization.

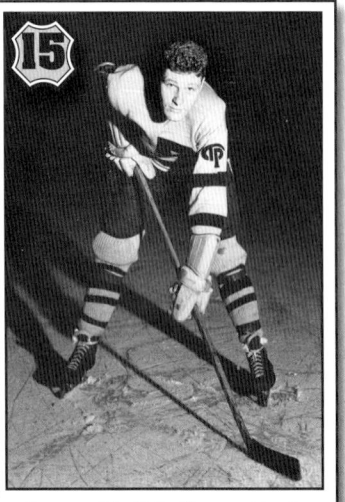

George (Red) Sullivan - Centre
17, born and played minor hockey in Peterborough. On Boston Bruins list.

Bill Buschlen - Centre/Wing
18, born in USA, raised in St. Catharines playing for 3 Ontario championship teams. He's a future Buffalo Bison.

Jim Maxwell - Right Wing
18, born in Toronto, but played minor hockey in St. Kitts on 5 championship teams. Is on reserve list of Detroit Red Wings.

Fiori (Fiery) Goegan - Defence
19, born in Fort William. Last year was with Falcons. Is on Boston Bruins list.

Tom Buck - Defence
17, born in St. Catharines. Played with 5 Ontario championship teams. Is on Toronto Maple Leafs list.

Jack McIntyre - Defence
17, comes from Listowel, Ont. Former junior B player with Listowel and Galt. Scouted by Boston Bruins.

Joe Krahulec - Defence
19, hails from Port Colborne where he played last year. He was scouted by Boston Bruins.

TEEPEES 1947-1948

Teepees Bump Dukes for 4-2 Win of Junior Opener in Scrappy Tilt

St. Catharines Standard headline and article appeared Saturday, November 1, 1947
- Bill Buschlen Scrapbook 2004.40.12(2-9)

Doug Mullens - Left Wing
19, comes from Toronto. Played on Ont. junior B championship teams in 1945-46 and 1946-47.

Wayne Service - Centre/L.Wing
19, played minor hockey in Toronto. Last season with Stratford Junior A team. Highly rated by Boston Bruins.

Andy Milne - Centre
19, born in Port Credit and played minor hockey in Toronto. Is on Boston Bruins list.

Bill Kodatsky - Right Wing
19, native of Crowland. Previous junior A experience with Port Colborne and Barrie. With St. Catharines Falcons last year.

Zellio Toppazzini - Right Wing
(Topper) 17, born and played Minor hockey in Copper Cliff, Ont. Scouted by Boston Bruins.

Fred Hildebrand - Left Wing
18, born in Sexsmith, Alberta. Played minor hockey in British Columbia. Property of Boston Bruins.

St. Catharines Teepees hit the victory mark in their home debut last night and despite counter attractions of a free city street parade, they catered to 2235 payees and doubled the score on the Toronto Marlboros of Hal Ballard and Staff Smythe at 4-2. It was fitting for Hallowe'en Night, that Art Jackson's golden Teeps rode the witches' broomsticks and turned out the bad goblins for the barber-pole Dukes. Only T-Ps used plenty of hickory and bodies with it, in their youthful flaming ardor. For their first home start (and they played far below the brand shown in Oshawa), they are going to be popular here, if for no other reason than they hit the enemy with all they have. Pacing that part of the program and yet not drawing a penalty was Fiero (Fiery) Goegan, who was in the Dukes hair all night and picked no soft spots whom he checked.

Teepees are scrappy, alright, but it will likely take them ten or a dozen games to burl off the rough edges and show the class the Stauffer-Jackson office hopes. The team still takes desperate chances, both on defence and attack and but for really brilliant work by Cec Gruhl, they would have been beaten here.

They are hard-hitting on defence, but quite loose in covering up and that stuck out like a sore thumb, when they gave up the first goal to Dukes, as a gift. T-P's signed Bill Kodatsky on Thursday and played him last night, with prospects when he works out more with the team. Both Billy Buschlen and Fred Hildebrand were hampered in the opener, the former in shooting (with his wrist in a cast) and the latter being boarded in the first period and retiring at the second siren.

Toronto Marlboros—Goal, Walmsley; defence, Bolton, Scruton; center, Timgren; wings, Hassard, Cooper; subs, McLagan, Lee, Kent, Ford, Pernfuss, McLaughlin, Clarke, French.

St. Cath. Teepees—Goal, Gruhl; defence, Goegan, Buck; centre, Sullivan; wings, Buschlen, Maxwell; subs, McIntyre, Krahulec, Mullens, Service, Milne, Hildebrand, Kadotsky, Toppazzini.

Referee, Bill Towne, Hamilton; linesman, Billy Mocha, St. Kitts.

Summary:
First Period
St. C.—Mullens (Milne) ... 5.58
Penalties—McLagan, Krahulec.
Second Period
Tor.—Pernfuss ... 9.07
St. C.—Service ... 11.27
Penalties—Goegan, Buck (major), Hassard (major), McLaughlin.
Third Period
Tor.—Clarke (French) ... 2.40
St. C.—McIntyre ... 4.52
St. C.—Goegan ... 7.20
Penalties — Buschlen, Buck (major), Clarke (major), McLagan, Pernfuss.
Goal stops—Walmsley (8-10-2) 20; Gruhl (16-7-7) 30.

From left to right, Bill Kodatsky, Wayne Service, Fiori Goegan, February, 1948
Courtesy of Bill Kodatsky

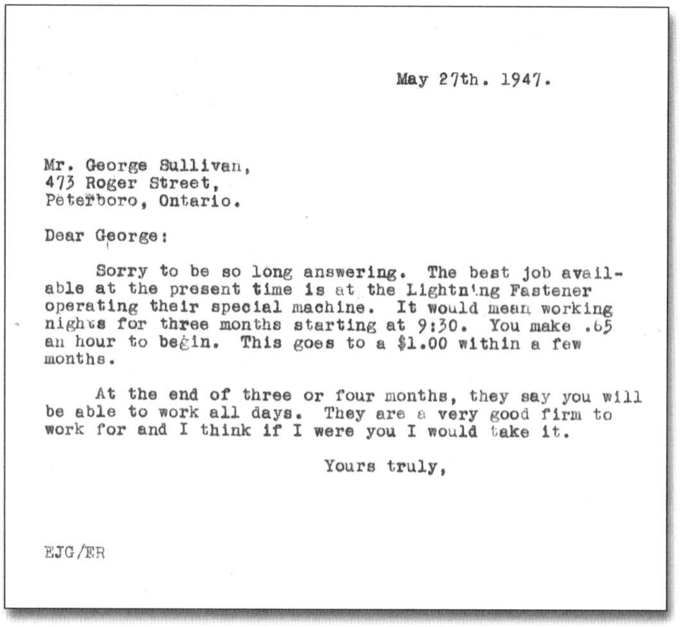

Letter to Red Sullivan from Ted Graves
St. Catharines Museum - Gatecliff Collection 2003.165

Continued from page 37

In his only season with the Teepees, Zellio Toppazzini led the team in scoring with 45 points. Toppazzini had two more years of junior eligibility, but Boston turned him pro in 1948, and the Teepees management wasn't happy.

The team was eliminated in the first round of the playoffs by Galt, 2-1, in the best of three series. Toppazzini was the top playoff performer with eight points.

Total attendance for the Teepees first season was excellent as 47,994 fans – 30,000 more than 1946-47 – watched their new team play 18 regular-season games and one playoff tilt.

At the conclusion of the season, Wayne Service, Bill Kodatsky, Joe Krahulec, and Fiori Goegan joined Boston Olympics, a Boston Bruins farm club. ■

Ivan McLelland
Spare Goaltender

ZELLIO TOPPAZZINI

Copper Cliff Ontario native Zellio Toppazzini, who played right wing in 1947-48 in St. Catharines, saw service in the NHL with Boston, New York Rangers, and Chicago.

In a pro career that spanned 16 years, 1948 to 1964, 12 seasons were spent with the AHL Providence Reds. He won an AHL scoring championship with Providence, earning 113 points and the Calder Cup in 1955-56.

Zellio Toppazzini in an AHL Providence Reds uniform
Ernie Fitzsimmons Collection

In 2000 he was voted Rhode Island Reds player of the century. As of 2006, Toppazzini was the AHL's thirteenth leading career points-getter with 786 in 785 games.

He passed away in Providence, Rhode Island, in 2001.

FIORI (FIERY) GOEGAN

One of the more popular players on the first Teepees team was Fort William native Fiori "Fiery" Goegan. The husky, barrel-chested defenceman was reported to be one of the strongest players ever to play junior A hockey in St. Catharines. His bruising body checks were a topic of conversation wherever he played.

St. Catharines Museum - Wendy Hyndman Collection 2004.127.27

Goegan played with the Falcons in 1946-47, and was the second leading scorer with nine goals and 21 points. In his first season with the Teepees, he improved to 14 goals and 29 points.

After graduating from the Teepees, he played minor pro for several teams and was a member of the 1959 world hockey champions, Belleville McFarlands.

Goegan died while playing hockey with his 22-year-old son in Belleville at age 47. His younger brother Pete played several seasons in the NHL with Detroit and Minnesota.

TEEPEES 1947-1948

BILL KODATSKY

In the fall of 1951, legendary Eddie Shore wanted ex-Teepee Bill Kodatsky to play for him in Springfield. Kodatsky had played for the Port Colborne Recs and then the Falcons before breaking his leg twice and being sidelined for almost two years. Shore wanted to pay the right winger $90 a week, but Kodatsky held out for $100. Finally Shore relented and sent the telegram pictured at right.

Kodatsky is one of the few players who can say that he took Shore for some money. Assuming that Shore couldn't remember every detail about running a hockey club, Kodatsky was able to extract his $75 train fare (from Welland to Springfield) from Shore twice! Kodatsky, who resides in Welland, is a member of the Welland Sports Wall of Fame.

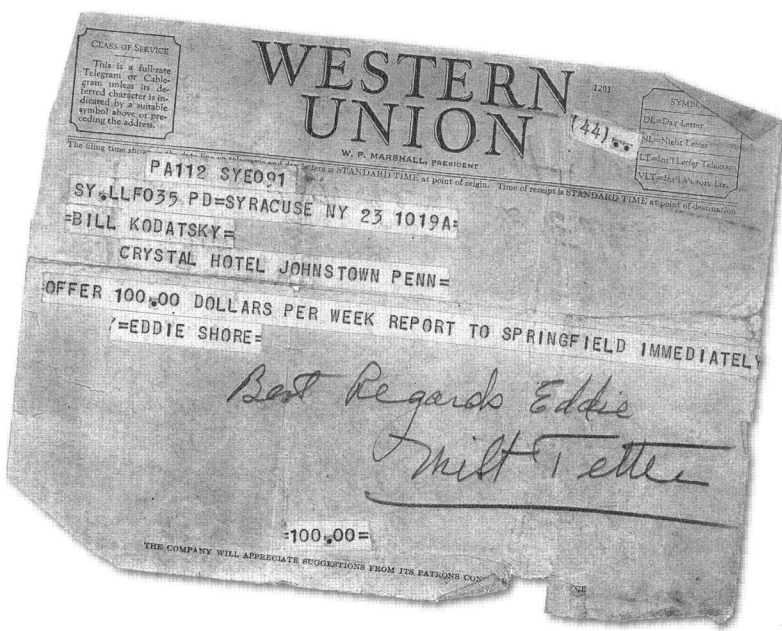

St. Catharines Museum - Wendy Hyndman Collection 2004.127.22

Courtesy of Bill Kodatsky

JACK McINTYRE

Jack McIntyre was born in Brussels, Ontario, but raised in Listowel. He was a defenceman/forward with the Teepees from 1947 to 1950. The former high school champion pole vaulter and outstanding baseball pitcher, who was drafted by the Cleveland Indians, started his pro career with Boston Bruins. They had signed him to a C form when he was 12.

He was traded to the Chicago Black Hawks in 1954, and then in 1957 he moved to the Detroit Red Wings with whom he ended his NHL career in 1960. He had his most productive year with the Hawks in 1956-57 when he earned 32 points, including 18 goals.

His NHL stats show 211 points earned in 499 regular-season games. He continued to play hockey until 1969, seeing action in AHL, EHL, WHL, CHL and OHA senior hockey. He coached Detroit-owned teams in the AHL and at the minor pro level.

After working for Molson Breweries, he became a car salesman in London. He was the first coach of the Junior A London Nationals who entered the OHA in 1965. Two of his sons, Rick and Randy, both saw action for the London Junior A club in the 1970s.

McIntyre passed away in London in 1998.

Jack celebrating four-goal game as a Boston Bruin March, 1953
Courtesy of Randy McIntyre

Action shot vs Chicago, 1953
Courtesy of Randy McIntyre

Jack McIntyre and son Randy with Chicago Black Hawks in 1957
Courtesy of Randy McIntyre

41

REX STIMERS

Former Niagara District Imperial Oil supervisor, Rex Stimers, joined radio station CKTB in St. Catharines in 1935. Nicknamed "The Lung," "The Throat," and "The Voice" by different sportswriters, Stimers was the radio voice of the Falcons, Teepees and Black Hawks. He broadcast both the 1954 and 1960 Memorial Cup games.

In the 1940s, he broadcast the St. Catharines Senior A Saints hockey games and made quite an impression on *Toronto Star* sports reporter Red Burnett. "To us, friend Stimers sounds like a cross between W. C. Fields and a side show barker. He can get hotter than the best man on the ice and there is no limit on the pitch that he raises his voice when the prides of the Miami of Canada turn on the heat…In fact, one almost expected the excited announcer to pop right out of the radio."

But his broadcasts were not limited to hockey. He also was on the air for lacrosse, bowling, baseball, basketball, wrestling and boxing. He was even on the air when the King and Queen visited St. Catharines to officially open the Queen Elizabeth Way.

Reporting on sports was not a job. "It was a way of life, a passion, a 24 hour-a-day proposition, 12 months of every year," former *St. Catharines Standard* sports editor Jack Gatecliff said.

Listeners tuned in to Stimers' broadcasts fully aware that his colourful game descriptions were anything but neutral. "I don't care who wins, as long as it's our team," Stimers was heard to say. Some tuned in just to hear him rant and rave.

Whether he was talking about "ten bell saves," "putting the biscuit in the basket," "the sin bin", or the virtues of "the Banana Belt", Stimers helped to put St. Catharines on the hockey map.

One of Stimers' most embarrassing moments came during a March 16, 1957 hockey game with the Toronto Marlboros. Teepee winger Johnny McKenzie scored a short-handed goal in the third period, and Stimers jumped for joy in the broadcast booth. In doing so, he lost his pants. "Just fortunate I wasn't on TV," Stimers said at the time.

What Foster Hewitt was to hockey in Toronto, Stimers was to sports in the Garden City. The Toronto native started his broadcasting career a few months after Hewitt in 1925.

For several years, he and his fellow broadcaster Tommy Garriock, who was also his brother-in-law, sat in radio station CKTB and simulated play-by-play lacrosse broadcasts using phone reports from the out-of-town games. The ghost broadcasts continued until one of the reporters, Haggis MacIntosh, didn't phone in a report after the third quarter of a road game. After stalling on the air for several minutes, Stimers reported that the game was called because of rain and sleet. That was the end of the reconstructed broadcasts.

Stimers died on April 1, 1966, a few weeks after his final Black Hawks broadcast. He was survived by his wife Flora, whom Rex had nicknamed Momma.

Stimers joined the Canadian Lacrosse Hall of Fame in 1971, and was inducted into the St. Catharines Sports Hall of Fame in 1991, and the Sports Media Canada Honour Roll in 2004.

"I was raised in Toronto, but the best thing that ever happened to me there was getting on the train which brought me to St. Catharines," Stimers told Gatecliff.

Bob Dunn's Cigar Store and Lunch Counter was located at the corner of Queenston Street and Thorold Road. (now Oakdale Ave.) This was a very busy corner as this was where people transfered from local buses to buses going to Merritton and Thorold.

As a young teenager, I worked for Bob, and used to open the store at 9:00 a.m. on a Sunday morning. On several occasions there would be a gentleman sitting in his car in front of the store, waiting for me to open up. He would come in and order his usual. One half cup of vinegar, half cup of water, two raw eggs, which I would put in the milkshake blender to mix up, and then he would drink it down.

If you knew this gentleman, you would understand why he would have such a concoction on a Sunday morning.

He was none other than Mr. Rex Stimers. The young teenager was Whitey Frick.

Bob Dunn had two brothers Lance and Jay, who owned Dunn's Florist.

– Whitey Frick

Rex Stimers on the air   St. Catharines Museum - *Tommy Garriock Collection N 10,240*

TOMMY GARRIOCK

Tom Garriock and Rex Stimers were not only brothers-in-law, they worked as a team on radio station CKTB. Garriock remembered exactly when his broadcasting career began. "My first broadcast was on June 26, 1938," Garriock told Jack Gatecliff. It was a ghost broadcast of a lacrosse game between St. Catharines Athletics and Orillia Terriers. Stimers and Garriock reconstructed the play-by-play using information relayed on the phone by Jay MacDonald, who was at the actual game.

St. Catharines Standard photo

From 1938 to 1966, the duo broadcast lacrosse, hockey, softball, basketball and baseball games. In the hockey booth at Garden City Arena, Tom would sit beside Rex and have dates, names and stats available for the radio broadcasts.

Sometimes he would replace Rex at the microphone if Rex lost his voice or became too excited. Sometimes there was no warning. Rex would just hand the microphone to his partner. "Tommy, take over, I'm exhausted," Stimers told Garriock one evening when nine-year-old Ralph Willis was a guest in the broadcast booth.

Garriock, the St. Catharines postmaster for 35 years, also reported sports news on CKTB at 11:15 p.m. nightly from February 7, 1947, to May 5, 1990. The sports roundup was scheduled for five minutes, but it often lasted for at least 30 minutes. Hockey scouts would often tune in to get all the details.

He retired from broadcasting in 1990 and was inducted into the St. Catharines Sports Hall of Fame in 1992. Garriock, who lived on a 73-acre farm on 11th Street Louth, died on May 26, 2005. He was in his ninetieth year.

Garriock with Elmer Vasko (left) and Stan Mikita (centre)
St. Catharines Museum - *Cheryl Steele Ref. File, February 27, 2006*

St. Catharines Teepee puck with "Pee Wee"
St. Catharines Museum - *John Brown Collection 2004.89.9*

One of the announcers at CKTB who read the commercials during junior A games, when Rex was doing the play-by-play, was Cec Linder. Linder later took on a new career as an actor and played Felix Leiter in the James Bond film *Goldfinger*. He also spent several years on the soap operas, *The Secret Storm* and *The Edge of Night*, in addition to many supporting roles in theatre, movies and TV.

Linder died in 1992 at age 71.

TEEPEES 1947-1948

The Standard, Saturday, October 12, 1985 — 11

Spectrum

Classical guitarist Liona Boyd goes commercial — Page 19
Rock video form is being grafted onto TV dramas — Page 17

K & M Autohaus
VOLKSWAGEN
SALES-SERVICE-PARTS
354-3829
4424 Montrose Rd., Niagara Falls
• SCIROCCO • CABRIOLET
• GOLF • JETTA • GTI

Radio untouched by time

If you want sports, Tommy says it all

By PETER CONRADI
Standard Staff

IN the world of modern radio, where brief is better, Tom Garriock is a fascinating anomaly. Since 1948, CKTB's late-night sportscast and the 70-year-old veteran behind the microphone have become an institution in the Niagara Region. As such, the program is probably unique in Canadian AM radio.

There is no slick production. Seldom are voice reports used. Interviews are rare. There isn't even a time limit. Every Monday to Saturday, Garriock, in his inimitable style, just goes from 11:10 p.m. until he's finished.

"A program like Tommy's is unheard of in radio these days," says CKTB station manager Pat Kiely. "When I first heard it, I was in favor of it because I'm interested in sports, and it provides such a complete dose of information that the real fan can't get anywhere else.

"But as a radio manager I was also surprised by it. It's long, it rambles at times, Tommy won't make much use of clips, and his delivery isn't pretty — it's rough and 'staccato.'

"But at the same time it is his personality that makes him successful. He is like Gordon Sinclair was. And there is no

"He's an institution, and we don't even try to compete with him. Our format doesn't allow us to. Our news, weather, sports package runs no longer than 15 minutes. But even though he's with the competition, I have to say that he's one of the finest gentlemen I've ever met in broadcasting. When I first came to this city he shook my hand and said if there is anything I can help you with, just call. That was 13 years ago and I'll always remember it."

☆ ☆ ☆

CKTB marks its 55th birthday this month, and Tom Garriock has seen 47 of them. He's been called a throwback to the days of early radio, and with good reason. He has been around almost since the beginning of radio in this city.

"The times may have changed, but I don't think I have too much. I'm no actor on the air, never have been. I don't get 'up' to go on. I don't have the golden voice. My style has always been to get on, get the message across, and get off.

"I use straight material. Most of it comes in about 30 minutes before I go on the air, so I don't often have time to mess around with things like voice reports and clips. I don't think I lose anything by not having them."

Growing up through the glory days of St. Catharines sports, Garriock has enough tales and anecdotes to fill a book.

"I've seen so many exciting games and amazing things. One thing that sticks out in my mind was what had to be the largest crowd for a sporting event in St. Catharines. It was in 1931 or '32. The Junior Ath-

44

TEEPEES 1948-1949

TEEPEES SET NEW ATTENDANCE RECORDS

ATTENDANCE FIGURES
Average per regular-season game: 3,469
Season's largest crowd: 4,097
Season's smallest crowd: 2,429

PLAYOFF ROUNDS:
2 - Beat Oshawa 2-0
Lost to Toronto Marlboros 3-0

1948-1949

GAMES PLAYED	WON	LOST	TIED	FOR	AGAINST	POINTS	FINISH
48	25	20	3	191	198	53	4/9

Leading Scorers

PLAYER	GOALS	ASSISTS	POINTS
George (Red) Sullivan	31	48	79
Fred Hildebrand	26	41	67
Bud Evans	29	25	54
Jerry Toppazzini	24	20	44
Bill Buschlen	18	23	41

Leading Goaltenders

PLAYER	GP	GA	SO	GAA
George (Porky) Douglas	27	123	0	4.55
Don Campbell	21	74	1	3.52

Teepees leave for Boston Bruins training camp in Hershey on Sept. 20, 1948. Front row: Wayne (Weiner) Brown, Jerry Toppazzini, Zellio Toppazzini. Back row: Ellard (Obie) O'Brien, Buddy Evans, George Scott, Marcel Clements, Jack McIntyre
St. Catharines Standard photo

In September, 1948, the Teepees held their training camp in Hershey, Pennsylvania. It was the first time a Canadian amateur team trained outside this country.

When the season started, there were six players who had come up through the St. Catharines minor hockey system: George (Porky) Douglas, Tom Buck, Ellard (Obie) O'Brien, Bill Buschlen, Connie Switzer, and Bill Altoft.

One new player, Bob Knowles, came from the Teepees archrivals, the Toronto Marlboros. While he was with the Marlies, coached by former NHLers Syl Apps and then Bob Davidson, players were encouraged to play an aggressive game, go into the corners and rough it up. If any player got cut playing rough, he would get $5 per stitch.

Back row: Carl Brunshaw (prop-man) Bill Altoft, Gord Byers, Ron Telford, Jerry Toppazzini, Tom Buck, Marcel Clements, Jack McIntyre, Obie O'Brien, Ron Rubic, Art Jackson Front row: Bob Knowles, Connie Switzer, Bud Evans, Porky Douglas, Don Campbell, Wayne Brown, Fred Hildebrand, Bill Buschlen

45

GEORGE DOUGLAS

George (Porky) Douglas defeated the St. Michael's College Majors twice in one weekend during the 1948-49 season. On Friday, January 7, 1949, the 5-foot-8, 129-pound goalie took a three-stitch cut over the eye in the game warm-up, but returned and played an outstanding game in front of 3,715 at Garden City Arena, winning 6-1. The next night in Maple Leaf Gardens, he led the Teepees to a 2-1 victory over the same team.

"His efforts in the Friday game looked considerably pale in comparison to the Houdini-like chore he did in Toronto on Saturday," The Standard reported.

"I was such a cute, round little fellow, my parents called me Porky," Douglas told Jack Gatecliff in 1982.

Porky was the netminder for a St. Catharines bantam club (1944) and two juvenile teams (1947 and 1948) that won All-Ontario championships before he joined the Teepees in 1948.

He worked at Thompson Products for 42 years, spending his spare time refereeing and coaching minor league hockey teams for 34 years.

He may be retired, but today the St. Catharines native stays active as a volunteer and he golfs regularly.

St. Catharines Museum - O'Brien Collection, C10,727

GORD BYERS

Eganville Ontario native Gord Byers played defence for the Teepees from 1948 to 1950. In 1949-50, he made a one-game appearance and recorded one assist with the Boston Bruins. In November, 1949, he was appointed team captain when Red Sullivan was called up to the Boston Bruins.

Gord's pro career included stops in the EAHL and the USHL before he returned to the amateur ranks. Byers closed out his career with the Senior A Sudbury Wolves in 1956-57.

He died in 2001 in Oklahoma.

St. Catharines Museum - O'Brien Collection, C10,729

Knowles, a former Marlboro teammate of ex-Toronto Maple Leaf star George Armstrong, graduated from the St. Catharines Collegiate, and when his junior career was over he worked for Thompson Products for several years.

In 1957 he and his wife Shirley moved to Rialto, California, where the father of five has operated a successful insurance business since 1965.

Another newcomer to the team was netminder Don Campbell, who was born in Calgary but raised in Toronto's west end. Campbell played his minor hockey for the Toronto Marlboros organization and when he turned 16, signed a C form with the Boston Bruins. Before coming to the Teepees, he won two Sutherland Cups with the Junior B Toronto De LaSalle club and then joined the Stratford Kroehlers for the 1947-48 season. He was traded to St. Catharines for Bibber O'Hearn.

Don Campbell *St. Catharines Museum - Toppazzini Collection, C10,615*

After Campbell finished his junior career in St. Catharines, he played for the IHL Grand Rapids Rockets, the EHL Boston Olympics, and finally the Senior A Charlottetown Islanders.

He retired at 24, returned to Fort Erie and worked for Campbell Construction, a firm partly owned by his dad. In 1954 he took over from his father and stayed with the company until 1993. He continues to reside in Fort Erie. "Just playing with the Teepees was an honour," Campbell said in 2006.

The team got off on the right foot by winning the season opener 4-3 over Galt in overtime. After nine games, the club had a record of 7-1-1 and was playing well, but it tailed off toward the end of the season and finished fourth. Goals-against continued to be a problem as the club allowed 198 goals, fourth highest in the league.

The team went two rounds in the playoffs, ousting the Oshawa Generals in two games in the first round. Red Sullivan scored four goals in the third period – three consecutive goals in 69 seconds – in the 9-5 win that eliminated the Generals. "Nothing, as far as I'm concerned, has since topped that moment," said Sullivan in 1961, when he was the New York Rangers captain.

Sullivan had an outstanding year leading the team in scoring with 79 points, including 31 goals. He added six more goals in the playoffs. It was quite an achievement after scoring 22 points in his rookie year. In the second round, Toronto Marlboros put the Teepees out in three straight games.

In 1948-49, a record for total attendance at Teepees home games was set as 91,795 attended 23 regular-season games and three playoff contests. This represented an increase of almost 44,000 fans after playing seven more games than in the 1947-48 season. The Teepees share of hockey revenue jumped to $44,669.24 from $15,813.43 the previous season.

■

Radio station CKTB broadcaster Rex Stimers (centre), kids around with Boston Bruins executives Art Ross, left and Weston Adams on January 7, 1949.

St. Catharines Standard photo

TEEPEES 1948-1949

Left to right: Bill Altoft, Connie Switzer, and Wayne Brown
St. Catharines Museum - Toppazzini Collection, C10,608

Left to right: Jerry Toppazzini, Bill Buschlen, and Marcel Clements
St. Catharines Museum - Toppazzini Collection, C10,626

Left to right: Buddy Evans, Red Sullivan, and Fred Hildebrand
St. Catharines Museum - Toppazzini Collection, C10,617

St. Catharines Museum - Wendy Hyndman Ref. File, July 12, 2004

Penalties And Speed Feature Junior Hockey Tilt

Four penalties in fast succession made the housing problem felt in the Maple Leaf Gardens penalty box this afternoon during the first period of the Toronto Marlboros - St. Catharines Tee-Pees OHA Junior A semi-final. Tee-Pees No. 12 Toppazzini has three Marlies for company — Windley (12), Pirie (15), Lee (3). There were 12 penalties in the game won by the Marlies 4-2.

– *appeared in* The Toronto Telegram *March 5, 1949*

Former Teepee Bill Buschlen signs a C Form (worth $100) on a ship in the Port Weller Dry Docks with the Buffalo Bisons Rudy Pilous on May 25, 1949.
St. Catharines Standard photo

St. Catharines Museum - O'Brien Collection, C10,722

JERRY TOPPAZZINI

Jerry Toppazzini, brother of Zellio, played for the Teepees in 1948-49 before moving on to the Barrie Flyers. In 1950-51 the right winger, nicknamed "Topper", scored 90 points with Barrie on the way to a Memorial Cup victory.

The Copper Cliff Ontario native played in 783 regular-season NHL games with Boston, Chicago and Detroit from 1952 to 1964, scoring 163 goals and 407 points. He had his best NHL season when he scored 49 points, including 25 goals, in 1957-58. He appeared in three NHL all-star games.

While in the NHL, he donned goalie pads for three different emergency situations and never gave up a goal. Ex-Boston Bruins netminder Don Simmons recalled one of those emergencies in a game against the Chicago Black Hawks, with a little over a minute to play. "Toppazzini took my gloves and my stick and my mask and they said to Bobby Hull and everybody: 'no slap shots'," Simmons said.

Today, Toppazzini, a former Sudbury Wolves OHA Junior A coach, lives in Sudbury.

BILL BUSCHLEN

Although he was born in Oak Park, Illinois, Bill Buschlen grew up in St. Catharines and was one of the city's outstanding hockey players.

Before joining the Teepees, the centreman played a leading role in winning two Ontario bantam titles and then an Ontario juvenile championship for the St. Catharines Lions in 1946-47.

He signed a C form with the AHL Buffalo Bisons for $100, and attended their training camp in 1949; however, he opted for a career in sales.

The former Garden City minor hockey coach retired in 1991 and lives in St. Catharines.

TEEPEES 1948-1949

Red Sullivan and Jerry Toppazzini, teammates in 1948-49, would soon both enjoy NHL careers.
St. Catharines Museum - *Toppazzini Collection, C10,622*

BOOSTER TICKETS NOW ON SALE TO THE GENERAL PUBLIC!

The Garden City Teepees, St. Catharines entry in the Junior O.H.A. League is the strongest ever this year! You'll want a booster ticket to guarantee that same good seat for every game!

- BOOSTER TICKETS ONLY $1.00
- OPENING GAME SOON
- ONLY 1500 BOOSTER SEATS WILL BE SOLD.
- Remember holders of this year's booster tickets get first chance next year!

NEW ADMISSION PRICES: Side Reds $1.25, Side Blues $1.00, Ends and Corners 75c.

PLEASE NOTE
To retain the privileges extended through purchase of a booster ticket, the holder must purchase his seat ticket for all but four of the regular scheduled games. Failure to do so forfeits the right to the Booster Ticket privileges.

St. Catharines Standard

The people sitting in the front row of Garden City Arena watching a Teepees game are (left to right) Boston scout Harold (Baldy) Cotton and St. Catharines boys, Ted Lott and Terry O'Malley. Sitting directly behind Lott is Teepees President George Stauffer. Sitting above Cotton is Boston Bruins President Weston Adams and above O'Malley is Bruins GM Art Ross.
Courtesy of Ted Lott

48

TEEPEES 1949-1950

STAUFFER CUTS TIES WITH BOSTON BRUINS

The Teepees came out of the gate strongly in their third season as they humbled the Galt Black Hawks 12-2 in the league opener, October 14, 1949, at Garden City Arena. "The attendance was 2,741 paid and would have another 1,000 had the absentees figured Art Jackson had a squad as full of ginger, vim, vigour, and team fight, mixed in with unselfish passing," the *Standard* reported. Listowell native Jack Mcintyre led the way with four goals. The next night the Teepees beat the Black Hawks in their own arena 7-2.

The team finished in third place with 58 points in 48 games, but was knocked out of the first round of the playoffs by Guelph Biltmores in five games. Future NHL star Andy Bathgate led the Biltmores to victory.

The difference with this Teepee team was its ability, as Rex Stimers would say, "to put the biscuit in the basket," as it scored 269 goals in 48 games and allowed 211.

The total attendance of 67,746 for the season saw 24,000 fewer fans at the 26 Teepees home games, compared to the 26 games played in 1948-49. For some reason, the team's share of revenue was reported to be only $1,500 lower than 1948-49.

Sullivan Jumps T-Ps
Red Sullivan Signed By Big Bruins
Club Shocks Teepees;
Will Centre For
Ed Sandford

In 1949-50, Art Jackson's last season as coach, the star of the team was Peterborough native George (Red) Sullivan who was leading the league in goals and assists in November, 1949. Sullivan never got a chance to win the league points championship because the NHL Boston Bruins, who had a working agreement with the Teepees, pulled the 19-year-old centre out of St. Catharines on Monday, November 14, 1949, without consulting Teepees officials.

"Sure enough the TPs were handed a lethal punch in the butt, but they'll come back the right way and win a lot of games for you folk before the cur-

ATTENDANCE FIGURES
Average per regular-season game: 2,516
Season's largest crowd: 3,803
Season's smallest crowd: 1,533

PLAYOFF ROUNDS:
1 - Eliminated by Guelph 3-2

1949-1950

GAMES PLAYED	WON	LOST	TIED	FOR	AGAINST	POINTS	FINISH
48	27	17	4	269	211	58	3/9

Leading Scorers

PLAYER	GOALS	ASSISTS	POINTS
Connie Switzer	35	77	112
Ellard (Obie) O'Brien	58	43	101
Norm Corcoran	33	36	69
Jack McIntyre	23	24	47
Jack White	20	23	43

Leading Goaltenders

PLAYER	GP	GA	SO	GAA
George (Porky) Douglas	24	109	1	4.54
Don Campbell	24	102	0	4.25

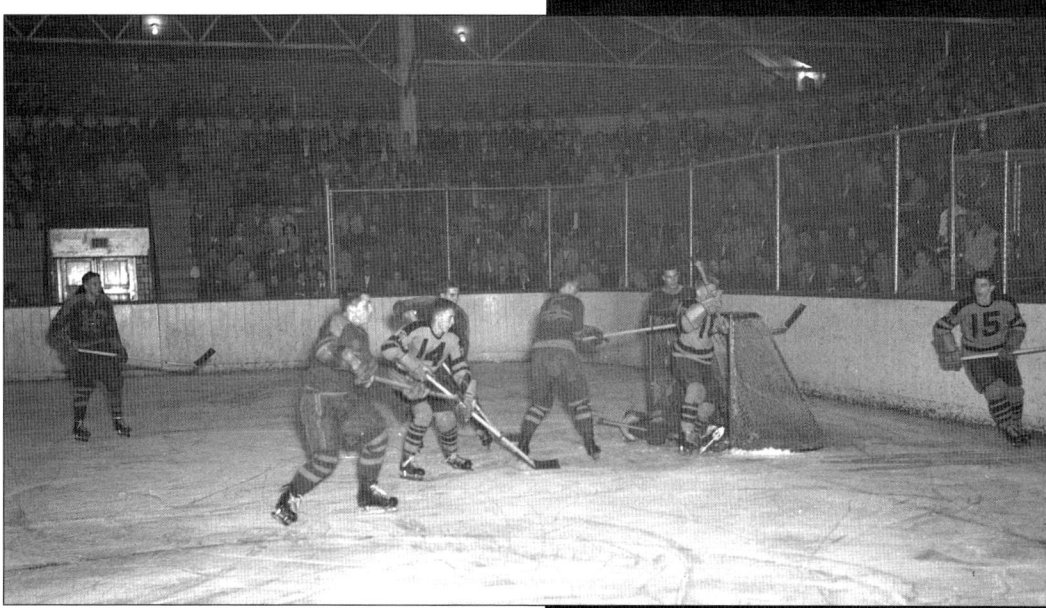

Red Sullivan
St. Catharines Museum - *Toppazzini Collection, C10,623*

Teepees Jack White (14), Buddy Boone (in the net) and Wayne Brown (15) swarm the Galt Black Hawks net in a 12-2 home-opener win October 14, 1949.

St. Catharines Standard photo

49

Teepees Coach/GM Rudy Pilous (left) signs an agreement with the AHL Buffalo Bisons on July 21, 1950, while Thompson Products executives Jack Leach (centre) and President George Stauffer (right) look on.
St. Catharines Standard photo

tain falls," wrote *Standard* sports editor Clayton Browne on November 15, 1949, after learning Boston had taken Sullivan out of St. Catharines.

Teammate Norm Corcoran remembered when Red Sullivan got the call. He was sitting in the Teepees dressing room when Sullivan told him he had a decision to make. "They [Boston management] want me to go with the Bruins. I don't know what to do," Sullivan said. "I told him to go," Corcoran recalled from his St. Catharines home on March 1, 2005.

"I was just told to pick up my skates from the Teepees dressing room, get a train ticket and go to Boston," Sullivan told *St. Catharines Standard* sports editor Jack Gatecliff in 1971.

In the fall of 2004, at the St. Catharines Junior A reunion, Sullivan made it clear that if he had to do it over again, he wouldn't have left the Teepees. "The biggest problem I had was getting my skates from (trainer) Jimmy Joy," Sullivan recalled from his home in Indian River, Ontario, 54 years later.

After playing only three games with the Bruins, Sullivan was sent to the AHL Hershey Bears. It was a move the Bruins would regret. Stauffer ended the Teepees agreement with Boston and connected with the AHL Buffalo Bisons on July 21, 1950. When Chicago Black Hawks added the Bisons to their farm system in 1955, they inherited the Teepees.

In the next few years, the Black Hawks, not the Bruins, would have Stan Mikita, Bobby Hull, Phil Esposito, Chico Maki, and many other Teepees move up to the NHL.

Sullivan won an AHL scoring championship setting a record for assists (89) and points (119) in 1953-54 while playing with the Hershey Bears. He played ten years in the NHL with Chicago, Boston and the New York Rangers, collecting 346 points in 557 games. He later coached 364 NHL games in New York, Pittsburgh and Washington.

"That's the best place [St. Catharines] I ever played hockey," Sullivan said. "If it wasn't for St. Catharines maybe I wouldn't have made it to the majors."

After Sullivan left the team, 5-foot-4 St. Catharines minor hockey product, Connie Switzer, caught fire and led the league in scoring until the final days of the season. He centred a line with two big wingers, St. Catharines native Ellard (Obie) O'Brien and Torontonian Norm Corcoran.

"Connie was like a flyweight boxer between two heavyweights, but the things he could do with the puck had to be seen to be appreciated," Gatecliff wrote in 1971.

When Switzer was nine, he entertained fans at Garden City Arena between periods of Masons Junior B games. He wowed the spectators with his smooth skating and expert stickhandling. "He was a wizard with the puck," said Switzer's close friend and former minor hockey teammate, Archie Katzman, the general manager of the St. Catharines Club.

Switzer and O'Brien were the first two St.

Teepees trainer Jimmy Joy was reluctant to let Red Sullivan take his skates out of the dressing room in Nov. 1949. He didn't know Sullivan was heading for Boston.
St. Catharines Museum - Wayne Brown Collection 2004.140.4

Connie Switzer
St. Catharines Museum - Toppazzini Collection, C10,264

Ellard (Obie) O'Brien
St. Catharines Museum - Toppazzini Collection, C10,621

OHA Junior 'A'

Final Standing

	P	W	L	T	F	A	Pts
Marlboros	48	37	9	2	253	119	76
Windsor	48	34	13	1	307	169	69
St. Catharines	48	27	17	4	269	211	58
Guelph	48	26	18	3	189	157	56
Barrie	48	21	24	3	164	213	45
St. Michael's	48	19	26	3	185	218	41
Stratford	48	14	31	3	144	265	31
Galt	48	14	32	2	160	262	30
Oshawa	48	12	34	2	160	262	26

Wednesday's Results
Windsor 5, Marlboros 1
Oshawa 10, St. Michael's 3
Stratford 8, St. Catharines 4

Future Games
Friday—Guelph at St. Catharines; Toronto St. Michael's at Barrie (playoffs).
Saturday—Windsor at Marlboros (Maple Leaf Gardens, 2:30 p.m.); St. Michael's at Barrie; St. Catharines at Guelph (playoff).

Scoring Leaders

	GP	G	A	Pts
Reibel, Windsor	48	53	76	129
Armstrong, Marlboros	45	64	51	115
Switzer, St. Catharines	48	35	77	112
Stankiewicz, Windsor	47	53	49	102
O'Brien, St. Catharines	48	58	43	101
Skov, Windsor	47	52	45	100
Grosse, Windsor	46	42	45	87
McKenzie, Marlboros	48	37	41	78
Flanagan, Stratford	46	33	36	69
Corcoran, St. Catharines	47	25	40	65
Plumb, Guelph				

Norm Corcoran
St. Catharines Museum - Frank Martin Collection, C10,747

Catharines Junior A players to go over 100 points in a regular season. Switzer finished third in the league with 112 points and was runner-up to George Armstrong for the Red Tilson Trophy. Left winger O'Brien was fifth with 101 points, including 58 goals, making him the first St. Catharines Junior A player to score 50 or more goals in a season.

Despite this high-scoring line, which earned 282 points, the Teepees were knocked out of the playoffs by Guelph in the first round in five games. Jack McIntyre led the team in playoff points with eight, including five goals. Norm Corcoran led the club in goals with six.

Switzer was deemed too small to make it in pro hockey, but he did travel to Scotland where he played for the Dunfermline Vikings and was one of the club's top scorers. After the Scottish league folded he left to coach in Switzerland, and returned to St. Catharines in 1956.

At one time he considered a career as a jockey, but he found he was too heavy. He ended up working for local businesses in his hometown.

Switzer, who had played with six consecutive OMHA championship teams, passed away in St. Catharines on July 9, 1995.

O'Brien, who started playing as a defenceman with the Teepees before switching to left wing and centre, turned pro and spent several years on left wing as captain with the AHL Hershey Bears, winning Calder Cups in 1958 and 1959. His best year as a pro came in 1954-55 when he collected 69 points, including 31 goals.

In 1955-56 he suited up for two games with the Boston Bruins. Boston was interested in keeping him with the Bruins, but the Bears were determined to keep him in Hershey.

Former teammate Corcoran described O'Brien as one of the best players offensively and defensively in the AHL; however, he got a bad break. "He spent eight years in Hershey when he should have been in the NHL," Corcoran said. "Boston offered four good players for him, but the Bears wouldn't let him go."

"Despite all the years in pro, my fondest memories are the late 1940s with the Teepees," O'Brien told Gatecliff in 1988.

After a successful sales career with Molson Breweries and working with the St. Catharines Black Hawks in the 1960s and 1970s, O'Brien retired and still lives in St. Catharines.

Corcoran spent 16 years as a pro from 1950 to 1966. He played 29 NHL games with Boston Bruins, Detroit Red Wings, and Chicago Black Hawks. The right winger also saw action in the 1955 NHL All-Star game. Although he played for American League teams in Springfield, Buffalo, Quebec, Pittsburgh and Providence, playing in Hershey was his favourite spot. He now resides in the Garden City. ■

The next week or two will be an important time in the lives of the young St. Catharines hockey players pictured above. all products of the St. Catharines Minor Hockey Association teams. These players have come up through the ranks of bantam, midget and juvenile, and last winter were all signed to try-out forms with Boston Bruins, of the National Hockey League. After a training session in Barrie, all will return to St. Catharines, some to continue with the Juvenile Lions of Stan Elliott and Vic Teal, and others to make the big jump into OHA Junior A with Teepees. Players above are (left to right): Bud Smith, Frank Toyota, Skip Teal, Jim Swain, Ralph Willis, Wayne Brown, Ernie Bodnar, and Ralph Markarian. The fellow dishing out words of wisdom in front is Coach Vic Teal while Jim Robertson kneels beside him so he won't miss a phrase. Frank Martin, another Garden City native to make the trip, was absent on holiday when picture was taken.

(Staff Photo, *Standard* Photo engraving.)

Teepee Connie Switzer (10) scores on Stratford goalie Boat Hurley in a Nov. 15, 1949 game played without leading scorer Red Sullivan who had left for Boston. The Falcons won 8-2.
St. Catharines Standard photo

18 THE ST. CATHARINES STANDARD, SATURDAY, OCTOBER 22, 1949

Fog Halts Tee Pee-Marlboro Classic

Teepees Deprived of Victory After 6-3 Lead in Second By Fog With Powerhouse Dukes

The toughest type of loss in the sports world is one over whom no one has any control and that's exactly what happened to St. Kitts Teepees last night at Garden City arena. In their first seasonal clash with the powerhouse Toronto Dukes, Art Jackson's gamecock youngsters built up a 6-3 lead by the end of the second period and then had the game called– because of fog. Under strict O.H.A. rules, the puck business must go three full periods, so some 3,615 wildly-cheering backers of the Teeps were as much disappointed as coach Art Jackson and the gold-black team. For the game has to be replayed later on, which gave patrons a break, as they were returned the equivalent of rainchecks.

TEEPEES UNVEILED IN ST. MIKE'S EXHIBITION

By the time you read this, the St. Catharines Teepees, 1949-50 class, will be officially participating in the Junior O.H.A. "A" race, under the able guidance of former National Hockey League star, Art Jackson. The "Teeps" enjoyed a fairish amount of prosperity last season, although they weren't exactly "hot" contenders for the league title.

But this is another year, and Mentor Jackson firmly believes that his 49-50 model is miles ahead of last season's team, and carries a much more potent punch, thanks to a few new additions and the inevitable improvement which comes with added experience.

Pre-season workouts, while disappointing at times, proved that Jackson has a team with great potentialities and given a few favourable nods from Dame Fortune will provide Garden City hockey addicts with a brand of the winter pastime which will eclipse all previous efforts.

The "Teeps" opened their season with an exhibition clash with their arch-rivals of last season, "Gentleman Joe" Primeau's Toronto St. Mikes, and wound up with a 7-3 triumph.

Elsewhere in these pages, CKTB's affable — and voluble — Rex Stimers discusses the Teepees on a more detailed basis — and so, on behalf of the publishers of this new Garden City Arena Programme and Sports Magazine, the best of luck to the Garden City Teepees for the new season.

St. Catharines Museum - *Wayne Brown Collection 2004.140.6*

St. Catharines Museum - *E.A. Donegan 2004.133.2*

TEEPEES 1950-1951

RUDY PILOUS NEW TEEPEES BENCH BOSS

ATTENDANCE FIGURES
Average per regular-season game: 1,981
Season's largest crowd: 3,972
Season's smallest crowd: 1,295

PLAYOFF ROUNDS: 2
Eliminated Guelph 3-2
Lost to Toronto Marlboros 3-1

In 1950 Rudy Pilous stepped back into the Teepees picture after the Falcons co-founder had won minor league championships with the Buffalo Bisons farm teams in Houston (1948) and San Diego (1949). Stauffer wanted him back, and after several months of negotiations hired him as the Teepees GM on August 1, 1950.

"After the first two or three years of junior A hockey, I came to two conclusions in particular. One, hockey was not my business. I therefore made arrangements for Rudy Pilous to take over the Junior A hockey club after he paid off some debts and won his first Memorial Cup," Stauffer wrote in a letter to Jack Gatecliff in October, 1997.

Before the start of the season, Stauffer announced that Art Jackson, who was Thompson Products director of personnel, was temporarily retiring as the Teepees coach due to business pressure. Pilous took charge behind the bench, and over the next eight seasons he became one of junior hockey's most successful coaches.

Pilous was also serious about cutting costs to make the club a financial success. "No more steaks for breakfast or overnight trips to Windsor by train," Pilous said at the time. "We were going to live within a budget."

One of Pilous' smartest moves before the season began was to sign Port Colborne native Don Simmons to play in goal. "Rudy Pilous came over to the house one day and asked me if I wanted to play in St. Catharines and I said 'sure,'" Simmons recalled on July 4, 2005, in Crystal Beach, Ontario. "Every time I'd see Rudy Pilous when he was alive, he would say, '35 Cross Street'. That's where I lived."

"There was no deal," the Ridgeway resident recalled. "Room and board and I think 35 bucks a week. I got a job at Thompson Products."

Simmons has never forgotten what CKTB broadcaster Rex Stimers used to say after his Teepee roommate Buddy Boone scored a goal. "Buddy Boone booted the biscuit into the basket to bottle up the ball game," listeners learned.

Simmons played 53 of the 54 regular-season games and earned five shutouts with a 3.41 goals-against average. Previously at 16, he had attended a Detroit Red Wings training camp where he competed with future NHL stars Harry Lumley and Glenn Hall.

In his first game as coach in 1950-51, Pilous guided the club to a 4-3 overtime win over the visiting Toronto Marlboros, and then the team tied archrival St. Michael's College Majors 1-1 in game two.

During the team's sixth game at Windsor on October 27, 1950, Pilous

1950-1951

GAMES PLAYED	WON	LOST	TIED	FOR	AGAINST	POINTS	FINISH
54	23	24	7	200	192	53	6/10

Leading Scorers

PLAYER	GOALS	ASSISTS	POINTS
Allan (Skip) Teal	32	28	60
Wayne (Weiner) Brown	29	24	53
Jim Robertson	16	30	46
Buddy Boone	27	14	41
Bill Young	21	16	37

Leading Goaltenders

PLAYER	GP	GA	SO	GAA
Don (Dippy) Simmons	53	181	5	3.41
Marv (Stinky) Edwards	1	11	0	11

Front row: Bibber O'Hearn, Frank Toyota, Skip Teal, Wayne Brown (captain), Bud Smith, Don Simmons, Bill Young, Jimmy Robertson, Buddy Boone and Gord Lomer
Back row: Bill Trojan, Chuck Marshall, Pierre Pilote, Frank Martin, Rudy Pilous (coach), Bobby Taylor, Orrin Gould, Ted Power, Jimmy Joy (trainer)

St. Catharines Museum - Frank Martin Collection, C10,80C

was given a ten-game suspension that lasted until December 3, 1950, for refusing to obey referee Frank Udvari who wanted him to put a man in the penalty box in the third period. The game was called with ten minutes remaining and awarded to the Windsor team, which was leading 5-2. OHA president Jack Roxburgh commended referee Udvari for the "excellent manner in which he ruled in a ticklish situation."

During the suspension, Pilous, who was banned from entering the arenas in which the Teepees played, sat outside the buildings, listening to games broadcast on CKTB (St. Catharines) by Rex Stimers. St. Catharines juvenile coach Vic Teal, Buffalo Bisons coach Leroy Goldsworthy, and Bisons GM Art Chapman took turns replacing Pilous behind the Teepees bench.

> WINDSOR, Oct. 28 (CP).—Following a prolonged delay which arose when St. Catharines Teepees Coach Rudy Pilous refused to send a player to the penalty box, referees called a junior OHA game here last night at 9:17 of the third period. Windsor Spitfires, their first home victory apparently in the bag, were leading 5-2, when officials Len Loree of Windsor and Frank Udvari of Kitchener broke up the contest.
> Loree called a banging-on-the-boards penalty against an unidentified St. Kitts player at 9:17. The bench did not budge and Loree then hiked the penalty to include a 10-minute misconduct. Still no St. Kitts player headed for the bench and a bitter verbal clash ensued between Pilous, players and the officials.
> Failing to ice a team after ordered to do so a second time, Pilous incurred the automatic forfeit rule. Loree and Udvari said they allowed Pilous two minutes after a warning and then invoked Rule 77 of Canadian Amateur Hockey Association. Pending official ruling of the OHA the game went to Windsor by forfeit.

By the end of the season, rookie Pierre Pilote had served 231 penalty minutes. Skip Teal led the team in scoring with 60 points, including 32 goals, but he left the Teepees the next season after a salary dispute with Pilous.

After finishing sixth in the ten-team league, the Teepees defeated the Guelph Biltmores in round one of the playoffs, three games to two.

This was quite an accomplishment considering Guelph had future NHL stars Andy Bathgate, referred to in *The Standard* as "Mr. Poison", Dean Prentice, Harry Howell, Ron Murphy, and Leaping Lou Fontinato.

In the fifth game of the series in Guelph, one of the few 1-0 games took place and the single tally couldn't have been more important. After a scoreless first period, Wayne Brown completed a three-way passing play with Jim Robertson and Chuck Marshall to give the Teepees a one-goal lead. For the next 33 minutes, Teepees netminder Don Simmons shut out the Biltmores to preserve the lead and enable the team to advance to the next round against the Toronto Marlies.

"For the first time in months, the loquacious Rudy was speechless...the tears were choking him and believe us, they were the real thing," *The Standard* reported after the Teepees eliminated the Mad Hatters.

Unfortunately, with future NHL stars, Ron Stewart, Parker MacDonald, Earl Balfour, and Eric Nesterenko (who scored eight points in four games), the Toronto Marlies eliminated the Teepees in round two, 3-1. Buddy Boone was the top producer for the Teepees in the playoffs, scoring seven goals and adding four assists. Wayne Brown also turned in a strong performance with five goals and three assists.

The largest crowd of the year, 3,972, showed up at the last playoff game with the Marlboros, but total Teepees attendance for 1950-51 dropped by 656 to 67,090, despite the fact they played five more home games than in 1949-50.

In a related note, a picture of the Edith Cavell city hockey champions appeared in the April 18, 1951 edition of the *St. Catharines Standard*, and in the front row was ten-year-old Stan Mikita, a future Teepee and NHL superstar.

In March, 1951, the Toronto Maple Leafs held their playoff workouts at Garden City Arena, and before one practice they were looking for a practice goalie. Teepees public announcer Pat Smith volunteered his services. "Smith claims one of the shortest goal-keeping records in history," *The Standard* reported.

"The arena disc jockey stopped one tremendous drive, then retired for good...He still carries the bruise." ■

Teepees line of (left to right) Bill Young, Skip Teal, and Jim Robertson
Courtesy of Jim Robertson

Teepees rearguards in 1950-51. From left to right: Frank Martin (2), Bobby Taylor (3), Orrin Gould (4), Pierre Pilote (5), and Charlie Marshall (6)
St. Catharines Standard photo

PIERRE PILOTE

Kenogami Quebec native Pierre Pilote joined the St. Catharines Teepees in 1950 and stayed for two seasons. He was a rushing defenceman who knew how to score, tallying 34 goals in two years.

Pilote's success on the ice came from watching others play and trying hard to find out what had to be done to become a better player. "He used to run on his skates," former Teepees teammate Jim Robertson said.

Making the Teepees in 1950 was a challenge for the 5-foot-8, 180-pound rearguard who had spent his youth playing baseball instead of hockey in Fort Erie. "I was rough around the edges," said Pilote, who started his junior career with the Niagara Falls Junior B club in 1949 as a forward, but stayed with the team because it needed a defenceman. "I wanted to make the club." And he was prepared to work hard and do whatever it took to make the grade, even if it meant hitting players whenever he could.

After several days of practice, Pilous signed him to a contract for $35 a week and arranged for him to work at Thompson Products. Years later, when he was with the Chicago Black Hawks, Hawks coach Pilous told Pilote how he really landed a job with the Teepees.

When the 1950 Teepees training camp opened, Art Jackson was coach and Pilous was GM. Pilous and Jackson had to make some cuts during camp and Pilote's name came up. Jackson wanted to cut him, but Pilous wanted to keep him. After their meeting, Teepees president George Stauffer decided to appoint Pilous as coach and employ Jackson full-time at Thompson Products. Pilous kept Pilote on the team.

Speaking in St. Catharines on July 18, 2006, Pilote revealed that he never knew how close he had come to being cut from the Teepees until Pilous told him. Pilous' decision changed his life.

In 1952 Pilote turned pro with the Chicago Black Hawks who placed him with the AHL Buffalo Bisons. He was called up to the Black Hawks in the 1955-56 season and stayed for 13 years.

He was a skilled playmaker who consistently ranked among the top-scoring defencemen of his day. His 59 points on 14 goals and 45 assists in 1964-65 was an NHL record for defencemen in the pre-expansion era. He was also one of the best defencemen in his own end of the ice.

For several years he was paired with another former St. Catharines Teepee, Elmer (Moose) Vasko. The duo has been ranked among the NHL's all-time top defence pairings.

While with the Hawks, Pilote won a Stanley Cup in 1961 and three consecutive Norris Trophies as the NHL's outstanding defenceman (1962-63 to 1964-65). The Hawks team captain from 1961 to 1968 was named to five first and three second NHL all-star teams from 1960 to 1967. In 1968 he was traded to the Toronto Maple Leafs and retired after one season.

In 890 regular-season NHL games, Pilote earned 498 points, including 80 goals.

Pilote, who now resides in Wyevale, Ontario, was inducted into the Hockey Hall of Fame in 1975.

Pierre Pilote, October 12, 1950 — St. Catharines Standard photo

Teepees Charlie Marshall (6) and Ted Power (9) watch a Pierre Pilote shot enter the Guelph Biltmores net in 4-1 playoff win March 17, 1951. — St. Catharines Standard photo

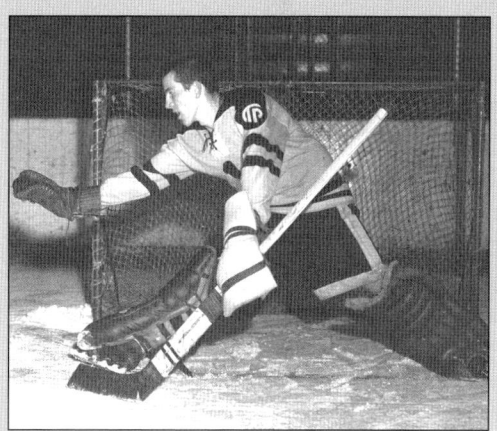

Don Simmons, January 3, 1951 — St. Catharines Standard photo

DON SIMMONS

Port Colborne native Don Simmons played goal for the St. Catharines Teepees in 1950-51. His pro career began with Eddie Shore's AHL Springfield Indians in 1951 and he didn't get a shot in the NHL until he joined the Boston Bruins in the 1956-57 season.

In 1961, after playing in two Stanley Cup finals against the Montreal Canadiens, led by Rocket Richard, Boston traded the goalie nicknamed "Dippy" to Toronto where he backed up Johnny Bower and earned Stanley Cups in 1962, 1963 and 1964. He ended his NHL career with the New York Rangers in 1968-69. In 247 regular-season NHL contests, he won 101 games and had 20 shutouts with a 2.93 goals-against average.

The former owner of Don Simmons Sports in Fort Erie now lives in Ridgeway, Ontario.

TEEPEES 1950-1951

Courtesy of Kay and David Fujiwara

FRANK TOYOTA

Frank Toyota was born in Duncan, British Columbia, in 1932. During WWII the Toyota family (three boys and seven girls) was detained at Hastings Park and interned at Slocan, British Columbia. In 1945, to avoid being sent to Japan, Mr. and Mrs. Toyota and six of their children moved to St. Catharines to work at the Tregunno farm.

Frank played minor hockey in the Garden City, winning an All-Ontario bantam and two All-Ontario juvenile hockey championships. He was the first Japanese-Canadian to play in the OHA Junior A League when he joined the St. Catharines Teepees in 1950. After one season with the Teepees, he ended his junior career with the Kitchener Greenshirts in 1952, finishing fourth in team-scoring with 58 points in 52 regular-season games.

The 5-foot-7, 170-pound right winger turned pro with the AHL Hershey Bears and then joined the EHL New Haven Nutmegs in 1952. He was the first Nisei to break into professional hockey. After playing with the IHL Johnston-Louisville team, he played with the EHL Washington Lions for two seasons and then retired.

"My uncle Frank was like a demi-god to me when I was a tyke," David Fujiwara, Frank's nephew, said in 2005. "Perhaps best of all he was a true gentleman and very thoughtful of others. He was a hero to a lot of Japanese Canadians."

Frank passed away in Montreal in 1976 at age 44.

Marlboros Oust Fighting Teepees From OHA Playoffs

Toronto Marlboros boasted too much over-all power for St. Catharines Teepees last night as they eliminated the Garden City Club from further OHA junior playoffs with a 7-3 victory in the fourth game of the semi-finals. Don Simmons, rated one of the best junior goalies in the province, did wonders to hold Marlboros off the score sheet completely in the first period of last night's game and here he is shown smothering a backhand shot from Eric Nesterenko (No. 12). Later Simmons didn't enjoy quite as much success. Despite their elimination, Teepees enjoyed one of their best season's since junior hockey was inaugurated in St. Catharines, astounding the hockey experts by knocking off the defending champion Guelph Biltmores in the first round.—Staff Photo, Standard Engraving.

St. Catharines Museum - Frank Martin Collection, C10,810

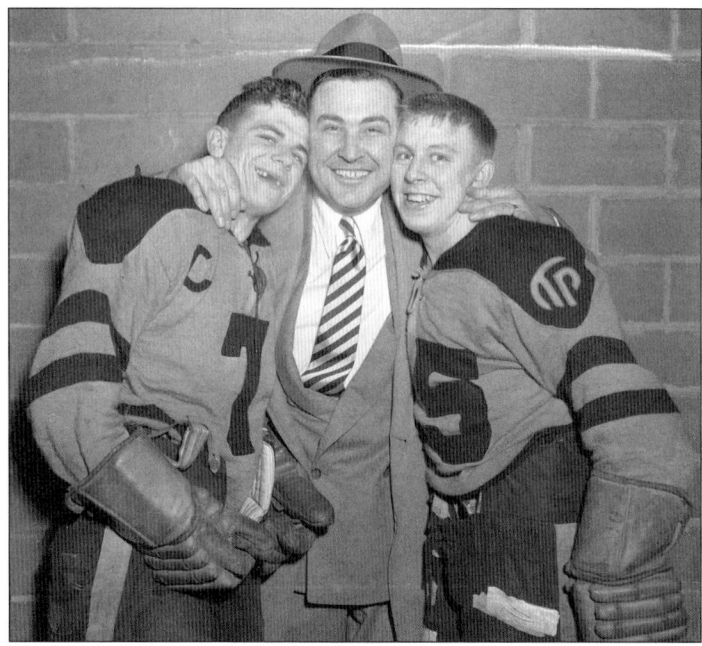

Teepees coach Rudy Pilous (centre), hugs captain Wayne Brown, left, and Buddy Boone after defeating Toronto Marlboros 5-4 in playoff action March 26, 1951.
St. Catharines Standard photo

RALPH WILLIS

In the fall of 1950, St. Catharines native Ralph Willis, who had played on several Ontario minor hockey championship teams coached by Vic Teal, was called up to the Teepees from his juvenile team. After three games, Teepees coach Rudy Pilous told the 17-year-old, who had signed an A form with the Boston Bruins for $300, that he wasn't ready for junior A hockey. Pilous' decision put Willis on the road to two Memorial Cup championships.

Courtesy of Ralph Willis

After Willis was sent back to his juvenile team, his dad contacted Vic Teal, who told Boston Bruins scout Baldy Cotton what had happened. Cotton made Barrie Flyers coach Hap Emms aware of the situation and soon Ralph was playing for the Barrie Junior B club and practising with the Flyers. His salary was $25 a week and he paid $15 for his room and board.

"Hap took me out West [to Winnipeg] in the spring of 1951," Willis said. He was part of the Memorial Cup championship team and was presented with a watch from Boston Bruins President, Weston Adams. "It was fantastic," he said. The first person he met after arriving at his Winnipeg hotel was Rudy Pilous.

In 1951-52 Willis was a regular with the Flyers, but Emms benched him for 20 games for talking back during a practice. "All I said was, 'What do you want me to do? Stand on my head?' " You didn't mess with Hap.

In 1952-53, the 6-foot-2, 200-pound, stay-at-home defenceman ended the season winning his second Memorial Cup with the Flyers.

Willis has not forgotten how controlling Hap Emms could be. Players were fined 25 cents every time they were caught swearing. No player could have a car. If you weren't going to school, you had to report to Hap's business every morning at 9:00 a.m. "I think he set up the CIA and the FBI," Willis said with a laugh. "I think that's who came to him. Hap had more spies around than anybody." There was a curfew every night and Hap would phone the boarding houses to check on the players. Sometimes he would drive up to see if the players were home.

In 1953 Willis turned pro with the AHL Hershey Bears and a year later he was sold to Eddie Shore. After playing for several teams that Shore owned, Willis retired in 1956. At that time he joined the family business, Grantham Packers, in St. Catharines, where he still lives today.

WAYNE BROWN

One of the Teepees graduates at the end of the 1950-51 season was defenceman-turned-winger, Wayne (Weiner) Brown, who had served as team captain during the year. Boston Bruins signed him to a three-way pro contract with a $1,500 signing bonus. "I got $3,000 if I played in the Pacific Coast Hockey League, $4,000 in the American League and $7,000 if I played in the NHL," Brown recalled from his home in Belleville in the spring of 2004.

St. Catharines Museum - Toppazzini Collection, C10,619

Brown started with the Pacific Coast Hockey League Tacoma Rockets in 1951, then moved to the Western Hockey League Seattle Bombers where he scored a league-leading 49 goals and 81 points, which led to a four-game call-up to the Bruins in the Stanley Cup semi-finals against the Montreal Canadiens in 1954.

In 1957-58, he was with the Belleville McFarlands when they won the Allan Cup, and was again with the club when it won the world championship in 1959 in Prague, Czechoslovakia. Former Teepees Marv Edwards and Fiori Goegan were Brown's teammates.

The Belleville resident was inducted into the Belleville Sports Hall of Fame in 2001.

Courtesy of Ralph Willis

ALLAN (SKIP) TEAL

Skip Teal, January 2, 1951 — St. Catharines Standard photo

Centre-left wing Skip Teal, son of legendary St. Catharines minor hockey coach Vic Teal, spent the 1950-51 season with the Teepees, and led the team in scoring with 60 points; however, the next year it was reported he was cut by the Teepees and suited up with the Barrie Flyers. That's not entirely true. According to Teal in an August, 2005 interview, his departure from the Garden City boiled down to a dispute over money. Pilous would not pay him what he wanted. He even lost his job at Thompson Products.

In his second year with Barrie, Teal scored 50 points in 36 regular-season games and sizzled in the playoffs with 18 points in 14 contests en route to Barrie's Memorial Cup victory. Aside from playing one NHL game for the Boston Bruins, from 1953 to 1963 Teal played in the AHL, WHL, QHL, EPHL and the EHL. His best pro season was in 1960-61 with the Clinton Comets with whom he scored 112 points, including 46 goals.

The former brewery and liquor salesman was the owner/operator of a restaurant in Astorville, Ontario, from 1989 to 2006. He died on July 8, 2006.

When the Barrie Flyers won the Memorial Cup in 1953, Ralph Willis' defence partner was future Hockey Night in Canada personality Don Cherry.

TEEPEES 1950-1951

Garden City Hockey Club Limited

G. A. STAUFFER . PRESIDENT
RUDY PILOUS . . GEN. MGR.
A. M. JACKSON . . . COACH
J. R. LEACH . . . SEC.-TREAS.

ST. CATHARINES "TEE PEES" JUNIOR O.H.A.

Dear Brian:

This is to inform you that you have been assigned to the Buffalo Hockey clubs Junior Hockey training camp for the coming season to be held here in St. Catharines.

It is customary for all amateurs to bring their own skates and boots. In this way you give yourself a fair chance to prove your hockey calibre on familiar skates.

Also, please acquire your release from your last year's club as it will eliminate unnecessary research if and when you make our Junior Club.

Your transportation will be forwarded to you in plenty of time to arrive at camp by Sunday September 10th. On your arrival at St. Catharines I will meet you at the station, otherwise please go immediately to the New Murray Hotel and check with me there for your hotel accomodations and reimbursement of any expenditure incurred enroute to the training camp.

If for any reason, such as illness, you are unable to report to camp, please advise me immediately.

Hoping this finds you in the very best of health, and looking forward to seeing you at camp, I am,

Yours sincerely,
GARDEN CITY HOCKEY CLUB LIMITED

R. Pilous
General Manager

RP/GM

Invitation to Brian Cullen

St. Catharines Museum - *Gatecliff Collection 2003.165*

TEEPEES 1951-1952

TEEPEES REACH OHA FINALS FOR FIRST TIME IN NINE YEARS

ATTENDANCE FIGURES
Average per regular-season game: 2,263
Season's largest crowd: 4,089
Season's smallest crowd: 712

PLAYOFF ROUNDS: 3
Eliminated Kitchener 3-1 and St. Mike's 3-
Lost to Guelph 4-1

In 1951-52 the Teepees added Ottawa native Brian Cullen to their lineup. In his first season he scored 25 goals and earned 53 points, finishing second in team scoring to Buddy Boone who had 66 points. He was voted the league's top rookie and the team's MVP. The best was yet to come.

The defence was solid with regulars Orrin Gould, Pierre Pilote, Frank Martin, and a newcomer who had been sent to the Teepees by Jim Hendy of the AHL Cleveland Barons. "Stauffer-Pilous interests have a hifalutin defenceman aboard, who could be the no. 1 rocker of the winter," *Standard* sports editor Clayton Browne wrote on September 27, 1951. "He is Al Kellogg of Cornwall. A six-footer…goes 205 on the hoof… and he shows he's been around." After an ordinary season, Kellogg turned it up a few notches in the playoffs and was one of the steadiest rearguards.

After his hockey career was over, Kellogg became heavily involved in old-timers hockey and in 1991, he was inducted into the Canadian Old-

Pierre Pilote (#5) comes out of the Teepees dressing room followed by Al Kellogg, (left) and Brian Cullen and trainer Jimmy Joy (right).
St. Catharines Museum - *Brian Cullen Collection N 5797*

St. Catharines Museum - *Al Kellogg Collection 2004.38.1.5*

1951-1952

GAMES PLAYED	WON	LOST	TIED	FOR	AGAINST	POINTS	FINISH
54	30	23	1	249	229	61	6/10

Leading Scorers

PLAYER	GOALS	ASSISTS	POINTS
Buddy Boone	42	24	66
Brian Cullen	25	28	53
Gord Myles	25	25	50
Pierre Pilote	18	30	48
Frank Martin	18	25	43

Leading Goaltenders

PLAYER	GP	GA	SO	GAA
Marv Edwards	48	199	2	4.15

Al Kellogg
St. Catharines Museum
- *Al Kellogg Collection 2004.38.1.5*

Front row: Bill Young, Bud Smith, Chuck Marshall, Buddy Boone, General-Manager and Coach Rudy Pilous, Gord Myles, Pierre Pilote, Marv Edwards, Brian Cullen. Back row: Trainer Jimmy Joy, Joe Schnurr, Willie Haas, Allen Kellogg, Frank Martin, Hank Ciesla, Orrin Gould, Gerry Foley and property man Billy Burnett. Seated, foreground, assistant property man Red Miller

St. Catharines Museum - *Betty Myles Collection, C10,82C*

TEEPEES 1951-1952

CARL (BUDDY) BOONE

Teepee Buddy Boone, who scored 42 goals during 1951-52, had a long pro career, including 34 regular-season and 22 playoff games with the Boston Bruins. Some might remember Boone as the player who scored the goal that helped Boston eliminate the Detroit Red Wings in the 1957 Stanley Cup semifinal series.

From 1952 to 1970, the 5-foot-7 right winger spent time in the AHL, QHL, EPHL, WHL and IHL. He had his most productive season in 1962-63 with the WHL Vancouver Canucks when he scored 80 points, including 44 goals.

Boone passed away in his birthplace, Kirkland Lake, in September of 1986.

St. Catharines Museum - Frank Martin Collection, C10,781

FRANK MARTIN

After three seasons with the Teepees, 1949 to 1952, defenceman Frank Martin turned pro in 1952. He spent part of his rookie season with the AHL Hershey Bears before making his NHL debut with the Bruins in February, 1953, at 19. He was the first graduate of the St. Catharines minor hockey system to make it to the NHL.

He was also an exceptional baseball pitcher who was invited to the Brooklyn Dodgers spring training camp in 1953, but stayed with hockey, joining Boston in the NHL's Stanley Cup finals against the Montreal Canadiens.

He spent six years in the NHL, playing 282 regular-season games with Boston and Chicago, collecting 57 points. He also saw action in the 1955 NHL All-Star game. From 1957 to 1965, the 6-foot-2 rearguard played in the AHL with Buffalo Bisons, Quebec Aces, and Cleveland Barons.

Martin, who worked for the City of St. Catharines after his hockey career was finished, died February 18, 2007.

St. Catharines Museum - Frank Martin Collection, C10,775

timers Hockey Hall of Fame. He was named St. Catharines Sportsman of the year in 1988 and has been a member of the St. Catharines Sports Hall of Fame since 1996.

On Friday, December 14, 1951, Garden City Arena, sometimes referred to as the Phelps Street Ice Palace, unveiled a new four-sided clock to keep track of the game details. Now everyone in the arena could see what was happening on the scoreboard.

The Teepees started the season poorly, losing the opener in Guelph 6-3, and their first home game 3-2 to Barrie. The good news was that 3,333 payees showed up to see the Teepees in action for home game number one. Early in the season the team was ninth in the ten-team league, but in the latter part of the year the club caught fire and had 16 wins in 19 games.

One of the team's leaders, game in and game out, was a veteran rearguard. "Once again it was the rugged, driving display of defenceman Pierre Pilote that proved to be the beacon by which the Teepees ship was guided," the *Standard* reported after a Teepees 5-3 victory over the Toronto Marlies on January 26, 1952.

On February 24, 1952, rookie Brian Cullen played his first pro game when he suited up with AHL Buffalo Bisons and received $50 for the game. A few days later, on February 5, 1952, he recorded his first hat trick as the Teepees whipped the Waterloo Hurricanes 11-1. Cullen's mother noted in her scrapbook that son Brian "got a lovely sports shirt for it."

Defenceman Frank Martin, who moved up to centre for the game, scored five goals.

Frank Martin, who has seen service both as a forward and defenceman with St. Catharines Teepees this year, turned in his top performance of the season last night as Teeps blasted out an 11-1 victory over Waterloo Hurricanes. Martin's contribution to the Garden City cause was five goals, a record number for any St. Catharines player during a game this season.—Photo by Simpson, Standard Engraving.

St. Catharines Museum - Frank Martin Collection, C10,813

Teepee captain Frank Martin (2) and netminder Marv Edwards look for the puck in 1952 playoff action.

St. Catharines Museum - Frank Martin Collection, C10,777

TEEPEES 1951-1952

Confusion Reigns as Teeps, Dutchies Tie

By The Canadian Press

Kitchener Greenshirts closed out their OHA junior A schedule last night in a game that has caused considerable confusion at league headquarters. By defeating third-place Galt Black Hawks, the Greenshirts moved into a fifth-place deadlock with St. Catharines Teepees.

Ontario Hockey Association regulations state that goal averages, figured out to three decimal points, decide the foremost team in case of a tie. Unofficial figures indicate both clubs' records work out to a .520 average. The next move is up to the OHA and phones were hot all morning.

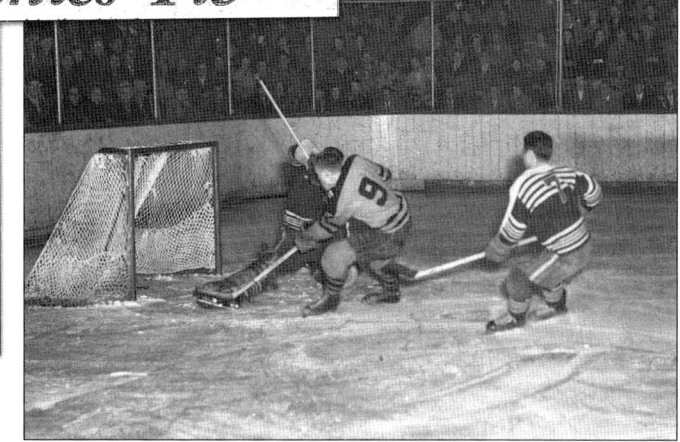

St. Catharines Standard

Teepee Hank Ciesla (9) goes to the net as his team eliminates the Guelph Biltmores from the playoffs on March 12, 1952.
St. Catharines Standard photo

Although the Teepees had risen as high as fourth place near the end of the season, the team finished the schedule tied with Kitchener for fifth place. After a controversial league decision and a toss of a coin to decide the placing of the two clubs, the Teepees were put in sixth place. Pilous protested, but the decision was final.

The club advanced three rounds in the playoffs in front of capacity crowds, eliminating Kitchener in four games and St. Mike's in five.

In the second game against St. Mike's, 4,089 people crowded into Garden City Arena to watch the visitors win 3-1. It was the first time in nine seasons that fans were turned away.

In the fifth game against St. Mike's, before a crowd of nearly 13,000 in Maple Leaf Gardens, the Teepees had a 6-1 lead after two periods. The Toronto club then scored four times in the third, narrowing the gap to one goal before Charles Marshall and Gerry Foley secured the victory and eliminated the Majors. It was the first time in nine seasons that a St. Catharines team had made it to the OHA Junior A finals.

In round three the Guelph Biltmores, led by future NHL stars Andy Bathgate, Dean Prentice, Ron Murphy, and Ron Stewart, were too much for the Teepees. Playing 14 playoff games in 23 days took its toll on the team.

Pierre Pilote and Charlie Marshall were the scoring leaders in the playoffs with 16 points, followed by Buddy Boone, Brian Cullen, Hank Ciesla, Bill Haas, and Gord Myles, who each earned 12 points.

While *Standard* sports reporter Jack Gatecliff was watching the Teepees being eliminated by the Biltmores in the fifth game on March 31, 1952, his wife Alice gave birth to their son John.

At the end of the season, speaking at a testimonial dinner held by the Garden City Hockey Club, Mayor John Franklin said: "I want to thank the Teepees and coach Rudy Pilous for the best hockey season St. Catharines has ever experienced."

Rex Stimers called the 1951-52 team "the greatest since 1943." Junior hockey fans in the Garden City seemed to agree with Rex as total attendance jumped from 67,090 in 1950-51 to 84,235 in 1951-52. No one was more aware of this increase than Pilous, whose team played six playoff games at home. In the final series with Guelph, Pilous was beside himself. "It's tickets, tickets, tickets," he moaned. "My phone has been ringing off the wall. We have one ticket for every ten requested." Now all he needed was a championship team. ■

Two great competitors, Marv Edwards of St. Catharines Teepees and Ed Chadwick of Toronto St. Michael's, shake hands at centre ice of Maple Leaf Gardens after the tremendous fifth and deciding game of the OHA junior "A" semifinals. Photo by Jimmy Simpson. Standard Engraving.
St. Catharines Museum - Frank Martin Collection, C10,812

ORRIN GOULD

Orrin Gould was a hockey, baseball and lacrosse star growing up in Cornwall, Ontario. He saw action on defence for the St. Catharines Teepees from 1950 to 1952.

From 1952 to 1959 he played in the AHL and IHL, spending five seasons with the Fort Wayne Komets.

After settling in Norwood, Massachusetts, he coached hockey at the high school and college levels. Today he operates a sports store in Norwood.

St. Catharines Standard photo

GORD MYLES

One of the leading scorers on the 1951-52 club, Gord Myles left the Teepees after one season. He played three years of minor pro before joining the Whitby Dunlops who won the 1957 Allan Cup.

In 1958 he was with the Dunlops when the team won the World Championship. Myles became a firefighter in Oshawa and a trainer with the Oshawa Generals.

He passed away in 1978.

St. Catharines Museum - Betty Myles Collection, C10,822

TEEPEES 1951-1952

JIM ROBERTSON

St. Catharines native Jim Robertson had a dream come true in 1950 when at 16 he became a regular with the Teepees and secured a job with Thompson Products.

The centre/left winger, who was a member of four St. Catharines championship teams (two bantam, one midget and one juvenile) and had seen action in a few Teepees games in 1949-50, couldn't believe he was following in the steps of former Teepee great, Red Sullivan.

Despite finishing the season as the team's third highest scorer, Robertson, who was on the Boston Bruins reserve list, was traded in December, 1951, to the Windsor Spitfires. "I was heart-broken," Robertson said on December 1, 2005. It wasn't where he wanted to play, so after a meeting with the OHA officials in the fall of 1952, he was awarded to Barrie Flyers for $1,000. It was the beginning of a love-hate relationship with Flyers coach/owner Hap Emms.

"Emms was a great coach. He had systems. Great on fundamentals," said Robertson. But he was also a controller who made the players sign in every morning and phone him for curfew every night. Even his roommate Don Cherry toed the line for Hap. "Everyone was so scared of him [Emms]. It was unbelievable," he said. "We called him 'The Bull Dog', but not to his face."

In 1953 Robertson was with the Flyers when they won the Memorial Cup.

After finishing his junior career in Barrie in 1953-54 with 114 points, including 54 goals, he played senior hockey and then turned pro with the AHL Hershey Bears. After two seasons in Hershey, he played in Victoria and Quebec before returning to his hometown to play senior hockey in Kitchener and then in Welland.

While working at the St. Lawrence Seaway, he coached for 14 years, including two years as bench boss of the St. Catharines Junior B Falcons. Unlike Emms he considered himself a coach with a heart. This was very rewarding.

Today the kid from Facer Street lives in the Garden City and is a member of the St. Catharines Sports Hall of Fame.

St. Catharines Standard photo

Courtesy of Jim Robertson

Coach Rudy Pilous and the three players grouped around him ... have every right to boast those wide grins. This "shot" was taken in the Teepee dressing room at Maple Leaf Gardens yesterday immediately after St. Catharines had eliminated St. Michael's from the OHA junior "A" semifinals in as dramatic a hockey game as one could imagine. Gerry Foley (12), Joe Schnurr (16) and Buddy Boone (15) were all two goal scorers. Schnurr is clutching the Teepee mascot, a rubber Indian, which has travelled with Teepees during their many ups and downs in the 1951-52 season. Immediately after the game, Pilous sent out for a new "headdress" for the Teepees most valued possession.
– Staff Photo, Standard Engraving.
St. Catharines Museum - Frank Martin Collection, C10,812

GERRY FOLEY

Gerry Foley was one of a few American-born players who played junior A hockey in St. Catharines. After playing his minor hockey in Northern Ontario, Foley spent the 1951-52 season with the St. Catharines Teepees.

In 1953 in his rookie pro season, the right winger was Western Hockey League rookie-of-the-year with the Seattle Ironmen. During his 17-year pro career, Foley spent eight seasons with the AHL Springfield Indians, winning three Calder Cups. He was inducted into the Springfield Hockey Hall of Fame in 1999. Earlier in his career he had won a Calder Cup with Pittsburgh in 1955.

He also saw action in the NHL with Toronto, New York Rangers, and Los Angeles Kings before retiring in 1969.

Teepees Oust St. Mike's in Thrilling Windup

Coach Rudy Pilous and his jubilant St. Catharines Teepees. They move against Guelph in final after beating St. Michael's, 8-5.
St. Catharines Museum - Frank Martin Collection, C10,817

62

TEEPEES 1952-1953

THE TEEPEES BUILD FOR THE FUTURE

1952-53 was a rebuilding year for the Teepees. There were only five veterans left from the 1952 OHA finalist team: Brian Cullen, Hank Ciesla, Charles Marshall, Marv Edwards, and Willard Haas.

During the season, Pilous insisted that all his players were to wear fedoras and topcoats on road games. Former defenceman Al Kellogg recalled that a couple of players showed up for one bus trip without their hats and coats. They were sent back to their boarding houses to get them.

At the start of the season, the Teepees were introduced to fans before each pre-game warm-up with a song which Rex Stimers began to use on his evening sports show on CKTB, *Spice of the Sports News*: "The Caissons Go Rolling Along," a grand old army march. Stimers had used "Wings Over the Navy" for the previous ten years as his introductory theme.

Stimers was convinced the 1952-53 Teepees would roll along to victory. The club lost its opening game 7-5 to its old nemesis St. Mike's, but would go on to improve its place in the league standings by the end of the season.

Sophomore centre Brian Cullen led the team in scoring with 42 goals and 76 points. Cullen played part of the year with Charlie Marshall and Ken Schinkel, who placed second and fourth respectively in team scoring. "There is little doubt that the Teepee trio is the most dangerous combination in Ontario junior hockey," Gatecliff wrote in January, 1953.

During the season, the Teepees played four teams from Quebec: Quebec Citadels, Montreal Royals, Montreal Canadiens, and Three Rivers Reds. The Teepees played in the Montreal Forum for the first time on January 20, 1953, and beat the Montreal Royals 3-0. Radio station

ATTENDANCE FIGURES
Average per regular-season game: 2,272
Season's largest crowd: 4,113
Season's smallest crowd: 1,385

PLAYOFF ROUNDS: 1
Eliminated by St. Mike's 3-0

1952-1953

GAMES PLAYED	WON	LOST	TIED	FOR	AGAINST	POINTS	FINISH
56	31	20	5	219	204	67	4/9

Leading Scorers

PLAYER	GOALS	ASSISTS	POINTS
Brian Cullen	42	34	76
Charlie Marshall	20	32	52
Willard Haas	28	23	51
Ken Schinkel	21	20	41
Hank Ciesla	19	22	41

Leading Goaltenders

PLAYER	GP	GA	SO	GAA
Marv Edwards	38	150	2	3.95
Norm Defelice	18	53	2	2.94

Opening game action as Teepees lose to St. Mike's 7-5 on October 10, 1952
St. Catharines Standard photo

Front row: Red Miller, Norm Defelice, Dan Poliziani, Rudy Pilous (coach), Brian Cullen, Marv Edwards, Jimmy Joy (trainer) Second row: Pop Steele, Alex Leslie, Bill Haas, Hank Ciesla, Joe Kastelic, Ian Cushenan, Jay MacDonald (publicity) Third row: Hugh Barlow, Ed Mateka, Bob Maxwell, Al Kellogg, Ken Schinkel, Charlie Marshall, Peter Kamula
St. Catharines Standard photo

TEEPEES 1952-1953

KEN SCHINKEL

Jansen Saskatchewan native Ken Schinkel played for the Teepees in 1952-53. From 1953 to 1959, the right winger played most of his hockey for the AHL Springfield Indians.

Courtesy of Bob Cornelius

From 1959 to 1973, he spent most of his time playing 636 regular-season NHL games with the New York Rangers and then Pittsburgh Penguins, collecting 325 points. He played in two NHL all-star games in 1968 and 1969.

After retiring, he coached the Penguins from 1972-73 to 1976-77. He spent a total of 21 years with the club, during which time he was general manager, director of player personnel, scout, chief scout, and director of player development. Jack Gatecliff called him "Mr. Everything of Pittsburgh Hockey."

He moved from Pittsburgh to the Hartford Whalers, who hired him as a pro scout. Now retired, he lives in Florida.

DAN POLIZIANI

Dan Poliziani spent one and a half seasons with the Teepees before being traded to the Barrie Flyers in 1953. In 1955 the right winger from Sydney, Nova Scotia, turned pro with the AHL Cleveland Barons. It was the beginning of a ten-year American League career with four games spent with Boston Bruins in 1958-59.

St. Catharines Museum - Bob Cornelius Collection, C10,676

He had his best pro season in 1960-61 when he collected 63 points in 63 regular-season games with the AHL Providence Reds.

Today he is involved in the training of racehorses, some of which are owned by former Teepees teammate Brian Cullen.

Left to right: Wilf Roberts, Brian Cullen, and Charlie Marshall
St. Catharines Standard photo

Left to right: Joe Kastelic, Alex Leslie, and Willard Haas
St. Catharines Standard photo

Pierre Pilote, ace defenceman of St. Kitts Junior Teepees, returned to Garden City arena to help out his "alma mater" club candidates and is pictured above demonstrating some fine points to five graduate St. Kitts Bison Juvenile champions. From left to right Mait Thompson, Ches Warchol, Pete Saliken, Pat Kelly, and Elmer Vasko ... all St. Kitts native sons but Kelly.
St. Catharines Standard photo

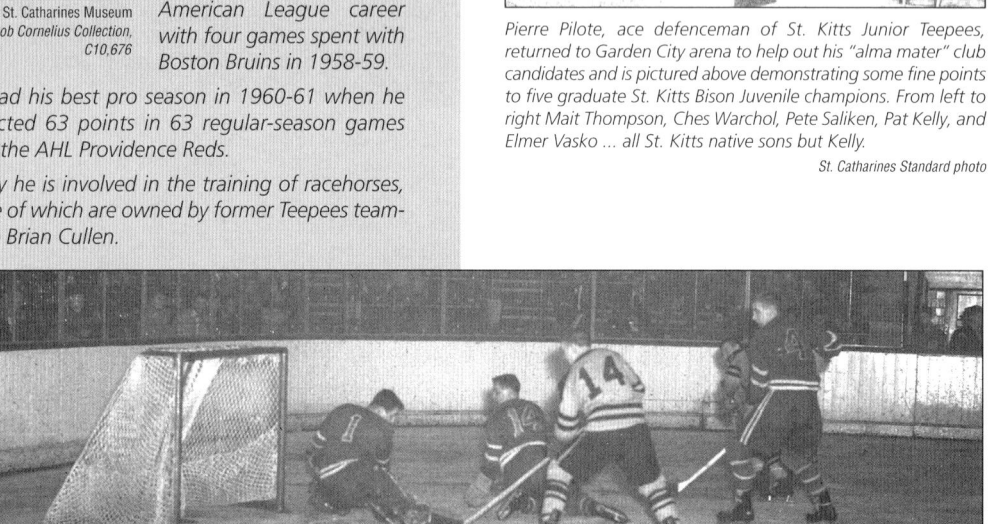

Teepee Brian Cullen (14) scores in 6-5 victory over Guelph Biltmores November 15, 1952.
St. Catharines Standard photo

CKTB broadcast the game. In the contests between the four Quebec clubs and the nine OHA teams, Quebec won 36, lost 30, and tied 3.

In January of 1953 the Citadels whipped the Teepees 14-2. A year later, in the Eastern Canada playoffs against another Quebec team, Pilous would remind his players of that one-sided defeat. Michel Labadie of the Citadels gained national attention when he scored eight goals in the victory. *Standard* sports editor Clayton Browne wasn't convinced the better team won. "They [Quebec] had every break in the book," said Browne, who was highly critical of the officiating.

The team finished fourth in the nine-team league with 67 points. The Teepees were eliminated in round one of the playoffs by St. Mike's in three straight games, but would meet the same team in the 1954 playoffs and see the series last eight games with a different result. Cullen scored four of the team's six playoff goals.

One Teepee player did, however, move on in the 1953 OHA playoffs – and it was a big surprise. After the Teepees were eliminated from the playoffs by St. Michael's College Majors, several of the players agreed to meet the next Saturday at the Henley Hotel to watch St. Mike's play Barrie Flyers on TV. Everyone, except goalie Marv Edwards, showed up. "Where is Edwards?" the players asked each other.

When they started to watch the game, they were stunned to see Edwards skate out with the Barrie Flyers. How did it happen?

Speaking from his Fort Erie home on November 14, 2005, Edwards recalled why he missed a few beers with his Teepees teammates that day. The Friday

64

TEEPEES 1952-1953

Teepee Wilfred (Wimpy) Roberts (12) moves in on goal in a 7-2 loss to the Quebec Citadels November 25, 1952.
St. Catharines Standard photo

before the game Barrie Flyers owner Hap Emms called and asked him to come to Maple Leaf Gardens. When he arrived just before the game, he met Dennis Riggin and Charlie Hodge, two other junior netminders who had also been summoned by Emms. All three men had their goaltending equipment. Emms told them to wait in the hall until it was decided who would play against St. Mike's.

When Emms emerged from the dressing room, he looked at Edwards and said, "Edwards, get in there and get dressed." After the game, which Barrie won, Edwards learned that the players voted on which of the three goalies they would prefer to be in the net. Ex-Teepees Skip Teal, Jim Robertson, and Ralph Willis were in the Barrie dressing room and no doubt helped to make Edwards the players' choice. "Marv was a good clutch goaltender," Jim Robertson said 52 years later. "He always came to play."

Edwards stayed with the club for the rest of the playoffs and ended up with his first Memorial Cup ring.

After the Teepees were eliminated from the playoffs, Willard Haas and Joe Kastelic played with the AHL Buffalo Bisons for the team's last five regular-season games. Brian Cullen played with the Bisons for two home games, but since he had played one game during the season, he couldn't play any more games without losing his amateur status.

Total attendance for the season dipped to 66,948, a drop of 17,307 from the previous year, but the club played four fewer games than in 1951-52. ■

Rudy Pilous, Brian Cullen, and George Stauffer look at a message from the manager of St. Mike's team after Teepees were eliminated from playoffs.
St. Catharines Museum - Brian Cullen Collection N5796

JOE KASTELIC

Kirkland Lake native Joe Kastelic joined the Teepees in 1952 after spending most of 1951-52 with the Oshawa Generals. In 1953, he turned pro with the IHL Fort Wayne Komets and would stay in the league for 15 years, playing with Troy, Louisville and Muskegon until 1968.

St. Catharines Museum - Don MacLean Collection, C11,169

With Muskegon Zephyrs from 1961 to 1965, he had seasons of 101 and 104 points, followed by two seasons with 94 points. He led the team to Turner Cup championships in 1962 and 1968. When he retired in 1968, he was the IHL's all-time leading goal scorer with 551 and fourth in assists with 583.

In 2001 the 68-year-old former right winger was inducted into the Muskegon Area Sports Hall of Fame.

NORM DEFELICE

Schumacher Ontario native Norm Defelice was with the St. Catharines Teepees in 1952-53 and earned a shutout in his first game.

From 1953 to 1970, he played in seven leagues with at least 15 different teams. In 1956-57 he played ten games with the Boston Bruins, replacing the injured Terry Sawchuk.

Courtesy of Norm Defelice

It was while playing for the AHL Springfield Indians that owner Eddie Shore introduced him to the experience of visualizing. Shore told him to stand in the net and make saves from every angle and from every type of shot. It was a unique practice session — there was no shooter and no puck. He was just visualizing and he did it for four hours. Nearly fifty years later, Defelice said that Shore was a way ahead of his time and visualizing did help him during his career, but he would never admit that to Shore.

It was in the EHL, mostly with Clinton Comets (eight seasons), that Defelice had the most success, earning seven all-star selections and winning the George L. Davis Trophy (for the fewest goals against) six times. He holds several goalie records with Clinton, which folded in 1973.

The ex-Teepee was with the Comets when they won three Mayor Walker Cups and one Atlantic City Boardwalk Trophy. In March, 1961, a testimonial was held at the Clinton Arena for the man who was described as "A Great Goaltender, Courageous Player, Top Sportsman and Good Fellow."

After his playing career ended, he played and then coached the Galt Hornets to an Allan Cup in 1971. He later scouted for the WHA Winnipeg Jets with whom he won an Avco ring in 1978.

After a successful sales career, Defelice now lives in St. Catharines, a stone's throw from Jack Gatecliff Arena (formerly Garden City Arena), where he shared netminding duties with Marv Edwards in 1952-53.

In April of 2008 Defelice was inducted into the St. Catharines Sports Hall of Fame.

TEEPEES 1952-1953

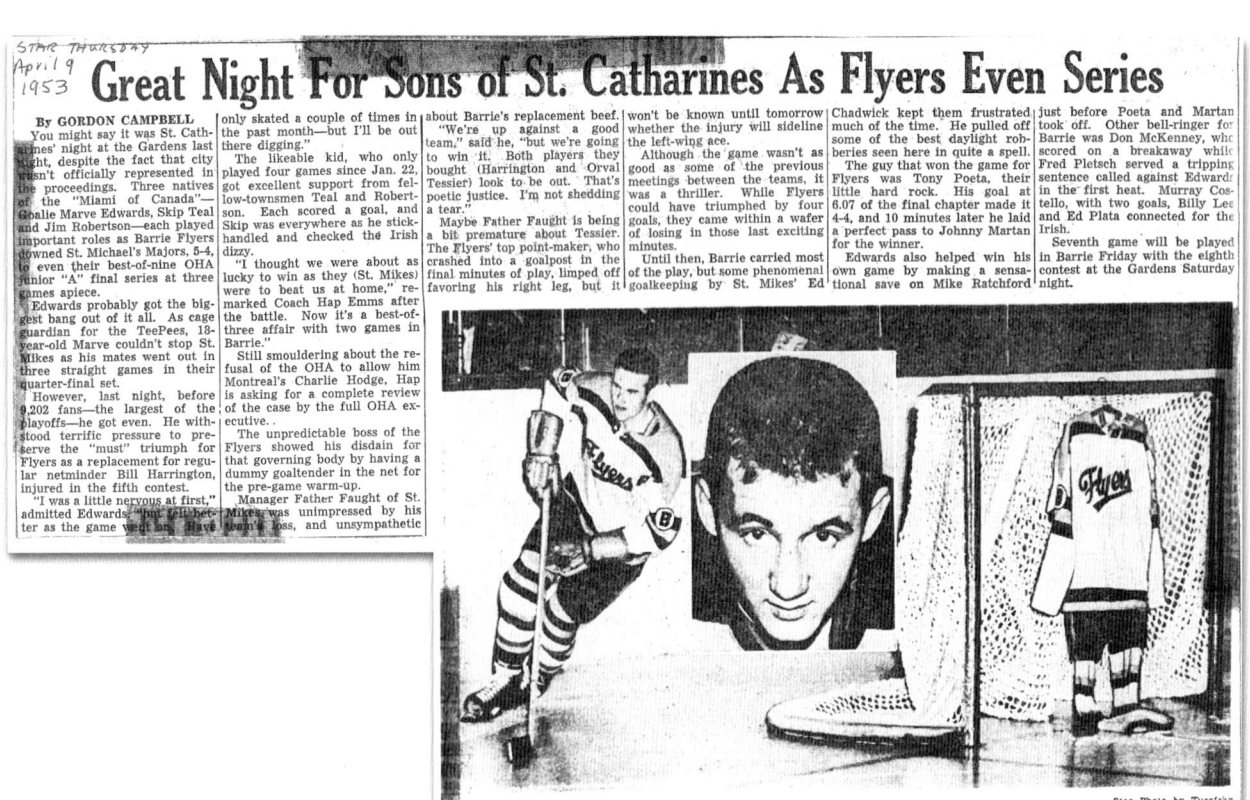

Great Night For Sons of St. Catharines As Flyers Even Series

STAR THURSDAY April 9 1953

By GORDON CAMPBELL

You might say it was St. Catharines' night at the Gardens last night, despite the fact that city wasn't officially represented in the proceedings. Three natives of the "Miami of Canada"—Goalie Marve Edwards, Skip Teal and Jim Robertson—each played important roles as Barrie Flyers downed St. Michael's Majors, 5-4, to even their best-of-nine OHA junior "A" final series at three games apiece.

Edwards probably got the biggest bang out of it all. As cage guardian for the TeePees, 18-year-old Marve couldn't stop St. Mikes as his mates went out in three straight games in their quarter-final set.

However, last night, before 9,202 fans—the largest of the playoffs—he got even. He withstood terrific pressure to preserve the "must" triumph for Flyers as a replacement for regular netminder Bill Harrington, injured in the fifth contest.

"I was a little nervous at first," admitted Edwards, "but felt better as the game went on. Have only skated a couple of times in the past month—but I'll be out there digging."

The likeable kid, who only played four games since Jan. 22, got excellent support from fellow-townsmen Teal and Robertson. Each scored a goal, and Skip was everywhere as he stickhandled and checked the Irish dizzy.

"I thought we were about as lucky to win as they (St. Mikes) were to beat us at home," remarked Coach Hap Emms after the battle. Now it's a best-of-three affair with two games in Barrie."

Still smouldering about the refusal of the OHA to allow him Montreal's Charlie Hodge, Hap is asking for a complete review of the case by the full OHA executive.

The unpredictable boss of the Flyers showed his disdain for that governing body by having a dummy goaltender in the net for the pre-game warm-up.

Manager Father Faught of St. Mikes was unimpressed by his rival's loss, and unsympathetic about Barrie's replacement beef. "We're up against a good team," said he, "but we're going to win it. Both players they bought (Harrington and Orval Tessier) look to be out. That's poetic justice. I'm not shedding a tear."

Maybe Father Faught is being a bit premature about Tessier. The Flyers' top point-maker, who crashed into a goalpost in the final minutes of play, limped off favoring his right leg, but it won't be known until tomorrow whether the injury will sideline the left-wing ace.

Although the game wasn't as good as some of the previous meetings between the teams, it was a thriller. While Flyers could have triumphed by four goals, they came within a wafer of losing in those last exciting minutes.

Until then, Barrie carried most of the play, but some phenomenal goalkeeping by St. Mikes' Ed Chadwick kept them frustrated much of the time. He pulled off some of the best daylight robberies seen here in quite a spell.

The guy that won the game for Flyers was Tony Poeta, their little hard rock. His goal at 6.07 of the final chapter made it 4-4, and 10 minutes later he laid a perfect pass to Johnny Martan for the winner.

Edwards also helped win his own game by making a sensational save on Mike Ratchford just before Poeta and Martan took off. Other bell-ringer for Barrie was Don McKenney, who scored on a breakaway while Fred Pletsch served a tripping sentence called against Edwards in the first heat. Murray Costello, with two goals, Billy Lee and Ed Plata connected for the Irish.

Seventh game will be played in Barrie Friday with the eighth contest at the Gardens Saturday night.

Barrie Flyers were not too keyed up over last night's game at the Gardens to get in a dig at the amateur hockey authorities who had blocked their efforts to bring in a substitute goalie from the outlawed Quebec league. When Flyers skated out for a warm-up, prior to facing St. Mikes in the sixth game of the OHA junior finals, they hung hockey pants, stocking and a Barrie sweater in their net. No goalie appeared. Later on, little Marvin Edwards of St. Catharines (inset) came out as the replacement for Barrie's injured goalie, Bill Harrington. Larry Thibault is the Barrie player shown at the left.

—Star Photo by Turofsky

Photo by Turofsky, Toronto Star, April 9, 1953

Teepees Marv Edwards (left) and Willard Haas stand in front of the St. Catharines train station. Both men might be wondering why the team had no dental plan.
St. Catharines Museum - Maxwell Collection 2004.67.27

Flooding Wagon
St. Catharines Museum - photo September 30, 2004 11-11A

TEEPEES 1953-1954

THE ROAD TO THE MEMORIAL CUP

ATTENDANCE FIGURES
Average per regular-season game: 2,277
Season's largest crowd: 4,264
Season's smallest crowd: 1,356

PLAYOFF ROUNDS: 4 - Eliminated St. Mike's 4-3-1, Toronto Marlboros 4-3, Quebec Frontenacs 4-2, Edmonton Oil Kings 4-0-1 to win the Memorial Cup

Stimers Said 7 And 11 Were The Teepees Lucky Numbers. He Was Right.

Before the 1953-54 season began, Teepees play-by-play broadcaster Rex Stimers made a prediction. His words can be found in the first Teepees program of the season under a column entitled: "A Natural".

"With the seventh year coming up of the wearing of the Gold and Black [the Teepees] and the eleventh year of junior "A" hockey hereabouts, I get the feeling that there's something NATURAL about this impending season. On October 1st, I can think of just one thing. When you talk about seven and eleven, you've got NATURALS and I for one, know for sure that naturals spell winner. If ever the omens were right, they are now."

When the 59-game regular season ended, Rex's prediction was looking good. The Teepees finished in first place with 86 points, 11 points ahead of the second place Toronto Marlboros. The Teepees had actually earned 96 points that season, but overnight they lost ten points (from five wins) when Quebec Citadels folded and dropped out of the league.

Brian Cullen won the Eddie Powers Trophy with 161 points, made up of 68 goals and 93 assists, setting league records in each category. The CBC line, made up of Brian and Barry Cullen and Hugh Barlow, accumulated 389 points during the regular season, establishing a record that would last for several years.

In the first round of the playoffs, the Teepees met the St. Michael's College Majors. The Majors and the Teepees had an intense rivalry that dated back to 1943 when the St. Catharines Falcons joined the league. Some of the most exciting and entertaining games at Maple Leaf Gardens and Garden City Arena featured the Double Blue and the Gold and Black. And they always drew a crowd.

The 1953-54 St. Michael's Majors had a talented club that which included Dick and Les Duff, Noel Price, Paul Knox, and netminder Gerry McNa-

1953-1954

GAMES PLAYED	WON	LOST	TIED	FOR	AGAINST	POINTS	FINISH
59	42	15	2	328	211	86	1/8

Leading Scorers

PLAYER	GOALS	ASSISTS	POINTS
Brian Cullen	68	93	161
Hugh Barlow	48	73	121
Barry Cullen	62	45	107
Hank Ciesla	39	29	68
Cec Hoekstra	24	35	59

Leading Goaltenders

PLAYER	GP	GA	SO	GAA
Marv Edwards	49	182	4	3.71
Reg Truax	10	29	1	2.90

Front row: Bob Maxwell, Hugh Barlow, Reg Truax, George A. Stauffer (owner and president), Brian Cullen (captain), Rudy Pilous (manager and coach), Marvin Edwards, Wimpy Roberts, Pete Koval
Second row: Dr. Michael Zaritsky (club physician), Ian Cushenan, Elmer Vasko, Cecil Hoekstra, Jack Armstrong, Hank Ciesla, Barry Cullen, Jay MacDonald (secretary)
Third Row: Frankie Banich (assistant trainer), Don McLean, Jack Higgins, Jimmy Joy (trainer), Chester Warchol, Nelson Bulloch, Jack Steele (equipment manager)

St. Catharines Museum - *McSloy Estate Collection 1971.682*

The CBC line: (left to right) Barry Cullen, Brian Cullen, and Hugh Barlow
St. Catharines Museum - St. Catharines Standard Collection N 5706

Teepees captain Brian Cullen and coach Rudy Pilous are initiated as warriors March 23, 1954.
St. Catharines Museum - Brian Cullen Collection N 5799

mara. The teams split the first two contests and game three was in Garden City Arena on March 23, 1954.

That was the night the Teepees experienced their own miracle on ice. With 25 seconds to go in the third period, the Majors were leading 5-4 and a faceoff was coming up in the St. Catharines end. It looked like a sure win for the Majors, but then Teepees coach Rudy Pilous did the unthinkable. He told captain Brian Cullen to tell goalie Marv Edwards to leave the net. Cullen was dumbfounded.

"The faceoff is in our own end," he told Pilous. "I know, but we still have time to get the puck down the ice and tie this game," Pilous replied. Cullen protested. "Who's coaching this team? You or me?" Pilous asked. "I said get him out of the net!"

"I was mad," Cullen recalled, but he did tell Edwards to leave the net.

"I thought it was just for instructions or to settle the team down," Edwards said. "When he [Pilous] opened the gate and told me to come in and sit for a while, I couldn't believe my ears."

Pilous replaced Edwards with another forward, leaving the Teepees net empty. The crowd was buzzing. Some fans were heading for the exits. "Nobody knew what was going on," recalled Andy Vasko, a spectator at the game. Rumour had it that Rex Stimers nearly fell out of the broadcast booth when he saw what Pilous was doing.

"If we don't win the faceoff, it doesn't really matter," Pilous said at the time.

"They [St. Mike's players] lined up just off the circle line," Edwards recalled. "They were going to hold us in. Big mistake. They should have jammed the faceoff, kept the puck in there."

Ex-Teepee Chester Warchol remembered what happened after the puck was dropped. "Hank Ciesla took the faceoff and skated up the middle of the ice and as he got to the blueline, he shot the puck in and it bounced off the backboards. [Cec Hoekstra pounced on the puck and passed it out front]. Hugh Barlow was there to put the rebound in to tie the score." The time was 19:48 of the third period.

The roar that signaled the goal was so loud, fans who had left the game ran back from as far away as Queenston Street. One fan claimed the walls of the arena were actually vibrating.

Suddenly Pilous was a genius. "It was a daring play by Pilous and one which places him alongside the inventor of the T-formation in football and the Williams shift in baseball," a *Standard* reporter wrote after the game.

After Pilous died in December of 1994, former St. Mike's goalie Gerry McNamara, who was the victim of Barlow's goal, attended Pilous' funeral and still remembered the event. "Rudy was the happiest guy in the rink," he said. "I couldn't smile for months."

Another ex-St. Mike's player, Dick Duff, was also at the funeral and had one short comment for Jack Gatecliff about Barlow's goal: "Tell everyone I wasn't on the ice when it happened."

In the overtime period – there was no sudden death, just ten minutes of play – Barlow scored at the fifty-five second mark, but at 8:18, with the Teepees a man short, the St. Mike's coach pulled his goalie, and ten seconds later the game was tied 6-6. There was no more scoring.

"I still think that one play won it [the Memorial Cup] for us," Marv Edwards said nearly 50 years later.

The Majors would go on to win the next two games, but that tie contest kept the Teepees alive. St. Catharines won games six and seven and then played number eight in Maple Leaf Gardens before 14,601 fans, the largest crowd to witness a hockey game up to that time. As Rex Stimers used to say, "It was a barn-burner!"

In the third period, the Majors Dick Duff scored to break a 3-3 tie. The Teepees were exhausted and once again it looked like St. Michael's was headed for victory. That's when Teepees winger Chester Warchol turned his game up a notch and led two rushes down the ice. On his first trip, the man, known as "Chet the Jet" scored to make it 4-4. On his second foray into enemy territory, he took a shot while on his knees, and linemate Jack Armstrong tipped the puck in to put the Teepees ahead 5-4. The Majors were out of the playoffs.

Next came the series against another bitter rival, the Toronto Marlboros. The Marlies, managed by Harold Ballard, had several future NHLers on the team, including Bob Baun, Billy Harris, Bob Pulford, and a football player on skates, Gerry James.

The Teepees won the first three games and then the Marlies won the next three, setting up game seven in Garden City Arena. That's when coach Pilous had an idea.

Chester Warchol scored a key goal in the series final game against St. Mike's.
St. Catharines Standard photo

"The night before the seventh game, I could tell that what I had to say wasn't making much of an impression," Pilous told *Blueline* magazine in 1957. "I asked Jack [Gatecliff] to interview each player and quote them on how they thought the team would do the next night. Each player, without exception, predicted we'd win. Jack bannered the story. I think each player, reading what he himself had said, had a lot to do with us winning 5-1. And Gatecliff deserved an assist on each goal."

Former Teepee Don McLean, now living in Sault Ste. Marie, recalled the interviews and the story in the *Standard* before the game. "Then we had to win," he said.

After the victory, captain Brian Cullen was presented with the J. Ross Robertson Cup for the club's first OHA Junior A championship. The Garden City went wild.

Then it was on to Quebec City to play the Quebec Frontenacs for the Eastern Canada champi-

Don McLean - Teepees ace penalty-killer
St. Catharines Museum - Brian Cullen Collection, C11,229

Teepees in front of Montreal-bound plane
St. Catharines Museum - Thompson Products Collection N 5710

onship. It took six games for the Teepees to eliminate the Frontenacs, but there was no doubt which team was better after a 9-1 Teepees victory in game five in Quebec. Barry Cullen scored four goals after flying to Quebec from the St. Catharines Collegiate where he had written a grade 13 exam earlier in the day. The team now had the Eastern Canada championship: The George T. Richardson Memorial Trophy.

There was, however, a loss off the ice. Rex Stimers lost his voice and had to be replaced by his sidekick and brother-in-law, Tommy Garriock. Would Stimers be able to broadcast the Memorial Cup championship game and see his prediction come true?

There was one more series to go to win junior hockey's most coveted trophy and it looked like it was going to be tough. Representing the West were the powerful Edmonton Oil Kings and they came to the East with a very impressive record. During the regular season they won 60 of 65 games and 18 of 19 playoff contests. Could the Teepees handle the club led by future NHLers Norm Ullman and Johnny Bucyk? It took one game to answer the question.

With fewer than 1,000 fans in Maple Leaf Gardens, the Teepees whipped the Oil Kings 8-2 in the first game. Former Oshawa Generals captain Jack (Red) Armstrong led the Teepees attack with a hat trick. It may have been his finest game in a Teepees uniform.

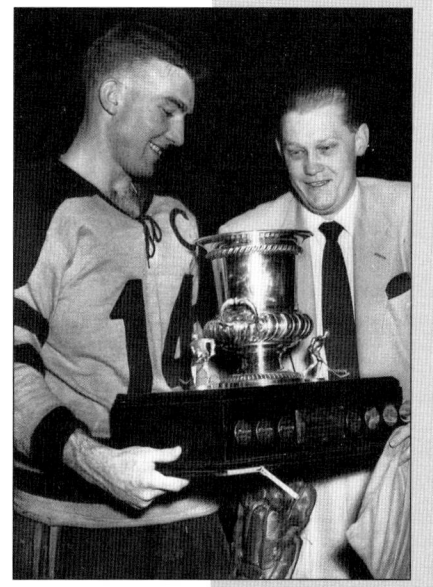

Brian Cullen with the Red Tilson Trophy
St. Catharines Museum - Brian Cullen Collection N 5803

BRIAN CULLEN

Ottawa native Brian Cullen joined the St. Catharines Teepees in 1951 and it didn't take him long to make an impression. In his first season, he was recognized as the OHA Junior A League's top rookie. The 5-foot-10, 165-pound centre never missed a game in three seasons. At the end of his third season, he had captained the Teepees to the city's first Memorial Cup and was recognized as one of the greatest players in junior hockey history.

Courtesy of Brian Cullen

In addition to winning the Red Tilson Trophy in 1954, as the league's most valuable player, Cullen won the Eddie Powers Trophy, setting new league scoring records with 68 goals, 93 assists and 161 points. Although these numbers would be erased by other OHA players in later years, they remain as records which were never broken in 34 years of St. Catharines Junior A hockey. He also centred the famed CBC line, which finished the 1953-54 season with a record 389 points.

He turned pro with the Toronto Maple Leafs organization in 1954 and stayed until 1959. He had his best pro season in 1957-58 when he earned 43 points, including 20 goals. In 1959 he was claimed by the New York Rangers. After two years in New York, he finished his career with the AHL Buffalo Bisons who won the Calder Cup in 1963.

Cullen, who was inducted into the St. Catharines Sports Hall of Fame in 1992, played in 326 regular-season NHL games and collected 156 points.

Since 1966, he has been a successful car dealer and today Brian Cullen Motors in St. Catharines is the largest GM dealership in Niagara. He also owns two GM dealerships in Niagara Falls and a Toyota car business in Cambridge.

For several years, he was a leading thoroughbred horse breeder and owner. In 1985 one of his horses, Pre Emptive Strike, placed third in the Queen's Plate.

Cullen lives in the Garden City.

TEEPEES 1953-1954

HUGH BARLOW

Hamilton native Hugh Barlow was the hero in one of the most exciting games ever played in Garden City Arena. On March 23, 1954, the left winger on the high-scoring CBC line scored the tying goal in a playoff game with St. Michael's College Majors with 12 seconds left in the game. In the overtime period, he potted the goal that resulted in a 6-6 draw.

The 5-foot-8 speedster scored 121 points in 1953-54 and finished second to teammate Brian Cullen in league scoring. In 26 playoff games, he scored 22 goals and earned 41 points.

Despite an outstanding junior career, Barlow never made it to the NHL. He plied his trade in the minors where he continued to be an offensive threat in the Western Hockey League.

In 1955-56 he was with the Western Hockey League champion Winnipeg Warriors and had his best year as a pro with 64 points. For part of that season the former Teepees CBC line was reunited.

After retiring from hockey, Barlow became a successful real estate salesman in Vancouver. Today he lives in Surrey, British Columbia.

St. Catharines Museum - Cornelius Collection, C10,634

IAN CUSHENAN

Ian Cushenan didn't start to play hockey in his hometown of Hamilton until he was 15, but it didn't take him long to adapt to the game. By 1952 the rugged reargard was playing with the St. Catharines Teepees, and in 1954 he was part of the city's first Memorial Cup team.

In 1954 he turned pro with the AHL Cleveland Barons and two years later was with the Chicago Black Hawks who traded him to the Montreal Canadiens, winners of the 1959 Stanley Cup. In 1960 and 1961, he won Calder Cups with the Springfield Indians and earned a third one with the Buffalo Bisons in 1963.

After retiring in 1966, Cushenan managed a steamship line for the New York Yankees owner, George Steinbrenner, and later he was involved in a number of businesses. Today he lives in North Olmstead, Ohio, and sells real estate in the Cleveland area.

St. Catharines Museum - Cornelius Collection, C10,661

Jack Armstrong
St. Catharines Standard photo

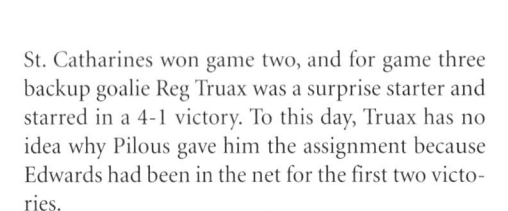

Reg Truax
St. Catharines Museum - Cornelius Collection, C10,678

St. Catharines won game two, and for game three backup goalie Reg Truax was a surprise starter and starred in a 4-1 victory. To this day, Truax has no idea why Pilous gave him the assignment because Edwards had been in the net for the first two victories.

After a 4-4 tie in game four, the Teepees won the Memorial Cup in convincing fashion in game five with a 6-2 victory seen by thousands on CBC Television. Rex Stimers was back in the broadcast booth to cheer on his beloved Teepees.

It is interesting to note who scored the last two Teepees goals in the third period. The second-last goal was scored by sweater number 7, Barry Cullen. The final marker was netted by number 11, Hugh Barlow. Seven and eleven, just like Stimers had predicted as lucky numbers for the Teepees at the beginning of the season. Hollywood couldn't have scripted a better ending.

The city's first Memorial Cup victory touched off a celebration that the Garden City had never seen before – and may never see again. Late on Sunday afternoon, May 16, 1954, bells were ringing and car horns were blaring throughout the city. Crowds were gathering along Geneva and St. Paul Streets.

People were hugging and kissing each other. Then-*Standard* sports reporter Jack Gatecliff described the scene as: "A spontaneous display of sheer pent-up emotion and enthusiasm which has never before been equaled in St. Catharines and the Niagara district."

During the celebrations in the city, a red Niagara, St. Catharines and Toronto bus, which had been followed along the Queen Elizabeth Way by a caravan of noisy cars decorated with gold and black streamers, slowly made its way to Garden City Arena. According to local resident Alex Ormston, the bus stopped at the corner of Geneva Street and Russell Avenue. Ormston, who was 11 years old at the time, saw Rudy Pilous and the players get off the bus and wave to Thompson Products President George Stauffer, who was standing in the window of his apartment. Apparently he had been too ill to attend the game in Toronto.

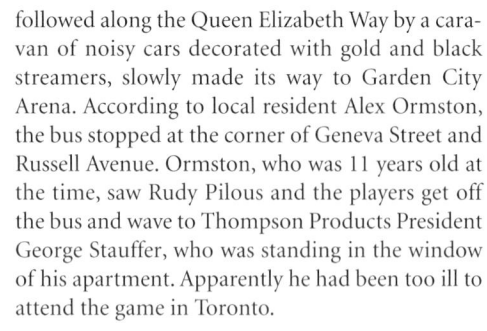

When the bus reached Garden City Arena, the occupants got out and entered the building. A crowd of 6,000 went wild as each of the 17 young men appeared. The city's newest heroes, the 1953-54 St. Catharines Teepees, were home.

Former Teepees goalie Marv Edwards remembered how he felt as he entered the arena that night: "My knees just about turned to jelly."

"It was mind-boggling," ex-Teepee Chester Warchol said.

"I got all the buttons torn off my sports jacket," former Teepees captain Brian Cullen recalled.

In the arena the players formed a semi-circle at centre ice, and Teepees broadcaster Rex Stimers kicked off the celebrations with the "Let's Go Teepees" chant while the Merritton Grenadiers pounded out the time on the drums.

"It was a night which those fortunate enough to be there will never forget," Brian Cullen said.

Stimers almost missed the excitement because his car broke down on the return trip from Toronto, but he was rescued by a police cruiser that pushed his car from outside St. Catharines to the parking lot behind the arena.

"There may be other Memorial Cups, but this was the first and there'll never be another like it," *Standard* reporter Craig Swayze said at the time. There are many Teepees fans who still believe it.

In addition to winning the Memorial Cup, the Teepees had their greatest year at the box office. Thirty-two regular-season games and nine playoff contests attracted 108,741 fans. One playoff game drew 4,264, the largest crowd ever to witness a junior A game in the club's 11-year history. The team's share of hockey revenue jumped from $47,749 to a whopping $74,332 because the club had played 12 more home games. ■

TERRY O'MALLEY: Almost A Teepee

St. Catharines native Terry O'Malley is the former chairman of the Toronto-based Vickers and Benson Advertising, now Vickers and Benson Arnold. O'Malley's creative talents helped to make the agency one of the leaders in its field.

Whether he was planning ad campaigns for McDonald's, Red Cap Ale, or the Liberal Party of Canada, O'Malley knew how to get the public's attention. A 30 second ad showing a hand sticking a lit cigarette into a globe of the planet earth won the distinction of entry into the Hall of Fame of the prestigious New York-based international advertising awards show, the CLIOS. On February 1, 2007, O'Malley was inducted into the Marketing Hall of Legends in Toronto.

Today O'Malley is semi-retired and still travels to Toronto twice a week to tutor admen in his former company. He is passionate about his hometown and is ready, willing and able to do whatever it takes to make St. Catharines a place of which we all can be proud.

So what's Terry O'Malley's name doing in a book all about junior A hockey? Well, part of the answer is that O'Malley was one of the main supporters of the St. Catharines Junior A reunion held at the St. Catharines Museum on September 25, 2004. The other reason is that he was almost a St. Catharines Teepee in 1953 and to this day, the former Harvard University hockey star wonders what his life would have been like if he had made the team.

How he came to be almost a Teepee, can best be explained by an article Terry wrote for the St. Catharines Standard on May 2, 1998. The column was entitled: "Taking the time to appreciate those who make a difference". This article will give readers some insight into not only O'Malley, but also the man who rescued junior hockey in St. Catharines, Thompson Products executive, George Stauffer.

Terry O'Malley was with the Harvard varsity hockey team for three years, and played twice in the NCAA final four championships. He was named All-Ivy defensive forward on two occasions. In 1955, he was the Crimsons second-leading scorer with 30 points.
Courtesy of Terry O'Malley

Terry O'Malley, a member of the Marketing Hall of Legends
St. Catharines Standard photo

VIEWPOINT
Saturday, May 2, 1998 B9

Taking the time to appreciate those who made a difference

Throughout our lives, there are those whose influences go far beyond any others. These are the people who so deeply change your actions, your perspective, your life.

They are our mentors, and it's important for us to acknowledge who these people have been, or are, and take the time to recognize and thank them. While you're thinking of who these may be in your career, let me indulge myself by proudly telling of those who have so profoundly affected me.

George Stauffer is a St. Catharines legend. I don't have to spend a lot of time telling you of his business impacts on this community, ranging from his role as Chief Executive of Thompson Products (now TRW), to his ownership of the renowned St. Catharines Teepees. He brought a profile and identity to this city we have lacked since their disappearance.

He has impacted charities, fund raising, the Hotel Dieu Hospital and virtually every professional corner of this town. What isn't registered and talked about is his quiet, thoughtful and generous impact on people. I was one.

No different than any other young male in this city, I wished for only two things, to play for the Teepees and to play in the NHL. Both would be difficult, because I wasn't all that talented, but I could at least dream and work hard. I applied the same ethic in the classroom, and was rewarded with a scholarship to a prestigious American university.

The magnitude of this opportunity didn't register on me, and I still had playing for the Teepees as a priority. I thought I could play both ends against the middle, and go to tryout camp before the mid-September opening of college. My idea was, if I made the team, I'd go back to high school for another year at least, and think about what Jack Gatecliff would say about me in The Standard and Rex Stimers would broadcast over CKTB.

Teepee tryouts were at Garden City Arena, two a day. The names of all players trying out, from goalies through to forwards, were printed carefully on large pieces of paper taped to a post in the dressing room. During each session, someone would go into the room and draw a line through the names of those being cut. So as you came into the room, sweaty, tired and anxious, you tried to avoid looking at the most recent markings, but it was invariably your first observation.

It seems in retrospect a rather cruel and barbaric approach. Anyone getting cut would have to endure that terrible period of failure and embarrassment as he removed his equipment and took that last shower, while those remaining looked on as though that person was now some other tainted species, from this point on forever on the outside.

I was surviving. Probably on about day three, Mr. Stauffer arrived to watch a practice. He wore his signature brown fedora, and had this handsome and I'm sure expensive camel coat casually draped over his shoulders, complimented by a tidy brown silk scarf to defend the cold arena air. Today it would be like George Steinbrenner coming into the locker room.

He was a handsome figure and inspired a mix of awe, admiration and fear in us. He knew who I was, and something of my background. I was never certain how he was privy to this, or why he cared, but like all successful people, he knew.

He asked me "What are you doing here, young man?" I responded with a nervous voice, completely intimidated by this figure, "Hoping to make the team, sir." Mr. Stauffer looked at me in a way that, if I'd had the sensitivity at the time, I would have clearly interpreted a look that yelled out: How foolish can you be?

He carefully explained to me I was in possession of the opportunity of a lifetime. What I did with it would be my business. The hockey equation wasn't quite as clear. Although I was hanging in, there were many cuts to come. Let's say I make it and get hurt, or during the season someone comes along who is better. There were no guarantees for the future. He told me, "Hockey might make you a star and it might make you a bum. I don't want you taking that chance."

With that, he went to the list on the pole and, with a simple but significant backward motion of his hand, stroked a line through my name, under the section called Wingers. He told me to get to school and come to see him in the summer.

Mr. Stauffer employed me for three summers. He put me into various departmental situations, and often times, with no warning, he would fire off a memo to me demanding my immediate perspective on a particular situation in that area of the business. He told me with these experiences I may not find out what I want to be for the rest of my life, but I'd find out what I wouldn't want to be, and that was just as important.

He took me to one-on-one lunches at his club in Niagara Falls, and proudly had me at his table at the St. Catharines Club. One time during our conversations I expressed an interest in corporate law. In his infallible way, he clicked that into his memory bank, and a few weeks later sent me to the head office in Cleveland, to meet with their legal staff and talk about what a career in that field might entail.

Flying was very, very special in those days, and to be in your teens travelling first class on business was pretty heady stuff. I remember that trip so vividly for another simple reason. I didn't have proper dress shoes, and I couldn't afford to just run out and get a pair, so I borrowed my Uncle Ted's. It forever gave him licence to tell everyone I knew how it felt to be in his shoes.

Mr. Stauffer continued to help me after I graduated, and when it appeared I had chosen a profession and a career path, he moved aside and allowed me my own experiences. Throughout my career I have carried the teachings of Mr. Stauffer with me, and have tried to be a considerate and sensitive mentor for others.

On different occasions, I have personally thanked him for the guidance and concern he gave to me. I hope, when you think of those who did the same for you, and you haven't said that thank you, you'll do it soon, before it's too late. I can't tell you how good it will make you feel. George Stauffer, a mentor who taught me direction.

In a future column, I want to tell you of four others who taught me lessons in other ways, and when you read them, I'm sure you'll see similarities in your own lives.

Terry O'Malley is a St. Catharines native whose commentary appears here regularly

TEEPEES 1953-1954

Win Four Games, Tie One

TEEPEES TAKE MEMORIAL CUP

Fans Cheered As Those Teepees Rolled Along

Brian Cullen accepts the Memorial Cup.

Courtesy of Jack Higgins

TEEPEES 1953-1954

Trainer Jimmy Joy with Teepees and the Memorial Cup
Courtesy of Jack Higgins

Rudy Pilous and George Stauffer with the Memorial Cup
St. Catharines Museum - *TRW Canada Collection N 5718*

Teepee players carry Rudy Pilous after the big win.
Courtesy of Jack Higgins

Teepees fans celebrate Memorial Cup victory
St. Catharines Museum - *Janine Muller Collection, C11,154*

TEEPEES 1953-1954

Memorial Cup showcase at Eaton's department store in St. Catharines
St. Catharines Museum - *TRW Collection N 5767*

Rudy waves his hat at Garden City Arena celebrations
St. Catharines Museum - *Janine Muller Collection, C10,881*

Left: Teepees in Garden City Arena for the Memorial Cup reception
St. Catharines Museum - *Janine Muller Collection, C10,883*

Jimmy Joy with Joy Juice, a cocktail with a secret formula designed to energize the players
St. Catharines Standard photo

1954 Memorial Cup champion Teepees at 1994 reunion
Front row: (left to right) Reg Truax, Bob Maxwell, Marv Edwards, Brian Cullen
Back row: Elmer Vasko, Chester Warchol, Don McLean, Cec Hoekstra, Jack Higgins
St. Catharines Museum - *Betty Maxwell Collection 2004.66.1*

TEEPEES 1954-1955

HANK CIESLA ENDS JUNIOR A CAREER WITH THE RED TILSON TROPHY

ATTENDANCE FIGURES
Average per regular-season game: 2,403
Season's largest crowd: 3,997
Season's smallest crowd: 1,579

PLAYOFF ROUNDS: 2
Eliminated St. Mike's 4-0-1
Lost to Toronto Marlboros 4-2

Although several of the Memorial Cup champions had graduated in 1954, there was every indication the 1954-55 team could capture another Memorial Cup. The club, with new gold and black sweaters featuring the word Teepees and with the character Peewee in the centre on the front, opened the season on a winning note, defeating the Kitchener-Waterloo Canucks 4-2. In goal for the Canucks was Reg Truax who had backed up Teepees netminder Marv Edwards in 1953-54.

The Standard reported after the opener that: "As the cigarette ad states…'They satisfied.'"

In the second game, the Toronto Marlboros whipped the Teepees 7-2; with future NHL stars, Bob Baun, Billy Harris, Bob Pulford, and Al McNeil, this team seemed to have a great future.

In January of 1955, Chicago Black Hawks GM Tommy Ivan visited St. Catharines before a Teepees game against the Galt Black Hawks, who were sponsored by Chicago at the time. As the new GM of the Hawks, Ivan was determined to build up a strong farm system, and acquired the AHL Buffalo Bisons. Ivan was pleased to have the Bisons because of their affiliation with the Teepees. In the summer of 1955, Chicago dropped its sponsorship of the Galt Black Hawks, and the Teepees became a major source of talent for the Chicago club.

For the second year in a row, the

1954-1955

GAMES PLAYED	WON	LOST	TIED	FOR	AGAINST	POINTS	FINISH
49	32	15	2	260	176	66	1/8

Leading Scorers

PLAYER	GOALS	ASSISTS	POINTS
Hank Ciesla	57	49	106
Barry Cullen	45	42	87
Cec Hoekstra	30	50	80
Ab McDonald	33	37	70
Chester Warchol	15	34	49

Leading Goaltenders

PLAYER	GP	GA	SO	GAA
Marv Edwards	47	162	1	3.45
Rodger Day	2	14	0	7.0

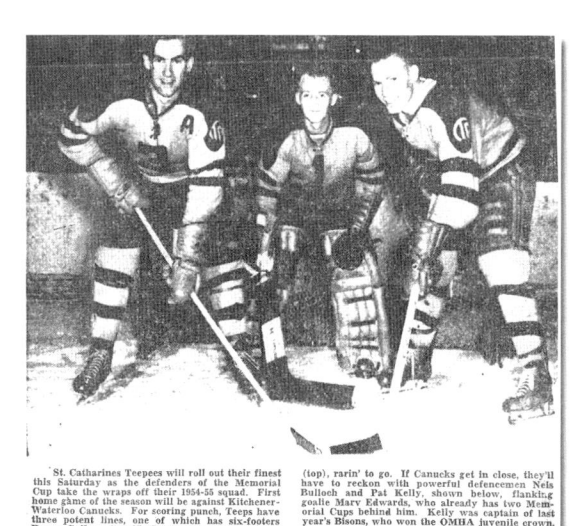

Marv Edwards with Nelson Bulloch (left) and Pat Kelly (right)
St. Catharines Standard

From the left, counter clockwise: Pete Hubbard, Ken Lamourie, Ed Hoekstra, Alex Viskalis, Roy Greenen, Bob Butler, Hank Ciesla (captain), Ab McDonald, Elmer Vasko, Cec Hoekstra, Barry Cullen, Nelson Bulloch, Maitland Thompson, Chester Warchol, Mitch Plata, Pat Kelly, Rodger Day, and Marv Edwards. Coach Rudy Pilous is in the middle of the lineup.

St. Catharines Museum - Standard Collection N 570

TEEPEES 1954-1955

BARRY CULLEN

Charles Francis (Barry) Cullen joined the Teepees in 1953 and for two years was one of the club's leading scorers, racking up 194 regular-season points, including 107 goals. Playing with older brother Brian and Hugh Barlow on the famed CBC line, the trio scored 389 points in 59 regular-season games en route to the Teepees 1954 Memorial Cup victory.

St. Catharines Standard photo

The right winger turned pro with the Toronto Maple Leafs in 1955. In his rookie season with Winnipeg Warriors he broke the Western Hockey League scoring record with 38 goals and won the league's top rookie award.

In 1956 he was reunited with his brother Brian in Toronto, but three years later was traded to the Detroit Red Wings. After one year in Detroit, he joined the AHL Buffalo Bisons. In 1961-62, he was an AHL First Team All-Star after scoring 41 goals and collecting 94 points. He was a member of Buffalo's Calder Cup team in 1963.

Since 1969 Cullen has owned a GM dealership in Guelph, Ontario, and lives just outside the city.

Cullen's son John, a former Boston University hockey star, played in the NHL with Pittsburgh, Hartford, Toronto and Tampa Bay. In 1990-91 he was the NHL's fifth leading scorer with 110 points. In 1999 John was presented with the Bill Masterson Award for his sportsmanship and dedication to hockey.

DENNIS RIGGIN

Kincardine native Dennis Riggin played Junior A hockey with Windsor and then Hamilton from 1951 to 1956. In the 1955 playoffs, he replaced Teepees netminder Marv Edwards after he was injured in a playoff game against the Toronto Marlboros.

Courtesy of Ernie Fitzsimmons Collection

After turning pro in 1956 with the WHL Edmonton Flyers, Riggin played for the Detroit Red Wings for nine games in 1959-60 and again in 1962-63. The 1957 WHL Prairie Division rookie-of-the year retired in 1963.

Riggin's son Pat played 350 NHL games with Atlanta, Calgary, Washington, Boston and Pittsburgh, winning 153 games with a goals-against average of 3.43.

St. Catharines-born players have an important part in the rebuilding plans of the Teepees this year. Here in the dressing room Coach Pilous gives out with a few words of wisdom . . . and wit . . . to Mait Thompson, Chester Lukasik, Mitch Plata, Roger Day, Pat Kelly and Chuck Stewart. All are St. Catharines boys and, with the exception of Stewart, all played with the juvenile T-P Bisons last season. Stewart was with the Brantford junior "B" club and led the league in goals and total points.
—Staff Photo (S)

St. Catharines Standard

Teepees with new fedoras   St. Catharines Museum - Pat Kelly Ref. File, 2004.09.21

St. Catharines' two greatest junior hockey players, Brian Cullen (left) and Doug McMurdy (centre) met briefly between periods of the Bison-Teepee game last night at Garden City Arena. McMurdy won the Red Tilson Memorial Trophy in the season 1944-45, the first year it was up for competition. Cullen was the almost unanimous choice last season. The trophy is presented each year to the player adjudged most valuable to his team in the OHA junior "A" circuit. McMurdy is now with Springfield of the AHL. Cullen is attempting to make a place with the Toronto Maple Leafs of the NHL. The smiling gent on the right is Rudy Pilous who coached both players the season they were named top of their class in hockey.
—Staff Photo (S)

St. Catharines Standard

Teepees finished the schedule in first place with 66 points. The club had a home record of 20 wins, only four losses and one tie. In the first round of the playoffs, the Teepees met St. Mike's, and disposed of their tough opponents in five games.

And then it happened. Teepees goalie Marv Edwards was injured in practice by a shot from Hank Ciesla. Without him, the team was eliminated from the playoffs by the Toronto Marlies in six games.

Dennis Riggin, the regular goalie for the Hamilton Tiger-Cubs, had played three playoff games for the Tiger-Cubs, two games for St. Mikes, and one game with the Marlboros versus the Teepees, before switching sides and joining the Teepees for the remaining games.

During the second game of the series in Toronto, Teepee Barry Cullen was accused of kicking Marlie Gary Aldcorn with his skates in a goal crease pileup. "I have never kicked with my skates since I started playing and never will," Cullen said after the game. Marlie defenceman Al McNeil jumped off his bench and attacked Cullen. Both teams left their benches. It was the biggest fight of the junior season.

When Marlies Manager Stafford Smythe tried to get at the Teepees bench, trainer and former Teepee defenceman Al Kellogg stopped him in his tracks. "I hit him with one punch," Kellogg recalled with a smile at the St. Catharines Junior A reunion in the fall of 2004. "The police were right there," Kellogg said.

"Don't you know who you hit?" a cop asked Kellogg, who didn't know who Smythe was at the time.

The penalty total was 413 minutes and included 9 minors, 33 majors and 23 misconducts. The Marlies were assessed 213 minutes and the Teepees 200.

In another third period incident, Teepee Pat Kelly tangled with Marlie tough guy Gerry James, and came out of the scrap with a badly gashed hand that later required surgery. "I'm sure that James bit me," Kelly said before heading to the St. Catharines General Hospital. "James must have a pretty fair set of molars," wrote *Standard* reporter Gatecliff.

Continued on page 78

TEEPEES 1954-1955

Penalties Total 413 Minutes in Game

An indication of things to come occurred early in the third period when Barry Cullen and Ron Casey tangled on the boards and finished up in a wrestling match. Cullen, in this picture, is on the bottom of the pile, while one of the linesmen attempts to pry the pair apart. The only person apparently enjoying the fight is a policeman in the background sporting a wide grin. Fourteen minutes later the entire rink was thrown into pandemonium as the biggest fight of the junior season broke out between the two clubs.

St. Catharines Museum - Pat Kelly Ref. File, 2004.09.21

St. Catharines Teepees, on the verge of elimination, defeated Toronto Marlboros 7-2 last night at Garden City Arena. Marlboros now lead the OHA Junior "A" finals 3-2. In a pre-game ceremony, Teepee captain Hank Ciesla was presented with the Eddie Powers Memorial Trophy by OHA past President Jack Roxburgh (right). The award goes annually to the leading point scorer in the junior series and was won last year by Teepees Brian Cullen. The smiling gent in the centre is Rex Stimers, who had an even broader grin three hours later.

St. Catharines Museum - Pat Kelly Ref. File, 2004.09.21

Most Valuable, Gentlemanly

Hank Ciesla Awarded Tilson Memorial Trophy

TORONTO (CP) — Centre Hank Ciesla of St. Catharines TeePees has been awarded the Albert Red Tilson Memorial Trophy as the most valuable and gentlemanly player in the Ontario Hockey Association Junior A. League, it was announced Friday.

The 20-year-old junior star, highest scorer in the league this season, becomes the second TeePee player to win the award in the last two years. Brian Cullen, now with the National Hockey League Toronto Maple Leafs, won it last season while with Teepees.

The six foot two inch Teepee Captain is the third player in St. Catharines junior hockey history to receive the award. Doug McMurdy, a member of the Falcons 11 years ago was the first winner of the Tilson Tropy. McMurdy is now playing with Springfield Indians of the American Hockey League.

Ciesla is the 11th player to be honored since the trophy was presented by The Globe and Mail to be awarded annually to the player regarded as the most valuable and gentlemanly in the league.

The trophy perpetuates the memory of Red Tilson, an outstanding player with Regina and Oshawa junior hockey teams who was killed in the Second World War. Sportswriters in the six league centres handled the voting.

Ciesla, a native of St. Catharines, is completing his fourth year with Teepees, defending Memorial Cup champions. He led all scorers this season with an unofficial total of 106 points — 57 goals and 49 assists — and was given five of a possible nine first-place votes.

Dennis Riggin, goalkeeper with Hamilton Cubs, was second. Others receiving votes were Bill McCreary of Guelph Biltmores, Bill Harris of Toronto Marlboros, Dick Duff of Toronto St. Michael's Majors, Harry Howell of Guelph, Hec Lalande of Galt Black Hawks and Les Duff of St. Michaels.

St. Catharines Standard

Hank Ciesla, captain of the Teepees and the OHA junior "A" scoring champion, has been named 1954-55 winner of the Red Tilson Memorial Trophy. Ciesla succeeds another Teepee captain, Brian Cullen, now playing with the Toronto Maple Leafs.

HANK CIESLA

St. Catharines native Hank Ciesla was a minor hockey league sensation. Before he joined the St. Catharines Teepees in 1951, the 16-year-old had won five Ontario Minor Hockey Association championships. In 1953-54 the talented 6-foot-2 centre played an important role in capturing the team's first Memorial Cup as he scored 39 goals in the regular season and had 26 points in 26 playoff games.

In 1954-55 he was the team captain and won the Eddie Powers Memorial Trophy for leading the league in scoring with 106 points. He was also the third St. Catharines junior to win the Red Tilson Trophy.

He turned pro with the Chicago Black Hawks in 1955, the first St. Catharines-born player to make it to the NHL. Two years later, he joined the New York Rangers. After two years with the Rangers, he spent the rest of his career with AHL teams, including Rochester, Cleveland, Pittsburgh and Buffalo.

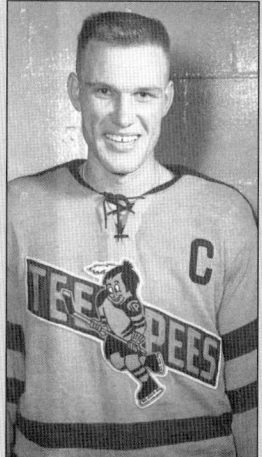

He was an AHL Second Team All-Star in 1963 after scoring 42 goals and collecting 98 points for the Cleveland Barons. He played 269 regular season NHL games accumulating 77 points, including 26 goals.

Ciesla passed away in St. Catharines in April of 1976.

St. Catharines Standard photo

TEEPEES 1954-1955

CEC HOEKSTRA

Winnipeg native Cec Hoekstra joined the Teepees after reaching the Memorial Cup finals with St. Boniface Canadians in 1953. The smooth-skating centre played a big role in the club's Memorial Cup victory in 1954. In his last season of junior hockey, 1954-55, he scored 80 points and enjoyed immense popularity in the Garden City.

St. Catharines Standard photo

In 1955 he turned pro with the Montreal Canadiens, but only saw action in a few NHL games because the NHL club was loaded with talented veterans who were on a five-year Stanley Cup winning streak.

He won a WHL championship with the Winnipeg Warriors in 1956 and after spending time in Montreal, Rochester, Buffalo, Pittsburgh and Calgary, he found a home in the AHL with the Cleveland Barons. He scored 20 goals four times and won a Calder Cup with the Barons in 1964.

After leaving Cleveland, he played with the Senior A Galt Hornets who won an Allan Cup in 1971.

Today the former supervisor of the ground crew for the Cherry Hill Golf Club in Ridgeway is retired and lives in St. Catharines.

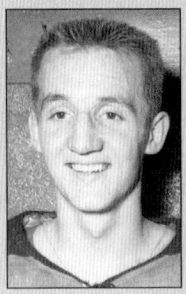

MARV EDWARDS

Marv Edwards was an outstanding netminder with the St. Catharines Teepees from 1951 to 1955. Early in his junior career, he let in some questionable goals and Teepees broadcaster Rex Stimers called him "Stinky." The name stuck.

In 1953, the St. Catharines native joined the Barrie Flyers in the playoffs and won a Memorial Cup ring. The next year he led the Teepees to their first junior championship.

St. Catharines Standard photo

Edwards played senior A hockey after leaving St. Catharines and in 1959 was with the Belleville McFarlands when they won the world championship. In the 1960s, he played in the Eastern Hockey League where he became a hockey legend, winning five EHL championships. He was a first team all-star four times and top goaltender three times.

Edwards played his first NHL game with the Pittsburgh Penguins in 1968 at age 33. Later, he played with the Toronto Maple Leafs and ended his career with California Golden Seals in 1974.

In 1996 he was the goaltending coach with the Peterborough Petes who won the OHL title.

Edwards, who lives in Fort Erie, was inducted into the St. Catharines Sports Hall of Fame in 1999.

Continued from page 76

Speaking from Charlotte, North Carolina, 50 years later, Kelly isn't sure what happened. What he does remember is that he didn't get on the operating table in St. Catharines until several hours after the game, and the pain was unbearable. And oh yes, the Teepees won the contest 3-0.

Eddie Bush was called in to replace Teepees coach Rudy Pilous who was suspended for two games because of the brawl. Marlboro coach Turk Broda was also suspended for two games and Al McNeil, who touched off the brawl, received a $10 fine and no suspension.

After being eliminated by the Marlboros, Pilous had nothing but praise for his troops. "I'm still proud of my kids," he said. "They really worked out there, but nothing seemed to go right."

Returning from Toronto, the Teepees and their supporters had to drive 10-15 miles an hour as the QEW was glare ice all the way to Oakville. It looked like a 30-mile funeral procession, the *Standard* reported.

Tilson Trophy winner Hank Ciesla sparkled in the playoffs, scoring 17 points in 11 games. Barry Cullen and Cec Hoekstra contributed 13 and 12 points respectively.

Total attendance for 1954-55 fell to 82,541, but the team played ten fewer games than the 1954 Memorial Cup champions. ■

Injured Teepee netminder Marv Edwards reads the Standard *sports section on March 15, 1955. Without Edwards in goal, the Teepees were eliminated from the playoffs by Toronto Marlboros.*

St. Catharines Standard photo

WIMPY ROBERTS

Popular Teepee was traded to Guelph during the 1954-55 season.

St. Catharines Museum
- Cornelius Collection, C10,702

Former Teepees Bob Maxwell (left) and netminder Marv Edwards, in action with the Nashville Dixie Flyers

St. Catharines Museum - *Maxwell Collection*
2004.74.3

TEEPEES 1955-1956

BOBBY HULL JOINS THE TEEPEES

ATTENDANCE FIGURES
Average per regular-season game: 2,475
Season's largest crowd: 3,672
Season's smallest crowd: 1,585

PLAYOFF ROUNDS: 1
Eliminated by Toronto Marlboros 4-1-1

On September 24, 1955, 58 players, not including the previous year's holdovers, checked into the Esquire Hotel in the Garden City, looking for jobs with the Teepees. "We'll also know where they are all the time," coach/manager Rudy Pilous said. It was the largest turnout in the club's history. Players who didn't make the team were farmed out to junior clubs with which the Teepees were connected in Simcoe, Brockville and Timmins.

One of the 58 hopefuls was Point Anne native Bobby Hull. In his Teepees debut, the 17-year-old had 11 goals and 18 points in the regular season. He added two assists in six playoff games.

The 5-foot-10 left winger wasn't ticketed to play for the Teepees at all. He was headed to the Galt Black Hawks, but the Chicago Black Hawks left Galt in 1955 during the off-season. Through the influence of George Stauffer and Rudy Pilous, the Chicago Black Hawks changed their affiliation to the St. Catharines Teepees.

Pilous had no trouble signing Hull to a playing certificate, paying him $35 a week while he was playing hockey and $10 a week from the end of the season to the end of the St. Catharines Collegiate school term.

Former *St. Catharines Standard* sports editor Jack Gatecliff recalled the first time he met Hull at the Esquire Hotel. "It was Bobby Hull, blond, muscular, already with the indelible stamp of a sports hero. His smile (he had all his teeth at 16

Tommy Ivan, Chicago Black Hawks GM, September 17, 1956
St. Catharines Standard photo

1955-1956

GAMES PLAYED	WON	LOST	TIED	FOR	AGAINST	POINTS	FINISH
48	28	17	3	219	197	59	1/8

Leading Scorers

PLAYER	GOALS	ASSISTS	POINTS
Ab McDonald	49	34	83
Art Stratton	37	42	79
Ed Hoekstra	22	31	53
Don Carter	15	26	41
Elmer (Moose) Vasko	9	31	40

Leading Goaltenders

PLAYER	GP	GA	SO	GAA
Roy Edwards	41	160	1	3.90
Rodger Day	5	22	0	4.40

Rudy Pilous, right, is one of the most successful coaches in hockey today. His St. Catharines Teepees just recently clinched their third straight first place finish in the tough OHA Junior A league. Above, Rudy shows some of his players a few of the intricacies of the game. Left to right, they are Ab McDonald, Elmer Vasko, and Pat Kelly.
St. Catharines Museum - Pat Kelly Ref. File, 2004.09.21

Front row: Len Ronson, Roy Edwards, Gary Eatough, Rudy Pilous (coach), Richard LaFontaine, Rodger Day, Pat Kelly
Middle row: Jay MacDonald (secretary), Bobby Hull, Matthew Plata, Pop Steele, Jimmy Joy (trainer), Don Ramsay, Matt Ravlich, Al Kellogg (property man)
Top row: Mait Thompson, Don Carter, Wayne Hillman, Roy Greenen, Ab McDonald, Elmer Vasko (captain) Ed Hoekstra, Rob Butler, Art Stratton
St. Catharines Standard photo

TEEPEES 1955-1956

BOBBY HULL

In 16 NHL seasons, playing 1,063 regular-season games, Bobby Hull scored 1,170 points, including 610 goals. He led the NHL in goals scored in seven seasons. He was the first to score 50 or more goals in a season more than once. He accomplished this four times.

His trophy collection includes: Art Ross (1960, 1962,1966), Hart (1965, 1966), a Lady Byng (1965) and the Lester Patrick (1969). He was named to ten first-all-star teams and two second teams. He was with Chicago when the Hawks won the Stanley Cup in 1961.

In 411 WHA games he collected 638 points, including 303 goals, and was the league's MVP in 1973 and 1975. He played on Avco Cup championship teams with the Winnipeg Jets in 1976, 1978, and 1979.

In 1983 Hull was inducted into the Hockey Hall of Fame. He is also a member of the Manitoba Hockey Hall of Fame and the Manitoba Sports Hall of Fame.

In 2005 he was named the commissioner of the new WHA, but it never got off the ground.

Hull in a Chicago Black Hawks uniform
St. Catharines Museum
- Standard Collection N 5696

St. Catharines Museum - Monica Smith Ref. File, 1998.05.04

Hull in first picture in Teepee uniform
St. Catharines Standard photo

years of age) would and did indeed melt the hearts of millions of young and not so young girls."

Chicago Black Hawks scout Bob Wilson, who had discovered Hull in a minor game in Belleville, knew the teenager was going to be a success. "There's a kid who'll be a great one," Wilson told Gatecliff in 1955.

Hull scored his first Teepees goal in an exhibition game against the Fort Wayne Komets on October 11, 1955. His first goal in a regularly-scheduled contest was scored against the Montreal Junior Canadiens. It was assisted by Len Ronson and Elmer Vasko.

Hull played centre, but he and Pilous had serious disagreements because Pilous wanted him to play left wing. Hull insisted on playing centre and went home twice during the season when Pilous kept switching him from centre to left wing.

Hull's plaque in Manitoba Hockey Hall of Fame
Courtesy of A. Phair

When Hull arrived in Chicago in 1957, with two years of junior eligibility remaining, Pilous convinced him to play left wing. Pilous also switched ex-Teepee Stan Mikita from right wing to centre. Both players ended up in the Hockey Hall of Fame.

In 1955-56 the Teepees iced another strong team, finishing first for the third straight year with 59 points. Ab McDonald led the Teepees in scoring with 83 points. He and Art Stratton finished third and fourth respectively in the league scoring race, but for the second year in a row the Teepees were ousted in the playoffs in six games by Toronto Marlies.

Jay MacDonald with prized souvenir - Bobby Hull's Teepee cheque for $35.
St. Catharines Standard photo

Standard sports editor Jack Gatecliff (temporary coach) lays the law down to Bobby Hull between periods of an exhibition game on October 1, 1964.
St. Catharines Standard photo

80

TEEPEES 1955-1956

During the playoffs the Teepees adopted Abigail Hoffman as the team mascot. Hoffman was a nine-year-old girl who had masqueraded as a boy with a Toronto Hockey League minor team named the Teepees.

In the second playoff game on Sunday, March 3, 1956, a brawl broke out in the last minute of play in overtime. Pat Kelly boarded Marlies Charlie Burns, and Gary Collins, Burns' teammate, swung his stick at Kelly. Players on both teams chose partners and for the second year in a row, Marlies manager Stafford Smythe became involved in the action near the boards when he grabbed Teepee Ab McDonald around the neck. Kelly came to McDonald's aid and silenced Smythe with a straight right to the jaw. Smythe was ordered out of Maple Leaf Gardens. Later, more fighting broke out in the overtime and all the players on the ice, except the netminders, received major penalties. The game ended in a 3-3 draw.

The Marlies, who were loaded with talented future NHLers like Al McNeil, Carl Brewer, Bobby Baun, Bob Nevin, and Bob Pulford, went on to win the Memorial Cup.

Total attendance for the season was 69,783, a decrease of 12,757 from the previous year, but the club played four fewer contests. At the end of the season, the *Hockey News* named Pilous the Hockey Executive of 1955-56. "Rudy's choice as the executive of the year is the finest tribute ever paid to junior hockey," Thompson Products President George Stauffer said at a banquet held for Pilous in January, 1957. Pilous was surprised when he was presented with the keys to a new Ford Monarch at the event.

When asked to suggest why the Teepees were one of the most successful junior A clubs in Canada, Jack Gatecliff had an answer. "Both [Rudy Pilous and Jay MacDonald] believe in promotion and dressing up for the games. Players must be suitably dressed at all times and have uniforms cleaned regularly." ∎

Pilous is honoured as Hockey's Top Executive for 1955-56.   St. Catharines Standard

PAT KELLY

Defenceman Pat Kelly graduated from the Teepees in 1956 after two seasons on the blueline. After one year with the Senior A Windsor Bulldogs, he turned pro with the QHL Three Rivers Lions in 1957. It was the beginning of a distinguished playing career that lasted until 1973.

St. Catharines Museum - Monica Smith Ref. File, 1998.05.04

In 1962 and 1963, he set an EHL record for assists and points by a defenceman. As a player/coach for Clinton Comets, he won three EHL championships and was a First Team All-Star in each of those years. He was honoured as league coach-of-the-year four times.

In 1967-68, his Clinton club won the EHL Northern Division title and had the all-time greatest single-season winning percentage (.861) of any minor hockey team in North America. The Comets won 57, lost 5 and tied 10 games during the regular season. In 1969-70, he was the Hockey News Minor League Coach of the Year.

In 1984-85 he guided the IHL Peoria Rivermen to a Turner Cup victory. He also had coaching stints in the WHA with the Birmingham Bulls and in the NHL with the Colorado Rockies from 1977-79.

In a 24-year period, he won 849 regular-season games.

In 1988 the Sioux Lookout native was the driving force behind the creation of the East Coast Hockey League and served as the league's president and commissioner for eight years. Today the ECHL champions receive the Kelly Cup, named in his honour.

Kelly has been inducted into six sports halls of fame: Greater Peoria (1990), Welland Walk of Fame (1998), Roanoke Valley (1998), and Greensboro Generals Hall of Fame (2002). He was the inaugural member of the Generals Hall of Fame and his number 5 sweater was retired. In 2008 he was an original inductee into the ECHL Hall of Fame as a builder. In the same year Kelly became a member of the Charlotte Checkers Hall of Fame as a coach.

Today Kelly lives in Charlotte, North Carolina.

Pat Kelly, former president and commissioner of East Coast Hockey League   Courtesy of ECHL

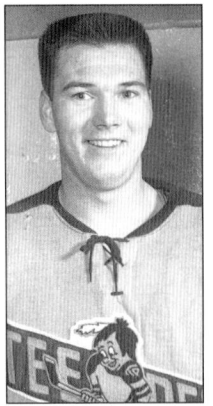

ALVIN (Ab) McDONALD

Winnipeg native Ab McDonald came to St. Catharines from the St. Boniface Canadiens in 1954. At the end of his second and final season with the Teepees, he was the team's leading scorer with 49 goals and 83 points.

The left winger turned pro with the Montreal Canadiens in 1957 and stayed with the organization, winning three Stanley Cups. He was traded to Chicago Black Hawks in 1960. In his first year with the Hawks, he won another Stanley Cup ring.

McDonald had his best years in Chicago playing on the Scooter line with Stan Mikita and Ken Wharram. From 1964 to 1972, he saw NHL service with Boston, Detroit, Pittsburgh and St. Louis before moving to the WHA with the Winnipeg Jets. In 762 regular-season NHL games, he scored 182 goals and collected 430 points. He played in five NHL all-star games.

After retiring, Ab owned a hotel and then ran an equipment rental store in Winnipeg. He was inducted into the Manitoba Hockey Hall of Fame in 1983 and the Manitoba Sports Hall of Fame in 1996.

Ab McDonald's plaque in the Manitoba Hockey Hall of Fame
Courtesy of A. Phair

DON CARTER

Torontonian Don Carter was with the Teepees in 1955-56 before embarking on a pro career that saw him star for the Greensboro Generals from 1959 to 1972.

The 5-foot-11, 185-pound defenceman/right winger had four seasons in which he scored more than 100 points. He won an EHL championship in 1963.

In November, 2003, the original Greensboro franchise member was inducted into the Greensboro Generals Hall of Fame and his number 14 sweater was retired.

ART STRATTON

Art Stratton came to the St. Catharines Teepees for the 1955-56 season after leading the Manitoba Junior Hockey League in scoring with 76 points. Teepees teammate Ed Hoekstra recalled that Stratton's nickname was "Magoo" because he wore contact lens at the time.

After playing one year of senior in North Bay, he turned pro with the Winnipeg Warriors and for the next 19 years was a minor league standout. He won the WHL Prairie Division's top rookie award in 1958. In 1963 he won a Calder Cup with the Buffalo Bisons. He was the AHL scoring champion and league MVP in 1965 and again in 1974. He is number 16 on the list of the top scorers in the AHL with 766 points in 669 games.

Stratton was the CHL MVP in 1966 and 1967. In 1976 he was selected as the SHL's most valuable player.

The centre/left winger also played 95 NHL regular-season games with New York Rangers, Detroit, Chicago, Pittsburgh and Philadelphia.

He now lives in St. Adolphe, Manitoba, and is a member of the Manitoba Hockey Hall of Fame.

Art Stratton with the AHL Buffalo Bisons
Courtesy of Ernie Fitzsimmons Collection

ELMER VASKO

Elmer Vasko was born in Duparquet, Quebec, but moved to St. Catharines when he was nine-years-old. He played his minor hockey in the Garden City and joined the Teepees in 1953 at age 17. His bruising bodychecks, solid clearing, and end-to-end rushes made him a crowd favourite.

After winning the Memorial Cup in 1954, the 6-foot-3, 200-pound defenceman spent two more years with the Teepees before moving up to the Chicago Black Hawks where public relations director Johnny Gottselig nicknamed him "Moose". For ten years he patrolled the blueline with another former Teepee, Pierre Pilote. Hockey Digest picked the duo among the top ten defence pairs in NHL history.

In 1961 he earned a Stanley Cup ring with the Hawks and was a Second Team NHL All-Star in 1963 and 1964. Minnesota North Stars selected him in the 1967 expansion draft. He retired in 1970 after he had accumulated 200 points in 786 regular-season NHL games.

The former owner of the Dog Patch, a Hillside Illinois fast food business, died of cancer in a Chicago hospital on October 30, 1998, just a few days before he was inducted into the St. Catharines Sports Hall of Fame.

LEN RONSON

Brantford native Len Ronson played with the Teepees in 1955-56 and then after three seasons with the IHL Fort Wayne Komets, made his debut in the NHL in October, 1960. It was a night to remember. The left winger, who was called up to the New York Rangers because three left wingers were injured, scored the winning goal in his first NHL game.

After 13 games it was back to the minors where he found a home with the WHL San Diego Gulls from 1966 to 1973. By the time he retired, he was the all-time leader in goals, assists and points for the Gulls.

Ronson now lives in Gresham, Oregon.

TEEPEES 1956-1957

RUDY PILOUS SIGNS 16-YEAR-OLD STAN MIKITA

Stan Mikita's Hockey Career Started With A Little Help From His Friends.

ATTENDANCE FIGURES
Average per regular-season game: 1,999
Season's largest crowd: 4,132
Season's smallest crowd: 1,207

PLAYOFF ROUNDS: 3
Eliminated Barrie Flyers 3-0 and Toronto Marlboros 3-2. Lost to Guelph 4-2

1956-1957

GAMES PLAYED	WON	LOST	TIED	FOR	AGAINST	POINTS	FINISH
52	25	25	2	184	193	52	3/8

Leading Scorers

PLAYER	GOALS	ASSISTS	POINTS
Johnny McKenzie	32	38	70
Ed Hoekstra	28	42	70
Bob Hull	33	28	61
Stan Mikita	16	31	47
Don Cosburn	22	23	45

Leading Goaltenders

PLAYER	GP	GA	SO	GAA
Roy Edwards	49	179	3	3.65
Gene Diotte	3	14	1	4.66

Stan Mikita and his Prince of Wales Public School championship hockey team. Mikita is the first person on the left in the second row. Coach and principal, Ashton Morrison, is the man with the fedora in the last row.
St. Catharines Standard photo

Unlike most young Canadian hockey players, making it to the NHL was not one of Stan Mikita's childhood dreams. Even suiting up with the St. Catharines Teepees never crossed his mind.

Growing up in St. Catharines was not an easy time for Stan Gvoth who had arrived in the Garden City with his cousin from Czechoslovakia in December, 1948. The children came to live with their aunt and uncle, Mr. and Mrs. Joseph Mikita, who gave them the Mikita surname after becoming their adoptive parents.

At age eight, Mikita was enrolled in Edith Cavell Public School, and from the beginning life was a struggle. In addition to not knowing the English language, he faced taunts and insults – which he often couldn't understand – and isolation from other children. It took him one week after he arrived in St. Catharines before he even had the nerve to venture out of his home and play street hockey.

He could have given up, but Mikita was determined to prove he was as good as those other kids.

It didn't take long.

He gradually picked up the English language, mainly from the street, and participated in all sports except hockey at Edith Cavell. By the time he was nine, he had never even tried on a pair of skates.

Front row: Don Grosso, goalie Bob Smith, Grant Morton, Captain Eddie Hoekstra, Bobby Hull, goalie Roy Edwards, Johnny McKenzie. Second row: Les Soloman, Pat Adair, Don Cosburn, Trainer Jimmy Joy, Wayne Hillman, Rino Robazza, Gary McDermott, Robert Corupe. Top row: Pop Steele, trainer, Chico Maki, Stan Mikita, Manager and Coach Rudy Pilous, Ronnie Quenneville, Matt Ravlich, trainer Billy Bennett. Missing are Guy Gendron and Bobby Ewer.
St. Catharines Standard photo

1956-57 Teepees forward line October 31, 1956. From left to right: Stan Mikita, Pat Adair and Bobby Hull. Mikita and Hull played together for one season in the Garden City.
St. Catharines Standard photo

Former Teepees trying out with the Buffalo Bisons September 18, 1956. From left to right: Don McLean, Don Carter, Chester Warchol, Pat Kelly, and Marv Edwards.
St. Catharines Standard photo

In 1949, his friend Archie Maybee read in the *St. Catharines Standard* that the Canadian Legion NHL minor hockey organization was registering players. "Why don't we go and sign up?" Archie said to Mikita. "Have you ever skated?" he asked.

"I said no," Mikita recalled from his Florida home in January, 2006.

The first time they tried to register, they were rejected. "Sorry to disappoint you, but we're looking for fellas 11½ to 12 and up," the man at one of the tables told them. But Archie suggested they should go back a week later. The next Saturday they applied again, only this time the two small youngsters went to a different man and said they were older. It worked and each boy was registered on a team. "I had not skated until these guys told me that I was going be on a hockey team," Mikita recalled.

Mikita's first club was the Rangers and the scrawny kid from Western Hill had to learn how to skate while learning the game on a pair of $13 second-hand skates that were two sizes too big." I had the same skates for about four years," Mikita said. It was the beginning of a hockey career that would see him play for his school, the Canadian Legion, and Conroy's bantam team, which won a provincial championship.

One of Mikita's first Canadian Legion coaches was Bill Buschlen, and the former Teepees player could see that Mikita had talent and the right attitude. "He listened," Buschlen said from his St. Catharines home.

After Mikita started to play for city teams, he met the man who had a great influence on his hockey career and his life. "I learned most of my skills mainly because of Vic Teal," Mikita said. Teal always carried a broom that Mikita soon learned was often used to get a player's attention. "But he was also one of the first ones, who as you came by, gave you a pat on the back too," Mikita said. "And Vic, to me, he was the greatest coach I ever saw, mainly because he taught you basics as a kid. He [Teal] said, 'Whatever you do, don't practise the things you can do. Practise the things you can't do.' I don't know if there is anything out there that's as good as he was with the kids."

He hasn't forgotten Ma Teal either. She used to make sandwiches for the players and she always had a hug for each of them.

By 16 Mikita was a Garden

St. Catharines Teepees twice fell one goal short in their weekend games against Toronto opposition. Saturday night the Teeps dropped a 4-3 decision to St. Michael's Majors. In this picture Bob Corupe, wedged between Lou Angotti of the Majors and Stan Mikita (9), manages to shove the puck into the left side of the net for the opening St. Catharines goal in the first period.
St. Catharines Standard photo, February 2, 1957

Vic Teal gives advice to a young player on March 15, 1955.
St. Catharines Standard photo

Proud pop and famous hockey-playing son. Joe and Stan Mikita sat together at Stan's testimonial dinner, June 23, 1971. St. Catharines Standard photo

Stan Mikita at his old school desk with his former principal Ashton Morrison on June 23, 1971 St. Catharines Standard photo

City Arena rink rat and a talented right winger with a lot of potential, but he was not thinking about a hockey future. "I thought I'd go to school, get my education, and become something from the educational side of it, not the sports side," he said.

A suggestion from a friend led to an audition with the St. Catharines Teepees. While at Garden City Arena one day, his friend Donnie Carr saw Teepees coach Rudy Pilous. Mikita didn't know who he was. Carr made a suggestion: "Why don't we go up and ask him if we can get a tryout?" Carr did most of the talking and Pilous took a good look at each of the boys. "You [pointing to Mikita], go take a good shower, scrub behind the ears, get a haircut, and I'll see you Tuesday after school, right here at the arena," Pilous said. The Teepees coach suggested Carr should look for a hockey future in Hamilton.

Mikita's first Teepees training camp in 1956 was not that intimidating. "I knew these guys from school or somewhere along the way," said Mikita, then a grade 10 student at the St. Catharines Collegiate. "They were approachable to me." At the time he was playing football at the Collegiate with Bobby Hull, who broke in with the Teepees a year earlier. Football was just one of many sports that Mikita played as a youth and he excelled in every one of them. He was a natural athlete.

He didn't really think he had a shot at making the Teepees, but Pilous was interested and signed him to a contract paying $15 a week. "If you're still with us at Christmas, I'll give you another $10 to $25 a week," Pilous said. Mikita thought he had struck gold. "I never gave it a second thought that someday I might be playing [pro] for money," he said.

Mikita doesn't remember his first junior A game, nor his first goal, but he stayed with the Teepees for the entire regular season, picking up 47 points and 129 penalty minutes in 52 games. The team made it to the OHA finals against Guelph Biltmores and the rookie collected 17 points in 14 games.

"Pilous was a real smart coach. He knew exactly what he was doing," the former NHL superstar said.

In 1957-58 Mikita turned it up a notch, earning 78 points in 52 regular-season games and he added nine more points in one round of the playoffs against Toronto Marlies. He was more mature and more confident.

In 1958-59 he was playing centre instead of right wing and soon became the talk of the league. He ended the regular season winning the Eddie Powers Trophy as the OHA's scoring champion with 97 points, including 38 goals. In addition, he received a majority of votes for the league's most prestigious award, the Red Tilson Trophy, which was presented to the OHA Junior A League's most valuable player. He also led the league in penalty minutes with 197. The amazing thing about all these achievements was that he played only 45 of 54 regular-season games after a season-ending shoulder injury in February, 1959.

At the time Mikita thought winning trophies was a bit of a bonus, showing he was a little bit better than the other guys, but he never thought of himself as being that much better. Those who played with and against him, knew he was a player with a future.

Without their star player, St. Mike's eliminated the Teepees in the first playoff round in 1959 and Mikita would not get a shot at the Memorial Cup, which the Teepees won a year later.

In the fall of 1959 Mikita was in the Chicago Black Hawks training camp and after scoring a hat trick against the New York Rangers in an exhibition game, he turned pro with Chicago, signing for $8,500 a year for two years with a $5,000 bonus. It marked the beginning of a 21-year NHL career that would make him one of the top 50 NHL players of all time.

And what does Mikita value after growing up and playing hockey in St. Catharines? "I think it's the people and the people I was involved with came through hockey," he said. "Also the school teachers."

One of those teachers was Ashton Morrison. "Stan had the most perfect co-ordination I have seen in an athlete. However, he had more than that. He had determination. That's what makes the difference between a good athlete and an outstanding athlete," Morrison told *St. Catharines Standard* sports editor Jack Gatecliff in 1962.

Before the 1956-57 season started, coach Rudy Pilous had a good feeling about the team. "We're as green as grass, but we may be the surprise team of the league," he said. "It may take a little patience to stick with these kids, but I don't think we'll have to wait too long."

Courtesy of family of Jack Reppen

Teepees line left to right: Stan Mikita, Bob Ewer, and Bob Corupe   *Courtesy of Bob Ewer*

St. Catharines Teepees had to wait until overtime in the last game of the schedule to score their first victory of the season over Toronto Marlboros. The win, accomplished before 3,400 fans at Garden City Arena, enabled the Teepees to finish third in the final standing and prevented the Marlboros from winning their first OHA junior "A" pennant. Four of the players who made victory possible are shown in the Teepee dressing room. From the left, Stan Mikita (one goal); Captain Ed Hoekstra (two goals); goalie Roy Edwards who made 43 stops; Bob Corupe, rookie St. Catharines left winger who scored the important overtime goal. The Teepees now meet Barrie Flyers in the Ontario quarter-finals. For story and pictures, see sport pages. —Staff photo (S)

St. Catharines Standard, March 2, 1957

Pilous had to be patient right off the bat because the Teepees lost their opening game and didn't register a win until their fourth contest of the season. In December, 1956, and January, 1957, the Teepees lost seven straight games, but eventually they ended up in third place in the league, 25 points behind the league-leading Guelph Biltmores.

During the season, Pilous put together an all-St. Catharines line (players who were raised, but not born in the Garden City) of Stan Mikita, Bob Ewer and Bob Corupe. Corupe was an outstanding local high school athlete who excelled in track and field, basketball, golf and lacrosse, in addition to hockey.

After a game on January 5, 1957, Bobby Hull was suspended for ten days. "He won't be back in the lineup until he shows an entirely different attitude," Pilous stated. A few days later, Hull asked to rejoin the club and returned to action on January 15, 1957, against the Guelph Biltmores.

During the season Pilous was concerned that Saturday night games should start at 8:30 p.m. instead of the regular 8:00 p.m. opening faceoff and asked fans to write to the *St. Catharines Standard* with their opinions. The 8:00 p.m. starting time wasn't changed until the playoffs when games did start at 8:30 p.m.

In the final game of the season, Grimsby native Bob Corupe scored in overtime to defeat the Toronto Marlboros 4-3 and in doing so, settled many issues in the 1956-57 OHA Junior A season. The goal, assisted by Mikita and Hull, lifted St. Catharines from fifth to third place in the league standings. It also meant that the Teepees wouldn't be meeting the Marlies or St. Mike's, led by future NHL superstar Frank Mahovlich, in the first round of the playoffs for the first time in four seasons. The Marlboros loss put them out of contention for the league pennant, which was won by Guelph.

Corupe's marker evened the Teepees record for the season at .500 with 25 wins, 25 losses and 2 ties. It also extended their longest winning streak at five and cut their losing streak with the Marlboros at seven straight – eleven if you counted the four straight playoff losses in 1955-56. "After scoring that one [overtime goal] against Ottawa, I never thought it would happen again and I still can't really believe it," Corupe said after the game.

Corupe suffered a stroke in the fall of 1992, but the former real estate consultant made a remarkable recovery and today lives in the Garden City. In 2005-06, his son Kenny played for the AHL Wilkes-Barre/Scranton Penguins, but he then moved to Italy for 2006-07.

Johnny McKenzie and Ed Hoekstra were the club's leading scorers in the regular season with 70 points each. Sophomore Bobby Hull was next with 33 goals and 61 points. Mikita made an impressive start in his rookie year with 47 points.

In the playoffs, the club advanced to the OHA finals against Guelph Biltmores after eliminating the Barrie Flyers and Toronto Marlboros.

In the last playoff game against Barrie, a dog took a front row seat in Garden City Arena and caused quite a disturbance by barking loudly at the players on the ice. "It had a blue ticket and was sitting in a red seat," explained the usher who evicted the boxer.

Guelph, led by netminder Bruce Gamble, "Terrible-Tempered" Eddie Shack, Bill Sweeney, and Dan Belisle, won the best-of-seven OHA final series, 4-2.

"We'll be back bigger and better than ever," Pilous said after being eliminated by the Biltmores.

Total attendance, with Mikita and Hull in the lineup and four more playoff games, rose to 76,052, an increase of 6,269 from the previous year.

Several Teepees put up impressive stats in the post-season. Ed Hoekstra led the way with 11 goals and 24 points, followed by Matt Ravlich with

21 points and Johnny McKenzie with 20. Stan Mikita and Bobby Hull, in their final junior season, had 17 and 15 points respectively.

Former Teepee teammate Don Cosburn has a special memory of Stan Mikita. "Stan Mikita invented the curved stick when I was there," claimed Cosburn in a story written about himself in the March 1995 issue of *Oldtimers' Hockey News*.

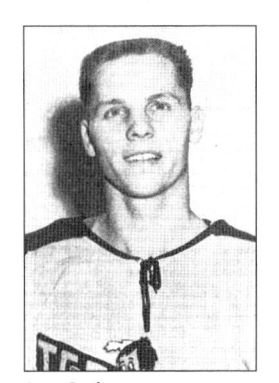

Don Cosburn
St. Catharines Museum
- Ron Quenneville Collection 2004.139.1

"One day after practice at the Garden City Arena, he put a wet stick under the dressing room door and started bending it," said Cosburn, whom coach Rudy Pilous had nicknamed the "Goose" because of his long neck. "He was the first guy to seriously try out the curved stick in practice and in games. Bobby Hull started to fool around with it, but as far as I am concerned, Stan Mikita should go down in the books as the guy who invented the curved stick."

In a January 2006 interview, Mikita recalled how his use of the curved stick really began. It was in Chicago. "It was an accidental thing that happened [in Chicago Stadium during a practice sometime in the 1960-61 season]," Mikita recalled. "My stick got caught in the boards and somebody hit me, so the stick twisted; the blade was in the boards. It was stuck. I couldn't get it out. Finally, I pull it out and it's bent into an angle."

On his way to get a new stick, he slapped a puck with the bent blade, trying to break the stick. "As it turned out, I caught it right and the sound it made against the boards and the velocity that was on there, I had never felt before." Right after that practice, Mikita took two sticks and started to bend the blades after heating them. About a month later, he tried one of his curved sticks in an NHL game. Bobby Hull also started to use a curved blade and soon they were being used by hockey players everywhere.

But wait a minute.

In 1999 Hall of Famer Andy Bathgate claimed that it was he, not Mikita, who first used a curved blade in the NHL when he was with the New York Rangers. "I know I was using a hooked stick three or four years before Mikita and Hull came into the league," Bathgate said in the book *The Blackhawks*, by Brian McFarlane.

In the same book, Tom Nease, former president of CCM, told the *Hockey News* that he watched Bathgate taking water-soaked blades and bending them under the dressing room doors in the early 1960s. "As much as I admire Stan Mikita …Andy Bathgate can correctly claim fame as the player who introduced the curved blade to the NHL," Nease said. "It was definitely later that Mikita, then Bobby Hull, started to use the curved stick."

In his 1969 book, *I Play To Win*, Mikita indicated that Bathgate was right. "Of course we weren't the first to use a bent stick. Apparently Andy Bathgate, who played for many years with the New York Rangers, also tried one," Mikita wrote.

Mikita went on to say, however, that it was a safe bet that he and Hull touched off the interest that led to the widespread use of the curved blade.

Cosburn's most memorable moment as a Teepee occurred in the 1957 playoffs against the Toronto Marlboros. "Coach Rudy Pilous put a $50 bill on the floor of the dressing room and said there'd be one for each player if we won. That was a week's pay," Cosburn said. "We won 4-2 and each of us got a $50 bill at practice the next day. The Marlboros were coached by Turk Broda and Rudy didn't like to lose to Turk." ■

Mikita in Teepee uniform
St. Catharines Museum - Standard Collection N 5773

Roy Edwards in a Chicago Black Hawks uniform, September 24, 1958
St. Catharines Standard photo

ROY EDWARDS

Roy Edwards was born in Seneca Township, Ontario, and came to St. Catharines in 1955 to play for the Teepees. In two seasons in the Garden City he played 90 of the team's 100 regular-season games, posting an average of 3.78.

After finishing his junior career he joined the Whitby Dunlops who won the 1958 World Championship. From 1958 to 1967 he played in the AHL, EPHL, CHL and the WHL, where he was a Prairie Division First Team All-Star and rookie-of-the year in 1959.

He began his NHL career with Detroit in 1967-68 and was with the Red Wings for five seasons and with Pittsburgh for one year before retiring in 1974. He played 236 regular-season NHL games, winning 97 and posting a 2.92 goals-against average.

Edwards died in Hamilton in 1999.

Teepee Roy Edwards with trophy for outstanding goaltending in 1955-56
St. Catharines Standard photo

TEEPEES 1956-1957

Bedlam reigned in the dressing room of the St. Catharines Teepees Sunday afternoon after the st. Catharines club had come from behind to defeat the Toronto Marlboros 4-2 in Maple Leaf Gardens. Here the Teepees are voicing their enthusiasm after the win was described as "the biggest upset of the Canadian hockey season." By their victory, the Teepees erased the Marlboro bid to become the first team in history to win three consecutive Memorial Cup championships. The Teepees now meet Guelph Biltmores in the OHA junior "A" finals, opening in Guelph Tuesday night.

St. Catharines Standard photo March 24, 1957

Teepee goal scorers celebrate after an 8-5 win over the Guelph Biltmores on March 27, 1957. Left to right: Stan Mikita, Bob Hull, Bob Corupe, Matt Ravlich, Ed Hoekstra

St. Catharines Standard photo

They Made Victory Possible on April 2, 1957
Four of the players who made victory possible for the Teepees are shown above. From the left Rino Robazza (1 goal), Matt Ravlich (2 goals), Stan Mikita (2 goals), Bob Hull (2 goals). The Teepees came from behind a 4-1 deficit to defeat Guelph Biltmores 7-4 in overtime and tie the best-in-seven OHA junior "A" finals 2-2. Fifth game is in Guelph.

St. Catharines Museum - Robazza Ref. File, 2004.08.16

TEEPEES 1957-1958

TEEPEES FINISH FIRST FOR THE FOURTH TIME IN FIVE YEARS

ATTENDANCE FIGURES
Average per regular-season game: 2,318
Season's largest crowd: 3,717
Season's smallest crowd: 1,399

PLAYOFF ROUNDS: 1
Eliminated by Toronto Marlboros 4-3-1

1957-1958

GAMES PLAYED	WON	LOST	TIED	FOR	AGAINST	POINTS	FINISH
52	32	14	6	246	174	70	1/8

Leading Scorers

PLAYER	GOALS	ASSISTS	POINTS
Johnny McKenzie	48	51	99
Ed Hoekstra	35	58	93
Stan Mikita	31	47	78
Matt Ravlich	38	35	73
Ron (Chico) Maki	21	19	40

Leading Goaltenders

PLAYER	GP	GA	SO	GAA
Denis DeJordy	52	174	1	3.34

Before the season started, Chicago Black Hawks GM Tommy Ivan decided that Bobby Hull would turn pro although he had two years of junior eligibility left. "We naturally had to weigh every angle before deciding to sign Hull to a Chicago contract," Ivan said at the time. "However, after watching him play for three weeks in our camp and several exhibition games, we decided that he was in fact ready for the big jump to professional hockey."

Without Hull, the Teepees got off to a good start, winning their first two games against St. Michael's College Majors. It was the team's best start in five years. Miss Tiger-Cat, Sylvia Swayze of Welland, dropped the puck to open the season. Stan Mikita missed the opening game because he was in Toronto playing for the St.

Continued on page 91

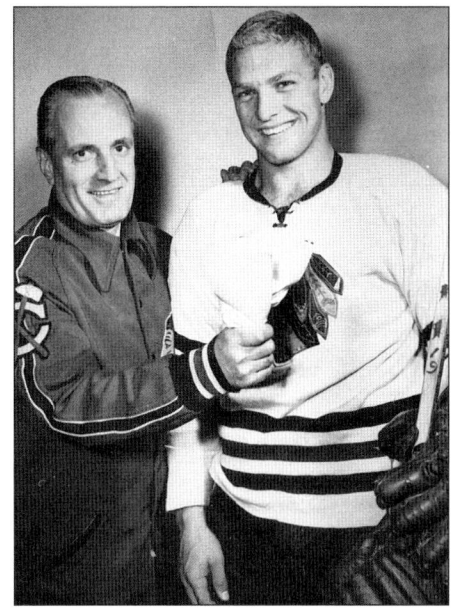

Bobby Hull signs his first pro contract with the Chicago Black Hawk GM Tommy Ivan.
St. Catharines Museum - Standard Collection R 5361

Stan Mikita (9) scores against the Toronto Marlies while future NHLer Carl Brewer to his left watches the puck enter the net in a 1-1 playoff game March 18, 1958.
St. Catharines Standard photo

Teepees coach Rudy Pilous (right) has some tips for defencemen Terry McGuire (left) and Wayne Hillman (centre) on October 23, 1957.
St. Catharines Standard photo

TEEPEES 1957-1958

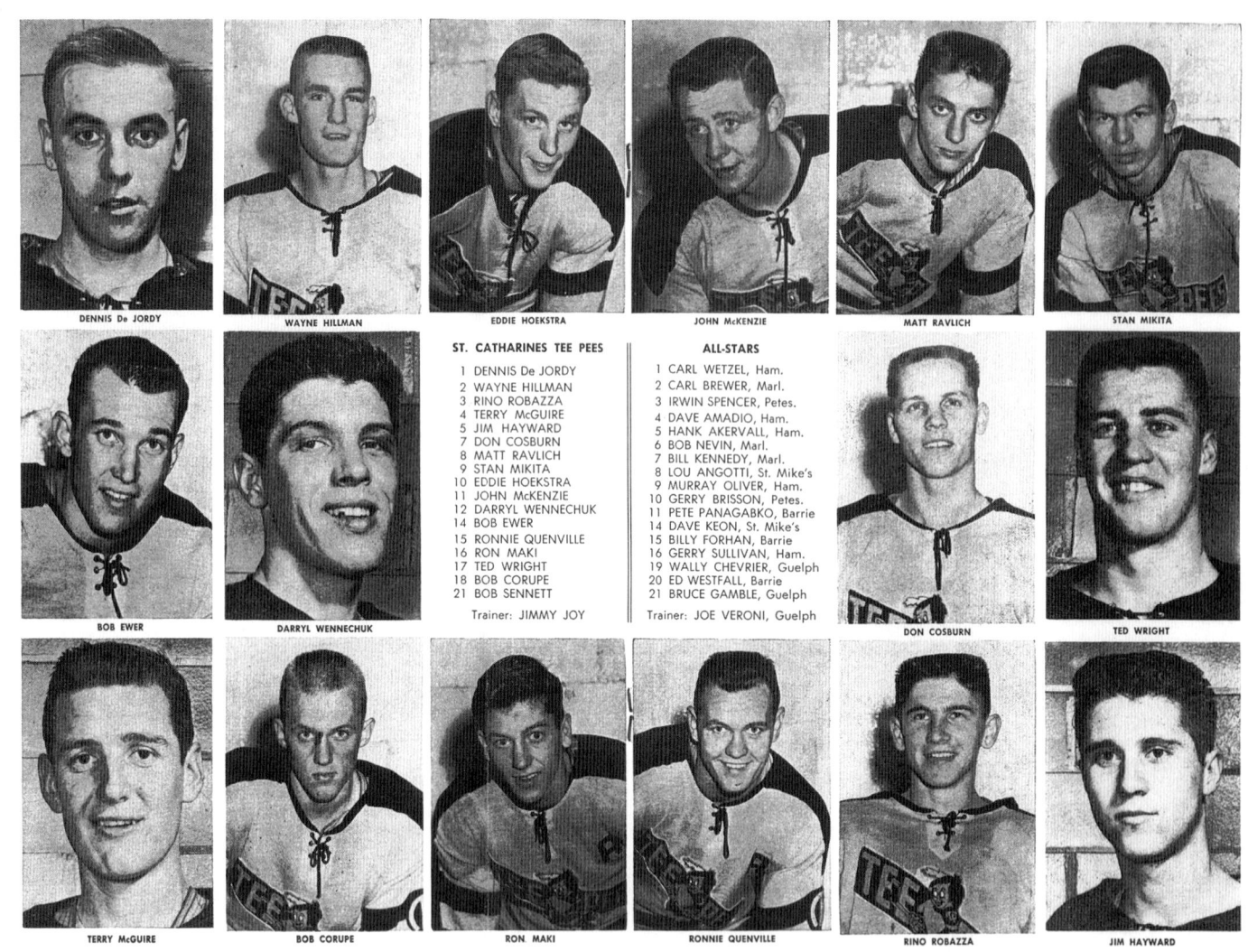

ST. CATHARINES TEE PEES	ALL-STARS
1 DENNIS De JORDY	1 CARL WETZEL, Ham.
2 WAYNE HILLMAN	2 CARL BREWER, Marl.
3 RINO ROBAZZA	3 IRWIN SPENCER, Petes.
4 TERRY McGUIRE	4 DAVE AMADIO, Ham.
5 JIM HAYWARD	5 HANK AKERVALL, Ham.
7 DON COSBURN	6 BOB NEVIN, Marl.
8 MATT RAVLICH	7 BILL KENNEDY, Marl.
9 STAN MIKITA	8 LOU ANGOTTI, St. Mike's
10 EDDIE HOEKSTRA	9 MURRAY OLIVER, Ham.
11 JOHN McKENZIE	10 GERRY BRISSON, Petes.
12 DARRYL WENNECHUK	11 PETE PANAGABKO, Barrie
14 BOB EWER	14 DAVE KEON, St. Mike's
15 RONNIE QUENVILLE	15 BILLY FORHAN, Barrie
16 RON MAKI	16 GERRY SULLIVAN, Ham.
17 TED WRIGHT	19 WALLY CHEVRIER, Guelph
18 BOB CORUPE	20 ED WESTFALL, Barrie
21 BOB SENNETT	21 BRUCE GAMBLE, Guelph
Trainer: JIMMY JOY	Trainer: JOE VERONI, Guelph

Teepees as they appeared in the 1957-58 All-Star program
St. Catharines Museum - Ron Quenneville Collection 2004.139.2

Rudy Pilous, Rex Stimers, and Bob Goldham open the Junior "A" season. Pilous presented Goldham with the "Oil Can Trophy" in a mid-ice ceremony.
St. Catharines Standard photo

Teepee Johnny McKenzie in the centre of the picture has something to say to the referee during a 2-1 win over St. Mike's during the Teepees home-opener on October 26, 1957. The St. Mike's goaltender on the ice, Cesare Maniago, also wants the referee's attention.
St. Catharines Standard photo

Continued from page 89

Catharines Collegiate Tricolours in the Red Feather game.

The team finished in first place in the league for the fourth time in five years with 70 points in 52 games and it was done without coach Rudy Pilous who left the club to coach the Chicago Black Hawks on January 2, 1958. He was replaced by Glen Sonmor whom Pilous had hired to coach the Junior Bees and assist with the Teepees.

PILOUS TO COACH BLACK HAWKS

"Rudy Pilous goes to Chicago with the full blessing and best wishes of the St. Catharines hockey club," said President George Stauffer. Pilous coached his last St. Catharines junior game on January 1, 1958, leading the club to a 5-2 win over St. Michael's College Majors. Before the start of the third period, the coach was given a tremendous ovation by the crowd of 3,000. "The part I liked about it most was the extra little handclap from my hecklers in section E [five vociferous fans who blistered Pilous even when he was winning]," Pilous said. "I've had my rough moments from that group, but believe me there's no hard feelings."

The Winnipeg native made a successful NHL debut coaching the Black Hawks to a 4-2 victory over the Toronto Maple Leafs in Maple Leaf Gardens on Saturday, January 4, 1958.

Sonmor made his Teepees coaching debut on Friday, January 3, 1958, and lost to the Guelph Biltmores 2-1. He won his first home game at Garden City Arena on January 4, 1958, beating Guelph 8-3. Teepee Matt Ravlich scored six goals, including a natural hat trick. Two weeks later, Ravlich repeated the same feat in a 15-4 win over the Barrie Flyers.

It's interesting to note that when Pilous did make it to the NHL, he recognized many of the players. He had at least one player whom he had coached in junior on each of the six NHL clubs, and 13 players in total.

Coach Sonmor and the game's star relax after an 8-3 win on January 4, 1958. Ravlich signifies his night's total goals with his fingers.
St. Catharines Standard photo

Teepees coach Rudy Pilous oils the team's dressing room door before leaving for Chicago.
St. Catharines Museum - Standard Collection R 5363

Best of Luck From Club President
G.A. Stauffer (right) president of the St. Catharines Teepees Hockey Club wishes coach Rudy Pilous "bon voyage" in this dressing room picture immediately following the game with St. Michael's College Majors New Year's afternoon. The game marked the end of Pilous' position as the coach of the Teepees although he will continue as team manager. Rudy will assume his new duties as coach of the Chicago Black Hawks today in Chicago. The Teepees made Pilous' final game a memorable one, defeating Toronto St. Michael's Majors 5-2 to open a nine-point lead in first place in the junior "A" standing.
St. Catharines Standard photo

JOHNNY McKENZIE

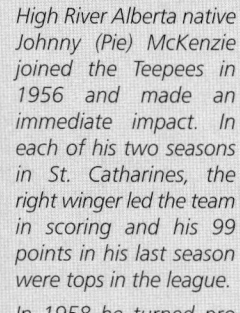

High River Alberta native Johnny (Pie) McKenzie joined the Teepees in 1956 and made an immediate impact. In each of his two seasons in St. Catharines, the right winger led the team in scoring and his 99 points in his last season were tops in the league.

In 1958 he turned pro with the Chicago Black Hawks, but after one season was claimed by Detroit.
St. Catharines Standard photo

Early in his NHL career McKenzie spent time in the off-season participating in rodeos, and earned the nickname "Cowboy".

He had his best NHL seasons with Boston Bruins, winning Stanley Cup rings in 1970 and 1972. In 691 regular-season NHL games, he scored 474 points, including 206 goals.

After 12 NHL seasons, he moved to the WHA where he played for Philadelphia, Vancouver, Minnesota, Cincinnati and New England.

McKenzie, who played in two NHL all-star games, now lives in Massachusetts.

GLEN SONMOR

Once a fine pro prospect, Glen Sonmor lost his left eye in February of 1955 as the result of a slap shop from his closest friend, Steve Kraftcheck. The pair were known as "the Hamilton Hard Rocks" when both were playing with the AHL Cleveland Barons. It was the end of Sonmor's playing career, but the Moose Jaw Saskatchewan native

New Chicago Black Hawks coach Rudy Pilous (left) helps new Teepees coach Glen Sonmor oil the team's gate on December 26, 1958.
St. Catharines Standard photo

went back to school and earned his bachelor of science degree.

After coaching the Teepees he taught high school in Hamilton, coached at the University of Minnesota, and had three coaching terms with the NHL Minnesota North Stars, winning 174 contests in 417 games.

Today he lives in Bloomington, Minnesota.

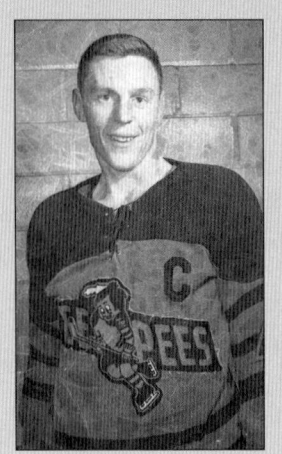

TEEPEES 1957-1958

ED HOEKSTRA

Ed Hoekstra, Cec Hoekstra's younger brother, was a high-scoring forward with the St. Catharines Teepees for four seasons from 1954 to 1958, earning 93 points in his last junior year.

While with the Teepees, teammate Chester Warchol urged the Winnipeg native to think of his future after hockey, so he attended a trade school in Toronto and became a carpenter before turning pro. "They're not going to hold a tag day for this cowboy," Hoekstra said with a smile in an interview in January of 2007.

In 1958 he turned pro with the QHL Trois Rivieres Lions and won the top rookie award in 1959. From 1959 to 1974 he saw action in the AHL, EPHL, WHL, WHA, SHL and one season with the NHL Philadelphia Flyers in 1967-68. Playing against some of the NHL's greats at the time including Howe, Orr and Hull, was one of the highlights of his career.

He was with the Calder Cup champion Buffalo Bisons in 1970 and the Springfield Indians in 1971. His best pro season came with the Springfield Kings in 1971-72 when he scored 85 points in 74 games.

Ed is retired and lives in St. Catharines.

St. Catharines Standard photo

MATT RAVLICH

On January 4, 1958, Sault Ste. Marie native Matt Ravlich scored six goals, tying the St. Catharines Junior A record which was held by Brian Cullen (1953-54) for the most goals scored in a single game. The defenceman /left winger repeated that amazing performance 14 days later.

After three seasons with the Teepees, 1955 to 1958, Ravlich went on to play defence in the NHL with Boston, Chicago, Detroit and Los Angeles. He was with the Bruins in 1972 when they won the Stanley Cup. In 410 regular-season NHL contests, he collected 90 points.

In 2004 he was sales manager for Jiminy Realty in Hancock, Massachusetts.

St. Catharines Museum - Cornelius Collection, C10.677

McKenzie, (left) the league's top point scorer, Hoekstra and Ravlich after last regular-season game
St. Catharines Standard photo

Teepees with goalie Denis DeJordy after first playoff game vs the Marlboros
St. Catharines Standard photo

Johnny McKenzie won the 1957-58 OHA scoring championship with 99 points and teammate Ed Hoekstra was second with 93. Sophomore Stan Mikita was fourth with 78 points. Goaltender Denis DeJordy played all 52 regular-season games, earning a goals-against average of 3.34.

In the playoffs the team only lasted one round as it was eliminated by the Toronto Marlies for the third time in four years, but it took eight games to decide the series. McKenzie led the team with 12 points in eight games. Matt Ravlich had ten points, followed by Mikita with nine and Maki and Hoekstra with eight each. St. Catharines native Doug Robinson made his Junior A debut in the playoffs on March 15, 1958, and almost scored his first goal.

Total attendance with three fewer games stood at 73,783, down 2,269 from 1956-57. The team lost only three home games all season, winning 21 and tying two.

At the end of the season Sonmor knew Pilous wouldn't be keeping him around, so he contacted owner George Stauffer and made a request: "Please don't let Mr. Pilous fire me," Sonmor recalled from his Bloomington Minnesota home in August of 2004. He wanted time to get another job and was successful when AHL Springfield Indians owner Eddie Shore hired him for the 1958-59 season.

Future Lady Byng Trophy winner Stan Mikita (left) being restrained by a linesman, gets ready to thump Toronto Marlie and future NHLer Carl Brewer in a playoff game on March 4, 1958. Referee Bill Friday, on the right, has a hold of Brewer.

St. Catharines Museum - Standard Collection N 5702

The First Annual OHA Junior "A" All-Star Game A Spectacular Success

The first-ever OHA Junior A All-Star game was played in Garden City Arena on Wednesday, January 8, 1958. It featured the league all-stars versus the Teepees.

Mikita was on the First Team and Johnny McKenzie, Ed Hoekstra, Matt Ravlich, and Wayne Hillman made the Second Team, but they played with the Teepees. Pilous returned to the Garden City from Chicago to coach the Teepees who lost the game 9-4 in front of 3,000 fans. Future NHLers, Murray Oliver (with a hat trick) and Dave Keon, led the junior all-stars, who had too much firepower for the Teepees. Money raised from the game was to be put into "The Injured Players Fund."

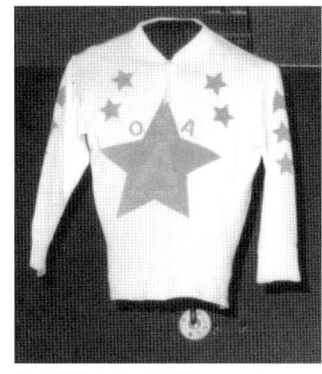

First OHA Junior A All-Star sweater worn by Pete Panagabko, number 11.
St. Catharines Museum - 1998.410

OHA President Lorne Cooke presents mementos to captains Ed Hoekstra (left) of the Teepees and Murray Oliver of the Stars.
St. Catharines Standard photo

St. Catharines Museum - Ron Quenneville Collection 2004.139.2

1958 All-Stars

CARL WETZEL — HAMILTON
MURRAY OLIVER — HAMILTON
GERRY SULLIVAN — HAMILTON

DAVE AMADIO — HAMILTON
HANK AKERVALL — HAMILTON
STAN MIKITA — ST. CATHARINES

ED HOEKSTRA — ST. CATHARINES
JACK McKENZIE — ST. CATHARINES
MATT RAVLICH — ST. CATHARINES

WAYNE HILLMAN — ST. CATHARINES
WALLY CHEVRIER — GUELPH
BRUCE GAMBLE — GUELPH

St. Catharines Museum - Ron Quenneville Collection 2004.139.2

TEEPEES 1958-1959

3, 1958   Aug 12/58

Harry Watson Named Coach

Announced At Noon Luncheon

George Stauffer, president of the St. Catharines Teepees Hockey Club, announced at a noon luncheon today the appointment of Harry Watson as coach of the junior "A" Teepees for the 1958-59 season.

Watson, a veteran of 14 seasons in the National Hockey League, succeeds Glen Sonmor who accepted the position of coach with Springfield Indians of the American Hockey League two weeks ago.

The new St. Catharines junior "A" coach will assume his official duties with the club when training season opens at Garden City Arena October 1.

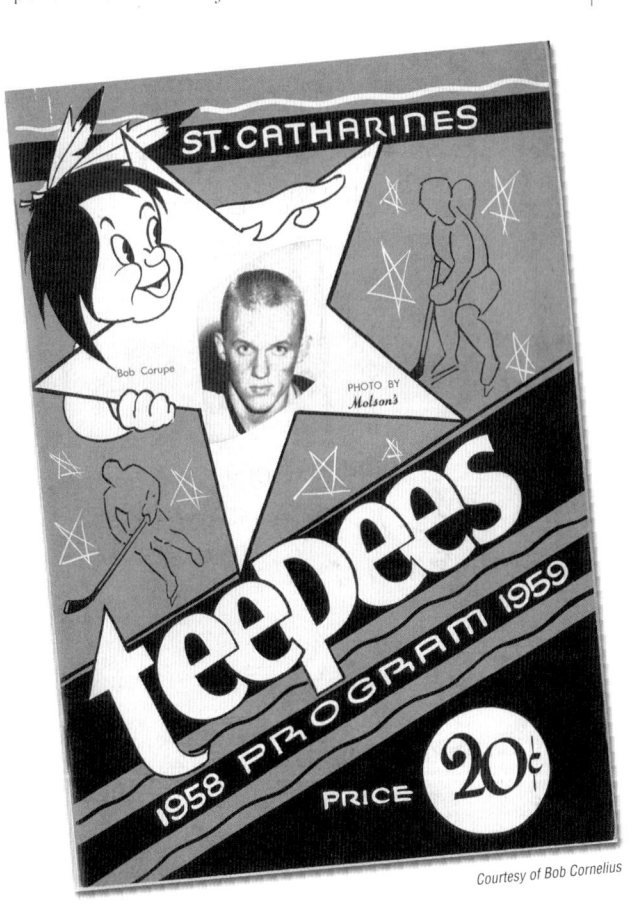

Harry Watson October 21, 1958
St. Catharines Standard photo

Courtesy of Bob Cornelius

In recognition of "Minor Hockey Week in Canada" two teams from the St. Catharines Legion Little American Hockey League played a 10-minute game during intermission of the Barrie-St. Catharines junior "A" game at Garden City Arena Saturday night. Here four members of the Teepees, all graduates of the Legion minor hockey system, talk things over with the two minor captains. From the left: Bob Corupe, Chiefs captain Stu Roberts, Stan Mikita, Ray Cullen, Bears captain Brian Stewart, Doug Robinson. The Chiefs won the short game 1-0 on a goal by Steve Rennie.

St. Catharines Standard photo

TEEPEES 1958-1959

MIKITA WINS SCORING TITLE AND RED TILSON TROPHY

ATTENDANCE FIGURES
Average per regular-season game: 2,190
Season's largest crowd: 3,773
Season's smallest crowd: 1,339

PLAYOFF ROUNDS: 1
Eliminated by St. Mike's 4-2-1

When the 1958-59 season started, former NHL star Harry Watson was behind the Teepees bench replacing Glen Sonmor.

He was the sixth St. Catharines junior coach since 1943. A native of Saskatchewan, Watson turned pro with the NHL Brooklyn Americans in 1941 and spent 14 years in hockey's top league, winning five Stanley Cups: one with Detroit and four with Toronto. In 809 regular-season NHL games, he collected 443 points, including 236 goals.

Watson was not your average hockey coach. He seldom raised his voice during a game or at practices. "The word gentleman describes him perfectly," Jack Gatecliff said. The ex-left winger, who was inducted into the Hockey Hall of Fame in 1994, died in 2002.

The Teepees opened the season October 18, 1958, with a 4-1 win over the Barrie Flyers, but Watson wasn't too impressed. "We still have a few rough spots," he said. The team was still awaiting the release of Don Grosso from the Guelph Biltmores and Fred Hilts was refused his release from the Edmonton Oilers because they wanted him to play there.

Nevertheless, the Teepees started the schedule strongly, winning seven straight and ten in total of their first 11 games. Grosso and Hilts were given their releases early in the season and both players made a significant contribution to the team's winning

1958-1959

GAMES PLAYED	WON	LOST	TIED	FOR	AGAINST	POINTS	FINISH
54	40	11	3	257	175	83	1/7

Leading Scorers

PLAYER	GOALS	ASSISTS	POINTS
Stan Mikita	38	59	97
Ron (Chico) Maki	41	53	94
Fred Hilts	37	31	68
Don Grosso	28	32	60
Wayne Hillman	8	30	38

Leading Goaltenders

PLAYER	GP	GA	SO	GAA
Denis DeJordy	53	169	1	3.19
Wayne Gibbons	1	6	0	6

St. Catharines Teepees meet Belleville McFarlands here Thursday night in the first exhibition game of the season for both teams. The McFarlands, Allan Cup champs, will represent Canada in world hockey competition next January. A line that could well take the place of the Hoekstra-Ravlich-McKenzie combination in the affections of the St. Catharines' fans, is pictured above. From the left, Chico Maki, Stan Mikita and Bob Maki have been the most consistent line in camp. Chico Maki and Mikita are returning for their third seasons with the Teepees while Bob Maki, Chico's brother, is making his debut in a St. Catharines uniform.
—Staff photo (S)
St. Catharines Standard

One line which will face the Allan Cup champion Belleville McFarlands tonight is pictured above. The Teepee trio, from the left, are Duke Harris, Ray Cullen and Bob Corupe. Harris and Cullen are making their junior "A" debut while Corupe is starting his third season in top flight provincial hockey.
—Staff photo (S)
St. Catharines Standard

TEEPEES 1958-1959

WAYNE HILLMAN

Defencenman Wayne Hillman moved from his hometown, Kirkland Lake, to join the St. Catharines Teepees in 1955 and stayed for four years.

The rugged rearguard turned pro with the Buffalo Bisons in 1959 and joined the Chicago Black Hawks in 1961, just in time to win a Stanley Cup.

After four seasons with the Hawks, he was traded to the New York Rangers and then moved to the Minnesota North Stars before spending four seasons with the Philadelphia Flyers. He played 691 regular-season NHL games accumulating 104 points. He closed out his career with the WHA Cleveland Crusaders in 1975.

Hillman passed away in 1990.

St. Catharines Standard photo

DENIS DEJORDY

St. Hyacinthe Quebec native Dennis DeJordy spent two seasons with the Teepees, 1957 to 1959, before turning pro with the EPHL Sault Ste. Marie Thunderbirds in 1959. He was an AHL First Team All-Star in 1962-63 with the Calder Cup champion Buffalo Bisons and won the Holmes Trophy for allowing the fewest goals. He was also the league's MVP.

In his first full year with Chicago Black Hawks in 1966-67, he shared the Vezina Trophy with Glenn Hall. After seeing action with Chicago from 1962-63 to 1970, he was traded to the Los Angeles Kings. In 1971 he moved to Montreal and then to Detroit Red Wings. When he retired in 1974, he had played 316 regular- season games with a 124-128-51 record, including 15 shutouts.

Today DeJordy lives in Quebec where he owns and operates a ferry service.

Courtesy of Fred Stanfield

Teepees coach Harry Watson (right) and Chicago Black Hawks scout Bob Wilson, centre, welcome new Teepee Fred Hilts on October 22, 1958.
St. Catharines Standard photo

Don Grosso
St. Catharines Standard photo

season that included only four home losses. Grosso, who had been on a one-year loan to Guelph, finished the year with 60 points in 49 games and Hilts scored 37 goals and 68 points, ending up as the club's third leading points-getter.

On November 18, the Barrie Flyers defeated the Teepees 5-2 and after the game, Flyers coach Hap Emms declared that he knew how to handle the St. Catharines team. "Tie up Mikita and you've got the Teepees licked," Emms said. His theory didn't hold up. The next time the two teams met, Mikita broke loose from the tight checking and scored a goal with two assists as the Teepees whipped Barrie 5-1.

On January 24, 1959, Emms made a farce out of a game with the Teepees when he refused to put a full team out for the final minute of the game. He sent the Flyers, who were losing the game, to the dressing room, and used two forwards and the goalie for the remainder of the game. The Teepees wanted Emms to be disciplined by the OHA council, but he wasn't because one council member said he added colour to junior hockey.

Emms was frustrated because his team, which cost $40,000 to run, was averaging 700 a game and he was charging $1 a seat. He threatened to move the Flyers to North Bay, but nothing happened until 1960 when he moved the team to Niagara Falls.

By the end of 1958, the Teepees had recorded 22 wins and were by far the strongest team in the league. The club got a scare when Mikita fractured his right wrist in a fall during the All-Star game on January 7, 1959, but he missed only part of one game as he played with a cast and continued to lead the team in scoring.

The second OHA All-Star game in 1959 was a genuine classic and ended in a 2-2 draw in front of 2,112 fans in Garden City Arena. All the scoring was done in the first period as Mikita scored both Teepees goals and St. Mike's Dave Keon scored a goal and

Teepees And All-Stars Play 2-2 Thriller

Outstanding Game Presented By Teen-Age Stars

All the work and effort which go into the preparation of the annual OHA junior "A" all-star game has been vindicated.

After a shaky start last season when the Stars scored a one-sided and uninteresting 9-4 win over the St. Catharines Teepees, the same two clubs (with many changes in personnel) produced an absolute classic here last night.

In a game packed with typical teen-age hockey action, the Stars and Teepees played to a pulsating 2-2 draw before a highly enthusiastic crowd of 2,112 fans.

All the scoring last night was confined to the first period but the thrills were equally distributed over the entire 60 minutes.

Stan Mikita, the leading points scorer in junior "A" hockey at the moment, gave the Teepees a 2-0 lead early in the opening period.

The St. Catharines centre directed a long shot from Pat Stapleton past Peterboro goalie Jacques Caron in the second minute of play, then picked the short side from a bad angle while St. Michael's Bruce Draper was serving a cross-checking penalty nine minutes later.

Tie Game

Dave Keon, the slick stickhandler from St. Michael's cut the Teepee lead back to 2-1 on a drive into the lower left corner 24 seconds after Mikita's man's partially-screened shot was picked off by Carl Wetzel.

With five seconds left Mikita once again gained control of the puck (this time to the left side of Wetzel's goal) but Stapleton's slap shot was inches wide of the mark.

Star Gazing . . . All players participating in the game were given mementos of the occasion with special awards to the two captains (Wayne Hillman of the Teepees and Wayne Connelly of the All-stars), the referees, trainers and coaches.

One of the biggest cheers of the night was occasioned when the announcement was made that Chicago had defeated New York 4-0 in a National Hockey League game in New York. . . Press, radio and the visiting dignitaries from th six teams

To the scorers go the laurels. And especially so following last night's second annual OHA Junior "A" All-Star Game. Here, young autograph-seekers surround Sandy McGregor of Guelph, who scored the second All-Star goal; Stan Mikita of Teepees, who came up with both St. Catharines goals and Dave Keon of St. Mike's, who potted the opening All-Star goal. Teepees and the All-Stars played to a 2-2 deadlock in an exciting outing before 2,112 fans at Garden City Arena.
—Staff photo (S

St. Catharines Standard

had an assist for the All-Stars. It was no surprise when these two men went on to star in the NHL.

APPLE NIGHT AT THE HAMILTON FORUM

On Thursday, February 5, 1959, the Teepees played the Hamilton Tiger-Cubs in a game at the Hamilton Forum. The game was rough, with plenty of penalties, and the Hamilton fans showed their displeasure with the visiting team by throwing debris on the ice. In the third period when they ran out of things to throw, they started to pelt the Teepees bench with apples which the Boy Scouts had been selling during the game. What were Hamilton officials thinking?

While Stan Mikita was sitting on the bench, one apple grazed his head and when he turned around, another came flying out of the crowd. That was all he was prepared to take. "In one motion, he [Mikita] skated to the boards and took off up into the crowd," *St. Catharines Standard*'s Craig Swayze reported. "Needless to say, the entire Teepees bench and most of the St. Catharines players who had been on the ice, followed." It was a scene reminiscent of the brawl between the Detroit basketball fans and Indiana Pacers during the final minute of a 97-82 Indiana win at the Palace of Auburn Hills, Michigan, on Friday, November 19, 2004.

It took 14 minutes to settle things down. Mikita received a game misconduct that meant he had to pay a $10 fine or serve a one-game suspension. And for those who might be interested, the Teepees won the game 6-4.

Two days later on February 7, 1959, the Teepees clinched their fifth league title in six years with a 5-2 win over the Peterborough Petes in a game viewed by 3,205 fans at Garden City Arena. There were eight games left in the schedule.

Was there another Memorial Cup on the horizon? Maybe not. On February 12, 1959, Mikita dislocated his right shoulder and was out for the season. At the time he was the OHA Junior A scoring leader and although he didn't play for the rest of the year, he won the Eddie Powers Trophy with 97 points in addition to the Red Tilson Trophy as the league's MVP. Teammate Chico Maki was just three points behind with 94.

Rookie Ray Cullen scored 33 points with 19 goals and it looked like the third Cullen brother was going to be an offensive force following in the footsteps of Brian and Barry. Netminder Denis DeJordy played 53 of the 54-game schedule, posting a 3.19 goals-against average; he was an OHA First Team All-Star along with defenceman Pat Stapleton and Stan Mikita.

Stan Mikita, the sidelined St. Catharines Teepee all-star centre, accepts the Eddie Powers Memorial Trophy from Jack Roxburgh of Simcoe, past-president of the Ontario Hockey Association, during a centre-ice ceremony at last night's OHA Junior "A" playoff here. The trophy went to Mikita as the leading point scorer in the league. He scored 38 goals and picked up 59 assists while playing 45 of the 54 Teepee games during the regular schedule. Roxburgh, in presenting the trophy and a smaller replica to Mikita, wished him "continued success in all walks of life". In a brief reply, the Teepee forward, out of action since Feb. 12 with a shoulder separation, paid tribute "to a couple of guys who deserve thanks too... my linemates, Fred Hilts and Chico Maki".

St. Catharines Museum - *Standard Collection N 5362*

The Teepees finished the season on a losing note, beaten 5-3 by the Toronto Marlies, but didn't lose two consecutive games all year, tying the record held by the 1953-54 Teepees. The calm, patient approach by coach Watson had paid off.

In the playoffs, the Teepees met St. Michael's College Majors who had finished the season with 33 fewer points than the league leaders, but without Mikita, the Majors, led by future NHL star Dave Keon, prevailed in seven games, 4-2-1. Only 13 goals were scored by the Teepees in seven games.

Looking back, many Teepees fans still think this was the team that should have won the city's second Memorial Cup.

After the season ended, Watson resigned as coach and moved to the Toronto area.

Total attendance for the season was 73,246, down slightly from 1957-58 – although there was one more home game. ∎

STAN MIKITA

Stan Mikita was an exceptional hockey player for several reasons. He turned pro with the Chicago Black Hawks at 19 with one year of junior eligibility left and stayed with the team for 21 years. He never played a game in the minors. His awards and trophies could fill a room.

St. Catharines Museum - *Standard Collection N 5360*

The 5-foot-9 centre who has a 1961 Stanley Cup ring, won the Lady Byng Trophy twice (1967 and 1968), the Art Ross Trophy four times (1964, 1965, 1967, 1968), the Hart Trophy twice (1967 and 1968) and the Lester Patrick Trophy (1976). He was the first NHL player to win the Art Ross, Hart, and Lady Byng trophies in one year and he did it twice (1967 and 1968). He was named to six first and two second all-star teams.

In 1,394 regular-season NHL games, he scored 541 goals and added 926 assists. The man nicknamed "Stosh" was inducted into the Hockey Hall of Fame in 1983.

Interestingly, Mikita who spent plenty of time in the "sin bin" while a junior, cleaned up his act in the NHL, and by 1966-67 when he won the scoring championship, had only 12 penalty minutes. He was rewarded with the Lady Byng Trophy. "I figured I'd proven myself. I was small when I came up and I didn't want anyone trying to take a piece of me. Now I get a few penalties but don't go out of my way to antagonize anyone," he told Jack Gatecliff in 1979, a few months before he retired.

Mikita, who has a Honourary Doctorate from Brock University in St. Catharines, was inducted into the City of St. Catharines Sports Hall of Fame in 1990. It's no surprise that he is an excellent golfer who now splits his time between homes in Illinois and Florida.

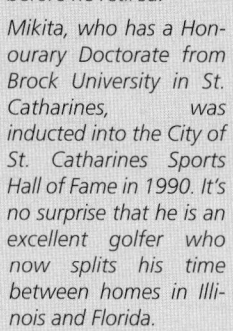

Stan Mikita talks hockey with St. Mike's goalie Cesare Maniago

St. Catharines Museum - *Standard Collection N 5701*

TEEPEES 1958-1959

St. Catharines Teepees whoop it up in the dressing room Saturday night after defeating Peterboro Petes 5-2 to clinch their fifth OHA Junior "A" hockey pennant in the last six seasons. It's the earliest the St. Catharines club has ever nailed first place to the mast. Teepee coach Harry Watson crouches in overcoat at the bottom front while right behind him, holding hat, is team trainer Jimmy Joy.
—Staff photo
St. Catharines Standard

Max Kaminsky
St. Catharines Standard photo

PILOUS OWNS THE TEEPEES

On July 21, 1959, Teepees GM Rudy Pilous announced that he was the new owner and president of the club, replacing George Stauffer of Thompson Products. Pilous had purchased the Teepees for $1.

"Rudy didn't have a dollar bill in his pocket to make the deal legal so he got one from [sportscaster] Rex Stimers," Stauffer told Jack Gatecliff in 1997. "Rex claimed to the day he died that Rudy never paid him back and, in effect, it was him who really owned the team." Well, Rex could dream, couldn't he?

Although Pilous had gained control of a team which had been watched by more than 1,00,000 fans over a 16-year period and had only missed the playoffs once, there was some doubt as to whether the Teepees would even play in St. Catharines in 1959-60. The cost of operating the club had risen to $75,000 in 1958-59. The St. Catharines Parks Board received $20,000 of that and there was a net loss of $1,000 despite the success of the team on the ice. Something had to be done to save junior hockey in the city.

Pilous was already making plans to send his players elsewhere if the club folded. The Chicago Black Hawks were making plans to hold their training camp in Sault Ste. Marie if a deal couldn't be worked out here. On September 1, 1959, Gatecliff published a story which indicated that only the willingness of both parties to give concessions kept the Teepees in the Garden City.

Rudy Pilous
St. Catharines Museum - C 11,268

Later that fall, the Chicago Black Hawks advanced $10,000 to the Teepees and also agreed to pay for scouts who brought players to the Garden City. In addition, the NHL team would pay for the operation of junior B and juvenile clubs in other cities from which the Teepees received players. It was estimated these benefits would cost the Black Hawks at least $25,000 per year.

In September, after the Parks Board and the Teepees settled their differences, it was announced that the new coach for the team was 46-year-old Max Kaminsky. Kaminsky was an outstanding baseball player and a former Niagara Falls junior and senior hockey star who had played in the NHL with Ottawa, St. Louis, Boston and Montreal. He had previous coaching experience with the AHL Pittsburgh Hornets, but had been out of hockey since 1955. When the call came to coach the Teepees, he was operating a restaurant/bar in Niagara Falls, New York. He was about to spend some sleepless nights coaching his first junior A club.

TEEPEES 1959-1960

MAX KAMINSKY LEADS TEEPEES TO A SECOND MEMORIAL CUP

The St. Catharines Teepees Road to the 1960 Memorial Cup

In the fall of 1959, the St. Catharines Teepees were off to a terrible start with two wins and six points in the first 12 games. The club was one point ahead of last place Hamilton Tiger-Cubs. The team was playing so badly, that on December 12, 1959, coach Max Kaminsky telephoned GM Rudy Pilous in Chicago and said he was going to resign. "I'm not a quitter," Kaminsky said. "I just know this is a better team than the way they've played and someone else can get more out of them."

Pilous had faith in his coach and refused to accept Kaminsky's resignation. His confidence in Kaminsky paid off as the Teepees, now wearing their new white sweaters with a wigwam in the centre, earned 22 points in the following 12 games, en route to a second place finish with the Barrie Flyers in the final league standings.

Captain Chico Maki was the league's scoring champion with 92 points and was the runner-up for the Red Tilson Trophy. Four Teepees of the six players on the 1959-60 OHA Junior All-Star Team were: Roger Crozier (goal), Pat Stapleton (defence), Vic Hadfield (left wing, tied with Pierre Gagne), and Chico Maki (right wing).

In round one of the playoffs the Teepees met the Guelph Biltmores who were led by future NHLers Rod Gilbert and Jean Ratelle. Teepee Ray

Continued on page 101

St. Catharines Standard photo

ATTENDANCE FIGURES
Average per regular-season game: 1,678
Season's largest crowd: 3,673
Season's smallest crowd: 835

PLAYOFF ROUNDS: 5
Eliminated Guelph 4-1, Peterborough 4-1, St. Mike's 3-1-2, Montreal Junior Canadiens 4-3-1, and Edmonton Oil Kings 4-2 to win the Memorial Cup

1959-1960

GAMES PLAYED	WON	LOST	TIED	FOR	AGAINST	POINTS	FINISH
48	25	19	4	209	191	54	2/7 (TIED)

Leading Scorers

PLAYER	GOALS	ASSISTS	POINTS
Ron (Chico) Maki	39	53	92
Ray Cullen	48	29	77
Vic Hadfield	19	34	53
Don Grosso	16	33	49
Pat Stapleton	12	35	47

Leading Goaltenders

PLAYER	GP	GA	SO	GAA
Roger Crozier	48	191	1	3.98

Seated in front: mascots Ricky and Brian Cibik. Front row: secretary-treasurer Jay MacDonald, Carlo Longarini, Pete Riddle, captain Chico Maki, owner-manager Rudy Pilous, coach Max Kaminsky, Pat Stapleton, Roger Crozier, Ben Greco, club physician Dr. Michael Zaritsky. Second row: Duke Harris, Peter Berge, Bill Ives, Ray Cullen, Bob Maki, John Brenneman, Don Grosso. Back row: assistant trainer Bill Burnett, Larry Burns, Murray Hall, property man Jack Steele, Vic Hadfield, Doug Robinson, Rich Predovich, assistant property man John (Skinner) McKenzie, Terry McGuire, Bill Speer, trainer Jimmy Joy

St. Catharines Museum - Standard Collection N 5704

Ricky Cibik (left) and his brother Brian pose at Garden City Arena on January 9, 1960.
St. Catharines Standard photo

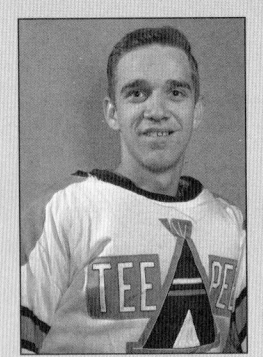

TEEPEES 1959-1960

ROGER CROZIER

St. Catharines Standard photo

In the fall of 1959, the St. Catharines Teepees had a goaltending problem. Coach Max Kaminsky and GM Rudy Pilous had auditioned several netminders, but were not impressed by any of them until Bracebridge native Roger Crozier arrived on the scene.

In his first season with St. Catharines, the 17-year-old led the club to its second Memorial Cup in six years, and was a 1960 OHA Junior A First Team All-Star.

After completing his third year with the Teepees in 1962, Crozier turned pro with the Chicago Black Hawks, who sent him to their St. Louis farm team. After being traded to Detroit in 1963-64, he split the season between the Red Wings and the AHL Pittsburgh Hornets. He had an outstanding season in Pittsburgh, winning the top rookie award and the Holmes Memorial Award for allowing the fewest goals-against in the league. He was also an AHL Second Team All-Star.

In his second year with the Wings, he was a First Team NHL All-Star and won the 1965 Calder Trophy as the NHL's top rookie. His sensational play in the 1966 playoffs wasn't enough to win the Stanley Cup, but he was awarded the Conn Smythe Trophy as the MVP in the playoffs.

In 1970, Crozier was traded to the Buffalo Sabres, an NHL expansion team. He played with the Sabres for six seasons, and in 1975 teamed with Gerry Desjardins to lead the Sabres to the Stanley Cup finals. He was inducted into the Buffalo Sabres Hall of Fame in 1980.

After being traded to the Washington Capitals in March of 1977, he played three games and then retired. In total, he had played 518 regular-season NHL games, winning 206, and recorded 30 shutouts with a goals-against average of 3.04.

Following retirement, he served as coach and then GM of the Capitals in 1981-82. The former netminder's distinguished hockey career has been recognized with the Roger Crozier MBNA Saving Grace Award given annually to the NHL's save percentage-leader.

Crozier forged a successful second career in the banking business with MBNA where he gained a reputation as "The Master Builder".

He passed away on January 11, 1996. He is a member of the Bracebridge Hall of Fame.

Former Teepees at 1959 Chicago Black Hawks camp. From left to right: Denis DeJordy, Stan Mikita, Wayne Hillman, Ted Wright
St. Catharines Museum - Brooks Collection, C 10,707

Teepees at first practice October 5, 1959. From left to right: Terry McGuire, Carlo Longarini, Bob Zupan, Roger Crozier, and Pat Stapleton
St. Catharines Standard photo

Teepees return home February 14, 1960, after three wins in three days.
St. Catharines Museum - Standard Collection N 5782

Teepees netminder Roger Crozier faces the Montreal Junior Canadiens.
St. Catharines Museum - Standard Collection N 5700

Teepees celebrate after first win in 1959-60, a 4-2 victory over St. Mike's on November 7, 1959. Front row left to right: Doug Robinson, Roger Crozier, and Vic Hadfield. Back row: Ray Cullen and Chico Maki
St. Catharines Standard photo

100

TEEPEES 1959-1960

Continued from page 99

Cullen, who had scored 48 goals in 48 games during the regular season, scored three winning goals in the series as the Teepees eliminated Guelph in five games.

In round two the Teepees faced the Peterborough Petes and Wayne Connelly, who had also scored 48 goals in the 1959-60 season. However, the Petes couldn't stop the Teepees, who won the series in six games.

Next came the St. Michael's College Majors, always a tough opponent for St. Catharines teams. The Majors had St. Catharines native Gerry Cheevers in the net and offensive stars like Dave Keon and Larry Keenan. The series was close with two tied games, but in game six, Ray Cullen once again scored the winning goal and the Teepees won the OHA Junior A championship. The J. Ross Robertson Cup was presented to the team for the second time in six years.

In the Eastern Canada final, the Teepees had all they could handle when they faced off against the Montreal Junior Canadiens. The Canadiens were led by future NHL stars Bobby Rousseau and Jacques Laperriere. If the Teepees were going to win the series, they would have to shut down Rousseau.

Teepees coach Max Kaminsky (centre) and Teepees captain Chico Maki (right) get their hands on the J. Ross Robertson Cup (OHA championship) on April 6, 1960.
St. Catharines Standard photo

The Teepees with the Robertson Cup April 6, 1960, in Maple Leaf Gardens
St. Catharines Standard photo

The Teepees celebrate the winning of the George T. Richardson Trophy on April 24, 1960.
St. Catharines Standard photo

PAT STAPLETON

Sarnia native Pat Stapleton finished his two-year Teepees career in 1960 with a Memorial Cup ring and a spot on the First OHA All-Star Team.

He turned pro with Chicago Black Hawks, but was claimed by Boston Bruins in 1961. In 1965 he was the WHL's top defenceman and a First Team All-Star.

St. Catharines Museum - Cornelius Collection, C 10,682

After being claimed by Chicago in 1965, for eight seasons he was one of the Hawks key players, winning three Clarence Campbell Bowls and two Prince of Wales Trophies. For six straight years he recorded a positive plus-minus rating, and no Chicago player has broken his record of six assists registered in a single game.

Stapleton played for Team Canada in the 1972 Summit Series and has possession of the puck which decided that series for Canada. He finished his NHL career in 1973 with 337 points in 635 regular-season NHL games. He saw action in four NHL all-star games.

From 1973 to 1977 he played in the WHA with Chicago, Indianapolis and Cincinnati. In 1974 he was named the league's top defenceman.

He now lives in Strathroy, Ontario.

VIC HADFIELD

Oakville native Vic Hadfield won a Memorial Cup in his second year with the St. Catharines Teepees in 1960.

The left winger turned pro with the Buffalo Bisons in 1960 and in 1961 was claimed by the New York Rangers. He closed out his career with the Pittsburgh Penguins in 1976. In 15 seasons with the two

St. Catharines Standard photo

NHL clubs, he collected 323 goals, 712 points, and 1,154 penalty minutes in 1,002 regular-season games.

He was the first Ranger to score 50 goals in a season, and the GAG (goal-a-game) line of Hadfield, Rod Gilbert, and Jean Ratelle finished third, fourth and fifth in NHL scoring behind Phil Esposito and Bobby Orr in 1971-72.

Today Hadfield owns and operates a golf driving range and teaching centre in Oakville, Ontario.

TEEPEES 1959-1960

RONALD MAKI

Sault Ste. Marie native Ronald (Chico) Maki spent four years with the Teepees, from 1956 to 1960, and twice scored more than 90 points in a season. In 1959-60, the All-Star right winger was the leading scorer in the league and runner-up for the Red Tilson Trophy, presented to the league's MVP. In the 1960 playoffs, Maki collected 56 points, including 19 goals in 31 games.

In his first pro season with the Buffalo Bisons, he was the AHL's 1961 rookie-of-the-year, and then he joined the Chicago Black Hawks in time to win a 1961 Stanley Cup ring.

From 1961 to 1975, Maki was a Chicago fixture, playing 841 regular-season games and collecting 435 points. He was a member of teams that won three Clarence Campbell Bowls and two Prince of Wales Trophies. He played in three all-star games and in 1970 tied Stan Mikita's Chicago record of scoring two short-handed goals in a game.

Maki, who is retired and living in Port Dover, Ontario, was inducted into the Norfolk County Sports Hall of Recognition in 2001.

St. Catharines Standard photo

Teepees Chico Maki (far left) and Ray Cullen (far right) in on goal
St. Catharines Museum - Standard Collection N 5776

Bill Ives
St. Catharines Museum - Cornelius Collection, C 10,662

Teepees celebrate a playoff victory over Montreal on April 13, 1960. Front row: Carlo Longarini, Pat Stapleton. Back row: John Brennenman, Duke Harris and Doug Robinson
St. Catharines Museum - Standard Collection N 5774

OHA immediate past president Jack Roxburgh presents the Eddie Powers Trophy (scoring championship) to Teepees captain Chico Maki on April 5, 1960.
St. Catharines Standard photo

The St. Catharines hockey fans line up at Garden City Arena for tickets for the first Memorial Cup game against the Edmonton Oil Kings on April 27, 1960. Walt Marsh (centre) holds up his four tickets.
St. Catharines Standard photo

Jack Roxburgh (left) presents the George T. Richardson Memorial Trophy (Eastern Canada championship) to Chico Maki with Coach Max Kaminsky, to the right. April 24, 1960.
St. Catharines Standard photo

The Teepees won the first three games of the series and then Rousseau came alive. In game four he scored two goals in a 4-3 Canadiens victory. In game five he scored four goals and added an assist as the Canadiens thumped the Teepees 10-5.

Then Teepee Bill Ives stepped into the picture as Rousseau's shadow. He followed Rousseau everywhere and it paid off. In the next three games, Rousseau scored only one goal and had one assist, and the Teepees won the series in eight games. After the final game Teepees coach Max Kaminsky said, "I can't single out any one boy for special praise, but I would like to say that Bill Ives did a great job shadowing Rousseau."

The Teepees were presented with the George T. Richardson Memorial Trophy for the second time in the club's history.

The Memorial Cup final got off to a rough start for St. Catharines as the Western Junior champion Edmonton Oil Kings, led by Bruce MacGregor, Ed Joyal, and Cliff Pennington, defeated the Teepees 5-3 in Garden City Arena before 3,660 fans.

The remaining games were played in Toronto's Maple Leaf Gardens and the Teepees took control, winning three of the next four games. They won the Memorial Cup with a 7-3 victory in game six before 7,745 fans. With five minutes left in the game, Rex Stimers became violently ill and had to turn the microphone over to an aide. He recovered in time to cover the final moments, but two hours later, he was still visibly shaken. "If we'd lost that one, I'd never made it to the seventh game," Stimers said at the time.

At the end of the game, captain Chico Maki grabbed a jug of trainer Jimmy Joy's Joy Juice and poured it into the Memorial Cup. One by one, each Teepee player drank a toast from the Cup before heading to the dressing room.

TEEPEES 1959-1960

Teepees owner Rudy Pilous presents a western hat to Teepees coach Max Kaminsky before the Memorial Cup series began with the Edmonton Oil Kings on April 27, 1960.

St. Catharines Standard photo

After a wild celebration in the dressing room, the team couldn't wait to get back to St. Catharines. "The Toronto Metro police with sirens screaming led the Teepee bus and its following cavalcade of cars from the front entrance of the Gardens to the western end of the Gardiner Expressway," Jack Gatecliff wrote on the front page of the *St. Catharines Standard* on Monday, May 9, 1960. It was drizzling when the team left Toronto, but nothing could put a damper on their celebration.

The Ontario Provincial Police then took over and escorted the parade to Ontario Street in the Garden City where the Grantham Township Police were waiting to take over and guide them to the Parkway Hotel on Ontario Street. Teepees players then jumped into open convertibles and St. Catharines policemen led the way down Ontario Street to St. Paul Street and on to Garden City Arena where 4,000 fans were waiting.

Standard reporter Al Dunn was in the crowd and remembered the homecoming. "The building shook with roars as loud as any inspired by TP goals during the season," he said.

Each player was greeted individually as he walked from the dressing room to the centre of the floor of the arena to be introduced by master of ceremonies Tommy Garriock. St. Catharines Mayor, Wilfred Bald, greeted the team and said St. Catharines was "the best little city in Canada" and that he was proud to have the best team in Canada.

"Kaminsky's deliberate, relatively mild coaching technique, together with the brusque drive of Pilous, formed a winning combination," Gatecliff said. It was eight days short of the sixth anniversary of the Teepees first Memorial Cup victory on May 16, 1954.

Total attendance for the championship year was 76,649, only 403 more than 1958-59. The team played seven more playoff games but three fewer regular-season games. ∎

Right: Brian Cullen (centre) holds the Memorial Cup as brothers Ray (left) and Barry (right) enjoy the moment on May 25, 1960.

Below: The 1960 Memorial Cup champion St. Catharines Teepees are honoured at a special dinner on May 25, 1960.

St. Catharines Standard photo

St. Catharines Standard photo

St. Catharines Museum - Bob Maki Collection 2004.63.1

103

THE WEATHER
MORE RAIN
Noon Temperature 48
Low Tonight 38, High Tuesday 50

The St. Catharines Standard

MAY

Sun	Mon	Tue	Wed	Thu	Fri	Sat
1	2	3	4	5	6	7
8	9	10	11	12	13	14
15	16	17	18	19	20	21
22	23	24	25	26	27	28
29	30	31				

SEVENTIETH YEAR — THIRTY-TWO PAGES — ST. CATHARINES, ONTARIO, MONDAY, MAY 9, 1960 — THIRTY-TWO PAGES — PRICE SEVEN CENTS

CITY HAILS MEMORIAL CUP CHAMPS

Teepees Given Tumultuous Welcome Home

By JACK GATECLIFF
Standard Sports Editor

St. Catharines Teepees, 1960 Canadian junior hockey champions, were accorded a tumultuous welcome early Sunday evening when they returned to the Niagara district from Toronto with the Memorial Cup.

Four police departments co-operated in escorting the teen-age hockey champions from Maple Leaf Gardens, where they defeated Edmonton Oil Kings 7-3 in the sixth game of the Memorial Cup finals, to Garden City Arena.

The Toronto Metro police, with sirens screaming, led the Teepee bus and its following cavalcade of cars from the front entrance of the Gardens to the western end of the Gardiner Expressway.

Provincial police hustled the St. Catharines group through the heavy Queen Elizabeth Way traffic to Ontario St. where Grantham Township police were...

...sociation "A" league to the very pinnacle of Canadian amateur hockey.

In the first 12 games of the regular schedule the Teepees accumulated three points on one victory and one tie.

Were in Seventh Place

Two weeks before Christmas they were in seventh place in the seven-team league, one point behind...

Victory was in the air—and so was the coach. Seconds after the final whistle blew at Maple Leaf Gardens yesterday, marking Teepees' second Memorial Cup...

ice, at left. At right, clutching the...

One of the first signs to gr...

Linhaven Drive In — TEE PEES MEMORIAL CUP CHAMPIONS

Thousands Brave Rain To Hail The Teepees

Parade Starts ... Toronto Ends

TEEPEE HILARITY

Too Much For Stimers

The Teepee victory was too much for CKTB sportscaster Rex Stimers.

With five minutes left in the third period and the Teepees leading 5-2, the excitable Stimers became violently ill and had to turn the broadcast over to an "aide" for the next three minutes.

He recovered in time to cover the final moments of the victory but was still visibly shaken at the tumultuous reception at Garden City Arena two hours later.

"If we'd lost that one," said Rex. "I'd have never made it to the seventh game."

And there were many who shared those sentiments.

...RNETT HELPS HARRIS FROM ICE
Winger Was Cut For Five Stitches

Eliminate Oil Kings 4-2

TEEPEES CANADIAN CHAMPIONS

Fans and Players Whoop It Up Following Victory

By CRAIG SWAYZE

TORONTO — It was really over when Chico Maki scored that fifth goal. And the St. Catharines fans seemed to sense it.

There was still six minutes to go, but the Teepee supporters were already whooping it up. This time they were sure.

Two more St. Catharines goals and the roar grew even louder. Then, as the big red second hand on the huge clock over centre ice swung into that final minute of play, they turned Maple Leaf Gardens into a bedlam of sound.

Louder and louder grew the roar. And this time they weren't waiting until those final few seconds.

With half a minute left, the fans began their countdown. Each second brought forth a stomping, chanting chorus that echoed to the roof and back.

Then, as those final moments arrived, the Teepee players joined in, whomping their sticks in time against the boards.

Then it was over.

St. Catharines Teepees had walloped Edmonton Oil Kings 7-3 and the Memorial Cup, emblematic of the junior hockey championship of Canada, was theirs.

And the Teepees were well aware of the fact. In one huge wave, the players broke from their bench over the boards and out on the ice.

Heading for Roger Crozier, they virtually buried their pint-sized goaltender under a mountain of pounding, shouting happiness. Back in the stands, the St. Catharines fans went wild.

Litter the Ice

Programs, hats, ribbons and rubbers littered the Gardens ice...

But soon the place was packed. Team officials, relatives and friends crowded in. It was all you could do to hear yourself think.

And through it all, Coach Max Kaminsky went quietly round, shaking hands and embracing each one of his boys.

More pictures were being taken. Reporters were trying to get comments. Well-wishers were attempting to reach their favorites.

In the space of a few minutes, the St. Catharines headquarters had turned from a subdued...

TERRY McGUIRE (LEFT) SCORES THIRD TEEPEE GOAL
Puck Can be Seen Crossing Goal Line Behind Gillow

WE WON!

Take Sixth Game Of Series 7-3 Before 7,745 Fans

By JACK GATECLIFF
The Standard Sports Editor

TORONTO — St. Catharines Teepees, a team which floundered in the basement of the Ontario Hockey Association junior "A" standing for the first month of the schedule, are the 1960 Canadian junior hockey champions.

Completing one of the most colorful chapters in St. Catharines sports history, the Teepees scored a decisive 7-3 win over Edmonton Oil Kings Sunday afternoon at Maple Leaf Gardens to capture the Memorial Cup four games to two.

This was the second St. Catharines team in six years to reach the absolute pinnacle of Canadian junior hockey. The 1953-54 Teepees, coincidentally, also defeated the Oil Kings in the Memorial Cup finals.

The victory Sunday afternoon, accomplished before 7,745 fans, was the climax of a fantastic climb from rock bottom by the Teepees.

After the worst start in the 17 years of junior "A" hockey in St. Catharines (three points in their first 12 games) the Teepees rocketed into a tie with Barrie Flyers for second place in the final standing, just five points behind the Toronto Marlboros.

They eliminated Guelph Biltmore in five games in the provincial quarter-finals; dethroned the defending Ontario champion Peterboro Petes in six games in the...

...position to block Chico Maki's shot on the rebound.

In the first seven minutes the Teepees had 11 shots on the Edmonton goal while the Oil Kings had exactly one from the blueline by Bruce MacGregor.

Dune McCallum, Edmonton defenceman, was penalized for high-sticking and Vic Hadfield followed him seconds later for hooking.

However it wasn't until both teams were at full strength that the Teepees finally scored...

Shutout Broken

TEEPEES 1960-1961

FORMER NHLER GUS BODNAR STEPS BEHIND THE TEEPEES BENCH

Gus Bodnar
January 13, 1961
St. Catharines Standard photo

ATTENDANCE FIGURES
Average per regular-season game: 1,491
Season's largest crowd: 2,481
Season's smallest crowd: 1,002

PLAYOFF ROUNDS: 1
Eliminated by St. Mike's 4-2

1960-1961

GAMES PLAYED	WON	LOST	TIED	FOR	AGAINST	POINTS	FINISH
48	18	24	6	167	204	42	5/7

Leading Scorers

PLAYER	GOALS	ASSISTS	POINTS
Murray Hall	35	41	76
Ray Cullen	24	50	74
Doug Robinson	36	30	66
George (Duke) Harris	15	22	37
Howard Kellough	13	24	37

Leading Goaltenders

PLAYER	GP	GA	SO	GAA
Roger Crozier	47.66	202	0	4.24

Ray Cullen (7) in on goal in opening game action against the Toronto Marlies on October 29, 1960. The Teepees lost 9-7.
St. Catharines Standard photo

After the 1960-61 season began, coach Max Kaminsky became ill and resigned as coach in November. For two weeks former Falcons coach Vic Teal handled the team until he was replaced by Phil Vitale on November 28, 1960. "Both Tommy [Chicago Black Hawks manager Tommy Ivan] and I feel that Phil is the right man for the job," Teepees GM Rudy Pilous said.

The Toronto-born former minor league player was an imposing figure behind the bench, standing 6-foot-4 and weighing 235 pounds. "For years I've had my heart set on coaching a junior hockey team," Vitale said. His dream of coaching junior A hockey soon became a nightmare as the team appeared to be going nowhere. After coaching the club to a record of 2 wins, 1 tie and 11 losses, he was fired on January 13, 1961, and replaced by Vic Teal, and then former NHLer Gus Bodnar. Chicago Black Hawks scout Bob Wilson was named manager of the team.

"I just couldn't get through to the players," Vitale said, when after six weeks as bench boss he learned of his dismissal. Vitale, who was at one-time Metro Toronto Hockey president, died in 1995.

Chicago Black Hawks scout Bob Wilson (centre) has some advice for Teepees coach Gus Bodnar (left) and Duke Harris (right) January 13, 1961.
St. Catharines Standard photo

On December 6, 1960, a Max Kaminsky Testimonial game was held at Garden City Arena. The Chicago Black Hawks faced a team made up of Teepees grads that included Bobby Hull, Stan

AUGUST (GUS) BODNAR

Fort William native Gus Bodnar won the NHL's Calder Trophy in 1944 and two Stanley Cups in 1945 and 1947 with the Toronto Maple Leafs. He was part of the blockbuster trade that saw Chicago Black Hawks swap Max Bentley and Cy Thomas to the Leafs for Bodnar and four other players in 1947.

The former Toronto Maple Leaf centre/right winger holds the distinction of establishing the NHL record for the fastest goal by a rookie: 15 seconds of the first period against the New York Rangers in 1943. His name also is in the record book for assisting on all three of Black Hawk Bill Mosienko's three quickest goals in NHL history. All three goals were scored in 21 seconds on March 23, 1952.

In 667 regular-season games Bodnar earned 396 points, including 142 goals. After his playing career, he was a successful junior coach winning a Memorial Cup in 1967 with the Toronto Marlboros. In 1983 he was inducted into the North Western Ontario Sports Hall of Fame, and in 1995 joined the Oshawa Sports Hall of Fame.

Bodnar passed away in Oshawa on July 1, 2005.

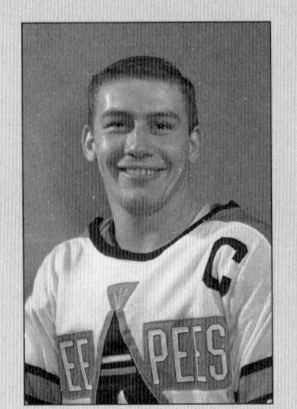

TEEPEES 1960-1961

RAY CULLEN

Like his older brother Brian, Ray Cullen was criticized for his lack of skating skills, but wherever he played, Cullen had a knack for scoring goals. In 1959-60, he scored 76 goals in 79 regular-season and playoff games. He played four years with the Teepees, 1958 to 1962, and captained the club for the last two. In 1961-62, he led the team in scoring with 78 points. In 34 years of junior hockey in the Garden City, Cullen is tied with Black Hawk Dave Gorman for fourth place as the all-time leading point-getters with 329.

In his first three years in the minors, after leaving the Teepees, Cullen scored 140 goals and won rookie of-the-year awards in the EHL (1963) and AHL (1965). By 1965, the high-scoring centre was in the NHL with the New York Rangers and then he spent time with Detroit Red Wings, Minnesota North Stars, and Vancouver Canucks.

The Ottawa native retired in 1971 at 29, the same age at which his brothers Barry and Brian decided to leave hockey. He was the most productive NHLer of the three brothers, scoring 92 goals and collecting 215 points in 313 regular-season NHL games.

Today Cullen owns a GM car dealership in London, Ontario.

St. Catharines Standard photo

New Teepees coach Phil Vitale (left) at practice with Ray Cullen and Chicago Black Hawks coach Rudy Pilous (right) on November 28, 1960.
St. Catharines Standard photo

Teepees line of Murray Hall, Howard Kellough, and John Brenneman
Courtesy of Fred MacKenzie

Bobby Hull, (left) poses with brother Dennis who is attending his first Chicago Black Hawks training camp, September 23, 1964.
St. Catharines Standard photo

Mikita, Pierre Pilote, and Elmer Vasko. Dennis Hull was brought up from the local Junior B club and played on a line with his older brother and Mikita. The game, which ended in a 2-2 draw, was attended by 2,883 fans who helped to raise $3,765 for the Kaminsky Trust Fund.

Kaminsky, who was in the Buffalo General Hospital at the time, died on May 5, 1961. He was known as one of the class guys in the game.

The club struggled during most of the year and won only nine games at home, but in the final 18 games finished strongly with the best record in the league, winning ten, losing four, and tying four. The team placed fifth in the league with 42 points. Murray Hall led the team in scoring with 76 points followed by Ray Cullen with 74.

To increase attendance and spark enthusiasm, the club brought a portable organ into the arena — and it was a hit. A contest to see which fan could shoot the puck through a slot in a board in front of the net was also started. There was a cash prize for the successful shooter each game, and if no one succeeded the prize was increased for the next game.

TEEPEES 1960-1961

Teepee Bill Ives on the right, scores on St. Mike's goaltender Gerry Cheevers, February 25, 1961.   St. Catharines Standard photo

In the first round of the playoffs, the Teepees were ousted by St. Michael's College Majors in six games. The Majors, led by St. Catharines native Gerry "Cheesie" Cheevers in goal, went on to win the Memorial Cup.

Murray Hall, Ray Cullen, Bill Ives, and John Brenneman were the top producers in the playoffs with five points each, followed by Doug Robinson, who had four goals.

At the end of the season, Bodnar gave up his coaching job because he found it too difficult commuting from his home in Lindsay where he owned a hotel. "Next to playing, I had my best hockey time commuting from Lindsay to St. Catharines as Teepee coach," Bodnar said in 1994.

Sunday afternoon hockey games had a curfew of 6 p.m. One of the Teepees playoff games with St. Mike's was cut short by the curfew. The game, which St. Mike's was leading 4-3, was washed out and had to be replayed.

Total attendance for 1960-61 was a disappointing 42,545, but the team played eight fewer home playoff games than the 1960 Memorial Cup champions.

Meanwhile, in Chicago, former Teepees coach and the present club owner Rudy Pilous led the Black Hawks to their first Stanley Cup victory in 23 years. Included on that championship club were former Teepees Stan Mikita, Bobby Hull, Ab McDonald, Chico Maki, Elmer Vasko, Pierre Pilote, and Wayne Hillman.

THE PILOUS SHIFT

In November of 1960, Chicago Black Hawks coach Rudy Pilous created a major shift in NHL coaching. During a game on November 17, 1960, the referee called a delayed penalty and Pilous pulled goalie Glenn Hall and sent out an extra forward. The plan worked and Murray Balfour scored for the Hawks. Today this strategy is a regular feature of hockey games everywhere. "It's strange that coaches haven't thought of this before," Gatecliff wrote at the time.

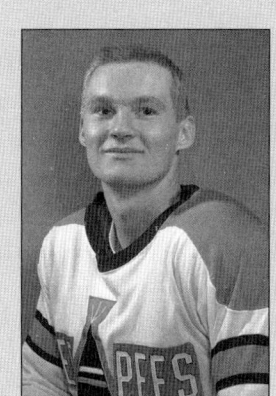

MURRAY HALL

St. Catharines Standard photo

Kirkland Lake native Murray Hall spent two years with the Teepees, 1959 to 1961, winning a Memorial Cup in his rookie year. Fifteen players from the 1960 Cup team had pro careers, but none of them played for as many teams or covered as much territory as the Teepees 1960-61 points leader.

In a 16-year pro career, the right winger played in six leagues with 14 different teams in ten American states and one Canadian province. Along the way, he won a Calder Cup with Rochester Americans and two Lester Patrick Cups with Vancouver Canucks.

In the NHL, Hall saw action with Chicago, Detroit, Minnesota and Vancouver before joining Gordie Howe and the WHA Houston Aeros in 1972. He won Avco Cups with Houston in 1974 and 1975.

Since retiring in 1978, Hall, a former associate pro golfer, has been involved with a number of golf clubs in the Burlington area where he now lives.

DOUG ROBINSON

St. Catharines Standard photo

Doug spent three years with the Teepees, 1958 to 1961, and won a Memorial Cup in 1960.

After one season with the EPHL Soo Thunderbirds, the Garden City native moved to the AHL Buffalo Bisons with whom he won the Calder Trophy in 1963. He was named the league's top rookie in the same year after collecting 73 points in 72 regular-season games. He led all playoff scorers in the 1963 playoffs with ten goals in 13 games.

From 1964-65 to 1970-71, the left winger saw action in 239 regular-season NHL games with Chicago, New York Rangers, and Los Angeles. His most productive pro season came in 1969-70 with the AHL Springfield Kings when the First Team All-Star earned 86 points, including 45 goals.

After an eye injury forced him to retire in 1972, he scouted for the Montreal Canadiens, eventually becoming their head scout.

He retired in 2002 and today lives in St. Catharines where he golfs and works up a sweat at the YMCA.

GERRY CHEEVERS

St. Catharines native Gerry (Cheesie) Cheevers enjoyed a great deal of local success playing goal in the Canadian Legion and CYO leagues, and with the Conroy bantams who won two All-Ontario championships. But his hockey future was not going to be in the Garden City. He was courted by the Toronto Maple Leafs, and at 14 he was enrolled in St. Michael's College in Toronto.

The youngster's dream of playing with the Teepees never had a chance. "That idea ended abruptly when I went to St. Mike's," Cheevers said on March 20, 2006, from his Massachusetts home. "There were some heated discussions [with his parents], but 14-year-olds never win those discussions."

At St. Mike's he came under the influence of Father David Bauer and before he left to turn pro, he had won four championships, including a Memorial Cup in 1961.

"Father Bauer was really ahead of his time," said Cheevers who would go on to win many awards and honours including a Calder Cup with Rochester Americans in 1965 and Stanley Cups in 1970 and 1972 with Boston Bruins.

He was inducted into the Hockey Hall of Fame in 1985.

It's interesting to note that Cheevers, like former Niagara Falls goalie Doug Favell, could play as a forward. Cheevers played several junior games on the wing in 1960-61; he remembered how rough it got on Friday, December 16, 1960, when he played right wing in a game against the Barrie Flyers while Dave Dryden took his place in the St. Mike's net.

Today Cheevers resides in Merrimac, Massachusetts.

Gerry Cheevers as a WHA Cleveland Crusader
Ernie Fitzsimmons Collection

Chicago forward Murray Balfour scored during a delayed penalty in a game on November 17, 1961.
St. Catharines Museum - C 11,260

TEEPEES 1961-1962

THE TEEPEES LAST SEASON

Pilous Steps Down As Teepees Owner;
Phil Esposito Plays with the Last Teepees Team

ATTENDANCE FIGURES
Average per regular-season game: 1,515
Season's largest crowd: 3,464
Season's smallest crowd: 722

PLAYOFF ROUNDS: 1
Eliminated by Hamilton 4-1-1

The Teepees challenge the Niagara Falls Flyers in opening game action on October 27, 1961.
St. Catharines Standard photo

1961-1962

GAMES PLAYED	WON	LOST	TIED	FOR	AGAINST	POINTS	FINISH
50	19	23	8	194	206	46	3/6

Leading Scorers

PLAYER	GOALS	ASSISTS	POINTS
Ray Cullen	36	42	78
Phil Esposito	32	39	71
George Standing	22	24	46
John Brenneman	12	30	42
Bill Ives	15	20	35

Leading Goaltenders

PLAYER	GP	GA	SO	GAA
Roger Crozier	44.33	174	1	3.92
Art Fegan	5	28	0	5.60

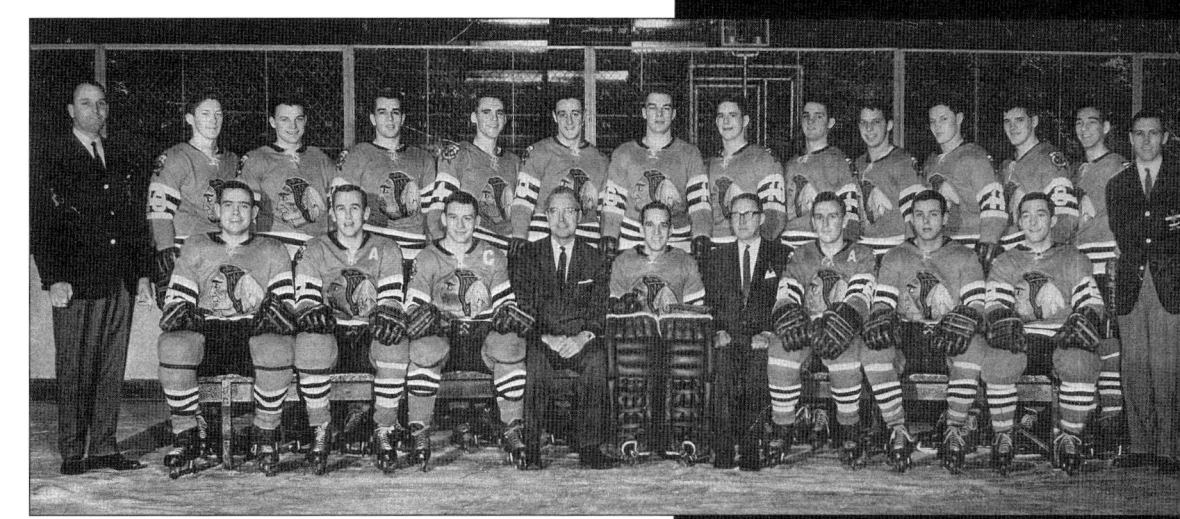

In 1961 the OHA Junior A League was in trouble. St. Michael's College Majors and Toronto Marlboros dropped out and joined three other clubs to form the Metropolitan Junior League. Father David Bauer of St. Michael's College felt that the goals of major junior A hockey were not compatible with the educational needs of his students and he withdrew from the league. The Majors were absent from major junior hockey for the next 36 years. Montreal joined the OHA Junior A League, so the season started with six teams.

The 1960-61 Teepees had only attracted 42,545 fans to 24 league and three playoff games compared to 76,649 in 33 games the previous season. The hockey club's share of the attendance revenue fell from $65,772.30 in 1959-60 to $36,012.73 in 1960-61. "Junior hockey was a losing proposition," said former Teepees director Ross Wilson from his home in Bobcayegon in May of 2004. Something had to be done to save the club from folding.

Rudy Pilous, busy coaching in Chicago, gave up his controlling interest in the Teepees, but the agreement with Chicago Black Hawks was to continue. The team was reorganized with 23 men as owners. Former Davis Cup captain Ross Wilson was the new president. "I went around to the men and asked, 'Would

Front row: Bill Speer, Bill Ives, Ray Cullen (captain), Ross Wilson (president), Roger Crozier, Bill Henry (one of Teepees owners), Poul Popiel, John Brenneman, Jim Sanko. Back row: Ken Campbell (coach), Fred Stanfield, Rick Lachowich, Dennis Berish, Brent Hughes, Phil Esposito, Ken Hodge, Doug Jarrett, Peter Ford, Dennis Hull, Jack Stanfield, George Standing, Chi-Chi Farenzena, unnamed person

St. Catharines Museum - Joan Bigger Collection 2004.16-

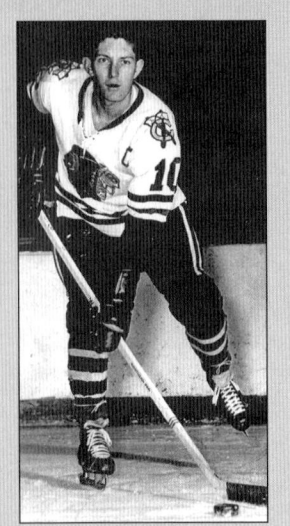

TEEPEES 1961-1962

FRED STANFIELD

In 1961-62 Toronto Township native Fred Stanfield played his Teepees rookie year with his older brother Jack. Fred would go on to lead the Hawks in scoring twice, win the Max Kaminsky Trophy (most gentle-manly player) and captain the team in 1963-64.

It looked like there might be a Stanfield in the hockey club's future for quite some time as five of Fred's and Jack's brothers, Jim, Joe, Vic, Paul and Gord, were all playing minor hockey at the time. As it turned out, only Jim made it to St. Catharines, but Fred, Jack and Jim each saw action in the NHL, with Fred having the most successful career.

After turning pro with Chicago in 1964, Fred was traded to Boston Bruins with Phil Esposito and Ken Hodge in 1967. It was his big break in hockey. He went on to win Stanley Cups with the Bruins in 1970 and 1972.

He played 914 regular-season NHL games with Chicago, Boston, Minnesota and Buffalo, scoring 211 goals and earning 616 points. His most productive season came in 1971-72 with the Bruins when he collected 79 points in 78 games. For six consecutive NHL seasons, he scored 20 or more goals.

Today the former office furniture storeowner is retired and lives in East Amherst, New York.

JACK STANFIELD

Toronto native Jack Stanfield, the eldest of three brothers who played in St. Catharines, spent the 1961-62 season with his brother Fred.

The left winger turned pro with the EHL Philadelphia Ramblers in 1963. For the next 11 years he played minor pro with the exception of one playoff game with Chicago Black Hawks and two seasons in the WHA, winning the Avco Cup with Houston Aeros in 1974.

Today he lives in Houston, Texas.

Chicago Black Hawks head scout Bob Wilson behind the Teepees bench
Courtesy of Fred Stanfield

Ken Campbell October 18, 1962
St. Catharines Standard photo

Name Ken Campbell St. Catharines Coach; Replaces Gus Bodnar

St. Catharines, Aug. 10 — Thirty-seven-year-old Ken Campbell of Pembroke has been named coach of St. Catharines Teepees of the Ontario Hockey Association Junior A League.

Campbell, playing-coach of Omaha Knights in the International League last season replaces Gus Bodnar who resigned following elimination of the Teepees by Toronto St. Michael's Majors last spring.

Born in Montreal, Campbell played junior and senior hockey with Montreal Royals and was a member of the 1946-47 Montreal team which won the Allan Cup.

He was playing-coach of Pembroke in the Quebec Senior League for seven years before taking over the same position with Troy, N.Y., in the International League in 1959-60.

Last year he took Omaha to third place in the seven-team International League after they had finished last the preceding season.

Campbell is married, and has two boys, 16-year-old Randy and 13-year-old Malcolm.

The family will move from Pembroke to St. Catharines later this month.

Teepees will open their pre-season training camp in the neighboring Stamford Arena, Aug. 28.

Coincident with releasing the name of the new St. Catharines coach, Ross Wilson, vice-president of the Teepees last season, announced a group of St. Catharines businessmen had agreed to take over the direction of the club.

Rudy Pilous, coach of Chicago Black Hawks, obtained controlling interest in the club two years ago from founder George Stauffer.

It is understood Pilous will remain as an advisor.

The Teepees also ratified their affiliation with the Black Hawks of the National Hockey League for another season.

St. Catharines Standard

---

you take a share and keep it for a year?'" Wilson recalled. "I just wanted to keep the thing going."

Ken Campbell became the Teepees new coach and GM.

Attendance was so low during the 1961-62 season that the club explored the possibility of playing games on Saturday afternoons. In 28 home games, 47,769 watched the last Teepees team to play in the Garden City. The club only won 11 of 25 home games.

Bill Henry, one of the owners, urged the Chicago Black Hawks to accept the club's financial responsibilities and over the next two years, 1962 to 1964, the parent team responded by paying off debts of $40,000.

In December, Campbell traded popular forward Duke Harris to the Guelph Royals for George Standing. Harris, who was with the Memorial Cup team in 1960, couldn't get untracked with the Teepees, but found new life in Guelph and ended the season as the Royals MVP.

During the season, the Teepees wore Black Hawks uniforms similar to those worn in Chicago, but only on away games. This started after an exhibition contest with St. Mike's Majors on December 3, 1961.

For the second straight season, the Teepees had a

Roger Crozier in action against Montreal, October 31, 1961
St. Catharines Standard photo

Coach Ken Campbell (centre) with defencemen Bill Speer (left) and Brent Hughes at a Teepees practice on October 17, 1961
St. Catharines Standard photo

TEEPEES 1961-1962

Ladies' Night at the Arena
St. Catharines Teepee president Ross Wilson pins roses on two lady hockey fans who have more than ordinary interest in the 1961-62 team. Mrs. Doug Jarrett, wife of Teepee defenceman Doug Jarrett, watches while a rose is affixed to Mrs. Roger Crozier's lapel. Roger has been the all-star junior "A" goalie with the Teepees the past two years. Some 500 ladies were given flowers when they entered the rink last night.
St. Catharines Standard photo, December 13, 1961

"How about that?" Bill Ives seems to be saying as he tugs at the Chicago Black Hawk uniform worn by Phil Esposito during Teepee practice here Tuesday. The St. Catharines OHA Junior "A" hockey club wore the Black Hawk sweaters for the first time last Sunday for their exhibition game against St. Michael's College Majors at Toronto. According to coach Ken Campbell, the Teepees will wear the uniform of their parent National Hockey League club for all away games the rest of the season. Ives has on one of the regular Teepee home sweaters bearing a big new "A" upon his recent appointment as an assistant captain.
—Staff photo
St. Catharines Standard

Ray Cullen with 300th-point puck on January 20, 1962
St. Catharines Standard photo

losing record, winning 19 and losing 23 games, but they still finished third in the six-team league with 46 points. Ray Cullen was the club's points-leader with 78 followed by Esposito with 71.

On January 20, 1962, Cullen recorded his 300th point, with two assists in a 4-2 victory over Niagara Falls. He was the second player to reach that total in the club's history. "I don't know why everyone is so excited," Cullen told Gatecliff at the time. "Brian [his older brother] scored more than 300 points and he was only in junior three years. It's taken me four years to get that many."

Roger Crozier was named to the 1961-62 First All-Star Team. It was the fifth time in a row that he had made the first team in mid-season as well as the end of each year. He was first chosen at the finish of the 1959-60 season. Phil Esposito made the Second All-Star Team.

The post-season was not successful as the Teepees were eliminated in the first round by Hamilton in six games. At one stage, in five of the six playoff games, the Teepees led the Wings, but lapses in the third period of four of those games were costly. The series was well attended at Garden City Arena with 3,465 fans showing up for the final playoff contest.

The fans were proud of the fight the team showed against the Wings, who would go on to win the Memorial Cup with future NHL stars, Pit Martin, Paul Henderson, and Lowell MacDonald. Ray Cullen led the Teepees with six points in the playoffs

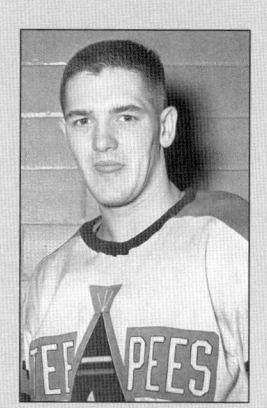

GEORGE STANDING

George Standing spent most of his junior career with the Toronto Marlboros and part of 1961-62 with the Teepees. He began his pro career with the Nashville Dixie Flyers in 1963 and played in the minors until 1972 with the exception of two games with Minnesota North Stars in 1967-68. 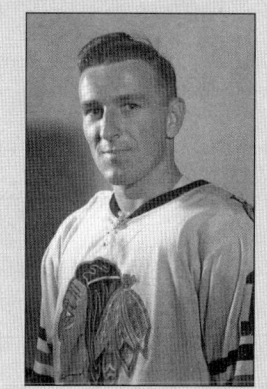
St. Catharines Standard photo

POUL POPIEL

Popiel, who was born in Sollested, Denmark, was a defenceman with the Teepees/Black Hawks from 1960 to 1963.

After turning pro with the Buffalo Bisons in 1963, he joined the St. Louis Braves and won the CHL's top rookie award in 1964.

He made it to the NHL in 1965-66 with Boston and then saw action in 224 regular-season games with Los Angeles, Detroit, Vancouver and Edmonton. He also spent six seasons with the WHA Houston Aeros where he played with Gordie Howe and won Avco Cups in 1974 and 1975.

He now lives in Houston, Texas. 
St. Catharines Standard photo

BRENT HUGHES

Defenceman Brent Hughes played for the St. Catharines Teepees from 1961 to 1963. He broke into the pro ranks with the EHL New Haven Blades and played in the minors until he made it to the NHL Los Angeles Kings in 1967.

After three seasons with the Kings, he was traded to Philadelphia. From 1972 to 1975 he saw action with St. Louis, Detroit and Kansas City, before moving to the WHA.
St. Catharines Standard photo

The Bowmanville native closed out his career with Cincinnati of the CHL in 1980. In 435 regular-season NHL games, he collected 132 points.

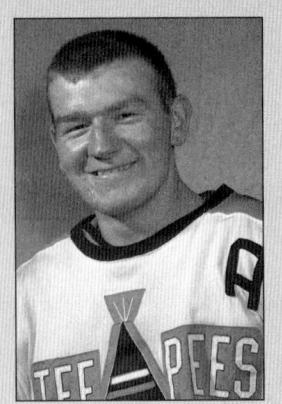

TEEPEES 1961-1962

GEORGE HARRIS

Duke Harris played three full seasons for the St. Catharines Teepees from 1958 to 1961, capturing a Memorial Cup in 1960. The Sarnia native finished his junior career with the Guelph Royals and then turned pro with the EPHL St. Louis Braves in 1962.

St. Catharines Standard photo

For the next 13 years he played in six different leagues for ten teams in six states and two Canadian provinces. From 1967 to 1970 Harris was on four consecutive championship teams. He earned Calder Cups with Pittsburgh and Rochester and two Lester Patrick trophies with the WHL Vancouver Canucks.

In the NHL the right winger saw action with Minnesota North Stars and Toronto Maple Leafs.

After retiring in 1975, Harris became a registered crane operator. Today he is retired and lives in Sarnia.

BILL SPEER

Lindsay native Bill (The Barber) Speer played for the St. Catharines Teepees and was the club's unofficial barber from 1959 to 1962, winning a Memorial Cup in 1960.

After turning pro in 1962 with the EHL Knoxville Knights, he embarked on a 12-year hockey journey that took him through six pro leagues with 14 different teams in nine American states.

Bill Speer with the AHL Buffalo Bisons
Ernie Fitzsimmons Collection

He spent 130 regular-season NHL games with Pittsburgh and Boston, winning a Stanley Cup with the Bruins in 1970. After two years in the WHA, he retired in 1974 and ran a barbershop in his hometown.

In 1989 he died in a snowmobile accident on a lake near Lindsay, Ontario. In 1993 he was inducted into the Lindsay Hall of Fame.

---

followed by Esposito who had five. "Not a word of criticism did we hear, and this we might add, is out of the ordinary when a team goes out in the first round," Gatecliff wrote at the time.

Eleven players graduated from the 1961-62 club, including captain Ray Cullen. Cullen's departure meant that it was the end of the Cullen era until 1976 when Brian Cullen's son Bob suited up with the St. Catharines Fincups. Brian Cullen played with the Teepees in 1951 and Ray was completing his fourth year with the team. The three Cullen brothers, Brian, Barry and Ray, amassed 931 points in regular-season and playoff games.

On June 7, 1962, steps were taken to keep junior hockey alive in the Garden City. The 23-man committee which owned the team was out. Conroy executive Bill Henry was in as president and majority owner. Others who had a stake in the club were Max Kaminsky, Howard Kamin, Hugh Feasby, and Jim Newman. Henry sent his son Bill Henry Jr. to pick up the shares from the 22 other owners.

Included among those who turned in their shares were Rudy Pilous, Jack Leach, and Ross Wilson.

The team's new braintrust consisted of Bill Henry, Fred Muller, Ken Campbell, Max Kaminsky, Hugh Feasby, Norm Lever, and Howard Kamin.

The team's new name was the St. Catharines Black Hawks and the new sweaters were identical to those of the Chicago Black Hawks (later Blackhawks) who were still affiliated with the club.

The 15-year association with the Teepees name was over. ■

For Services Rendered

Captain Ray Cullen and goaltender Roger Crozier, who have a total of seven years of service with the St. Catharines Teepees, were honored last night between the second and third periods of the Red Wing-Teepee playoff game. Cullen is chosen most popular player on the 1961-62 club by a player by the press-radio representatives. Assisting with the presentations were Ross Wilson, president of the St. Catharines Teepee Hockey Club, left, and Jack Aitken, who presented the Esquire Hotel Trophy to the brilliant St. Catharines goalie. Both players will complete their outstanding junior hockey careers this season.
—Staff photos

St. Catharines Standard

Teepees coach Ken Campbell puts defenceman Bill Speer on the scales. November 3, 1961.
St. Catharines Standard photo

Ray Cullen trims the hair of Bill (The Barber) Speer on October 20, 1960.
St. Catharines Standard photo

TEEPEES 1961-1962

Meet The Junior Black Hawks!
New Name, New Owners For Teepees

Junior "A" hockey will continue to operate in St. Catharines during the 1962-63 season.

However it will be under new managment and a new club name.

Sale of the St. Catharines franchise in the Ontario Hockey Association junior "A" league to five local businessmen was announced at a noon luncheon meeting Thursday.

Known as the Teepees since George Stauffer and Thompson Products Ltd assumed ownership in 1947, the team has been re-named the St. Catharines Black Hawks.

St. Catharines Standard

Spring Change-Over
Chicago Black Hawk Manager Tommy Ivan, seated extreme left, signs new agreement with the St. Catharines junior hockey club. The St. Catharines club, known as the Teepees for 14 years, will henceforth be called the Black Hawks. With Ivan are, back row, left to right, St. Catharines directors Howard Kamin, Max Kaminsky and Vice-President Hugh Feasby. Seated: Ivan, St. Catharines President Bill Henry, Chicago Chief Scout Bob Wilson, Director Jim Newman.
St. Catharines Standard photo

The Teepees final banquet on March 19, 1962. Front row: Fred Stanfield, Teepees treasurer Bill Henry, Doug Jarrett, and coach Ken Campbell. Back row: John Brenneman, Teepee executive Norm Lever, and Chi-Chi Farenzena
St. Catharines Standard photo

Phil Esposito (left) digs for the puck in front of Niagara Falls Flyer netminder Wayne Rutledge on October 27, 1961.
St. Catharines Standard photo

Phil Esposito with hands raised behind the Montreal Canadiens net celebrates a Teepees goal on November 18, 1961. The Teepees lost 5-4.
St. Catharines Standard photo

Teepees captain Ray Cullen (right) watches teammate Phil Esposito get mugged behind the Montreal net by Canadiens captain Jacques LaPerriere on November 18, 1961.
St. Catharines Standard photo

PHIL ESPOSITO

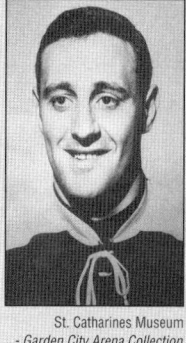

St. Catharines Museum - Garden City Arena Collection R 5686

Six-foot-one, 201-pound Phil Esposito made his Junior A debut with the Teepees in 1961. The Sault Ste. Marie native had attended the 1960 Teepees training camp, but after breaking curfew, he was sent to Hap Emms in Niagara Falls. In his book, Phil Esposito: Thunder and Lightning, Esposito recalled Emms' words after he skated for the Flyers owner: "I want you to get off this ice and get the hell out of here".

Esposito ended up with the Sarnia Junior B team and after a productive season earned a second shot with St. Catharines in 1961. He was sent home by Rudy Pilous and told if he lost 28 pounds, he would be signed and given $60.00 a week. After losing 27 pounds, Esposito said he was given $57.50 a week. The sum of $2.50 had been deducted for the one pound he didn't lose.

He finished his rookie season as the second-highest Teepees scorer with 32 goals and 71 points. He made the second OHA All-Star Team as a centre. "Not since Chico Maki...has this city had a player who possesses the ability to lift the club when things aren't going right," Gatecliff wrote in November, 1961.

Esposito would go on to become an NHL superstar, seeing action with Chicago, Boston, with whom he won two Stanley Cups in 1970 and 1972, and the New York Rangers, from 1963 to 1981. He was the first player to break the 100-point-barrier with 126 points in 1968-69 and he led the league in goals for six seasons. In 1970-71 he had 76 goals and 76 assists, setting records for goals, assists and points, 152 in total. In 1,282 NHL regular-season games, he scored 717 goals and collected 1,590 points.

He won five scoring championships (1969, 1971, 1972, 1973 and 1974), two Hart Trophies (1969 and 1974), two Lester B. Pearson Awards (1971 and 1974), and the Lester Patrick Trophy (1978). He was selected on six first and two second NHL all-star teams.

In the 1972 Summit Series, he scored 13 points in eight games and was Team Canada's inspirational leader in the memorable eight-game showdown.

He was inducted into the Hockey Hall of Fame in 1984.

Today Esposito resides in Tampa Bay, Florida, where he helped put together that city's first NHL team in 1992. He was a colour commentator for Tampa Bay when it won the Stanley Cup in 2004 and in 2007 he was a hockey commentator on satellite radio.

JIMMY JOY - Trainer Extraordinaire

Jimmy Joy, a veteran of World War I and winner of the Military Medal, was the first trainer of the first Junior A team in St. Catharines in 1943. He looked after junior hockey players for over three decades.

Nicknamed "The Bulldog", he had the players' respect. "Never had any trouble with that gang [1954 Memorial Cup team]," Joy said. "Maybe they didn't agree with my suggestions, but they certainly never questioned them."

The London England native created a special drink named Joy Juice for the players in 1954, and many thought it helped their performance. The special drink became a fixture with future junior teams.

Joy was a trainer in several sports, including football, rowing, boxing and baseball. His sports year knew no season.

In 1920 he was working as a photographer for the Welland Canal, and in 1929 he became the official photographer until he retired in 1959.

In 1962 a special night was held for Joy in the St. Catharines Canadian Legion. Hundreds turned out to pay their respects to the man who had helped so many athletes over a period of 42 years. He was one of the best-known trainers in Canada.

Jimmy Joy passed away in September of 1967 and today is survived by his son Jimmy Junior and daughter Jean Garriock.

Teepees trainer Jimmy Joy with jackets, October 6, 1953
St. Catharines Standard photo

Jimmy Joy tests the strength of the Smelle brothers, Carl (left) and Tom.
Courtesy Tom Smelle

Jimmy Joy and his wife Jane are surrounded by local politicians on his big evening.
St. Catharines Standard photo

Teepees trainer Jimmy Joy, in the centre of the photo, is honoured at his appreciation dinner held on September 13, 1962.
St. Catharines Standard photo

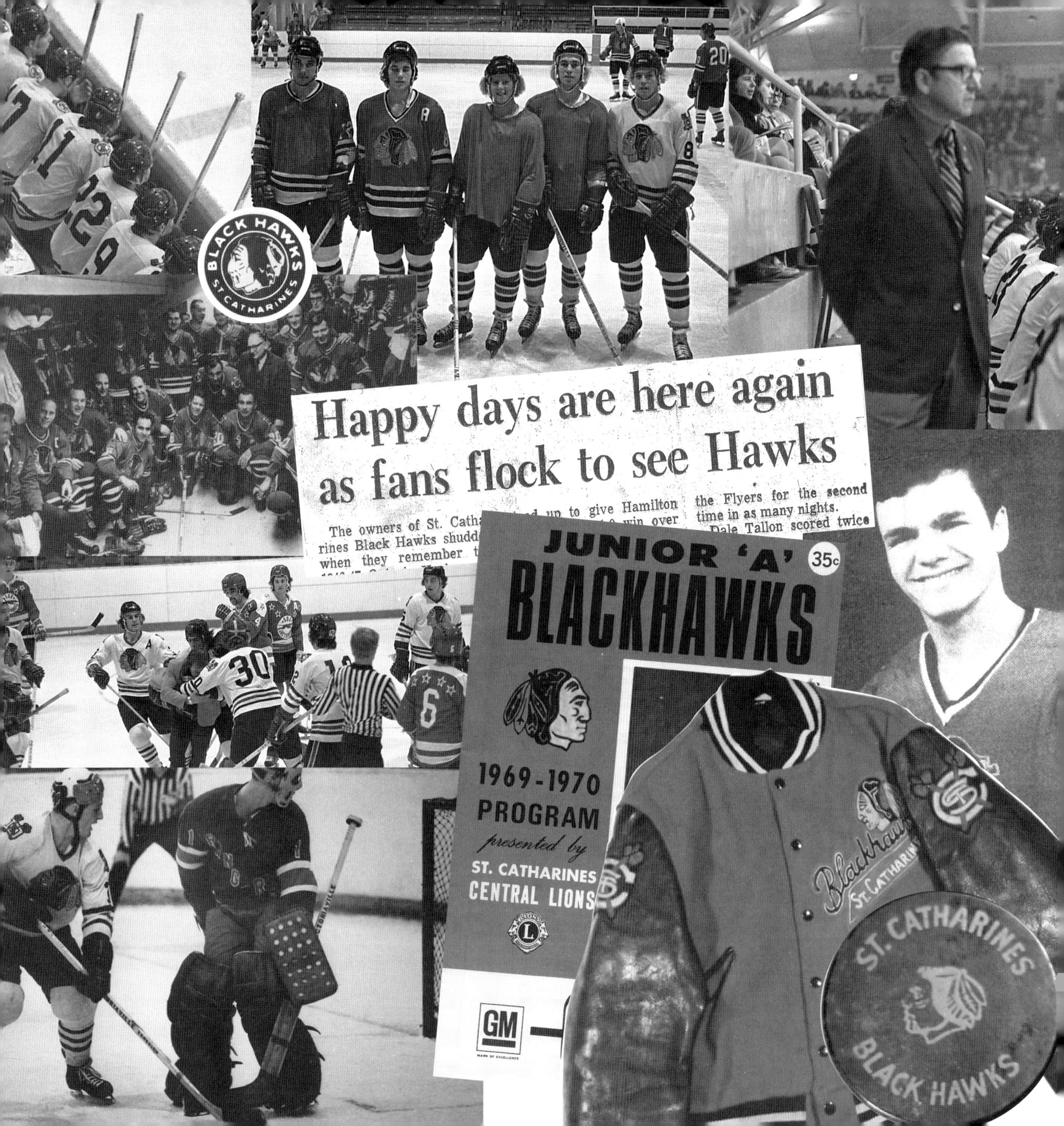

Happy days are here again as fans flock to see Hawks

JUNIOR 'A' BLACKHAWKS
1969-1970 PROGRAM
presented by
ST. CATHARINES CENTRAL LIONS

FRED MULLER
THE SECOND MAN TO SAVE JUNIOR HOCKEY IN ST. CATHARINES

St. Catharines Museum - Janine Muller Collection, C11,075

Hawks owner Fred Muller steps behind the bench for suspended coach Frank Milne and leads his club to an 8-1 victory over Oshawa on November 8, 1970.

St. Catharines Standard photo

He was a businessman turned hockey executive who drove a big car and loved a good cigar, but there was a lot more to Fred Muller than met the eye. He was the second man who saved Junior A hockey in St. Catharines.

In 1961, Muller, a longtime junior hockey fan and Teepee executive since 1958, was the first of 23 men who agreed to be a director of the hockey club; this occurred after Thompson Products had ended its sponsorship and Rudy Pilous was no longer the team's president. The directors took on the responsibility of sharing any losses incurred by the Teepees.

One year later the Teepees became the St. Catharines Black Hawks. Muller became president of the Black Hawks in 1964 after former majority-owner Bill Henry resigned. The Yugoslavian native left his position at Niagara Glass and went into hockey full time. "There's something about the game which gets into your blood and now I'm hooked," Muller said in 1967.

"And believe me he worked very, very hard, was intensely interested and this resulted in his success," Bill Henry told Jack Gatecliff in 1987. The hockey club was losing money and only funds from the Chicago Black Hawks were keeping the club afloat. Henry had turned his shares in the hockey club over to Chicago in 1964. Forty years later, Henry couldn't remember how much the Hawks had paid for those shares. He passed away on September 3, 2005.

By 1967 the Junior A Black Hawks owed $50,000 to Chicago, and it looked like the club might fold because NHL sponsorship was to end that year. That's when Muller, who became the Hawks GM, rolled up his sleeves and went to work.

In the next few years, working with former Teepee star Obie O'Brien, Dr. Archie Manoian (the club's vice-president and team dentist), and Ken Campbell (a former Hawks coach and then Chicago Black Hawks director of playing personnel), Muller put the team's finances in order. When the debt to Chicago was repaid, the shares of the club were returned to Muller and Campbell.

Muller set up an extensive scouting system and traveled thousands of miles recruiting players such as Marcel Dionne, Pierre Guite, Bob MacMillan, and Mike Bloom. Sometimes the players boarded at Muller's home on Highway 8, west of St. Catharines. One of his hockey boarders, Brian McDonald, married his daughter Marlene.

"The players loved Fred Muller," said former Hawks coach Frank Milne. When Milne was suspended for four games in 1970, Muller stepped behind the Hawks bench with no coaching experience and walked away with a perfect 4-0 record.

According to Gatecliff, Muller was a walking and talking public relations department. He never stopped promoting the club — and it paid off. He talked Gladys Crowe, nicknamed the "Swinging Granny" by Gatecliff, into forming the Black Hawks Supporters' Club that followed the team and hosted a variety of activities to drum up attention and support for the Hawks. Trophies were awarded to outstanding players at the end of each season and this practice continued until 1977.

Muller also worked with the Central St.

Catharines Lions Club, which sold programs for home games. Season ticket sales increased steadily as the team improved over the next few years. St. Catharines Junior A hockey once again became a hot ticket in town.

In the spring of 1971, the Hawks won the OHA Junior A championship and faced the Quebec Remparts in the Eastern Canada finals. The abusive actions of fans in games three and four in the Quebec Colisée ended the team's Memorial Cup dream.

After the Hawks won game five decisively in Maple Leaf Gardens, Muller took full responsibility for refusing to return to Quebec for game six and forfeiting the series to the Remparts. "He stood up and took a stand," said Muller's daughter, Marlene McDonald. But it came with a price. The Canadian Amateur Hockey Association suspended Muller for one year.

In 1971 Muller bought Ken Campbell's shares and became the sole owner of the hockey team, but one year later he sold the Hawks to former Niagara Falls Flyers owner Hap Emms. Emms kept the team in the Garden City until 1976 when he moved it to Niagara Falls. In 1978 he sold the Flyers to businessman Reg Quinn. Four years later, the team was in North Bay. The North Bay Centennials were relocated to Saginaw, Michigan, in 2002, and the team was renamed the Saginaw Spirit.

"I'd just been going at it too hard and too long," the 1971 St. Catharines Sportsman of the Year told the *Standard* at the time. "When it started to affect my health, I figured it was time to get out."

Muller stayed retired for a few months before taking on the job of GM for the North American Hockey League Binghamton Dusters. He traveled across Canada recruiting players, often using a helicopter supplied by the Dusters owner Jim Matthews. He was largely responsible for Binghamton's box office success in 1973-74 and was rewarded with a new car for his efforts. While with the Dusters, he was voted the top hockey executive in New York State.

In addition to helping establish pro hockey in Binghamton, Muller found time to act as a consultant for the classic hockey film, *Slap Shot*. After one year with the Dusters, he retired for the second time, dividing his time between Parry Sound and Florida.

In 1987 he died at his home in Ajax, leaving behind his second wife Janine, two daughters, a son and 14 grandchildren.

He's gone but not forgotten. "He was a good character," said former Binghamton Dusters owner Jim Matthews. "He never did any damage to anybody. He only made life interesting for people."

BLACK HAWKS 1962-1963

Junior "A" in Their Future?

Six St. Catharines area boys are included among the 26 trying for places with the Junior Black Hawks this season. Four of them are pictured above. From the left, forward Brian Desbiens, defenceman Art Graham, forwards Jim O'Brien and Don Snider. The Junior Hawks open their pre-season schedule of exhibition games at Garden City Arena Saturday night against the Memorial Cup champion Hamilton Red Wings. Sunday afternoon they move into Hamilton for their second game. Also working out with the club are St. Catharines goaltenders Doug Favell and Tom Purser.

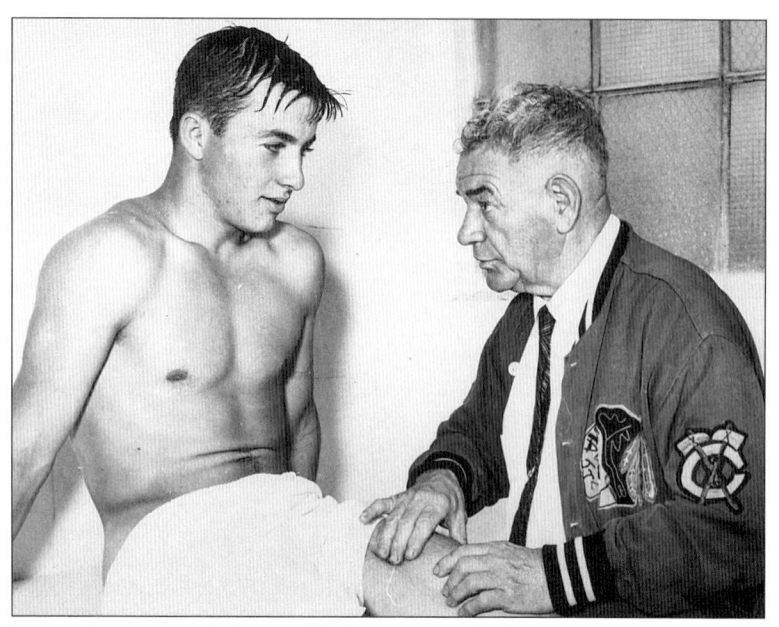

St. Catharines Standard photo

Hawks trainer Jimmy Joy treats one of his players. St. Catharines Museum - *Standard Collection N 5778*

Hawks and Niagara Falls Flyers players battle in the season's first game, a 9-3 loss for St. Catharines on October 26, 1962.

St. Catharines Standard photo

118

BLACK HAWKS 1962-1963

FIRST BLACK HAWKS TEAM MISSES THE PLAYOFFS

ATTENDANCE FIGURES
Average per regular-season game: 1,420
Season's largest crowd: 2,779
Season's smallest crowd: 624

PLAYOFF ROUNDS: 0

1962-1963

GAMES PLAYED	WON	LOST	TIED	FOR	AGAINST	POINTS	FINISH
50	15	24	11	172	224	41	5/6

Leading Scorers

PLAYER	GOALS	ASSISTS	POINTS
Fred Stanfield	28	39	67
John Brenneman	31	27	58
Dennis Hull	19	29	48
Ken Hodge	23	23	46
Poul Popiel	11	34	45

Leading Goaltenders

PLAYER	GP	GA	SO	GAA
Jim Horton	24	90	1	3.75
Jim Keough	21	112	0	5.33

Hawk Ken Laidlaw (7) scores in a 5-2 win over Guelph Royals on November 10, 1962. Behind the net is Dennis Hall (9).
St. Catharines Standard photo

When the first season for the Black Hawks started, the official name for the club was the St. Catharines Hockey Club Limited, with Bill Henry as president and secretary-treasurer. Hugh Feasby was vice-president and Ken Campbell was the general manager.

With 11 graduating players gone from the 1961-62 team and five new netminders trying to replace Roger Crozier, it appeared that the season could be a losing one. It was – starting with the season's opening game, a 9-3 loss to the Niagara Falls Flyers.

For the season's opener at home, a 6-6 tie with Niagara Falls, an Indian head, similar to the one on the Chicago Black Hawks crest, was painted at centre ice in Garden City Arena. The 1,415 fans in attendance were impressed.

One newcomer to the Hawks was 1961-62 Niagara District Junior B scoring champion Jim O'Brien, who had set a new league record with 46 goals. One of the prospects in goal was Doug Favell who played in his first Hawks game against the Guelph Royals in December, 1962. Two St. Catharines Lions Midget hockey players, Stu Roberts and Bill Young, dressed for their first junior A hockey action in the final game of the season.

Low attendance continued to be a concern for the Black Hawks, so the club decided to move home games to Sunday afternoons, starting on December 30, 1962. The first Sunday afternoon contest only attracted 1,498

Hawks Fred Stanfield (10) and Ken Laidlaw (7) on the attack in a 4-3 loss to Niagara Falls Flyers January 20, 1963.
St. Catharines Standard pho

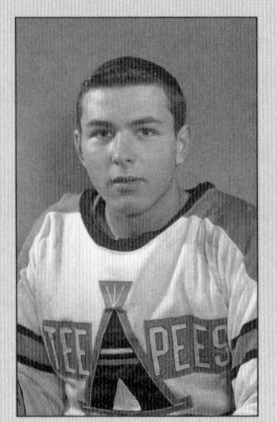

BLACK HAWKS 1962-1963

JOHN BRENNEMAN

John Brenneman broke into the St. Catharines Teepees lineup at age 16 and remained with the team for four seasons, 1959 to 1963. Brenneman had speed to burn.

In 1962-63, the left-winger was the team captain and had his most productive year, scoring 58 points in 48 games.

St. Catharines Standard photo

After turning pro with the CHL St. Louis Braves in 1963, he collected 75 points and was named the league's top rookie and a First Team All-Star. From 1964 to 1969, he saw NHL action in 152 regular-season games with Chicago Black Hawks, New York Rangers, Toronto Maple Leafs, and Oakland Seals. He also played in the CHL, AHL, WHL and IHL. A back injury led to his retirement at age 28.

Today he lives and works in Mississauga.

DON SNIDER

Kitchener-born Don Snider played with the Black Hawks in 1962-63, but an injury sidelined him for most of 1963-64. In 1964, he joined the EHL Nashville Dixie Flyers and his outstanding play led to a front-page picture on the February 20th, 1965 edition of The Hockey News.

Front page courtesy of the Hockey News

After winning the EHL championship with Nashville in 1966, he decided to devote his time to his business, Snider Engraved Specialities (later it was renamed McGee Marking Devices). He also found time to play with the Galt Hornets who won the Allan Cup in 1969.

Today Don lives in Fonthill, Ontario.

For Services Rendered
It was awards' night for St. Catharines Black Hawk players Saturday as they completed their season with a solid win over Hamilton Red Wings. From the left, John Brenneman, most popular player; Fred Stanfield, most valuable player and leading points scorer; Poul Popiel, outstanding defenceman.

St. Catharines Standard photo, March 4, 1963

Billy Reay — St. Catharines Museum, C11,081

fans, but that was the second largest crowd of the season up to that time. A disappointing total of 35,506 fans watched the Black Hawks in 25 home games during the season.

New trophies were created during the season to honour Hawk players. The Hotel Esquire Trophy was awarded to the club's MVP and the first recipient was Fred Stanfield. The Murray Walters Trophy for the team's most popular player went to John Brenneman, and the Constable Transport Trophy for the highest Hawk scorer was awarded to Fred Stanfield. Poul Popiel received the John Steele Memorial Trophy as the club's outstanding defenceman.

The Teepees finished the schedule 28 points behind the league-leading Niagara Falls Flyers, who had future NHLers Bill Goldsworthy, Ron Schock, Gary Dornhoefer, and Terry Crisp in their lineup. For the second time in the city's Junior A history, the team missed the playoffs, finishing in fifth place in the six-team league with only 41 points.

The Hawks lost $15,000 during the season. Rumours were circulating around the city that the Black Hawks would be moved, perhaps to London, and Ken Campbell would be fired. "There's absolutely no truth to any of it," President Bill Henry said. "We're sticking with Ken Campbell and the Hawks are staying in St. Catharines."

In related events outside of St. Catharines, former St. Catharines Teepees coach/manager Rudy Pilous was fired by the Chicago Black Hawks on May 21, 1963, after 5½ seasons in the Windy City. He was replaced by Billy Reay.

Former Teepees boss George Stauffer had his own ideas as to why Pilous got the axe in Chicago. "I think the animus started when Jim Norris wanted Rudy as coach against Ivan's [Chicago Black Hawks GM] wishes," Stauffer wrote in a letter to Jack Gatecliff in May, 1994. "As you know, he negotiated through Conn Smythe [30 mile radius from Toronto]. Thus Rudy was not only started at a higher salary than his boss, but went on to not only win the Stanley Cup, but higher accolades from the press and fans. What an ignominious position for little Tommy! Shortly thereafter, Jim Norris had a debilitating heart attack, putting Ivan in the

BLACK HAWKS 1962-1963

saddle and never to be forgotten revenge, even in the face of Rudy's devastating health and family problems."

Although things were not going well in St. Catharines, former Teepees players were being recognized in pro hockey's best leagues. Four Teepee graduates were on the First and Second NHL All-Star Teams (Stan Mikita, Pierre Pilote, Elmer Vasko, and Bobby Hull). Four of the 12 spots on the AHL's 1963 First and Second Teams were taken by former St. Catharines Junior A players.

The new NHL hockey draft had come into effect on May 31, 1963. Under the new rules, only minor players 17 or over could be approached by the six NHL clubs. Each NHL team could draft up to four teenagers, but had to pay the minor league team $2,000. The beginning of the draft spelled the end of NHL sponsorship that came about in 1967.

Attending a St. Catharines Junior A game in the photo above are from left to right: Art Crooks, "The Bell Ringers" (John and Helen Brown), and Anne Lindsay.

St. Catharines Standard photo, March 16, 1957

St. Catharines Museum - *Bill Argent Collection 2004.95.2*

The Bell Ringers

If you couldn't see them, you could certainly hear the "Bell Ringers" in Garden City Arena. The Bell Ringers were Helen and John Brown, who never missed a St. Catharines Junior A game from 1952 to 1977.

Rudy Pilous named them the Bell Ringers, and they were easy to spot because they wore white Hudson Bay coats to hockey games. Sitting in section M, row B, seats 18 and 19, they rang the bells for the Teepees, Black Hawks, and finally, the Fincups.

After games, the Browns would talk to the players, establishing friendships that lasted long after the players left St. Catharines.

With the loss of major junior hockey in the Garden City, the couple switched their allegiance to the AHL Hamilton Bulldogs.

The bells used by Helen and John are now retired and resting at the St. Catharines Museum. So are the familiar Hudson Bay coats.

On May 16, 2004, the Bell Ringers were part of the procession that led the 1953-54 Teepees to the outdoor ceremony held at the St. Catharines Museum to honour the team which had won the city's first Memorial Cup.

121

DOUG FAVELL: The Goalie Who Got Away

He won a Memorial Cup in 1965 and spent 12 seasons in the NHL, but for the St. Catharines Black Hawks, Doug Favell will always be the goalie who got away.

In the fall of 1962, the St. Catharines Black Hawks were in need of a goalie to replace all-star netminder Roger Crozier, who had played for the team from 1959 to 1962. Coach/GM Ken Campbell invited five goalies to camp and among them was Doug Favell, a 17-year-old St. Catharines native who had enjoyed a very good 1961-62 season with the St. Catharines Junior B team.

"We were told the job was wide open and all of us would get a chance," Favell recalled in August, 2005, in his Garden City home. At the end of training camp, Jim Keough, Jim Horton, and Favell made the team and were told there would be a rotation to see who would stay with the club.

After a long wait, Favell finally got his turn on Friday, December 7, 1962, in a road game against the Guelph Royals. Campbell also told him he would be starting against the Peterborough Petes on Saturday, December 8, 1962, at Garden City Arena.

In his junior A debut, the teenager faced 26 shots in a 2-2 draw. "Favell performed in excellent fashion," the Standard reported.

The Sir Winston Churchill Secondary School student was excited to be playing his next game at home, but when he got to the arena that night, his sweater was not hanging in the dressing room. Netminder Jim Horton's was. When Favell asked Campbell why he wasn't playing, Campbell said, "We changed our minds. You played last night and we want you to play junior B on Sunday afternoon."

"What did I do not to play?" Favell thought to himself. His dad, Doug Favell Sr., asked the same question. "They're screwing the kid," friend Joe Cheevers told Favell's father.

Into the picture stepped Niagara Falls Flyers owner Hap Emms. Emms had seen Favell play against his Stamford Junior B club the previous season and was looking for a replacement for his regular goalie, George Gardner, for 1963-64. He suggested Favell get his release and join the Stamford team for the rest of the season. The young netminder didn't want to leave St. Catharines, but he also wanted to play. Getting his release wasn't going to be easy.

Ken Campbell told Favell Sr. that he didn't have the authority to release his son, and he would have to talk to Billy Reay who was head of scouting for the Chicago Black Hawks at the time.

A few days later, Campbell, Reay and Favell Sr. met at Garden City Arena. Reay was adamant that the young goaltender would stay in St. Catharines and do what he was told. After Campbell left, Favell and Reay continued their discussion in a corner of the arena while a game was going on. Frustrated by Reay's refusal to release his son, Favell grabbed Reay by the tie and the disagreement became physical. In the presence of fans standing and watching the game, Reay was told there would be more of the same every time he (Favell) saw Reay until he released his son. The next day, Doug Favell Jr. got his release, joined Stamford, and started practising with the Flyers.

In the next two seasons, 1963 to 1965, Favell and future NHL star Bernie Parent shared the Flyers netminding duties, and in the spring of 1965 they won Memorial Cup rings. That same year, St. Catharines Black Hawks were eliminated in the first round of the playoffs by Peterborough Petes.

"Hap Emms gave me a chance," Favell said. "I learned a lot."

After turning pro with the Oklahoma Blazers in 1965, Favell made his first start in the NHL in the Philadelphia Flyers first league game in 1967 and stayed for six years. In 1973 he was traded to the Toronto Maple Leafs and then it was on to Colorado where his NHL career ended in 1979. He played 373 regular-season NHL games, winning 123 with a goals-against average of 3.17.

During his hockey career, Favell also excelled as a high-scoring lacrosse forward. He won a Minto Cup with the Oshawa Green Gaels in September of 1964.

"Lacrosse was my love, my passion," he told the St. Catharines Standard in 2005. In October of 2005 Favell was inducted into the Ontario Lacrosse Hall of Fame.

Today Fav runs a wholesale car brokerage business and lives in his hometown. He's the one who got away and it changed his life.

Doug Favell (left) with Niagara Falls coach Bill Long (centre) and Bernie Parent
Courtesy of Doug Favell

Black Hawks goaltending candidates for 1962-63, October 9, 1962. From left to right: Jim Keough, Bob Groh, Jim Horton, Doug Favell, and Tom Purser
St. Catharines Standard photo

BLACK HAWKS 1963-1964

HAWKS TOP SCORER FRED STANFIELD WINS THE MAX KAMINSKY TROPHY

ATTENDANCE FIGURES
Average per regular-season game: 1,470
Season's largest crowd: 3,637
Season's smallest crowd: 678

PLAYOFF ROUNDS: 2
Eliminated Oshawa 4-2
Lost to Montreal Junior Canadiens 4-2-1

1963-1964

GAMES PLAYED	WON	LOST	TIED	FOR	AGAINST	POINTS	FINISH
56	29	20	7	244	215	65	3/8

Leading Scorers

PLAYER	GOALS	ASSISTS	POINTS
Fred Stanfield	34	75	109
Dennis Hull	48	49	97
Ken Hodge	37	51	88
Brian McDonald	31	44	75
Doug Jarrett	10	51	61

Leading Goaltenders

PLAYER	GP	GA	SO	GAA
Bob Sneddon	51.33	184	4	3.59
Bob Groh	4.33	25	0	5.77

Hawks coach Ken Campbell with his players at practice on September 29, 1963. Left to right: Ken Campbell, Bob Groh, Fred Stanfield, Dave Green, and Brian McDonald
St. Catharines Standard photo

For the 1963-64 season the Black Hawks scheduled home games for Sunday afternoons, despite the announcement that Toronto Maple Leafs road games would be carried at the Capitol Theatre in downtown St. Catharines on Sunday evenings.

Toronto Marlboros were re-admitted to the league and the Oshawa Generals also returned, bringing the number of clubs up to eight. Oshawa played its home games in Trenton and Bowmanville until a new arena was built in Oshawa. The Guelph franchise was switched to Kitchener.

Fifteen-year-old Parry Sound native Bobby Orr made his OHA Junior A League debut with the Generals and made an immediate impact. He was picked for the OHA First All-Star Team with Black Hawk Doug Jarrett, who would go on to star in the NHL with Chicago Black Hawks.

At the beginning of the season things did not go well for the Hawks. The team lost three of its first four games and coach Ken Campbell was not

Hawk Doug Shelton (15) tests the Peterborough Petes netminder in a 4-3 win December 15, 1963.
St. Catharines Standard photo

BLACK HAWKS 1963-1964

DOUG JARRETT

6-foot-3 defenceman Doug Jarrett spent four years with St. Catharines (1960 to 1964) before turning pro with the Chicago Black Hawks in 1964.

He was the first London Ontario native to make it to the NHL and spent 11 years with the Hawks and two seasons with the New York Rangers. He came to be known as Chairman of the Boards for his bruising checks along the boards.

St. Catharines Museum - Standard Collection N 5680

His career, which included 775 regular-season NHL games and 220 points, ended with a Guy Lafleur slap shot that hit his ankle and damaged his back in 1976-77.

BOB SNEDDON

Montreal-born Bob Sneddon won 29 games with the St. Catharines Black Hawks in 1963-64.

His pro career began with the IHL Port Huron-Muskegon team in 1964. In a minor pro career that lasted 13 years, Sneddon was a First Team IHL All-Star in 1966 and won the James Norris Memorial Trophy (fewest goals-against) in the same year. He had a five-game stint with the California Golden Seals in 1970-71.

St. Catharines Standard photo

After his pro career was finished, he played OHA Senior A hockey with the Brantford Alexanders in 1977-78.

---

satisfied with goalie Bob Groh and St. Catharines Junior B netminder Tom Purser.

In the meantime, former Windsor Junior B goalie Bob Sneddon turned down an opportunity to be the backup netminder for the Hamilton Red Wings. Detroit Red Wings assigned him to the IHL Windsor Bulldogs and removed him from their protected list. Chicago Black Hawks immediately put Sneddon on their protected list, and five hours later he was in the net for St. Catharines, leading the club to a 6-1 win. Campbell had found the goalie he needed to make the "big save" for the Hawks.

As the Black Hawks improved on the ice, attendance picked up. The club earned 16 of a possible 18 points in January and February, and a home crowd of 3,000 showed up on February 2, 1964.

The Kaminsky Trophy (most gentlemanly player), which was created in honour of former Teepees coach Max Kaminsky, was presented to Fred Stanfield in 1964. It was replaced with the William Hanley Trophy in 1974 and was named in honour of the man who had been the secretary-manager of the OHA for 25 years.

Stanfield led the team in points for the second

DOUG JARRETT (5) SPRAWLS AMONG FOREST OF ARMS, LEGS
Close Play Came in First Period at Hawk End of Rink

St. Catharines Standard, November 25, 1963

consecutive season with 109 and was voted the club's MVP.

After finishing in third place in the standings, the Teepees met Oshawa Generals in the first round of the playoffs. The Hawks eliminated the Generals in six games and then faced the Montreal Junior

1963-64 Black Hawks high-scoring line of (left to right) Chuck Kelly, Brian McDonald, and Ken Hodge, November 10, 1963

St. Catharines Standard photo

BLACK HAWKS 1963-1964

Canadiens who won the series in seven games. Fred Stanfield had an outstanding playoff, scoring 27 points, including 15 goals in 13 games. Ken Hodge collected 23 points. Brian McDonald and Doug Jarrett with 17 points each and Dennis Hull with 16, also had strong playoff performances.

With an increase in overall attendance of 23,000, the 1963-64 club almost broke even and had helped to re-establish junior A hockey as a major sport in the Garden City. ■

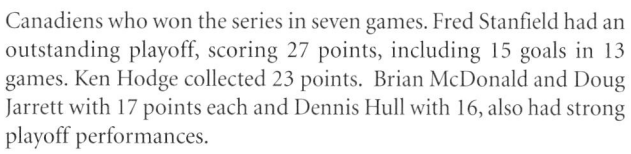

Fred Stanfield, most valuable player and leading scorer 1963-64
St. Catharines Standard photo

Award Winners 1963-64
(Left to right) Doug Jarrett (outstanding defenceman), Fred Muller (Hawks president), Fred Stanfield (top scorer), Bill Henry (Hawks immediate past president), and Dennis Hull (most popular)
St. Catharines Standard photo

Brian McDonald, the Hawks top rookie of 1963-64
St. Catharines Museum - Hewitt Collection, C10,716

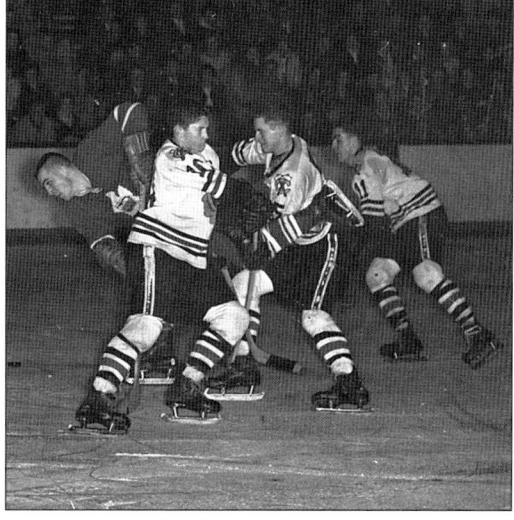

Hawk players Fred Stanfield (left), and Doug Jarrett (right), sandwich Toronto Marlie Grant Moore during a 5-2 victory February 2, 1964.
St. Catharines Standard photo

DENNIS HULL

Dennis Hull, who followed his brother Bobby to St Catharines in 1960, spent four seasons in the Garden City and closed out his junior career in 1964 with 48 goals and 97 points.

Dennis, who some say had a harder shot than his brother Bobby, had a very successful 14-year NHL career, mainly with the Chicago Black Hawks. He played 959 regular-season games and accumulated 654 points, including 303 goals. In seven seasons, the Point Anne Ontario native had 20 or more goals, hitting a high of 40 in 1970-71. In the playoffs Hull was outstanding, collecting 67 points in 104 contests.

In 1972 Hull played with Team Canada in the famed Summit Series, scoring four points in four games. It was the highlight of his hockey career. The left winger also saw action in five NHL all-star games between 1969 and 1974.

After graduating from Brock University in St. Catharines, he taught school in Canada and then the USA. Today, Dennis, who lives on a cattle farm in Cobourg, Ontario, is a popular speaker, master of ceremonies, and head table guest, traveling throughout North America. You can learn more about Dennis in his book, The Third Best Hull.

Hull in a Teepees uniform October 17, 1960.
St. Catharines Standard photo

Dennis Hull (9) scores against the Niagara Falls Flyers in a 5-5 tie December 8, 1963.
St. Catharines Standard photo

BLACK HAWKS 1963-1964

18 THE ST. CATHARINES STANDARD, Monday, Feb. 24, 1964

OPPOSING OLD TIMER TEAMS FACE CAMERA

The National Hockey League Old Timers pose in a group photo before their game here last night. Front row, from the left, John Henderson, Roy Conacher, Sid Smith, Gus Bodnar, Herbie Cain, Gus Bodnar, Wally Stanowski, Murray Henderson, Cal Gardner. Back row, Bob Goldham, Harry Watson, Brian Cullen, Jackie Hamilton, Murray Ezzard, Coach Hank Goldup, Trainer John Lunau.

St. Catharines Standard, February 23, 1964

Fans line up for a hockey game at Garden City Arena on January 6, 1963.
St. Catharines Standard photo

Opposing the NHL team in the Grantham Optimist-sponsored game was a group of former St. Catharines Junior A players augmented by Junior Hawk Coach Ken Campbell and scout John Choyce. Front row from the left: Skip Teal, Ken Croft, Carl Smelle, John Choyce, Connie Switzer, Al Kellogg. Second row, Porky Douglas, Jim Dawdy, Denny White, Bibber O'Hearn, Archie Katzman, Tom Buck, Ken Campbell, Nip O'Hearn. Back row: Trainer Jimmy Joy, Bill Altoft, Tom Smelle, Bill Buschlen, Dean McBride, Obie O'Brien, Jack Gatecliff, and Coach Vic Teal.

St. Catharines Standard photo, February 23, 1964

New Garden City Arena monster ice cleaner, January 7, 1964
St. Catharines Standard photo

126

FRED MULLER - THE HAWKS NEW PRESIDENT

Former Hawks President Bill Henry (left) shakes hands with new President Fred Muller (right) while GM Ken Campbell stands between the two men.

St. Catharines Museum - *Janine Muller Collection, C11,022*

ATTENDANCE FIGURES
Average per regular-season game: 1,612
Season's largest crowd: 2,809
Season's smallest crowd: 821

PLAYOFF ROUNDS: 1
Eliminated by Peterborough 4-1

1964-1965

GAMES PLAYED	WON	LOST	TIED	FOR	AGAINST	POINTS	FINISH
56	19	28	9	236	253	47	6/8

Leading Scorers

PLAYER	GOALS	ASSISTS	POINTS
Ken Hodge	63	61	124
Brian McDonald	47	61	108
Wayne Maki	29	48	77
Mickey Cherevaty	17	26	43
Bob Sicinski	10	26	36

Leading Goaltenders

PLAYER	GP	GA	SO	GAA
Bob Groh	20	86	0	4.30
Bob Taylor	18	89	0	4.94

In April of 1964, Hawks president Bill Henry resigned because of illness and business responsibilities. He sold his shares to the Chicago Black Hawks. Hawk players had often dropped into Henry's recreation room in his Russell Avenue home to relax and enjoy themselves.

In June of 1964, Fred Muller was appointed president of the Black Hawks. He replaced Henry, who had held the post for three years. At the same time, coach/GM Ken Campbell was named the Chicago Black Hawks director of player personnel. Campbell turned his coaching duties over to former hockey player Chirp Brenchley, but maintained his position as the St. Catharines GM.

In the fall of 1964, crowds were averaging about 1,500 at the start of the season, but promotional work by Fred Muller and George Bird resulted in attendances of 2,000 at home games by the end of the year. Overall, the club drew 4,000 more fans than in the 1963-64 regular-season games, despite finishing the season in sixth place, three notches lower than the previous year.

It's interesting to note that there was a curfew for Saturday night hockey games in Toronto. No hockey contest could be played between 12 midnight and 1 p.m. Sunday.

Early in the season, winger Garry MacMillan became known as "The People's Choice" because his robust play, hard body checks, and tireless effort created a stir every time he stepped onto the ice. At the end of the season he was voted the club's most colorful player.

On December 15, 1964, the Hawks played the first OHA Junior A game in the new Oshawa Civic Auditorium, losing to the Generals 6-4. In 2005 Oshawa city council announced plans for a new arena in the

Familiar Faces

Six members of the 1964-65 St. Catharines Black Hawks are working out with Buffalo Bisons and St. Louis Braves at Garden City Arena this week. From the left, Tom Reid, Dave Reid, Ross Eichler, Mickey Cherevaty, Brian McDonald and Wayne Maki. In background are Ian Cushenan and Jim O'Brien, also former members of St. Catharines junior teams. The Bisons open their exhibition schedule here Friday against the American Hockey League champion Rochester Americans.

—Staff photo
St. Catharines Standard

BLACK HAWKS 1964-1965

EDGAR BRENCHLEY

"Chirp" Brenchley, a native of London, England, grew up in Niagara Falls and played in the Eastern Hockey League for 15 years.

His hockey career highlight occurred in the 1936 Olympics when he played with the British team that stunned the hockey world by beating Canada 2-1 on an outdoor rink in a heavy snowstorm. Brenchley scored the winning goal against Canadian netminder Dinty Moore of Port Colborne. The British club went on to win the European and World championships the same year.

After coaching junior hockey from 1967 to 1974, he scouted for the Pittsburgh Penguins and the Washington Capitals.

Brenchley, who was inducted into the Niagara Falls Sports Wall of Fame in 1990, passed away in 1975.

Chirp Brenchley with Hershey in the EAHL
Ernie Fitzsimmons Collection

BRIAN McDONALD

Brian McDonald played with the St. Catharines Black Hawks from 1963 to 1965, collecting 183 points in those two seasons.

His pro career began with the CHL St. Louis Braves in 1965. After 20 games in the NHL with Chicago Black Hawks and Buffalo Sabres, he spent five years in the WHA. He also played in the WHL and the NAHL.

The 5-foot-11 centre had his best pro year with the CHL Dallas Black Hawks in 1967-68, scoring 69 points, including 24 goals. He was with Dallas when it won the league championship in 1969, scoring 13 points in 11 playoff games

The Toronto native is retired and lives in St. Catharines.

St. Catharines Museum - Hewitt Collection, C10,715

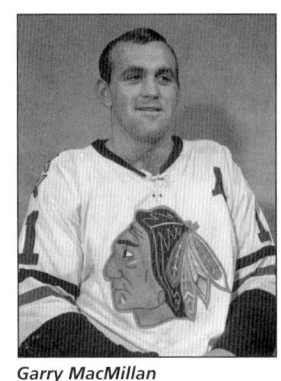

---

downtown district, and on Friday, November 3, 2006, the new General Motors Centre was officially opened, with the Generals hosting the Owen Sound Attack.

The Hawks scored 236 goals, but allowed 253 compared to the Memorial Cup-winning Niagara Falls Flyers who gave up only 168. Two of the club's netminders, Bob Groh and Jim Keough, who had played 38 of the team's 56 regular-season games, left the team in 1965 to play university hockey in the United States on hockey scholarships.

Ken Hodge was the league's leading points-getter with 124 points, including 63 goals. Brian McDonald with 108 and Wayne Maki with 77 points were the team's second and third leading scorers respectively.

The Hawks lasted one round and five games in the playoffs against the Peterborough Petes. Hodge led the team in playoff scoring with ten points in five games, followed by Maki, who had seven. The Petes were led by future NHL stars Mickey Redmond, Andre Lacroix, and Gary Monahan.

Although the club lost $31,000 at the end of the year, Chicago picked up the tab. Muller was convinced that the team could be put back on a paying basis. ■

Garry MacMillan
St. Catharines Standard photo

Captain Ross Eichler
St. Catharines Museum - Cornelius Collection, C10,649

Hawks 1964-65 defence duo of Bill Carson (3) on the left and Paul Terbenche (5) on the right, February 3, 1965
St. Catharines Standard photo

Netminder Bob Groh in action February 3, 1965
St. Catharines Standard photo

Hawk forward Bob Sicinski takes a shot at Oshawa goalie Dennis Gibson during a 6-1 win on February 7, 1965.
St. Catharines Standard photo

BLACK HAWKS 1964-1965

Hawk Ken Hodge (16) drills the puck at the Montreal Canadiens goalie Fernand Rivard. Ross Eichler (4) and Stu Roberts (9) are in on the play. Hawks lost 4-3 on January 1, 1965.
St. Catharines Standard photo

Hawk Wayne Maki (18) on the ice scores against the Hamilton Red Wings. Celebrating the goal are Ken Hodge (16), Bob Sicinski, to the right of the net, and Brian McDonald jumping for joy to the extreme right. The Hawks won the game 4-3 on February 14, 1965.
St. Catharines Standard photo

KEN HODGE

In 1964-65 Birmingham England native Ken Hodge became the Hawks team leader, and in his fourth season with the team, led the league in scoring with 124 points, including 63 goals. He was a unanimous choice for the OHA All-Star Team on right wing.

Hodge went on to enjoy a distinguished NHL career playing 13 seasons with Chicago, Boston, where he won Stanley Cups in 1970 and 1972, and New York. He played in three NHL all-star games. His most productive NHL years were 1970-71 and 1973-74 when he collected 105 points each season. In 881 regular-season contests, he collected 328 goals and 800 points.

Today Hodge lives in Massachusetts.

St. Catharines Museum
- Janine Muller Collection, C11,056

WAYNE MAKI

Sault Ste. Marie native Wayne Maki followed in the footsteps of his brother Chico and played with the St. Catharines Black Hawks in 1964-65.

The left winger turned pro with the St. Louis Braves in 1965 and joined the Chicago Black Hawks in 1967-68. From Chicago, he moved to St. Louis, and then to Vancouver, where he ended his career in 1973. He had his best year with the Vancouver Canucks in 1970-71 when he earned 63 points, including 25 goals. In 246 NHL regular-season games he had 136 points.

Maki died in 1974 from a brain tumor.

St. Catharines Museum
- Cornelius Collection, C10,667

CARL LINDROS

In the fall of 1964, Ken Campbell signed Chatham native Carl Lindros to a junior contract. Lindros made the team, but decided to return to his hometown. He would go on to star with his Chatham high school football team and then the Western University Mustangs.

Twenty-seven years later, his son Eric starred with the Oshawa Generals and was named 1991 Canadian Major Junior Player of the Year. He began a distinguished NHL career with the Philadelphia Flyers the next year, scoring 41 goals in his rookie season.

BLACK HAWKS 1964-1965

PAUL TERBENCHE

Port Hope native Paul Terbenche starred on defence for the St. Catharines Black Hawks from 1964 to 1966.

He started his pro career with the CHL Dallas Black Hawks in 1966 and made his NHL debut with Chicago a year later. In 1969 he was with Dallas when it won the league championship.

From 1970 to 1974 he was with the Buffalo Sabres and then joined the WHA for five seasons, winning an Avco Cup with the Winnipeg Jets in 1979. He finished his career with the CHL Birmingham Bulls in 1981.

Today he lives in Cobourg, Ontario.

St. Catharines Museum - Cornelius Collection, C10,683

BOB TAYLOR

Calgary native Bob Taylor spent part of the 1964-65 season with the St. Catharines Black Hawks. The netminder did not play the next season because of injuries, and then after two years of senior hockey in Calgary turned pro with the EHL New Jersey Devils in 1968.

Taylor didn't play a game in the NHL until 1971-72 when he donned the pads for six games with the Philadelphia Flyers. For the next five years he was in and out of the Flyers lineup before finishing his NHL career with Pittsburgh in 1975-76. He played 46 regular-season NHL games, winning 15 and posting a 4.10 goals-against average.

After his pro career, Taylor was a colour analyst for Philadelphia radio and television broadcasts.

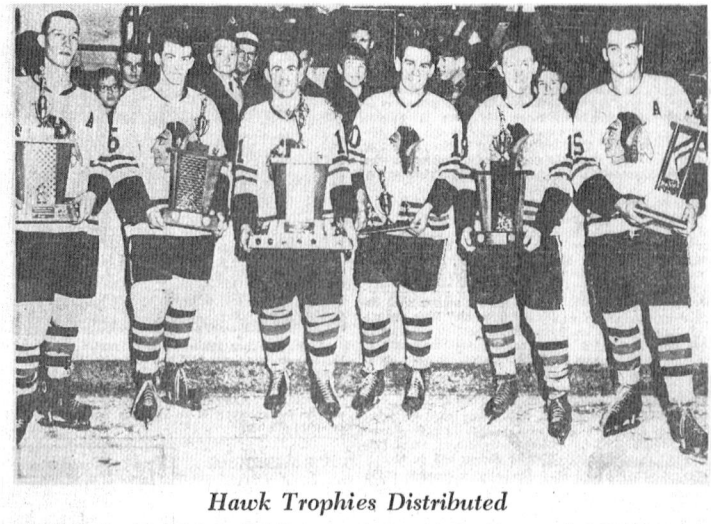

Bob Taylor with the EHL New Jersey Devils
Ernie Fitzsimmons Collection

Hawk Trophies Distributed

The six members of the St. Catharines Black Hawks who were awarded team trophies Sunday are pictured here. From the left, Ross Eichler, most gentlemanly player; Paul Terbenche, outstanding defenceman; Garry MacMillan, most colorful player; Bob Sicinski, most improved player; Wayne Maki, outstanding rookie; Ken Hodge, top points scorer.
—Staff photo

St. Catharines Standard

Hawk players whoop it up after a 7-3 win over Toronto Marlies on February 2, 1965.

St. Catharines Standard photo

BLACK HAWKS 1965-1966

BRENCHLEY OUT AND O'FLAHERTY IN AS HAWKS COACH

ATTENDANCE FIGURES
Average per regular-season game: 1,734
Season's largest crowd: 2,979
Season's smallest crowd: 1,089

PLAYOFF ROUNDS: 1
Eliminated by Oshawa 4-3

1965-1966

GAMES PLAYED	WON	LOST	TIED	FOR	AGAINST	POINTS	FINISH
48	15	26	7	182	231	37	8/9

Leading Scorers

PLAYER	GOALS	ASSISTS	POINTS
Doug Shelton	36	24	60
Ken Laidlaw	25	34	59
Bob Sicinski	17	32	49
Kerry Bond	20	21	41
Paul Terbenche	5	31	36

Leading Goaltenders

PLAYER	GP	GA	SO	GAA
Peter McDuffe	24	126	0	5.25
Larry Holmes	23	99	0	4.24

Hawks brass watch the team practise on September 17, 1965. Front row: Obie O'Brien, coach Chirp Brenchley and Fred Muller. With a notepad, in the next row up, is Hawks GM Ken Campbell.
St. Catharines Standard photo

Hawks coach Chirp Brenchley talks things over with Kerry Bond October 27, 1965. St. Catharines Standard photo

Chicago Black Hawks did not hold their training camp in St. Catharines in the fall of 1965 for the first time since 1956. Strained relations between the two clubs were rumoured to be the reason for the shift.

The OHA Junior A League opened with nine teams with the addition of the London Nationals. Rudy Pilous was back in the league as coach/manager of the Hamilton Red Wings, but only for one season. Another former Teepees coach, Gus Bodnar, was the bench boss of the Toronto Marlboros.

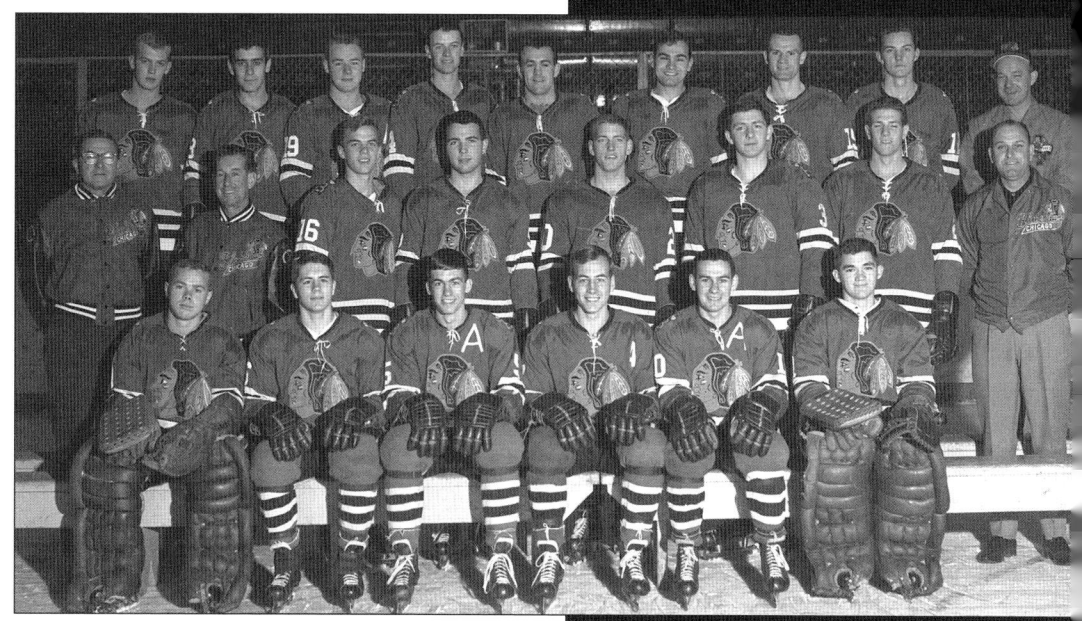

Front row: Peter McDuffe, Barry Salovaara, Paul Terbenche, Ken Laidlaw, Bob Sicinski, Larry Holmes. Second row: Fred Muller (president), Chirp Brenchley (coach), Ritchie Bayes, Andy Culligan, Kerry Bond, Glen Sherwood, Tom Reid, Ken Campbell (GM). Back row: Bobby Taylor, Jan Popiel, Maurice (Moe) L'Abbe, Willie Terry, Garry MacMillan, Steve Latinovich, Doug Shelton, Jim Stanfield, Bruce Beaupit (trainer)
St. Catharines Standard photo

BLACK HAWKS 1965-1966

JOHN (PEANUTS) O'FLAHERTY

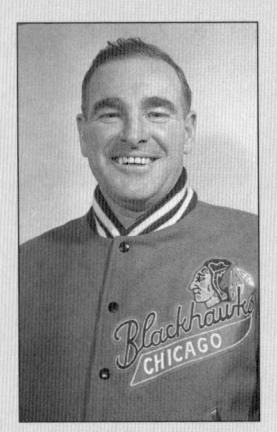

As a youngster, John O'Flaherty sold peanuts in Maple Leaf Gardens during NHL games and someone called him "Peanuts." The name stuck.

The Toronto native, who took the Black Hawks coaching reins on December 20, 1965, had a long playing career, winning a Memorial Cup with the Toronto Nationals in 1936 and playing in the AHL along with a few NHL games with the New York Americans and Brooklyn Americans from 1940 to 1942.

Before coming to the Garden City, O'Flaherty had coached at nearly every level. He was GM of the Toronto Marlies from 1961 to 1963, before taking over the coaching duties for the Junior B Dixie Beehives in 1964.

The father of nine children (six boys and three girls) died July 16, 2008 in Mississauga, Ontario.

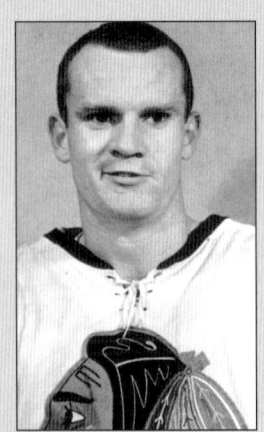

St. Catharines Standard photo

DOUG SHELTON

Doug Shelton was born in Woodstock, Ontario, and played one year of junior B before joining the Hawks in 1963. After two so-so seasons, Shelton scored 36 goals and earned 60 points to lead the team in his last junior year, 1965-66.

The right winger spent most of his four-year pro career in the AHL, CHL and WHL, with the exception of five games with Chicago Black Hawks in 1967-68.

His best pro year was with Dallas Black Hawks in 1967-68 when he collected 58 points in 65 regular-season contests. He was with Dallas when it won the CHL championship in 1969.

He now resides in Dallas, Texas.

Ernie Fitzsimmons Collection

Hawks Jan Popiel (8), J.P. LeBlanc (19), and Doug Shelton (15) are on the attack in a 9-8 win over Oshawa Generals January 16, 1966. Lying on the ice to the extreme right is future NHL superstar Bobby Orr.
St. Catharines Standard photo

Chicago Black Hawks scout Jack Davison (left) gives some advice to Hawk players.
St. Catharines Museum - Janine Muller Collection, C11,024

Black Hawks team bus used in 1965-66 season
St. Catharines Standard photo

Obie O'Brien
St. Catharines Museum - Janine Muller Collection, C11,076

At the start of the season, the Hawks executives bought three station wagons and made road trips by car instead of bus. The club hoped to save $5,000 by making the switch.

On December 3, 1965, coach Chirp Brenchley was fired because he couldn't get his hockey knowledge through to the players. He was given a job scouting for Chicago Black Hawks. "We feel we have sufficient talent to be at, or near the top of the Junior A League," manager Ken Campbell said.

Brenchley was replaced first by former Teepee and Hershey Bear star, Ellard (Obie) O'Brien, the twelfth coach in the 23-year history of the club, and then by Dixie Beehives coach Johnny (Peanuts) O'Flaherty on December 20, 1965.

O'Brien, who had captained the AHL Hershey Bears for six seasons and had two Calder Cups on his resume, had enjoyed two successful seasons coaching the St. Catharines Junior Bees. The St. Garden City native had a

BLACK HAWKS 1965-1966

Hawks GM Ken Campbell (hat) introduces Peanuts O'Flaherty to the players. (Left to right) Ken Laidlaw, Kerry Bond, Brian McKenny, Peter McDuffe, Barry Salovaara, Lou Polgrabia, Bob Sicinski, Ritchie Bayes
St. Catharines Standard photo

Fred Muller, Obie O'Brien, Peanuts O'Flaherty, Jack Davison, and Ken Campbell look over Hawks contracts.
St. Catharines Museum - Janine Muller Collection, C11,041

permanent sales job and filled in until 46-year-old O'Flaherty took over behind the bench.

"Don't think he [O'Flaherty] wasn't chosen carefully," Black Hawks GM Ken Campbell said. "I had 40 applicants. He's the kind of coach who keeps the players on their toes."

O'Flaherty soon had the attention of his players. "He is easily the most demonstrative coach in hockey, constantly hollering encouragement and various other things at his players," former *Toronto Star* hockey reporter Frank Orr wrote at the time.

Hawks president Fred Muller was convinced that O'Flaherty could shatter a plate glass window at 90 paces.

Despite a poor start by the club with only six wins in its first 21 games, attendance was up slightly from the previous year. On Sunday, February 6, 1966, CFTO televised the first live hockey game in St.

JIM STANFIELD

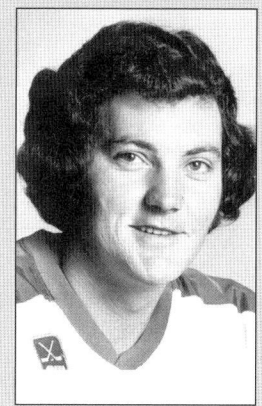

Jim Stanfield played for the Black Hawks from 1964 to 1966 and finished his junior career with the London Nationals in 1967.

The Toronto native began his pro career with the CHL Dallas Black Hawks in 1967 and won the league championship in 1969. In 1971 he won a Calder Cup with the Springfield Kings.

Jim Stanfield with the WHL San Diego Gulls
Ernie Fitzsimmons Collection

Although he spent most of his ten-year career in the WHL, he did see action with the Los Angeles Kings in seven games. His most productive season was with the Spokane Jets in 1974-75 when he earned 102 points in 47 regular-season games.

The centre/right winger retired in 1977 and now lives in Spokane, Washington.

BARRY SALOVAARA

Defenceman Barry Salovaara played for the Black Hawks from 1965 to 1968 and was the team's captain in his last year.

The Cooksville native started his pro career with the EHL Greensboro Generals in 1968. He had his best pro year with the Generals in 1970-71 when he earned 68 points in 72 regular-season games.

St. Catharines Standard photo

He also played in the CHL and AHL until he debuted in the NHL with Detroit Red Wings in 1974-75. He retired in 1976 after his second season with the Wings.

He now lives in Dorset, Ontario.

133

BLACK HAWKS 1965-1966

BILL BIRD

Growing up in St. Catharines, Bill Bird loved sports, and after graduating from Ryerson's three-year course in Radio and Television Arts, he got the opportunity to start a sports broadcasting career that lasted for more than 35 years.

While attending Ryerson, Bird got his first real experience with sports broadcasting when he was hired by the Toronto Maple Leafs to act as gofer at home games for his broadcasting idol, Foster Hewitt, who did the play-by-play in the gondola located high above the ice surface in the Gardens.

While still in school in 1964-65, he was hired by local radio station CKTB to read the news, act as a deejay, and perform other duties around the studio on weekends. This led to a full-time job in 1965. He started out by reading the news and covering newsworthy events such as city council meetings.

At the time, Rex Stimers, who had been broadcasting St. Catharines Junior A hockey games for years, decided to do the play-by-play for home games only. Bird was asked if he would like to do the road games, and he jumped at the chance to do something he had dreamed about as a youngster.

"Rex was a character," Bird said. "He would have been the equivalent of Don Cherry back then, except he did the play-by-play." Bird recalled that whenever someone asked Stimers what he did all day, because he was heard only once a day on his sports show, Rex would say, "I'm out doing research."

Stimers died in April of 1966 and Bird then became the play-by-play announcer for all St. Catharines Black Hawks games from 1966 to 1974. His colour man during that time was Stimers' former pal and brother-in-law, Tommy Garriock. Sometimes Standard sports editor Jack Gatecliff would be in the broadcast booth with him.

In 1974 CKTB decided it was no longer going to broadcast Hawks games. At the same time, Bird, who had been appointed sports director at CKTB in 1967, was encouraged by his friend Terry O'Malley to apply for a sports announcing position at Global, Toronto's new TV station. He got the job and covered the sports scene for Global for the next 25 years, leaving in 1999.

After writing for the Ontario Jockey Club for several months, in 2001 Bird landed a job with CBC Radio in Toronto, where he currently reads the news and also does some writing for TV News.

Bill now lives in Pickering, Ontario.

St. Catharines Standard photo

Catharines. The Hawks defeated the Toronto Marlboros 4-3 before a crowd of 2,003 at Garden City Arena.

For the first time since 1960, the OHA held an all-star game in 1966 in Niagara Falls. The All-Stars defeated the Niagara Falls Flyers 8-4. Paul Terbenche and Doug Shelton represented the Hawks on the All-Star Team.

By the end of the season, the club finished eighth out of nine teams. Starting on January 2, 1966, all Sunday games were played in the afternoon and the club didn't lose a Sunday contest in the last nine weeks of the season. However, the overall attendance was down about 1,300 from 1964-65. Doug Shelton led the team in scoring with 60 points, including 36 goals.

The Black Hawks lasted one round in the playoffs as they were eliminated by the Oshawa Generals, who were led by future NHL superstar Bobby Orr, Wayne Cashman, Nick Beverley, and Danny O'Shea. In the seven-game series, Ken Laidlaw led the team in scoring with ten points, followed by Kerry Bond and Ritchie Bayes who had seven points each.

"It wasn't a tremendously successful year, but I think I'm safe in saying we provided a lot of good entertainment for the fans," president Fred Muller said.

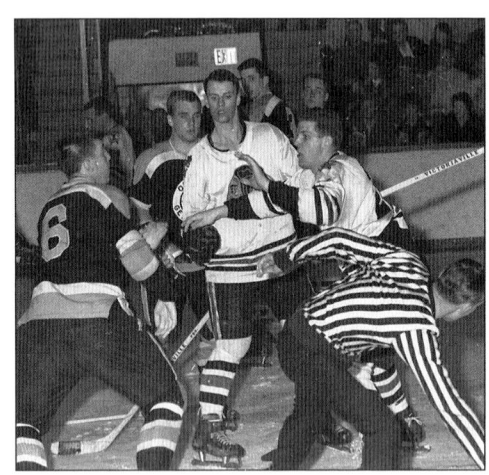

Oshawa General Barry Wilkins (6) goes at it with Hawk Tom Reid (right) while defenceman Willie Terry stands in the middle. The Hawks won the March 18, 1966 playoff game 4-3.
St. Catharines Standard photo

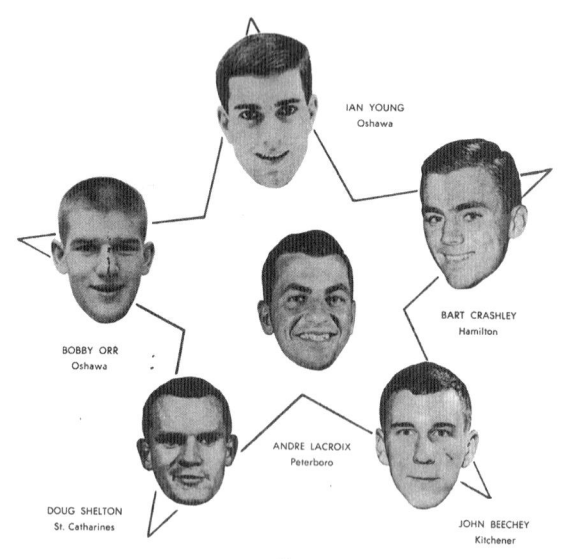

OHA All-Stars
IAN YOUNG - Oshawa
BART CRASHLEY - Hamilton
BOBBY ORR - Oshawa
ANDRE LACROIX - Peterboro
DOUG SHELTON - St. Catharines
JOHN BEECHEY - Kitchener
St. Catharines Museum - *Saveall Collection 2004.88.30.2*

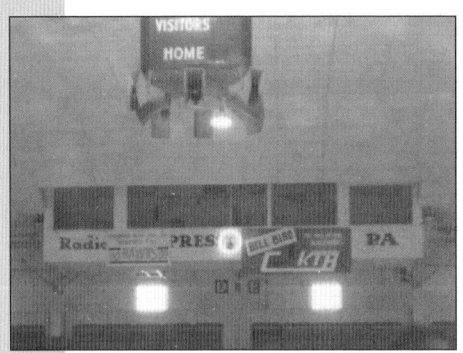

CKTB broadcasting booth in Garden City Arena
Janine Muller Collection

Black Hawks broadcasters, reporters and photographers taken shortly before Rex Stimers' death on April 1, 1966. Front row: Tommy Garriock, Rex Stimers, Bill Bird. Back row: Craig Swayze, John McTaggart, Jack Gatecliff, Don Sinclair
St. Catharines Museum - *Garden City Arena Collection N 5681*

BLACK HAWKS 1965-1966

Hawks celebrate after clinching a playoff spot with a 3-2 win over London on February 27, 1966.
St. Catharines Standard photo

TROPHY WINNERS — 1965-66
Front row: Doug Shelton – Most Points; Garry MacMillan – Most Popular Player; Ken Laidlaw – Most Valuable; Back row: Willie Terry – Most Gentlemanly Player; Ritchie Bayes – Rookie-of-the-Year (tie); Barry Salovaara – Rookie-of-the-Year (tie); Larry Holmes – Most Improved; Paul Terbenche – Best Defenceman
St. Catharines Standard photo

BLACK HAWKS 1966-1967

ST. CATHARINES BLACK HAWKS
Garden City Arena, St. Catharines — Ontario
Farm Club of Chicago Black Hawks

TEAM RULES

PLAYERS MUST BE DRESSED AND READY TO GO ON THE ICE 5 MINUTES BEFORE PRACTICE.

GAMES
PLAYERS MUST BE DRESSED WITH SHIRT AND TIE AND SUIT OR SPORTS JACKET FOR GAME. FOR ROAD GAMES THEY MUST WEAR SPORTS JACKET OR SUIT WITH SHIRT AND TIE OR SPORTS SHIRT.

HOME GAMES
SUNDAY GAMES- PLAYERS MUST REPORT TO THE DRESSING ROOM BEFORE 6 P.M.

TUESDAY GAMES- PLAYERS MUST REPORT TO THE DRESSING ROOM BEFORE 6.45 P.M.

IF ANY PLAYER IS NOT DRESSING FOR THE GAME, HE MUST STAY REGARDLESS.

PLAYERS MUST CARRY THEIR GATE PASSES AT ALL TIMES AND NOT LEND THEM TO ANYONE.

ROAD GAMES
PLAYERS MUST REPORT TO DRESSING ROOM ½ HOUR BEFORE BUS DEPARTURE.

ALL PLAYERS MUST ACCOMPANY TEAM WITH EQUIPMENT READY TO PLAY.

DRESSING ROOM
PLAYERS MUST HANG UP THEIR OWN EQUIPMENT AFTER GAMES AND PRACTICES.

THE TEAM TRAINER IS IN CHARGE OF THE DRESSING ROOM AND COMES UNDER THE JURISDICTION OF THE COACH.

CURFEW
ALL PLAYERS MUST BE IN THEIR HOMES BEFORE 11.00 P.M. NIGHT BEFORE GAME. NO PLAYER WILL LEAVE THE CITY UNLESS PERMISSION IS GRANTED. PLAYERS ARE EXPECTED TO ACT GENTLEMANLY AND COURTEOUS AT ALL TIMES. CURFEW AFTER GAMES 12.00 P.M. SUNDAYS 12.30 P.M. WEEK NIGHTS

SCHOOL BOYS
NO PLAYER SHALL BE ABSENT FROM SCHOOL UNLESS BY SPECIAL PERMISSION. THE SCHOOL MEN ARE ASKED TO NOTIFY THE TEAM EXECUTIVE IF A PLAYER MISSES ANY CLASS AT SCHOOL.

GENERAL MANAGER.

Team Rules — St. Catharines Museum - Saveall Collection 2004.88.27.2

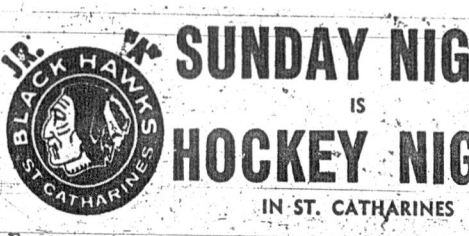

Niagara Glass and Paint
21 King Street
St. Catharines, Ontario
P.O. Box 363   Phone: 684-7481

November 17, 1966

Mrs. Saveall,
74 Carlton Street,
St. Catharines, Ontario.

Dear Mrs. Saveall:-

On behalf of the St. Catharines Hockey Club I would like to take this opportunity to thank you for looking after Tom Reid, Don Burgess, and Pete Mara. Without your co-operation our hockey club would not be a success.

Please be free to call either Ken Campbell or myself at any time regarding the boys.

Please find enclosed a set of rules that all boys must adhere to also a copy of the hockey schedule. As you can see from our schedule there should be no reason for the boys to miss any school with the exception of the two more trips we will be taking to Peterborough.

Yours truly,
ST. CATHARINES HOCKEY CLUB,

Fred Muller
General Manager

FM/mp

Letter to Mrs. Saveall — St. Catharines Museum - Saveall Collection 2004.88.27.1

SUNDAY NIGHT IS HOCKEY NIGHT IN ST. CATHARINES

Everyone is going to the newly renovated

GARDEN CITY ARENA
SO WHY NOT YOU?

FOLLOW THE CROWDS...

SEE... the future "TORONTO MAPLE LEAFS"

TORONTO MARLBOROS vs.
The High Flying ST. CATHARINES BLACK HAWKS

SUNDAY, NOVEMBER 6, 7.15 P.M.

All Seats Reserved — 1.75 - 1.50 - 1.25 Series 534

Students with Cards Under 16 and Children 50¢ (In Section 3 Only)

St. Catharines Standard, November 5, 1966

GOALIE PETER McDUFFE IS LEAGUE'S TOP NETMINDER

Peter McDuffe in action — St. Catharines Museum - *Janine Muller Collection, C11,069*

ATTENDANCE FIGURES
Average per regular-season game: 2,815
Season's largest crowd: 3,852
Season's smallest crowd: 1,946

PLAYOFF ROUNDS: 1
Eliminated by Kitchener 4-1-1

1966-1967

GAMES PLAYED	WON	LOST	TIED	FOR	AGAINST	POINTS	FINISH
48	19	20	9	175	155	47	5/9

Leading Scorers

PLAYER	GOALS	ASSISTS	POINTS
Jean-Paul LeBlanc	18	26	44
John Fisher	16	25	41
Stu Roberts	21	17	38
Bob Sicinski	10	25	35
Steve Latinovich	17	17	34

Leading Goaltenders

PLAYER	GP	GA	SO	GAA
Peter McDuffe	30.66	90	2	2.93
Larry Holmes	17.33	65	1	3.75

Before the 1966-67 season began, the nine OHA Junior A owners took steps to save junior hockey in the province. Student players were to receive $20 for room and board plus $10 expenses a week. Players not in school would be paid a maximum of $50 a week. With the end of NHL sponsorship coming on July 1, 1967, it was expected that some teams would fold.

The NHL and the CAHA made a deal to terminate the use of A, B and C forms which tied young players to certain pro organizations. In their place would be a universal draft and players could sign with the clubs drafting them.

The St. Catharines Black Hawks had lost $30,000 in 1965-66 and $8,000 had been spent on the local Junior B team. Therefore, to cut costs, there was no St. Catharines Junior B club from 1966 to 1968.

The Hawks started the season strongly and after ten games led the league with seven wins and 16 points. The team's success on the ice started to bring in the fans who were able to cheer on four hometown boys: Stu Roberts, Bill Young, Lou Polgrabia, and Skeeter Teal.

One of the players who caught the fans' attention in the first home game was Pete Mara, who received three standing ovations for his rocking body checks and tenacious forechecking.

Front row: Peter McDuffe, Jan Popiel, Jean-Paul Leblanc, Steve Latinovich, Stu Roberts, Bob Sicinski, Barry Salovaara, Peter Mara, Larry Holmes. Middle row: Ken Campbell, GM, Fred Muller (president), Victor Teal, Jim Stanfield, Bob Forester, John O'Flaherty (coach), Larry Gibbons, Maurice L'Abbe, Willie Terry, Obie O'Brien, Dr. Archie Manoian. Top row: Tony Cammarata, assistant trainer, John Fisher, Lou Polgrabia, Glen Sherwood, Jerry Korab, Tom Reid, Bill Young, Ron Anderson, Don Burgess, Harry Argent (property manager)

St. Catharines Standard photo

BLACK HAWKS 1966-1967

TOM REID

One of the grads of the 1966-67 team was Fort Erie native Tom Reid. The 6-foot-1, 200-pound stay-at-home defenceman, a three-year veteran and a 1966-67 First Team OHA All-Star, turned pro with the Chicago Black Hawks in 1967. In 1969 he was traded to the Minnesota North Stars and stayed with the club for ten seasons.

St. Catharines Standard photo

While playing with the North Stars, Reid was afflicted with a skin rash that made him allergic to his hockey equipment. The illness caused him a great deal of pain and forced him to retire in 1978.

In 701 regular-season NHL contests, he accumulated 130 points.

Today Reid is a color analyst for the Minnesota Wild and owns Tom Reid's Hockey Pub in St. Paul, Minnesota.

JEAN-PAUL LeBLANC

The leading scorer for the Hawks in 1966-67 was centre J. P. LeBlanc, a native of South Durham, Quebec. After two years in the Garden City, he turned pro with the CHL Dallas Black Hawks who won the league championship in 1969 and again in 1972.

J.P. LeBlanc in a Dallas Black Hawks uniform
Ernie Fitzsimmons Collection

He had his most productive pro season in 1971-72 when he collected 90 points in 70 games. During his pro career, the smooth play-making centre's assists outnumbered his goals by a wide margin.

In 1972 he jumped to the WHA, playing for Los Angeles Sharks and then Baltimore-Michigan. From 1975 to 1981, he was with Detroit Red Wings or their farm clubs in Kansas City and Adirondack.

In 1981 LeBlanc and Tom Webster coached the AHL Adirondack Red Wings to a Calder Cup victory.

Today LeBlanc lives in Syracuse, New York.

Bill Young
St. Catharines Museum - Skeeter Teal Ref. File, 2004.09.27

Victor (Skeeter) Teal
St. Catharines Standard photo

Lou Polgrabia
Courtesy of Lou Polgrabia

Pete Mara
St. Catharines Museum - Janine Muller Collection, C11,064

Mara played pro hockey from 1968 to 1977 and had his most successful season with the IHL Des Moines Capitols in 1973-74. The First All-Star Team centre was the league's scoring champion and MVP with 115 points, including 44 goals, leading Des Moines to a Turner Cup victory.

On Sunday, November 20, 1966, 3,852 fans attended the game, the largest crowd since 4,018 had crammed into the arena in a 1956-57 game against the Guelph Biltmores. After eight home games, the club had attracted 23,766 fans, more than half of the 41,000 fans who had attended 24 home games the previous season.

The Hawks lost 20 games, nine games by one goal and ten by two.

The team improved to fifth place in the standings and allowed the fewest goals in the league, 155. Milton native Peter McDuffe starred in goal with a sparkling 2.934 goals-against average in 31 games, the best in the league. He beat Kitchener Rangers netminder Robbie Irons who had an average of 2.938 and if McDuffe had allowed one more goal in the season's last game, Irons would have been the winner.

Hawk Jerry Korab (16) watches the action in front of Niagara Falls goalie Phil Myre. The game ended in a 4-4 tie December 11, 1966.
St. Catharines Standard photo

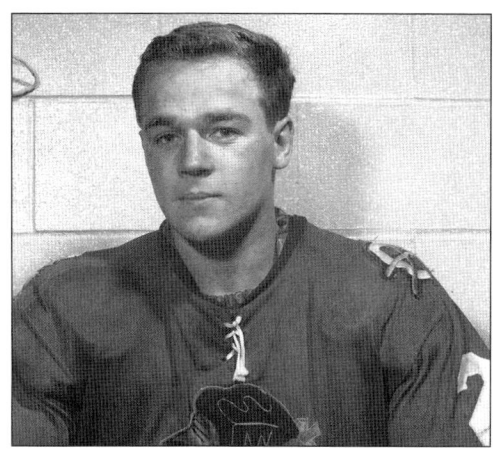

BLACK HAWKS 1966-1967

Moe L'Abbe
St. Catharines Standard photo

Hawk Ron Anderson played with Chicago and Cleveland in the WHA
St. Catharines Standard photo

J.P. Le Blanc led the team in scoring with 44 points.

The improved play of the team in 1966-67 and promotional efforts by Fred Muller paid off with an overall increase in regular-season attendance of 25,947. But once again, the team made no impact in the playoffs, losing in the first round to the Kitchener Rangers, led by future NHLers Walt Tkaczuk, Tim Ecclestone, Don Luce, and Mike Robitaille. Moe L'Abbe was the top playoff scorer for the Black Hawks with ten points, followed by Steve Latinovich with eight and Bill Young with seven.

By the time the 1967-68 season was to begin, Chicago Black Hawks had spent an average of $20,000 a year to keep junior hockey alive in St. Catharines. The club guaranteed payment of any outstanding debts at the end of the season, but as of July 1, 1967, NHL sponsorship was over and each junior team had to find a way to keep operating on its own.

Hawks president Fred Muller enlisted the help of the St. Catharines Lions Club to sell season's tickets and bring in more money. In 1966 there were 200 season's tickets sold, but in 1967 the number had jumped to 1,000 and the goal for 1968 was 2,000.

Muller received an offer of $30,000 to sell the Hawks, but he was determined to make the team a success on and off the ice. The club was gaining new popularity as evidenced in attendance figures for 1966-67, which showed total attendance for 24 home games of 67,563 (an average of 2,815) compared to 41,616 (an average of 1,734) in 1965-66. This reflected a growth of 62.3% in 12 months.

The playoff games attracted 9,292 fans, an increase of 1,290 for three games in each season. During the season, overall attendance for St. Catharines Junior A hockey from 1943 to 1967 went over the 1,000,000 mark.

Over the next few years, Muller paid off $56,000 in debts to Chicago Black Hawks, and as a result, the shares in the St. Catharines Black Hawks were returned to him and Ken Campbell, who became the sole owners. ■

Hawks Peanuts O'Flaherty on the ice with his players
St. Catharines Museum - Janine Muller Collection, C10,882

PETER McDUFFE

Peter McDuffe spent three full seasons with the St. Catharines Black Hawks and in 1966-67 posted the best goals-against average in the league with 2.93.

In 1968 the Milton native turned pro with the EHL Greensboro Generals and he was an EHL South First Team All-Star selection and rookie-of-the year in 1969. In 1971 he shared the CHL MVP award with three other players and was again a First Team All-Star. He won CHL championships with Omaha in 1970 and again in 1971.

McDuffe played in the minors until he made his NHL debut with the St. Louis Blues in 1971-72. In 1972 he shared the WHL's leading goaltender award. From 1972 to 1975, he saw action with New York Rangers, Kansas City Scouts, and Detroit Red Wings. He ended his career with the WHA Indianapolis Raiders in 1977-78. He played 57 regular-season NHL games, winning 11, and posted a 4.08 goals-against average.

McDuffe lives and works in Milton, Ontario.

St. Catharines Standard photo

STU ROBERTS

St. Catharines native Stu Roberts is the brother of Wilfred (Wimpy) Roberts who played with the 1953-54 Teepees, the Memorial Cup champions. The right winger saw action with the Black Hawks over four seasons from 1963 to 1967 and had his best year in 1966-67 when he scored 38 points, including 21 goals.

Courtesy of Stu Roberts

In 1967 he turned pro with the EHL Greensboro Generals and for seven seasons was a scoring machine, collecting 307 goals and 613 points. The Generals finished first in their division three years in a row, 1968 to 1970.

Today Roberts is retired and lives in Greensboro, North Carolina.

BLACK HAWKS 1966-1967

STEVE LATINOVICH

Welland native Steve Latinovich played left wing for the Black Hawks from 1965 to 1967 while he was attending Brock University.

After one season with the CPHL Dallas Black Hawks, in 1968 he returned to Brock University where he earned his bachelor of arts degree and played for the school's hockey team. He ended the season as the club's MVP and was tied for the OIAA scoring hockey championship.

For the next three years he attended Osgoode Hall and was an OUAA All-Star playing for the York University hockey team.

In 1972 he was named to the Canadian team that played in the World University Games, earning a silver medal.

After securing his law degree in 1972, he turned down NHL and WHA offers to act as a player/coach with Biel/Bienne in the Swiss National League. Two years later he was invited to the Buffalo Sabres camp and was offered a contract, but turned it down to pursue a law career that was interrupted by playing/coaching jobs in Switzerland from 1976 to 1983.

After guiding Swiss teams to A and B championships, he settled into his law firm. He did return for one last coaching stint during the 1987-88 season.

Steve, who has coached several Welland minor hockey teams, including the local Junior B club, is a partner with the law firm of Flett Beccario.

Ernie Fitzsimmons Collection

Chicago scout Jack Davison, January 22, 1967
St. Catharines Standard photo

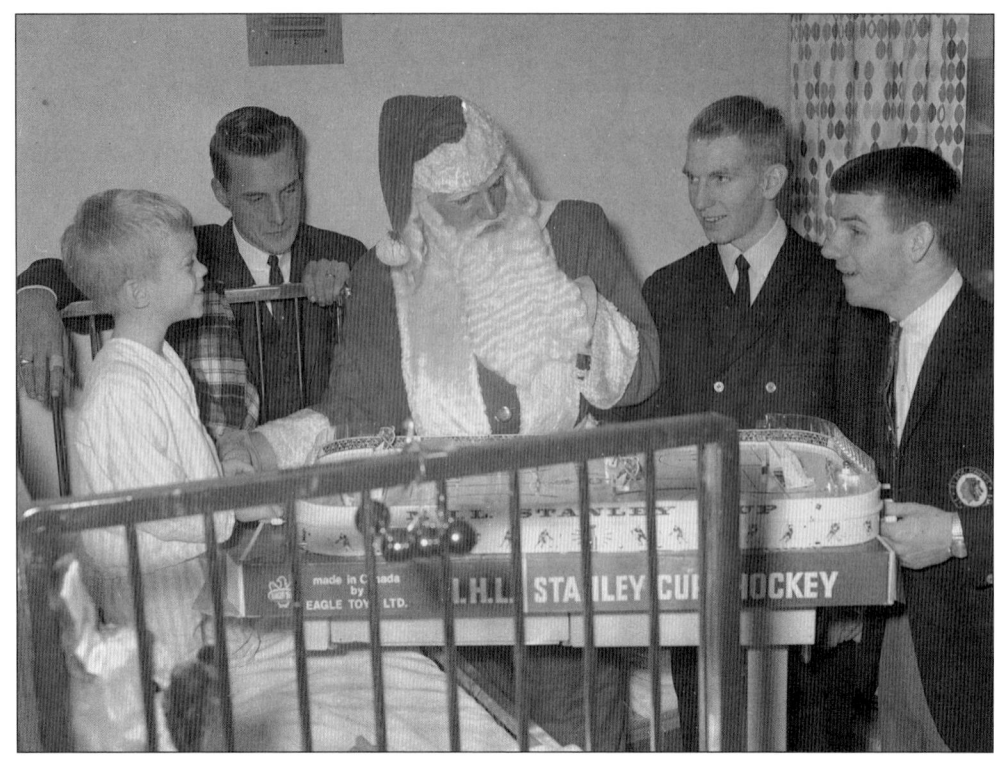

Five-year old Greg Campbell (left) plays a hockey game with Black Hawks Skeeter Teal and Stu Roberts (right), while Gary Campbell, Greg's dad, and Santa watch on December 25, 1966.
St. Catharines Standard photo

Chicago Black Hawks coach Billy Reay (left) and Tommy Ivan (right) watch St. Catharines Black Hawks play March 16, 1967.
St. Catharines Standard photo

FRED MULLER REPLACES KEN CAMPBELL AS GM

The 1967-68 schedule called for 54 games, up from 48, and the Hawks played the majority of their home games on Sundays. Also, the Ottawa 67's entered the league, bringing the number of teams to ten.

There was a feeling of optimism for the club before the season started. "We have a solid club, probably the best balance since I've been here, and there seems to be more team spirit than last season," coach Peanuts O'Flaherty said.

Fred Muller took over the Hawks GM duties from Ken Campbell, who had his hands full as director of playing personnel for the Chicago Black Hawks. Now that Chicago no longer had scouts providing players for the Junior Hawks, Muller drove all over Ontario and Quebec in search of players for his team. At that time, only two branch-to-branch transfers were allowed.

For previous training camps, Chicago had paid the $10,000 in expenses,

Fred Muller, October 6, 1967 — St. Catharines Standard photo

ATTENDANCE FIGURES
Average per regular-season game: 2,188
Season's largest crowd: 3,080
Season's smallest crowd: 1,332

PLAYOFF ROUNDS: 1
Eliminated by
Montreal Junior Canadiens 4-0-1

1967-1968

GAMES PLAYED	WON	LOST	TIED	FOR	AGAINST	POINTS	FINISH
54	21	30	3	200	210	45	6/10

Leading Scorers

PLAYER	GOALS	ASSISTS	POINTS
Victor (Skeeter) Teal	34	29	63
John Fisher	27	34	61
Maurice (Moe) L'Abbe	27	23	50
Dale Power	18	29	47
Jerry Korab	10	34	44

Leading Goaltenders

PLAYER	GP	GA	SO	GAA
Peter McDuffe	50.66	192	0	3.79
Jim Douglas	3.33	19	0	5.70

Welcome To The Club

Dennis Giannini, centre, is welcomed to the St. Catharines Black Hawk dressing room by two of last year's players Peter Mara (right) and Maurice Labbe. Giannini set an Ontario junior scoring record last season with 83 goals while playing with Kitchener Greenshirts of the Western Ontario B league. Mara is starting his second year with the Hawks, Labbe is in his fourth season of junior in St. Catharines. The Hawks open their exhibition schedule in Hamilton Saturday afternoon, then meet the Wings here next Friday night. President Fred Muller said this morning that those who buy season tickets before the first exhibition game will be given free admission.
—Staff photo

Note: Peter Mara is on the left. — St. Catharines Standard

Peanuts O'Flaherty (right) at the chalk board with Barry Salovaara (left) and Dave McDowall — St. Catharines Museum - Janine Muller Collection, C11,07

BLACK HAWKS 1967-1968

JERRY KORAB

Six-foot-3 Jerry Korab spent 1966 to 1968 with the St. Catharines Black Hawks.

The defenceman turned pro with the IHL Port Huron Flags in 1968 and broke into the Chicago Black Hawks lineup in 1970-71.

After three years with the Hawks, he moved on to Vancouver before finding a home with the Buffalo Sabres for seven seasons. In 1980 he was traded to Los Angeles Kings, but finished his career with the Sabres in 1984-85.

His most productive NHL season was in 1974-75 with the Buffalo Sabres when he scored 56 points in 79 regular-season games. The Soo native, who played in the 1975 and 1976 NHL All-Star Games, scored 455 points in 975 regular-season games.

Today Korab is in the packaging business in Chicago.

St. Catharines Standard photo

PIERRE JARRY

Montreal Quebec native Pierre Jarry played most of his junior career with the Ottawa 67's, but in March, 1968, he was acquired by the Black Hawks as a replacement for Barry Salovaara who had been injured. In the playoffs, he scored three goals and collected four points.

Jarry turned pro with the CHL Omaha Knights in 1969 and was a First Team All-Star with 92 points when the Knights won the league championship in 1971.

In 1971-72 he was in the NHL with New York Rangers who traded him to the Toronto Maple Leafs during the season. From 1973 to 1978, he saw action with Detroit Red Wings and Minnesota North Stars.

In 344 regular-season NHL games he collected 205 points.

Pierre Jarry in an OHL Ottawa 67's uniform
Ernie Fitzsimmons Collection

Hawk goalie Peter McDuffe lunges at puck as Kitchen Ranger Don Luce comes out behind the net. Other Hawks in the picture are captain Barry Salovaara (6) and Jerry Korab (2). The Rangers won the December 10, 1967 game 5-4.
St. Catharines Standard photo

Hawk Al McDonough, to the left of Niagara Falls goalie Phil Myre, steers the puck into the net. Number 14 is Don O'Donoghue. The Hawks lost the game 5-3, February 11, 1968.
St. Catharines Standard photo

Al McDonough (left) signs his first junior contract with Hawks President Fred Muller looking on.
St. Catharines Museum - Janine Muller Collection, C11,068

but now the Junior Black Hawks were on their own. To attract more fans and raise revenues, Muller encouraged 66-year-old Gladys Crowe to form a fan support group and the woman whom Jack Gatecliff nicknamed the "Swinging Granny" took the job to heart. In 1968 there were 100 members, but before the 1968-69 season began, there were 200. The group followed the team on road games, held dances to raise money, and at the end of the season created special awards and trophies for the players.

At the start of the 1967-68 season, timekeeper Ashton Morrison was replaced by Bernie Cibik and Ozzie Hill. Morrison timed the first St. Catharines Junior A game played in Garden City Arena on November 19, 1943.

After NHLer Bill Masterson died from a head injury in January of 1968, the OHA Junior A League debated the compulsory use of helmets for its players. In the end, the league decided to urge players to wear protective headgear, but did not make this mandatory until 1970.

The OHA Junior A All-Star Game was played in Niagara Falls on January 31, 1968, and it featured the Eastern Team All-Stars versus the Western Team All-Stars. Black Hawks Peter Mara, Jerry Korab, Barry Salovaara, Skeeter Teal, John Fisher, and Maurice L'Abbe were chosen to play for the Western squad.

At the end of the 1967-68 season, Skeeter Teal was the team's scoring leader with 63 points, and the club finished in sixth place. It was eliminated in the first round of the playoffs by Montreal in five games. The Canadiens had a very strong club that included several players who would make it to the NHL, including Gilbert Perreault, Marc Tardiff, Rejean Houle, Guy LaPointe, and Pierre Bouchard. Skeeter Teal and Moe L'Abbe were the top playoff scorers with six points each.

Total attendance had dipped to 63,452 from 76,855 in 1966-67, but the arrival of a teenager from Drummondville in time for the 1968-69 season was about to change the on-and off-ice fortunes of the Black Hawks. ■

142

BLACK HAWKS 1967-1968

Bernie Cibik (left) and Ozzie Hill, winners of the 1979 St. Catharines Sportsman of the Year Award
St. Catharines Standard photo

Hawks team dentist, Dr. Archie Manoian, October 24, 1966
St. Catharines Standard photo

Watch Exciting JR. "A" HOCKEY

Sunday, January 14, 7.15 p.m.
GARDEN CITY ARENA
Oshawa Generals vs.
St. Catharines Black Hawks
Avoid Lineups... Get Your Tickets Early!

Series 575
All Seats Reserved
Reds 2.00
Blues 1.75
Greens 1.50
Children and Students under 16 with cards 75¢ in Section "J" only

St. Catharines Museum - Wilma Brown Collection 2004.86.1.1

Team trophy winners for 1967-68 (left to right) John Fisher (most valuable and most gentlemanly player), Larry Gibbons (most improved), Al McDonough (top rookie forward), Jerry Korab (most colourful), Skeeter Teal (top scorer), and Moe L'Abbe (most popular). Absent were Dave McDowall (top rookie defenceman) and team captain Barry Salovaara (outstanding defenceman).
St. Catharines Museum - Janine Muller Collection, C11.035

GLADYS CROWE

London England native Gladys Crowe was one of the reasons for a renewed interest and support of junior hockey in St. Catharines in the late 1960s and 1970s.

In the 1967-68 season, Black Hawks president Fred Muller asked Mrs. Crowe to form the St. Catharines Black Hawks Junior A Supporters' Club, and she was more than willing to take on the job. She loved hockey and was a loyal follower of the Black Hawks and other city teams. "I should have got this Supporters' Club started years ago," she told Jack Gatecliff in January, 1969. "At my age [66], I can't be expected to carry on forever you know."

St. Catharines Standard photo

Mrs. Crowe arranged bus trips for road games, wrote bulletins that were inserted into the hockey programs, and trained fans to be cheerleaders. After the club attracted a few hundred members, she arranged dances and social evenings to raise money for a team banquet at the end of each season. Her club also presented awards and plaques to the players and team personnel. Gifts were given to any players who had to spend time in the hospital.

The "Swinging Granny" had five children, seventeen grandchildren, and ten great grandchildren, six in Canada, two in South Africa, and two in England.

Her support of the team continued until 1977 when the city's last team, the St. Catharines Fincups, returned to Hamilton.

BLACK HAWKS 1968-1969

Marcel Dionne
St. Catharines Standard photo

Front and back of Dionne's 1968-69 player's registration card October 17, 1968
Janine Muller Collection

Garden City Arena, Dionne's new home from 1968 to 1971
Janine Muller Collection

BLACK HAWKS 1968-1969

NEW COACH BRIAN SHAW LAYS DOWN THE LAW

ATTENDANCE FIGURES
Average per regular-season game: 3,306
Season's largest crowd: 4,117
Season's smallest crowd: 2,506

PLAYOFF ROUNDS: 3
Eliminated Toronto Marlboros 3-1-2 and Niagara Falls 3-2-2.
Lost to Montreal Junior Canadiens 4-0-1

1968-1969

GAMES PLAYED	WON	LOST	TIED	FOR	AGAINST	POINTS	FINISH
54	31	11	12	297	206	74	2/10

Leading Scorers

PLAYER	GOALS	ASSISTS	POINTS
Marcel Dionne	37	63	100
Bobby Sheehan	44	41	85
Victor (Skeeter) Teal	30	53	83
Dennis Giannini	37	44	81
Dick Redmond	33	45	78

Leading Goaltenders

PLAYER	GP	GA	SO	GAA
George Hulme	37.66	137	0	3.64
Rick Carpenter	16.33	69	0	4.22

Shaw at the Hawks bench St. Catharines Museum - *Skeeter Teal Collection, C 10,965*

Hawks president and GM Fred Muller never played much hockey, but he had an eye for hockey talent. After the 1968-69 season began, Muller was able to arrange the transfer of Quebec junior star Marcel Dionne to the Black Hawks from Drummondville, Quebec. It wasn't easy. Dionne spoke no English and Muller spoke no French, but Dionne was impressed when Muller paid a visit to his home to talk to his parents. The Montreal Canadiens only sent a letter to him and paid no visit. For Dionne, it was easy to see who really wanted him.

"The acquisition of Marcel Dionne by the Black Hawks promises to be one of the biggest breaks for Junior A hockey in St. Catharines in a great many years," Gatecliff wrote, after it was announced that Dionne would be coming to the Garden City. The *Standard* sports editor was right.

It was rumoured that Dionne's release from Drummondville came at a price of $100,000. At the time, the Canadian Amateur Hockey Association did not allow branch-to-branch transfers, so Dionne's mother and the family moved to St. Catharines for a legitimate family relocation – at least for a while. They quietly

Front row: Marcel Dionne, Dick Redmond, Skeeter Teal (captain), Brian Shaw (coach), Dr. Archie Manoian, Dave Burrows, Dave McDowall, Bob Sheehan; Second row: George Hulme, Keith Pallett, Don O'Donoghue, Rick Dudley, Al McDonough, Don McCulloch, Doug Rombough, Dennis O'Brien, Garry Cunningham, Rick Carpenter, Harry Argent (property manager); Back row: Dr. Robert Orr, Charlie Paul (bus driver), Howie Beaupit (assistant trainer) Bob Goss, Dennis Giannini, Wayne Ego, Brian McKenzie, Bob McMahon, Alan Young, Dean Bayne, Dr. H. Dyck

St. Catharines Museum - *Hulme Collection, C 10,708*

BLACK HAWKS 1968-1969

HARRY ARGENT

Hamilton native Harry Argent was an up-and-coming baseball player in his youth and later he managed and sponsored baseball teams in the Garden City. At one time he owned and operated the city's baseball team in the Niagara District Senior League.

After interest in baseball declined, Argent became more involved in hockey; he acted as a manager for the St. Catharines Junior B club in the 1950s. Later, he joined forces with Jack Steele, father-in-law of Rudy Pilous, looking after the Teepees equipment and sharpening skates. As well as holding down a job at General Motors, he continued as property man for the Black Hawks in 1962 and stayed on the job until his death in 1972.

Argent loved being around the junior players. "They're a great bunch of kids and it makes me feel young just being with them," Argent said. "Few if any men gave as much of themselves to sport in this city than the late Harry Argent," Gatecliff wrote after his death.

St. Catharines Museum - Garden City Arena Collection N5682

DAVE BURROWS

Defenceman Dave Burrows spent the 1968-69 season with the St. Catharines Black Hawks and began his pro career with the Dallas Black Hawks in 1969. In 1971 the Toronto native was claimed by the Pittsburgh Penguins and stayed with the team for seven seasons.

The 6-foot-1 rearguard had a reputation as a rock-solid defender who could be relied upon in all situations. In 1978 he was traded to the Toronto Maple Leafs where he suffered a serious knee injury. He ended his career back in Pittsburgh in 1981.

In 724 regular-season games, he earned 164 points and appeared in three all-star games.

St. Catharines Museum - Hulme Collection, C 10,708

It's Harry Argent Appreciation Night at Garden City Arena March 9, 1969. Taking part in the presentation were (left to right) Ken Campbell, Hap Walters, Mrs. Argent, Harry, Linda Lepp and Dr. Archie Manoian.
St. Catharines Standard photo

Hawks coach Brian Shaw (right) confers with stars Bob Sheehan (left) and Marcel Dionne, the day after the 1968-69 season ended with a 5-3 win over Hamilton Red Wings. March 10, 1969
St. Catharines Standard photo

St. Catharines Black Hawks added one defenceman to the six already on their roster last night as Dick Redmond made his debut at the Hawk practice. Redmond was obtained from Peterborough in exchange for centre Dale Power. With coach Brian Shaw in the picture above are defencemen Don McCulloch, Garry Cunningham, Dave Burrows, Bob McMahon, Dennis O'Brien, Redmond and Dave McDowall.
St. Catharines Standard photo

returned home after four months in the Garden City.

From the moment the French-Canadian teenager stepped onto the Garden City Arena ice, he was an instant hit. Once again OHA Junior A hockey became a hot ticket in the city. "The darling of Drummondville became the darling of St. Catharines, spoiled and worshipped," *MacLean's* magazine reported in its March 24, 1980 issue.

Muller was also able to get junior star Bobby Sheehan's release from the Halifax Junior club and it turned out to be a wise decision – on the ice. The "Weymouth Whirlwind" was a concern off the ice.

BLACK HAWKS 1968-1969

Thirty-seven-year-old Brian Shaw replaced Peanuts O'Flaherty behind the bench in the fall of 1968 and was given the title of manager as well.

Muller actually wanted ex-Teepees defenceman Pat Kelly to coach the team. However, Kelly, who was coaching in the Eastern Hockey League, was offered more money by Minnesota North Stars GM Wren Blair, and was promised that he would advance in the Minnesota organization. It never happened for Kelly who eventually became one of the founders and the first president and commissioner of the East Coast Hockey League.

Black Hawks executives (Muller, Vice-President Dr. Archie Manoian, and Secretary-Treasurer Ken Campbell) believed the upcoming season could be "the year of the Hawks."

On the first day of the 1968 training camp in September, Shaw took control. He gave 12 of the 74 players at camp 24 hours to crop their hair and trim their sideburns. "This is a hockey camp, not a fashion show," said Shaw, who had his own hair cut once a week.

Shaw, who had come to the Black Hawks after three successful years coaching the Junior A Moose Jaw Canucks, was described by CHSC Radio Sports Director Karl Edmands in 1968 as: "A swinger who knows his business, but a swinger nonetheless."

And there was more about the bachelor who dressed with a flair. "Brian Shaw likes to live life first class. He drives a gold Lincoln Continental and lives in a plush penthouse apartment, completely furnished in a manner that would make Hugh Hefner content," Edmands wrote. Years later, Shaw's controversial life style was the subject of featured articles in the *St. Catharines Standard*, but by then Shaw was dead.

The team opened the season with a 5-3 loss to Peterborough, but in the home-opener, the Hawks

Hawk George Hulme reaches behind to grab a shot from Toronto Marlie Dale Tallon. Hulme was brilliant in a 4-0 playoff victory on March 20, 1969.
St. Catharines Standard photo

Hawk Coach Lowers Boom
Sideburns, Long Hair Must Go Orders Shaw

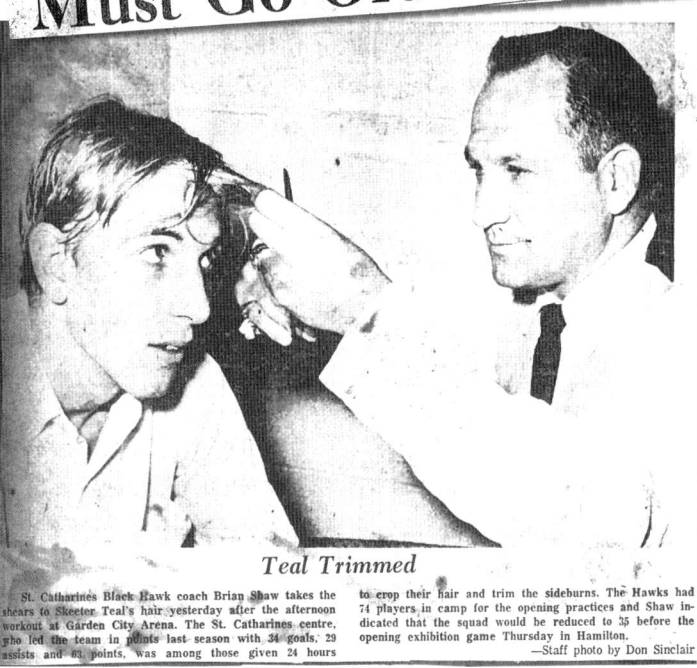

Teal Trimmed
St. Catharines Black Hawk coach Brian Shaw takes the shears to Skeeter Teal's hair yesterday after the afternoon workout at Garden City Arena. The St. Catharines centre, who led the team in points last season with 34 goals, 29 assists and 63 points, was among those given 24 hours to crop their hair and trim the sideburns. The Hawks had 74 players in camp for the opening practices and Shaw indicated that the squad would be reduced to 35 before the opening exhibition game Thursday in Hamilton.
—Staff photo by Don Sinclair

St. Catharines Standard, Saturday, September 14, 1968

GEORGE HULME

One year after backstopping the Toronto Butter Beeps to the Canadian Centennial Midget Hockey Championship in 1967, Scarborough native George Hulme joined the Black Hawks, and it didn't take him long to make an impression. He was the club's MVP in his rookie season. In his sophomore year, he was a member of the OHA Junior A First All-Star Team, and the next year he starred in goal as the club won the OHA championship.

In 1971 he was drafted by the Detroit Red Wings and won a Turner Cup with the Port Huron Wings in 1972. After spending time in the AHL, CHL and NAHL, he retired in 1976 and now lives in the Garden City.

Hulme and former Hawks Skeeter Teal and Bill Cheropita established the St. Catharines Teepees/Black Hawks Alumni Golf Reunion in 1980 and it's still going today.

VICTOR (SKEETER) TEAL

Right winger Skeeter Teal spent three seasons with the Hawks and was the club's leading scorer in 1967-68 with 63 points. In his last year, 1968-69, the St. Catharines native captained the team and one of his jobs was to keep an eye on teammate Bobby Sheehan. Sheehan ended up living with Skeeter's parents, who tried to keep track of the Massachusetts native because he loved to have a good time off the ice.

Teal was the third choice of the St. Louis Blues in the 1969 Amateur Draft, but saw action in only one NHL contest with the New York Islanders. After a minor league career in the CHL, AHL and NAHL, he ended his pro career in 1977. His best season came in 1973-74 with the CHL Fort Worth Wings when he collected 76 points, including 33 goals in 72 regular-season games.

He now lives in the Garden City.

BLACK HAWKS 1968-1969

GUY DELPARTE

Sault Ste. Marie native Guy Delparte split the 1968-69 season between the London Knights and the St. Catharines Black Hawks. The left winger helped teammate Marcel Dionne learn English during his stay in the Garden City.

After being taken by the Montreal Canadiens in the 1969 Amateur Draft, he spent most of his career in the EHL with the Johnstown Jets, and then with the AHL Nova Scotia Voyageurs and the Maine Mariners with whom he won a Calder Cup in 1978. His most productive season was in 1969-70 when he collected 70 points, including 31 goals with the Johnstown Jets.

He did get a taste of NHL action with the Colorado Rockies in 1976-77 before retiring in 1981 with the AHL Springfield Indians.

Guy Delparte in an AHL Maine Mariners uniform
Ernie Fitzsimmons Collection

DON O'DONOGHUE

After spending two seasons with the Black Hawks, 1967 to 1969, right winger Don O'Donoghue was drafted by the Oakland Seals in 1969. The Kingston native spent parts of three seasons with the California Golden Seals before moving on to play in the AHL, WHA, CHL and the SHL from 1971 to 1978.

The former owner of OD's Kitchen in Gilroy, California, died on June 4, 2007.

St. Catharines Museum - O'Donoghue Collection, C 11,253

tied the Petes 4-4 with American-born Bobby Sheehan in the lineup. Sheehan scored a goal and became an immediate hit with the fans. The club, however, went six games before winning its first contest.

Muller, who was determined to make the club a success, worked with the St. Catharines Central Lions Club to bring in the fans. Thirty Lions Club members were directly involved in selling season tickets, booster tickets, programs and program ads. Usually, eight to nine club members worked in various roles at each home game. Money from the sale of Hawks programs helped to fund the Lions Club's various community projects.

The Junior Chamber of Commerce also assisted by providing ushers at home games. Each usher was paid $3.50 a game, and at the end of the season the $1,400 earned was turned over to the Chamber's

Marcel Dionne (9) and linemate Dennis Giannini (7) look for the puck in action against the Kitchener Rangers.
St. Catharines Museum - Standard Collection N5365

Hawks scorers in a November game (left to right) Skeeter Teal, Marcel Dionne, Al McDonough, Dennis Giannini, and Bob Channell
St. Catharines Museum - Standard Collection N 5779

BLACK HAWKS 1968-1969

Ways and Means Committee.

It wasn't long before the exciting play of Dionne, Sheehan, newcomer Dick Redmond from the Peterborough Petes, and talent at every position started to draw the crowds. On November 25, 1968, 3,887 attended the game. It was the largest crowd since the 1956-57 season when Bobby Hull played for the Teepees.

For many games the Standing Room Only sign was a common feature as the club was in the thick of a fight for first place throughout the season. On February 18, 1969, 4,116 fans jammed into Garden City Arena to see the Hawks beat the Montreal Junior Canadiens 7-3. It was the largest crowd for a junior game since 1954, and according to Jack Gatecliff, it was a hockey classic.

On the last game of the season, March 9, 1969, veteran Hawks property man Harry Argent was honoured with a "Harry Argent Appreciation Night". One of the many presents that the Hamilton native received was a Gold Stick Award from Ontario Hockey Association President Jack Devine. The 3,563 fans in attendance gave a standing ovation to the 74-year-old. "I had a long talk prepared but I am so overcome I can't remember a word I was going to say," Argent said at the ceremony.

The team finished second in the league standings with 74 points, which was the highest number of points earned by a team since the Teepees had 86 in 1953-54.

Despite missing a few games at the start of the year, Dionne was the team's point leader with 100, followed by Sheehan with 85. Teal with 83 and Giannini with 81 points finished third and fourth respectively.

Success followed in the 1969 playoffs with victories over the Toronto Marlies in six games and the Niagara Falls Flyers in seven. The Hawks were defeated in the OHA Junior A final by Montreal, and were only able to tie one game. The fifth and final game of the series drew 17,557 fans to the Montreal Forum. In the playoffs, Dennis Giannini led the way with 38 points in 18 games, followed by Dionne with 36 and Dick Redmond with 28.

Attendance soared to 89,257 for 27 home games, breaking the 1948-49 record of 79,797 in 24 home games. Attendance records show that 32,749 fans crowded into Garden City Arena for nine playoff games, breaking all previous attendance records. The team's share of gate receipts which totaled $79,758 in 1967-68, jumped to $160,856.23 in 1968-69.

Massachusetts native Bobby Sheehan scored 44 goals in 44 games and Marcel Dionne finished second in the OHA scoring race with 100 points. He was voted the top rookie in the OHA. It was the highest scoring total by a rookie in OHA Junior A hockey history.

The club had only 11 losses and tied the record for consecutive games without a loss (14) held by the 1953-54 Teepees. The Hawks scored the second highest number of goals during the regular season, 297. ∎

Trophy Time For Hawks

Ten members of the St. Catharines Black Hawks were recipients of team trophies last night for excellent play during the 1968-69 Ontario Hockey Association junior A schedule and playoffs. Front row, from the left, Dennis Giannini, tied with Wayne Ego as outstanding playoff performer; Bob Sheehan, most colorful; Marcel Dionne, outstanding rookie and top points scorer; George Hulme, most valuable. Back row, Al McDonough, most gentlemanly; Wayne Ego; Dave Burrows and Dick Redmond, tied as outstanding defencemen; Brian McKenzie, most improved; Alan Young, most popular. —Staff photo

St. Catharines Standard

DENNIS O'BRIEN

Port Hope Ontario native Dennis O'Brien spent 1968-69 on defence with the Black Hawks. The Minnesota North Stars made him their second selection in the 1969 Amateur Draft, and he played with the team until 1977.

He also saw NHL action with Colorado, Cleveland, and then Boston, where he ended his career in 1980.

The veteran of 592 regular-season NHL games, with 122 points, lives in Port Hope, Ontario.

Ernie Fitzsimmons Collection

DICK REDMOND

Kirkland Lake native Dick Redmond set a St. Catharines record for defencemen with 33 goals and was a First Team All-Star in his only season with the Black Hawks in 1968-69.

After graduating to the NHL in 1969-70, he played 771 games with Minnesota, California, Chicago, St. Louis, Atlanta and Boston, accumulating 445 points during his 13-year career. His most productive year in the NHL came in 1973-74 when he collected 59 points in 76 regular-season games.

Ernie Fitzsimmons Collection

BLACK HAWKS 1968-1969

RICK DUDLEY

Left winger Rick Dudley was a lacrosse star who spent only part of 1968-69 with the St. Catharines Black Hawks.

After apprenticing for three years in the minors and winning a Calder Cup with the AHL Cincinnati Swords in 1973, he made his way up to the NHL. He played five full seasons with the Buffalo Sabres and collected 174 points in 309 NHL games.

He had his best NHL season with the Sabres in 1974-75 when he earned 70 points, including 31 goals.

He spent four years with the WHA Cincinnati Stingers with whom he collected 277 points in 270 games.

Former Black Hawk Rick Dudley suits up with the Buffalo Sabres on September 14, 1973.
St. Catharines Standard photo

Since retiring in 1981, the Toronto native turned to coaching, first in the Atlantic Coast League (three championships), and then to Flint and three seasons with the Buffalo Sabres. Dudley moved into management with NHL GM positions in Ottawa, Tampa Bay, and then Florida until 2004.

In 2005 he was director of playing personnel for the Chicago Blackhawks and today is the Hawks assistant GM.

Dudley is a member of the Cincinnati Hockey Hall of Fame for his work with the AHL Swords and the WHA Stingers.

He is also the only NHL player who was a winning contestant on the long-running American TV Game To Tell the Truth. Dudley and two other men, the imposters, appeared as Rick Dudley, a two-sport major athlete (an NHL and National Lacrosse League player). The four panelists had to guess who was the real Rick Dudley.

When Dudley didn't know the maximum length of a lacrosse stick, the TV panel decided he wasn't a lacrosse and hockey star and chose someone else.

Today Dudley lives in Lewiston, New York.

BOBBY SHEEHAN

The 1968-69 club was one of the most exciting and entertaining teams ever to play in St. Catharines. For many fans, watching Weymouth Massachusetts native Bobby Sheehan play was worth the price of admission alone.

"He [Sheehan] combines some pretty fair hockey ability with a show business attitude, which, at times, looks like a combination of the old Ice Follies comedy team of Frick and Frack," Gatecliff wrote in the fall of 1968.

Hawks owner Fred Muller had pried Sheehan away from the Halifax Junior A Canadiens in 1968 by playing two exhibition

Bobby Sheehan in a WHA Edmonton Oilers uniform
Ernie Fitzsimmons Collection

Bobby Sheehan (14) scores his 16th goal against the Montreal Canadiens on December 1, 1968.
St. Catharines Standard photo

Hawk Bobby Sheehan (right) is checked into the boards during a 5-3 win over the Montreal Canadiens December 1, 1968.
St. Catharines Standard photo

games in Halifax with proceeds going to the Halifax team.

After leaving for St. Catharines in the fall of 1968, somehow Sheehan ended up at the Niagara Falls Flyers training camp. "I guess I was a little mixed up," Sheehan said at the time.

There was no mixup. Niagara Falls Flyers owner Hap Emms actually had sent transportation money to Sheehan. Emms wanted Sheehan to stay, and even told him to hide under his bed when Hawks owner Fred Muller sent his captain, Skeeter Teal, to bring him to St. Catharines. Emms, however, did eventually contact Muller and gave up his claim to the former Halifax star.

Sheehan came to the Garden City and enrolled at Brock University to acquire deferred status and avoid the American draft and the possibility of being sent to Vietnam.

Keeping track of Sheehan off the ice was a frustrating task for team officials because he liked to have a good time. They hired a detective to follow him, but Sheehan wasn't intimidated. On one occasion he invited the detective, who was tailing him, to have a drink, and that was the end of the surveillance that night.

"Give me the money and maybe I'll stay home," Sheehan recalled telling Hawks officials, when he was interviewed in front of the Atlantic Ocean in Hingham, Massachusetts, on June 8, 2004.

In January of 1969, Sheehan and winger Don O'Donoghue were suspended indefinitely by coach Brian Shaw. Shaw had experienced disciplinary problems with both players in previous weeks and decided enough was enough. "It's just a case where the rules are made for 20 boys and we can't make exceptions for one or two," Shaw said. It was Sheehan's second suspension in a month. When Sheehan was playing in Halifax before coming to St. Catharines, Halifax manager Fred McGillvary had suspended him during the Memorial Cup playoffs. Some speculated that this was the main reason McGillvary released Sheehan in 1968 and allowed him to hook up with the Hawks.

Sheehan made it to the NHL, but didn't stay very long with any one team. He suited up with seven different clubs in 13 years. In 310 NHL regular-season games, he earned 111 points and 185 in 241 WHA contests. He won a Stanley Cup ring with the Montreal Canadiens in 1971.

Today he works for the Massachusetts State Lottery – and he still likes to have a good time.

BLACK HAWKS 1969-1970

THE BLACK HAWKS GET BIGGER AND STRONGER

ATTENDANCE FIGURES
Average per regular-season game: 3,396
Season's largest crowd: 4,038
Season's smallest crowd: 2,721

PLAYOFF ROUNDS: 2
Eliminated Kitchener 4-2
Lost to Montreal Junior Canadiens 4-0

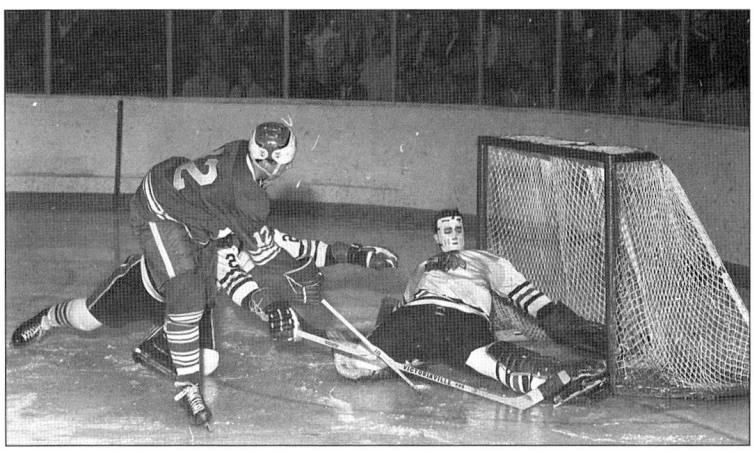

1969-1970

GAMES PLAYED	WON	LOST	TIED	FOR	AGAINST	POINTS	FINISH
54	30	18	6	268	210	66	3/10

Leading Scorers

PLAYER	GOALS	ASSISTS	POINTS
Marcel Dionne	55	77	132
Al McDonough	47	56	103
Pierre Guite	31	30	61
Brian McKenzie	17	41	58
Dennis Giannini	20	30	50

Leading Goaltenders

PLAYER	GP	GA	SO	GAA
George Hulme	49.5	175	1	3.61
Jim Steele	3	18	0	6

Hawk goalie George Hulme does the splits on a shot by Toronto Marlie Mike Murphy in a 10-7 loss in the Hawks season opener October 5, 1969. During the game Hulme was hit in the mask on a shot from Dale Tallon and required 12 stitches.
St. Catharines Standard photo

In 1969-70 there were ten teams in the league. Sixty hopefuls, led by Shaw who had signed another one-year contract, showed up for the training camp. For the second season opener in a row, the Hawks lost to Peterborough Petes 2-1, and didn't win a game until October 12, 1969, when the club defeated Hamilton Red Wings 7-5. A victory over Niagara Falls on October 19th marked the beginning of a nine-game winning streak that lasted until November 14, 1969. It set a new team record previously held by the 1953-54 Teepees.

Muller had strengthened the club by securing a release from the Quebec Junior Hockey league for Sorel Junior Pierre Guite and for Mike Bloom from the Northern Ontario Hockey Association. Both of these transfers didn't come without some tough negotiations. Guite only got his release

Hawks coach Brian Shaw adds a touch of class behind the bench during a 7-2 win over Niagara Falls Flyers on January 1, 1970.
St. Catharines Standard photo

Front row: George Hulme, Brian McKenzie, Dr. Archie Manoian, Marcel Dionne, Brian Shaw (coach), Al McDonough (captain), Fred Muller (co-owner), Bob McMahon, Jim Steele. Second row: Dr. Robert Orr, Garry Cunningham, Bill Ellis, Don McCulloch, Mike Bloom, Doug Rombough, Pierre Guite, Fran McKey, Ron Woodhouse, Harry Argent (property manager). Back row: Charlie Paul (bus driver), Howie Beaupit (assistant trainer), Brian Thorne, Tim Jacobs, Duane Wylie, Paul Shakes, Jim Pearson, Clyde Simon, Glen Crichton, Pete Zaroda, Bob Scott, Dr. H. Dyck

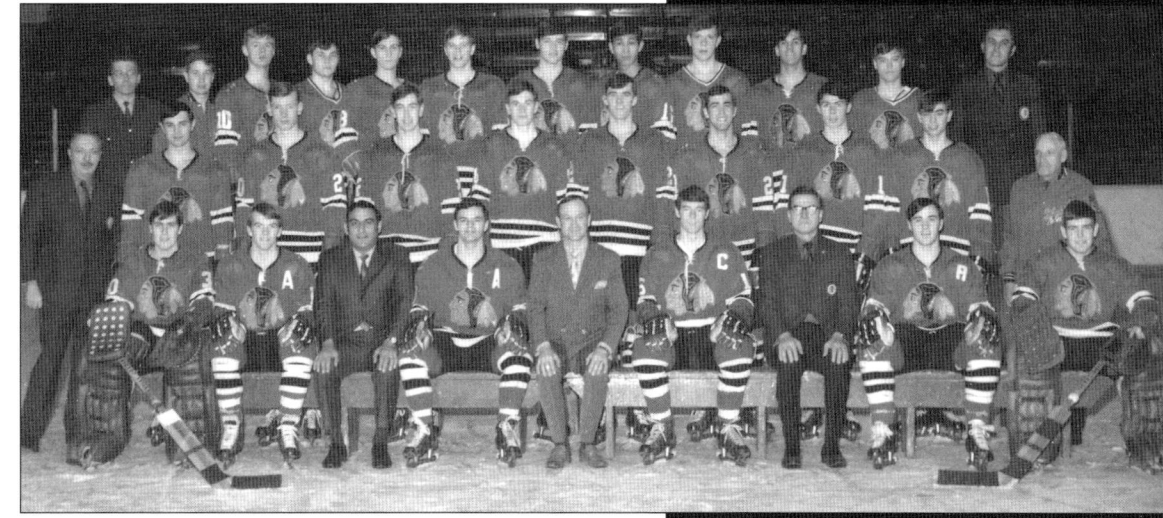

St. Catharines Museum - Hulme Collection, C10,70

BLACK HAWKS 1969-1970

DUANE WYLIE

Spokane Washington native Duane Wylie came from Western Canada to play one season for the Black Hawks in 1969-70, and then turned pro with the IHL Flint Generals in 1970.

The centre/left winger spent most of his career in the CHL with the Dallas Black Hawks with whom he won the league championship in 1974. His best year as a pro came in 1975-76 with Dallas when he recorded 70 points in 76 games.

He was called up for 14 games with the Chicago Black Hawks before retiring in 1978.

He currently lives in Richardson, Texas.

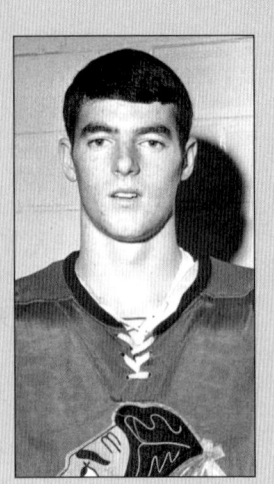

Duane Wylie with the IHL Flint Generals
Ernie Fitzsimmons Collection

AL McDONOUGH

Al McDonough was born in Copetown, outside of Hamilton, but raised in St. Catharines. He played for the Black Hawks from 1967 to 1970 and was club captain and an OHA First Team All-Star in his last season, when he collected 103 points in 53 regular-season contests. "We were looking for a boy whose conduct both on and off the ice was beyond question. Someone whom the players could look up to," coach Brian Shaw said.

He was the Los Angeles Kings first choice in the 1970 Amateur Draft and won a Calder Cup with the Springfield Kings in 1971. After parts of two seasons with Los Angeles, he moved to Pittsburgh, then Atlanta, and finally Detroit after three years in the WHA.

He had his best NHL season in 1972-73 with the Penguins when he earned 76 points, including 35 goals in 78 games. In 237 regular-season NHL games, the right winger collected 161 points.

Today McDonough is executive vice-president of Programmed Insurance Brokers Inc. and resides in Kitchener.

Ernie Fitzsimmons Collection

from Sorel by appealing to the CAHA. Both of these players added to the club's offence, and their ability to take care of themselves and their teammates made other clubs think twice before gooning it up.

On December 27, 1969, Shaw wanted a right winger for Dionne, so he traded Dennis Giannini, who was not happy playing for Shaw, to London for Clyde Simon.

Clyde Simon
St. Catharines Museum - O'Brien Collection, C11,083

Dennis Giannini
St. Catharines Museum - O'Brien Collection 2004.59.5

Simon was a perfect fit. He scored the winning goal in his first game as a Hawk, 19 goals in his first season, and 44 in 1970-71.

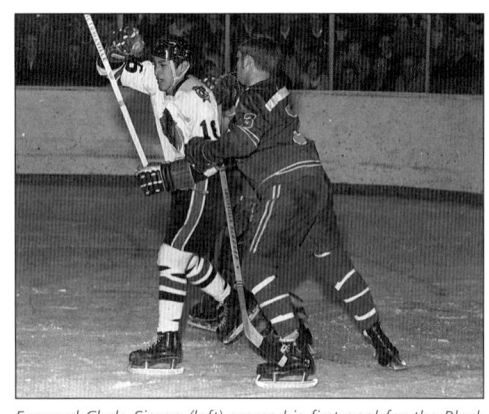

Forward Clyde Simon (left) scores his first goal for the Black Hawks after being traded by London. His new team beat Oshawa 4-2 on December 28, 1969.
St. Catharines Standard photo

Fran McKey
St. Catharines Museum - Muller Collection, C10,671

In the Hawks second game in Ottawa, Hawk forward Fran McKey suffered a fractured skull and broken collarbone after his head hit the ice following a fight with Ottawa 67's future NHLer Dennis Potvin.

On Friday, October 24, 1969, for the first time in the 27-year history of St. Catharines Junior A hockey, Hawks team officials announced that protective headgear would be mandatory for all players. The league required all teams to wear helmets by January 1, 1970.

In November of 1969, Hawks owner Fred Muller incurred the wrath of the nine other OHA Junior owners. In 1968 the OHA Junior Council had agreed not to recruit players from the independent Western Canada Junior League. Fully aware of the agreement, Muller, nevertheless, arranged to send two Western defencemen, Glen Irwin and John Stewart, to Sorel in the Quebec League for 1968-69 with the idea of bringing them to St. Catharines for 1969-70. The other league owners knew what Muller was doing and told him he couldn't get away with it. They told Muller he had better send Irwin, who did report to St. Catharines in the fall of 1969, back to Sorel. Some owners talked of forming an independent league that would exclude the Hawks.

Muller went beyond OHA regulations and appealed to the CAHA for the transfer of the two players for 1969-70. He won a partial victory, but he would lose the war.

The CAHA approved Irwin's transfer, but not Stewart's, and the OHA gave Irwin clearance to play and issued his playing card. Toronto Marlboros GM Tommy Smythe's immediate reaction was to boycott the Marlies next game against the Hawks if Irwin dressed; however, he changed his tune when he was told that his club would be hit with a big fine.

In the end, Muller, who was not very popular with other owners before the controversy, traded Irwin to the Peterborough Petes several days after he had played with the Hawks. There was a regulation forbidding the trade of a player who was transferred, but in this case the rule was relaxed. Irwin was devastated and decided to return to Western Canada rather than report to the Petes.

Montreal Junior Canadiens, who had defeated the Hawks in the 1968 OHA final, angered Black Hawk fans on a visit to St. Catharines on December 9, 1969. During the game some yahoos in the crowd bombarded the Montreal players with eggs, programs and paper cups. The game was delayed on numerous occasions and took three hours and ten minutes to complete. During the second period, vandals had set the Montreal bus on fire and another bus had to be brought in to transport the players.

After the game Shaw made the Hawks practice from 11:30 p.m. to 2 a.m. because the club had given up a 5-2 lead in the second period. In the spring of 1971 Hawk players would experience similar treatment

BLACK HAWKS 1969-1970

Three Star Selection
The three St. Catharines Black Hawk players selected to the 1969-70 Ontario Hockey Association Junior A team are all smiles after hearing the good news before practice at Garden City Arena last night. From the left, Junior A scoring champion Marcel Dionne, named centre on the Second All-Star Team; goaltender George Hulme and right winger Al McDonough chosen for the First All-Star Team.
St. Catharines Standard photo

Hawk Marcel Dionne accepts the 1970 Eddie Powers Trophy from Frank Doherty OHA Vice-President on March 31, 1970.
St. Catharines Standard photo

given to the Canadiens in Quebec City. The difference was that in Quebec City, many Hawk players feared for their lives and refused to return to the Colisée.

At the end of the 1969-70 season, netminder George Hulme and right winger Al McDonough, the Hawks captain, were chosen as OHA First Team All-Stars. Centre Marcel Dionne, who won the league scoring championship and placed second to Gilbert Perreault for the Red Tilson Trophy, was picked for the Second Team.

The Hawks defeated Kitchener in the first round of the playoffs in six games, but once again were eliminated in round two by Montreal in four straight games. Three of the losses to the Canadiens were by identical 5-4 scores after a 13-2 whipping in the Montreal Forum.

Dionne was the club's top scorer with 32 points in ten playoff contests, followed by Clyde Simon and Duane Wylie with 15 and 14 points respectively.

Total attendance fell to 106,743 because of fewer playoff games, but the team was still extremely popular. ■

Trophy Time For Hawks
St. Catharines Black Hawk centre Marcel Dionne not only led the Ontario Hockey Association Junior A League in points during the 1969-70 season, but was also No.1 last night in trophy collection. During the annual St. Catharines Supporters' Club post-season dinner Dionne was awarded team trophies as most valuable player, most popular player, and the team's leading scorer and he shared the most valuable playoff trophy with Duane Wylie. The major award winners are shown here, from the left, Clyde Simon, most gentlemanly; Jim Pearson, co-winner of best defenceman; Wylie, most improved; Dionne; Paul Shakes, co-winner of best defenceman; Pierre Guite, most colourful.
St. Catharines Standard photo

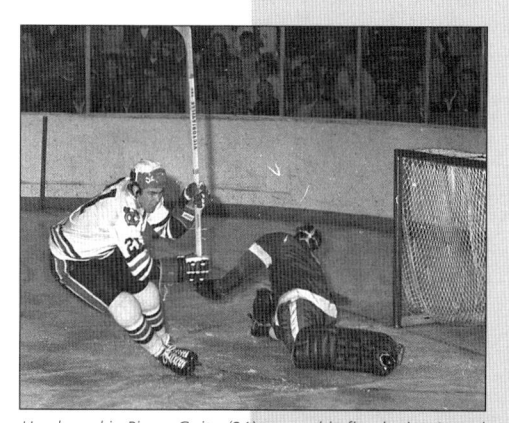

Hawk rookie Pierre Guite (21) scores his first junior A goal against Hamilton Red Wings in a 7-5 win October 12, 1969.
St. Catharines Standard photo

DOUG ROMBOUGH

After two seasons with the Black Hawks, 1968 to 1970, centre Doug Rombough was drafted by the Buffalo Sabres in 1970. He won a Calder Cup with the Cincinnati Swords in 1973, scoring 18 points in 14 playoff games. In 1978 he won the CHL championship with the Fort Worth Texans.

Doug Rombough in a CHL Dallas Black Hawk uniform
Ernie Fitzsimmons Collection

From 1972 to 1976 the Fergus native played in 150 regular-season games with the Sabres, New York Islanders, and Minnesota North Stars. He retired in 1978.

PIERRE GUITE

Pierre Guite spent two seasons with the Black Hawks and had a great deal of success on and off the ice. When the Montreal native arrived in St. Catharines in 1969, he was determined to learn English. He not only succeeded, but was selected as Mr. Collegiate of 1971 in his second year at the St. Catharines Collegiate.

St. Catharines Museum - Cornelius Collection, C10,652

"He was a great scholar and a credit to the Black Hawks and the school," the Collegiate principal said.

Guite collected 112 points in his two seasons with the Hawks, but was not happy in his last season.

"They [Hawks] wanted me to fight all the time and I didn't want to," Guite said.

He was drafted by the Detroit Red Wings in 1972, but turned pro with the WHA Quebec Nordiques with whom he won an Avco Cup in 1977. After seven years in the WHA, collecting 200 points, he retired in 1978 at 27.

Today Pierre lives and works in Florida. His son Ben was called up to the Colorado Avalanche in 2007.

BLACK HAWKS 1970-1971

Hawk goalie Keith Pallett deflects a shot from London's number 8, Bob Wright, during a 6-3 Hawks win on December 20, 1970.
St. Catharines Standard photo

Marcel Dionne (centre) is congratulated by teammates Brian McKenzie (left) and Clyde Simon (right) for winning his second straight league scoring championship, March 28, 1971.
St. Catharines Standard photo

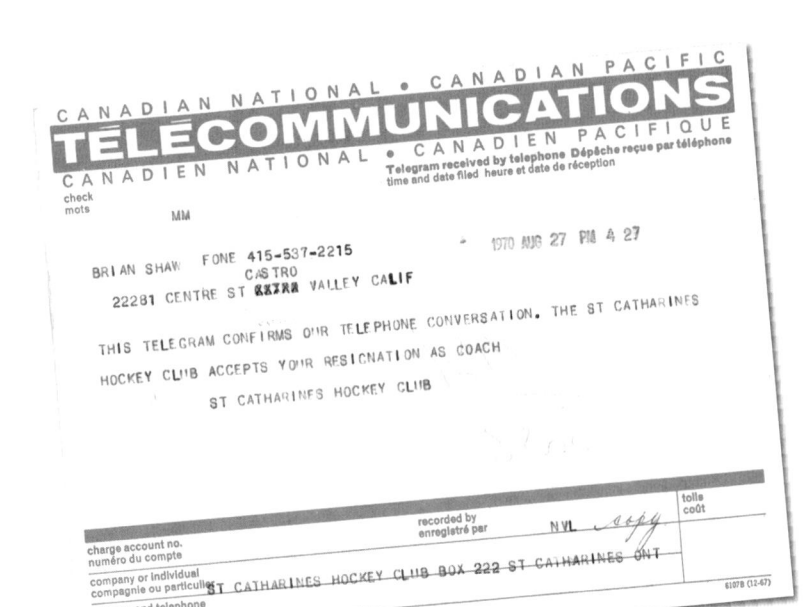

Telegram confirming Brian Shaw's resignation as the Hawks coach
Janine Muller Collection

17 new usherettes make their debut at Garden City Arena on October 4, 1970.
St. Catharines Standard photo

St. Catharines Mayor Mac Chown drops the puck at the Black Hawks home opener on October 4, 1970. Taking the faceoff for the Hawks is Marcel Dionne (9) and for the Kitchener Rangers, Bill Barber (12). The Hawks won the game 5-3.
St. Catharines Standard photo

BLACK HAWKS 1970-1971

HAWKS WIN THIRD OHA TITLE

Before the season started, 1,000 season tickets had been sold, the largest number in the history of Junior A hockey in the Garden City. Each club in the league was to play eight more games in 1970-71, making the 62-game schedule the longest since 1953-54 when teams played 59 games. Bob MacMillan joined the team from Prince Edward Island and came through with 103 points. Pierre Guite and Mike Bloom gave the club plenty of muscle and scoring power. George Hulme was solid in goal and there was a strong defence corps made up of Paul Shakes, Dave Fortier, Bob McMahon, Brian McBratney, and Tim Jacobs.

The Hawks lost the season opener against the Peterborough Petes 6-5, for the third straight year, but it didn't take the club long to show it would be a force to be reckoned with that season.

In the first home game, the club had a new look. During the opening ceremonies, the crowd was introduced to four of several mini-skirted usherettes who replaced the male usherettes from previous seasons. The usherettes drew almost as large an ovation as the Hawks players.

• • •

In 1970-71 it looked like the Hawks had a real shot at winning the Memorial Cup, but it was Frank Milne, not Brian Shaw, behind the Hawks bench when the season began. Shaw's departure was unexpected as the 1969-70 team had responded to his coaching methods and finished third in the league standings with 66 points. There were plenty of stories circulating as to why Shaw left the Garden City, but nobody was talking – publicly. It was alleged at the time that Shaw was fired amid rumours of sexual misconduct.

In 1997 when Sheldon Kennedy accused Swift Current Junior A coach Graham James of sexual assault, Shaw's name came up; there were allegations of sexual misconduct with players while he was coach/GM and owner in the Western Hockey League. Three former WHL

Front row: Peter Crosbie, Paul Shakes, Bob McMahon, Fred Muller (president and GM), Marcel Dionne (captain), Frank Milne (coach), Brian McKenzie, Bob MacMillan, George Hulme. Second row: Harry Argent (property manager), Fred Litzen (chief scout), Max Hansen, Gary Running, Pierre Guite, Mike Bloom, Brian McBratney, Glenn Cickello, Dr. Bob Hannah (team dentist), Dr. H. Dyck (team doctor). Back row: Howie Beaupit (assistant trainer), Bob Peppler, Jerry Andreatta, Tim Jacobs, Mike Ballanger, Dave Pay, Dave Fortier, Clyde Simon, Jeff Jacques, Ron Dionne, Gary Stevens (trainer).

ATTENDANCE FIGURES
Average per regular-season game: 2,991
Season's largest crowd: 3,361
Season's smallest crowd: 1,970

PLAYOFF ROUNDS: 4
Eliminated Kitchener 4-0, Montreal Junior Canadiens 4-3 and Toronto Marlboros 4-0. Forfeited Eastern Final to Quebec Remparts who led the series 3-2

1970-1971

GAMES PLAYED	WON	LOST	TIED	FOR	AGAINST	POINTS	FINISH
62	40	17	5	343	236	85	2/10

Leading Scorers

PLAYER	GOALS	ASSISTS	POINTS
Marcel Dionne	62	81	143
Brian McKenzie	39	85	124
Bob MacMillan	42	61	103
Clyde Simon	44	36	80
Bob Peppler	38	35	73

Leading Goaltenders

PLAYER	GP	GA	SO	GAA
George Hulme	53.75	207	2	3.85
Peter Crosbie	3	12	0	4

St. Catharines Museum - *Hulme Collection 2004.71.3*

BLACK HAWKS 1970-1971

FRANK MILNE

Frank Milne, a former minor pro player who won a Calder Cup with the AHL Cleveland Barons, was hired by Muller after he had coached the Dixie Beehives to the Junior B provincial title in 1970. In 1971 Milne guided the Hawks to the OHA Junior A championship and a controversial Eastern Canada final appearance against the Quebec Remparts.

After leaving the Hawks in 1973 he founded Milne and Associates, which became one of the top players' agents in North America. Over the years, his firm represented 500 players.

In 1991 he introduced hockey to North Charleston, South Carolina, with the East Coast Hockey League's South Carolina Stingrays. The team was an instant success with 5,600 season ticket holders, but it was sold for a tidy profit in 1995. Later, Milne held executive positions with the Raleigh Ice Caps and Louisiana Ice Gators in the ECHL.

Off the ice, Milne was a part owner and president of Blueliner Stables Inc. The star of the stables was standardbred trotter Twin B Playboy with $800,000 in earnings and the holder of several track records.

During his hockey career Milne has been honoured for his achievements by New York City and the governor of South Carolina. In 2005-06 he was director of player development for Pensacola Ice Pilots of the ECHL.

Frank died in St. Catharines on June 13, 2008

St. Catharines Museum - Janine Muller Collection, C11,072

Hawks coach Frank Milne (left) and trainer Gary Stevens watch the action in a 6-3 win over Montreal October 13, 1970. St. Catharines Standard photo

players made accusations against Shaw, including ex-Edmonton goalie Larry Hendrick who played for Shaw in 1971-72. "Advances or suggestions were made openly and blatantly," Hendrick told hockey writer Robin Brownlee.

Shaw was the Western Hockey League's chairman of the board of governors for several years and at no time did the league take action against him, despite the rumors of misconduct.

No one in St. Catharines who played for Shaw came forward with charges of sexual abuse or misconduct, but there were plenty of stories concerning Shaw's tyrannical rule when he coached the Hawks from 1968 to 1970.

Shaw didn't want his players going out with girls, but Marcel Dionne, who had been warned by team owner Fred Muller not to get too friendly with Shaw, told his coach it was too late because he had found the girl he was going to marry.

In interviews with *St. Catharines Standard* reporters, former Black Hawks defender Bob McMahon remembered how Shaw told him to run certain players like Bobby Sheehan from his own team into the boards during practice if they weren't hitting in games. Ex-goaltender George Hulme recalled Shaw ordered a practice with damp uniforms at 3 a.m. in St. Catharines after losing a one-goal game to Montreal. Former Hawks captain Skeeter Teal loved playing for team owner Fred Muller. "But when he [Muller] wasn't around, it was a scene straight from hell," Teal said in 1997.

Jack Gatecliff said that Muller told him that he wanted to fire Shaw after his first season in St. Catharines, but the Chicago Black Hawks threatened to withdraw support if he let Shaw go. According to Gatecliff, after Shaw's second season Muller decided to fire Shaw and went to the OHA. The OHA came to an agreement with Shaw that he would not be prosecuted if he accepted a suspension from hockey in Ontario. Shaw left the province. Muller alleged that the Canadian Hockey Association knew all about Shaw's reputation, but still allowed him to coach in Western Canada.

Shaw died in 1993 of AIDS-related brain cancer. According to writer Laura Robinson on the web site *play the game.org*, the Western Hockey League paid tribute to Shaw after his death by giving him its "Humanitarian of the Year Award." In 1997 it is alleged that the league quietly removed his name.

• • •

After Marcel Dionne broke his collarbone on December 11, 1970, Brian McKenzie assumed a leadership role. "McKenzie picked that team up by the bootstraps," recalled ex-teammate Dave Fortier. During Dionne's absence, the Hawks won eight, lost four, and tied two games.

On Sunday, December 6, 1970, Marcel Dionne scored four points against the Peterborough Petes and broke Brian Cullen's regular-season points record (290) with 293 and Cullen's career points total (359) by accumulating 361 points.

The Hawks finished the season strongly, winning 16 and tying two of their last 20 games to take second place with 85 points, five fewer than the league-

Hawk goalie George Hulme may be playing in a fog, but here he stops Montreal's Hartland Monahan and the Hawks went on to win 6-3. The game played on October 13, 1970, was delayed 20 times by the fog. St. Catharines Standard photo

Dionne, McKenzie and Hulme before second 1971 playoff game. St. Catharines Standard photo

St. Catharines defenceman Paul Shakes (6) clears the puck from own end of rink; Gavin Kirk (14) of Toronto Marlboros sprawls on top of Black Hawk centre Marcel Dionne. St. Catharines Standard photo

BLACK HAWKS 1970-1971

leading Peterborough Petes. The team attracted a record 125,152 fans during the regular season and playoffs, an increase of 15,084 from 1969-70.

Marcel Dionne won his second OHA Junior A scoring title with 143 points, including 62 goals. What made this an amazing achievement was that he missed about six weeks of the schedule with a broken collarbone. Once again, he was runner-up for the Red Tilson Trophy won by Marlie Dave Gardner, who finished second to Dionne in the scoring race with 137 points. There were many hockey observers who felt that Dionne had been robbed of the honour for the second time in two years. "It's just one of those things that's hard to understand," a disappointed Dionne said upon learning he placed second in the voting for the Tilson Trophy.

In the playoffs, the Hawks disposed of Kitchener, Montreal, and then Toronto Marlies, to win the OHA Junior A championship for the third time in the team's history. George Hulme's outstanding goaltending was a feature of the sweep of the Marlies in four games.

Eliminating the Montreal Junior Canadiens in seven games was especially satisfying because the Canadiens had ousted the Hawks from the playoffs in the three preceding seasons. Dionne led all OHA playoff scores with 55 points, including 29 goals.

Dionne with OHA Championship Cup — St. Catharines Standard photo

Frank Milne celebrating Cup win — St. Catharines Standard photo

Hawks fans line up at Garden City Arena for playoff tickets on April 24, 1971. — St. Catharines Standard photo

THE GOOD, THE BAD AND THE UGLY

Next came the Eastern Canada final against the Quebec Remparts. When the series started it was understood that the Memorial Cup was at stake. Earlier in the season the OHA and the QJHL had decided not to play the Western Canada Junior champions for the Memorial Cup because of concessions awarded to those teams by the Canadian Amateur Hockey Association.

What attracted national interest in the series was the matchup between two junior superstars: Rempart right winger Guy Lafleur and Hawk centre Marcel Dionne. Lafleur and Dionne would be the first and second choices respectively in the 1971 Amateur Draft. Both would have outstanding NHL careers and end up in the Hockey Hall of Fame.

Owner Fred Muller was tempted to open the series in Maple Leaf Gardens, where the Hawks could have earned $6,500 after the

CO-OWNERS FRED MULLER, KEN CAMPBELL GRASP ONTARIO CUP WITH COACH FRANK MILNE Club Physician Dr. H. H. Dyck (Left), Players And Other Personnel Celebrate Victory In Dressing Room

Milne Dunked In Shower

Bedlam In Hawk Room After Clinching Victory

St. Catharines Standard

BRIAN McKENZIE

St. Catharines native Brian McKenzie played for the Black Hawks from 1968 to 1971. In his last junior year the left winger led the league in assists with 85, and earned 124 points, prompting the Pittsburgh Penguins to make him its first choice in the 1971 Amateur Draft.

St. Catharines Museum - Janine Muller Collection, C11,070

He played six games with the Penguins in 1971-72, but never got another shot in the NHL. From 1971 to 1978, he played in the AHL, CHL, WHA, NAHL and the IHL. He won a Central League championship with the Omaha Knights in 1973.

His most productive pro-season came with the IHL Toledo Goaldiggers in 1976-77 when he earned 90 points in 77 games.

He now lives in Bedford, Nova Scotia.

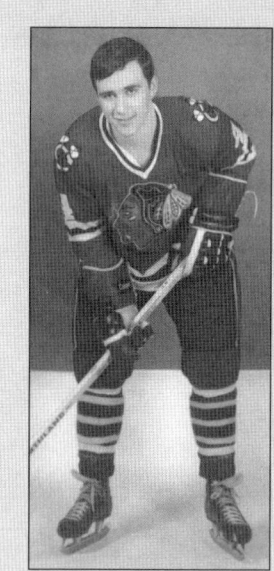

BOB McMAHON

St. Catharines native Bob McMahon was a steady Hawk rearguard from 1968 to 1971. He was also a high-scoring lacrosse star.

In 1970 he was the youngest player in the North American Lacrosse League to score 90 goals (with 50 assists), breaking lacrosse legend Gaylord Powless' goal-scoring record.

Bob was following in the footsteps of his dad Jim, who is a member of the Ontario and Canadian halls of fame.

Courtesy of Bob McMahon

After being drafted by the Boston Bruins in 1971, he played in Oklahoma City, Dayton, Baltimore, Muskegon and Charlotte.

Today he works at TRW (Thompson Products) and resides in Thorold, Ontario.

BLACK HAWKS 1970-1971

DAVE FORTIER

Sudbury's Dave Fortier spent one year with the St. Catharines Black Hawks in 1970-71 and impressed the Toronto Maple Leafs who made him their second choice in the 1971 Amateur Draft.

The stay-at-home rearguard spent 205 games in the NHL with the Leafs, New York Islanders, and the Vancouver Canucks, in an eight-year pro career that ended in 1979.

Today he is a firefighter with the Sudbury Fire Department.

St. Catharines Museum - Janine Muller Collection, C11,053

DAVE PAY

Wayne Gretzky saw Dave Pay celebrate a St. Catharines Junior B goal with a kick and a pump when he was ten-years-old. "I thought everything Dave Pay did was cool, so I started doing it," Gretzky said in his book, Gretzky: An Autobiography.

After playing with the St. Catharines Junior B Falcons and Junior A Black Hawks, Pay enrolled at the University of Wisconsin and was a member of the Badgers hockey team that won the National Collegiate Athletic Association championship in 1973.

Today Pay is a firefighter in St. Catharines.

St. Catharines Museum - Janine Muller Collection, C11,078

DENNIS VERVERGAERT

Hamilton native Dennis Ververgaert started the 1970-71 season with the St. Catharines Black Hawks, but was soon traded to the London Knights. After scoring 141 goals in 187 games for London, the right winger was the Vancouver Canucks first choice in the 1973 Amateur Draft.

In 583 regular-season NHL games with the Canucks, Philadelphia Flyers, and Washington Capitals, Ververgaert earned 392 points, including 178 goals. The former OHA all-star had his best season in 1975-76 when he scored 71 points in 80 games for Vancouver.

Dennis Ververgaert in an OHL London Knights uniform
Ernie Fitzsimmons Collection

CAHA took 60 per cent of the gross gate. He wanted to reward Hawks fans, however, and let them see their team at home. To help defray the costs of traveling to Quebec, student ticket prices were doubled to $1.50 and all other tickets were increased by $1.50. Before tickets went on sale for the first game May 2, 1971, at 10 a.m., fans started lining up at 4:30 a.m.

The teams split the first two games in St. Catharines and then the series moved to the Quebec Colisée. The scores of games three and four were a small part of the news coming out of Quebec. Both games featured major brawls on and off the ice.

Hawk players feared for their lives in game four when Hawk Mike Bloom struck a policeman with his stick at the end of the game. Bloom said it was an accident, but it didn't matter. The players were forced to flee and seek refugee from the mob in their dressing room. The Quebec police couldn't or wouldn't lay down the law. When the Hawks finally reached their bus, it was pelted with bottles. A parade of angry fans in cars followed the Hawk bus to the team's hotel and stayed for several hours in the parking lot. Players were told to keep the curtains closed in their rooms and stay away from the windows. It was a nightmare.

Game five was played in Maple Leaf Gardens and the Hawks thumped the Remparts 6-3, but there would be no game six in Quebec City. Team President and General Manager Fred Muller would not go to Quebec and endanger the lives of his players. The parents of several players would not allow their sons to return to Quebec even if Muller changed his mind. The OHA president at the time supported Muller's decision, but it made no difference. The series was forfeited to the Remparts who then reversed their decision not to play the Western champions for the Memorial Cup.

The Remparts defeated the Edmonton Oil Kings in a best-of-three-series and won junior hockey's most coveted trophy. It was a bitter pill to swallow for the Black Hawks who were convinced they could have beaten the Remparts.

Muller was suspended by the CAHA for one year for refusing to go to Quebec, but in St. Catharines he was named the 1971 Sportsman of the Year.

In the 1971 post season, Dionne established playoff records for goals, 33, and total points, 64. ■

Fred Muller with Sportsman of the Year Award
St. Catharines Museum - Janine Muller Collection, C11,073

The Ontario Junior A hockey champion St. Catharines Black Hawks and St. Catharines Falcons, who finished first in the Niagara District Junior B League, received individual awards last night during the annual post-season banquet sponsored by the St. Catharines Junior Hockey Supporters' Association. Front row, from the left, Bob MacMillan, rookie of the year; Brian Campbell, Falcons most valuable player; Hawk captain Marcel Dionne, most valuable player and Junior A scoring champion; Paul Shakes, outstanding defenceman and most gentlemanly player. Back row, Mike Bloom, most popular player; Bob Peppler, most colourful player; Bob McMahon, outstanding defenceman in playoffs; Dave Fortier, most improved player. Peppler and goaltender George Hulme also received special awards from the Supporters Association.

St. Catharines Standard photo

BLACK HAWKS 1970-1971

MARCEL DIONNE

In the fall of 1968, St. Catharines Black Hawks owner Fred Muller brought Marcel Dionne to St. Catharines and the move changed the Drummondville native's life. From the moment the 17-year-old centreman stepped onto the Garden City Arena ice, he was a fan favourite and the player who packed the arena for three straight seasons.

In 1970 and 1971, he won the OHA Junior A scoring title, and as captain led the team to the 1971 OHA championship. In the 1971 Amateur Draft, he was picked second overall by the Detroit Red Wings behind Guy Lafleur.

From 1971 to 1989, Dionne was a superstar in the NHL, first with Detroit Red Wings, and then Los Angeles Kings, and finally, New York Rangers. When he retired, he was the Kings all-time leader in goals, assists and points.

In 1,348 NHL regular-season games, he scored 731 goals and collected 1,771 points. He won the Art Ross Trophy in 1980 with 53 goals and 137 points. Dionne also won the Lady Byng Trophy twice, in 1975 and 1977, and the Lester B. Pearson Award in 1979 and 1980. He was named to two first and two second NHL all-star teams and represented Canada seven times in international tournaments. In 1992 he was inducted into the Hockey Hall of Fame.

Today the head of Marcel Dionne Enterprises Ltd. resides in Niagara Falls, Ontario.

Marcel Dionne with Hawks supporter Walt McCollum
St. Catharines Museum - Janine Muller Collection, C11,074

Points Champion Hits Bonanza

Marcel Dionne, 1970-71 captain of the Ontario Junior A champion St. Catharines Black Hawks, was signed to his first professional contract today by Detroit Red Wings. Lawyer Alan Eagleson, who represented Dionne, said that it was the highest contract ever given a first-year player in the National Hockey League. Dionne will reportedly receive a guaranteed $50,000 plus incentive bonuses which could bring him an additional $20,000. He is shown here with the Eddie Powers Memorial Trophy awarded annually to the leading points scorer in the Ontario Hockey Association Junior A League. Dionne was the first player to win the points title two successive years since Billy Taylor of Oshawa Generals in the late 1930s.

St. Catharines Standard photo, April 17, 1971

MIKE BLOOM

Ottawa native Mike Bloom played three seasons in St. Catharines, 1969 to 1972, before turning pro with the Boston Bruins in 1972.

Bloom had a very good reputation as a fighter in junior, but he just wanted to play hockey in the NHL.

Ernie Fitzsimmons Collection

After two seasons in the minors, he was claimed by the Washington Capitals and then was traded to Detroit Red Wings. From 1975 to 1978, he played with the Wings or their farm clubs, winning the CHL championship with Kansas City Blues in 1977.

He had his best year as a pro in 1977-78 with Kansas City Red Wings, scoring 23 goals and collecting 77 points.

After two seasons in Europe, he retired from hockey at age 28. Today he makes his home in Marina, California.

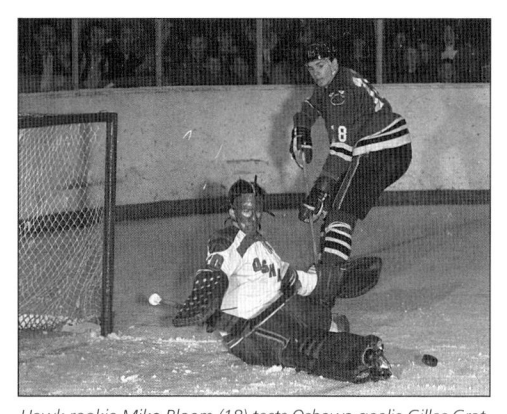

Hawk rookie Mike Bloom (18) tests Oshawa goalie Gilles Gratton in a 8-5 victory February 22, 1970. Bloom scored a hat trick in the game.
St. Catharines Standard photo

BOB MacMILLAN

Bob MacMillan was a Prince Edward Island native who had nine Ontario junior teams bidding for his services in 1970 before ending up with the St. Catharines Black Hawks. He made an impressive debut, collecting 103 points in his rookie year.

St. Catharines Museum - Janine Muller Collection, C11,062

He decided to turn pro with the WHA Minnesota Fighting Saints in 1972, but found his way to the NHL in 1974 with the New York Rangers. From 1975 to 1985, MacMillan played with five different NHL clubs: St. Louis, Atlanta (which became Calgary), Colorado, New Jersey, and Chicago.

The right winger had his most productive NHL year with the Atlanta Flames in 1978-79 when earned 108 points, including 37 goals. He also won the Lady Byng Trophy that year.

In 753 regular-season NHL games, he recorded 577 points, including 228 goals.

Bob resides in Charlottetown, Prince Edward Island, where he is a successful businessman and former Tory MLA in the P.E.I. legislature.

Hawk rookie Bob MacMillan (14) gets up close and personal with Kitchener goalie Glen Sperich in a 6-5 win on November 1, 1970.
St. Catharines Standard photo

159

BLACK HAWKS 1971-1972

EARLY SEASON ACTION

Hawk Bill Best (15) scores his first junior A goal against Toronto Marlie goalie Kevin Neville in a 6-3 loss, October 5, 1971.
St. Catharines Standard photo

New York City native Max Hansen (11) pokes the puck against Hamilton netminder Mike Veisor in a 6-2 loss, October 24, 1971.
St. Catharines Standard photo

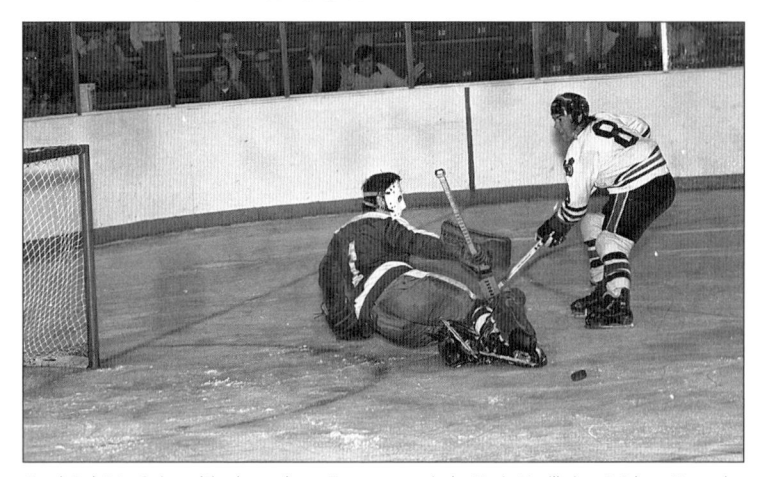

Hawk Bob MacGuigan (8) takes a shot a Toronto netminder Kevin Neville in a 3-2 loss, November 16, 1971.
St. Catharines Standard photo

Hawk right winger Dave Gorman (12) just misses Ottawa goalie Bunny Larocque. The game ended in a 2-2 draw on November 28, 1971.
St. Catharines Standard photo

BLACK HAWKS 1971-1972

GOALTENDING PROBLEMS AND INJURIES WEAKEN THE HAWKS

ATTENDANCE FIGURES
Average per regular-season game: 2,224
Season's largest crowd: 2,839
Season's smallest crowd: 1,752

PLAYOFF ROUNDS: 1
Eliminated by Peterborough 4-1

Accident On Meaford Farm
Black Hawk Official Dies When Tractor Overturns

By JACK GATECLIFF
Standard Sports Editor

Chicago Black Hawk director of player personnel Ken Campbell was killed early yesterday afternoon in an accident on his farm near Meaford.

The 47-year-old Campbell had been co-owner of St. Catharines Black Hawks of the Ontario Hockey Association Junior A league for four years until he sold his 50 per cent interest in the club to his partner Fred Muller less than seven weeks ago.

According to reports from the scene of the tragedy Campbell was removing stumps of trees from an apple orchard, clearing the ground for a swimming pool.

KEN CAMPBELL

St. Catharines Standard

1971-1972

GAMES PLAYED	WON	LOST	TIED	FOR	AGAINST	POINTS	FINISH
63	25	31	7	253	308	57	7/10

Leading Scorers

PLAYER	GOALS	ASSISTS	POINTS
Paul Shakes	20	48	68
Mike Bloom	25	40	65
Jeff Jacques	26	31	57
Dave Gorman	31	24	55
Bob MacMillan	12	41	53

Leading Goaltenders

PLAYER	GP	GA	SO	GAA
Brian Cousineau	24.16	141	0	5.83
Mike Ralph	24	108	0	4.50

In 1971 Fred Muller gained complete control of the Hawks by buying Ken Campbell's shares. Later that summer, Campbell, director of player personnel for the Chicago Black Hawks, was killed as a result of an accident on his farm.

Without Dionne, Pierre Guite, and six other graduating players, the Hawks were a much weaker team. The club dropped its season opener in Peterborough and lost four in a row before winning in the team's third home game.

By November 19, 1971, the team had lost nine straight, and owner Fred Muller was worried about the effect poor team performance was going to have on attendance. "I just have to commend them [the spectators] for their patience," Muller said after the eighth loss.

One player who earned the praise of Hawks fans and team officials throughout the season was defenceman Tim Jacobs, who could also play effectively on a forward line if necessary. "If we had 19 like Timmy we'd have no trouble," coach Frank Milne said on January 1, 1972.

Earlier in November, the St. Catharines Central Lions Club purchased an organ for the arena and it was used for the first time on November 21, 1971. Music added to the enthusiasm of the crowd and the Hawks broke their losing streak with a 9-2 win over Niagara Falls. The Hawks never lost another home game until January 2, 1972. Muller considered bringing in more organs and a piano if he thought it would keep the team winning!

Injuries to veterans during the season forced Milne to bring up players from the local Junior B team. Bob MacMillan was forced to sit out six weeks with hepatitis and he no

St. Catharines Mayor Mac Chown drops the opening faceoff puck between the Hawks Bob MacMillan (14) and London's Wayne Elder (3) on October 3, 1971. There were several fog problems in the game won by London 5-2.

St. Catharines Standard photo

161

BLACK HAWKS 1971-1972

PAUL SHAKES

In his sophomore season with the Hawks in 1970-71, defence-man Paul Shakes was chosen the club's best defenceman and most gentlemanly player. In his last year, the Collingwood native was the team's leading scorer with 68 points and a OHA Junior A First Team All-Star defenceman with future NHL star Dennis Potvin.

St. Catharines Museum - Janine Muller Collection, C11,082

He was selected by the California Golden Seals in the 1972 Amateur Draft and saw action in 21 regular-season NHL games during his four-year pro career. In 1975 he and former St. Catharines teammate Tim Jacobs won a Calder Cup with the AHL Springfield Indians.

A serious back injury ended his career in 1975 and since then he has been involved in training and racing standardbred horses from his Maple Lane Farms in Stayner, Ontario.

TIM JACOBS

Keswick native Tim Jacobs played for the Black Hawks from 1969 to 1972. While with the Hawks, he played defence and was a forward when needed.

After being drafted by the California Golden Seals in 1972, he started his pro career with the Western Hockey League Salt Lake Golden Eagles.

St. Catharines Museum - Janine Muller Collection, C11,060

In 1975, he and former Hawk teammate Paul Shakes were members of the AHL Calder Cup champion Springfield Indians. In 1975-76 he played 46 games with California, but after an injury he never got another chance to play in the NHL.

He retired in 1979 and became a head pressman with MacLean Hunter in Aurora.

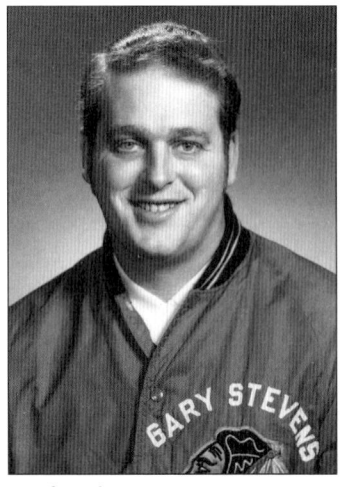

Hawks trainer Gary Stevens
St. Catharines Museum - Janine Muller Collection, C11,151

Hawk players line up for a haircut on November 4, 1971. From left to right: Brian Cousineau, Mike Bloom, licensed barber and assistant trainer Ken Egerter, and Danny Blair.
St. Catharines Standard photo

Hawk goalie Mike Ralph slides out to make a save in a 2-2 tie with Peterborough Petes on January 9, 1972. Also in the photo are Hawks Tim Jacobs (3) and Garry Lariviere (4).
St. Catharines Standard photo

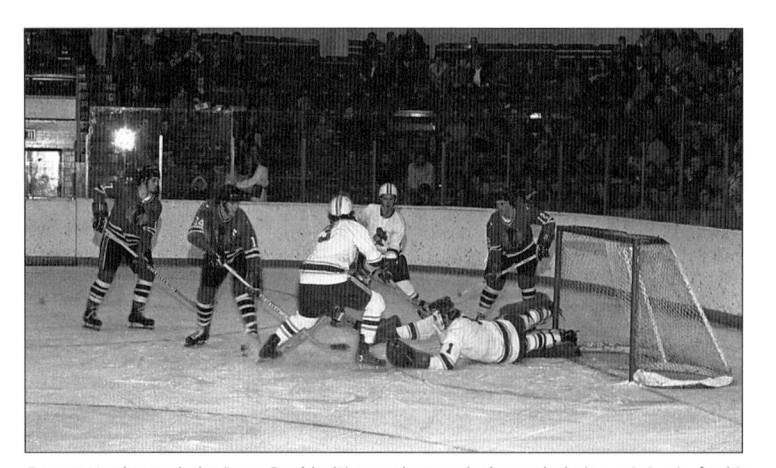

Former Hawk netminder Peter Crosbie (1) sprawls to grab the puck during a 3-2 win for his new club, the London Knights, on January 23, 1972. Hawks Dave Gorman (12) and Bob MacMillan (14) are looking for a loose puck.
St. Catharines Standard photo

sooner returned than Mike Bloom suffered a broken bone in his wrist and was out for more than a month. Jeff Jacques seemed to have the most bad luck, as he suffered injuries to both knees, a shoulder separation, concussion, broken nose, and lacerated ear at various times during the season.

Goaltending was unsettled as five netminders saw action. On March 21, 1972, the club's three regular goalies, Mike Ralph, Brian Cousineau, and Gord Back, left the team. Milne wasn't worried about the walkout. "The goaltending just hasn't developed as I'd hoped and lately the bad games have outnumbered the good," he said. Cousineau and Black rejoined the team, but by then Milne had turned to young goalie Bill Cheropita who had outstanding performances in the club's last two regular-season contests with a goals-against average of 1.0.

162

Despite the team's problems, it finished the 1971-72 season in seventh place with 57 points. Defenceman Paul Shakes led the team in scoring with 68 points, followed by Mike Bloom with 65. It was the first time in 29 years that a defenceman had led the team in points.

Bloom appeared in a Quebec court on December 15, 1971, to settle his assault charge from the 1970 playoff game in Quebec; he was fined $200 for the incident involving a Quebec City policeman.

Lack of interest in the club was evident as the number of season tickets sold fell to 1,400, down 200 from the previous year. Attendance, which totaled 68,944 during the season and 5,045 during the playoffs, dropped drastically from 1970-71's totals of 92,712 and 32,440. To be fair, the previous year the Hawks had gone as far as the Eastern Canada final and played eight more playoff games.

Promotional events staged throughout the season such as a stick night and a puck night for youngsters, the selection of a Miss Black Hawk (Wendy Jane Rose), and a "win a pony night", didn't seem to help.

In the playoffs, the Hawks were eliminated by the Peterborough Petes in five games. One bright spot for the club was the excellent play of netminder Bill Cheropita and rookie Dave Gorman, who scored five goals in the post season after collecting 55 points, including 31 goals in the regular season.

At the conclusion of the 1971-72 season, Fred Muller sold the team to former Niagara Falls Flyers owner Hap Emms for $230,000. Emms had sold his Niagara Falls Flyers to Sudbury. "I'd just been going at it too hard and too long," Muller told the *St. Catharines Standard*.

1971-72 Black Hawks Award Winners, April 11, 1972
Left to right: Dave Gorman, top rookie; Jeff Jacques, most valuable player; Mike Bloom, most colourful; Gladys Crowe, Tim Jacobs, most under-rated; Garry Lariviere, most improved; Paul Shakes, best defenceman and leading scorer.
St. Catharines Standard photo

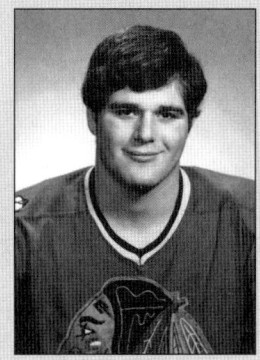

RON SERAFINI

Defenceman Ron Serafini came from Michigan to play two seasons with the Black Hawks from 1971 to 1973.

The second choice of the California Seals in the 1973 Amateur Draft, Serafini only played two games with the Seals in a pro career that lasted from 1973 to 1977 in the WHL, CHL, WHA and SHL.

Janine Muller Collection

TERRY CASEY
(THE ENERGY GUY)

Toronto native Terry Casey spent two years with the Hawks, 1971-72 and 1973-74, after one year with the Sudbury Wolves. "He [coach Frank Milne] called me the energy guy. When things got a little flat, he would give me the tap," Casey said.

Janine Muller Collection

The right winger didn't mind playing for Hap Emms in his second stint with the Hawks. "He taught me to be a hockey player, but he also taught me to be frugal," Casey recalled.

After his pro hockey career ended at 21, Casey used Emms' cost-cutting ideas to eventually set up his own consulting business, Better Bottom Line, based in Surrey, British Columbia. He flies across North America advising airlines and manufacturers on how to manage their money. Hap would be proud.

Hawk Terry Casey (16) reaches for the puck around the Kitchener Rangers net in a 4-3 victory January 30, 1972.
St. Catharines Standard photo

BLACK HAWKS 1972-1973

Hawk Greg Craig (23) is stopped by Peterborough goalie Frank Salive in a 3-3 tie on February 18, 1973.
St. Catharines Standard photo

Hawk Gord Titcomb (left) and Sudbury's Randy Holt collide during a 5-5 tie, October 15, 1972. Dave Gorman scored all 5 goals for the Hawks.
St. Catharines Standard photo

Hawk Wilf Paiement (9) and Gord Titcomb (17) close in on Soo netminder Bill Thompson in a 6-2 win on November 26, 1972. Number 8 is Bob MacGuigan.
St. Catharines Standard photo

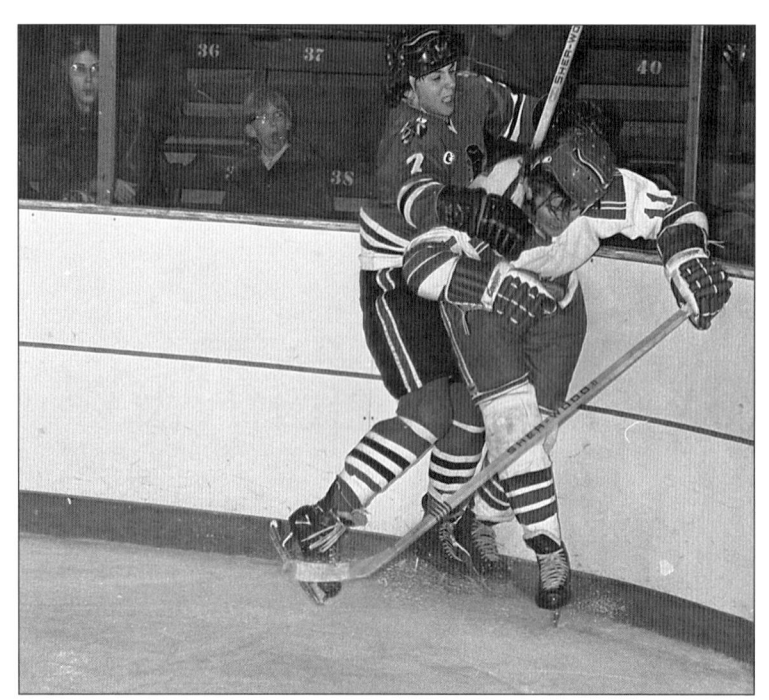

Hawk Dave Salvian (7) clashes on the boards with Kitchener Ranger Roger Bourbonnais (11) in a 7-3 loss on March 4, 1973.
St. Catharines Standard photo

Max Hansen was from the Bronx in New York City. In 1969-70 he played for the Brooklyn Stars.
Ernie Fitzsimmons Collection

164

BLACK HAWKS 1972-1973

HAP EMMS BUYS THE BLACK HAWKS

With eight OHA Junior A championships and two Memorial Cups, Hap Emms knew how to win. But he also had a reputation as an owner who was tight with the buck, and the question was whether or not he could keep junior hockey afloat in the Garden City with a limited budget.

For the 1972-73 season, the Montreal franchise had been transferred to Sault Ste. Marie, and Sudbury Wolves took the place of Niagara Falls. In Emms' first year as owner, the Hawks finished fifth with 59 points and were eliminated in the first round of the playoffs by Toronto Marlies in four games.

Attendance, which had averaged 2,991 in 1970-71 and 2,224 in 1971-72, fell to 2,063 (63,944 in 31 games) in 1972-73. The NHL Buffalo Sabres and Tier 2 hockey in Welland, along with plenty of hockey on TV, contributed to the attendance decline, which was also being felt around the OHA Junior A League.

There were, however, some good signs for the following year. Rick Adduono led the team with 109 points and Dave Gorman was right behind with 103. With the return of Dave Salvian, Garry Lariviere, Wilf Paiement, and Bill Cheropita, there was every indication that this team would be a contender in 1973-74.

Paul Emms and owner Hap Emms
St. Catharines Standard photo

In April of 1973, Hawks coach Frank Milne got his walking papers from Hap Emms who decided to give the coach's responsibilities to his son, Paul, who had been the club's general manager. ■

ATTENDANCE FIGURES
Average per regular-season game: 2,063
Season's largest crowd: 3,099
Season's smallest crowd: 1,331

PLAYOFF ROUNDS: 1
Eliminated by Toronto Malboros 4-0

1972-1973

GAMES PLAYED	WON	LOST	TIED	FOR	AGAINST	POINTS	FINISH
63	24	28	11	280	319	59	5/10

Leading Scorers

PLAYER	GOALS	ASSISTS	POINTS
Rick Adduono	45	64	109
Dave Gorman	46	57	103
Jeff Jacques	32	46	78
Bob MacGuigan	26	28	54
Wilf Paiement	18	27	45

Leading Goaltenders

PLAYER	GP	GA	SO	GAA
Brian Cousineau	28	136	0	4.87
Jim Pettie	30	152	1	5.04

Supporters' Club Trophy Winners 1972-73, April 7, 1973
From the left: Dave Gorman, most gentlemanly; Rick Adduono, top rookie; Wayne Chrysler, most valuable player; Dave Salvian, most improved; Jeff Jacques, most popular; Rick Hampton, outstanding defenceman; and Bob MacGuigan, most colourful
St. Catharines Standard photo

Hawk Jeff Jacques flips the puck over Peterborough goalie Rolly Kimble in a 7-3 win on October 29, 1972.
St. Catharines Standard photo

165

BLACK HAWKS 1972-1973

RICK ADDUONO

During his three seasons with the Hawks, Thunder Bay native Rick Adduono led the club in scoring twice and shared the OHA scoring championship in 1974 with 135 points.

He has the third highest points total, 343, in the history of St. Catharines Junior A hockey, behind Marcel Dionne and Brian Cullen.

After an injury-filled season in 1974-75, the centre was taken by the Boston Bruins in the 1975 Amateur Draft, but Adduono's NHL career never materialized as he played only a few games with the Bruins and Atlanta Flames.

He spent seven years in the minors, playing mostly in the AHL. In 1977-78 he shared the AHL scoring championship with 98 points while with the Rochester Americans. He scored 20 goals and had 53 points in his one year in the WHA with the Birmingham Bulls.

In the 1980s, Adduono played on three Allan Cup winners with the Thunder Bay Twins.

After ending his playing career, Adduono was a very successful coach in the ECHL with the South Carolina Stingrays (two Kelly Cups) and the Greensboro Generals. In 2004-05 he was the bench boss of the United Hockey League Port Huron Beacons, and in 2005-06 he spent part of the season coaching the ECHL Pensacola Ice Pilots. In 2006-07 he was the coach of the Long Beach IceDogs.

St. Catharines Standard photo

Hawk Rick Adduono (18) scores on Peterborough goalie Mike Kasmetis in a 5-3 win on October 6, 1974.
St. Catharines Standard photo

PAUL EMMS

Paul Emms, Hap's son, was a former Barrie Flyer who had won a Memorial Cup in 1951 while playing for his dad. The younger Emms was following a musical career when his dad asked him to manage the Niagara Falls Flyers in 1965.

St. Catharines Standard

In 1967 Hap persuaded Paul to coach the team. He had no experience. The rookie coach surprised everyone by leading the Flyers to the Memorial Cup in the spring of 1968.

After Hap bought the St. Catharines Black Hawks in 1972, Paul managed the club before taking over the coaching reins from Frank Milne in 1973. In his first season, he guided the Hawks to a Memorial Cup appearance in Calgary.

Since 1977 he has resumed his music career and is based in Port Severn, Ontario.

SUZANNE EMMS

Hamilton native Suzanne Emms, wife of Hawk general manager Paul Emms, was team secretary since the 1967-68 season when the Emms family owned the Niagara Falls Flyers. Mrs. Emms looked after the correspondence, attended all home games and as many on the road as possible. Paul and Suzanne met in Barrie while she was attending a figure skating school.

St. Catharines Standard

JEFF JACQUES

After three seasons with the Black Hawks, 1970 to 1973, Preston native Jeff Jacques was drafted by the California Golden Seals, but opted to make a deal with the WHA Toronto Toros.

After playing in Jacksonville and then Mohawk Valley, Jacques was called up by the Toros. He scored four goals and added an assist in his WHA debut in 1975 at the Cow Palace in Houston, Texas.

Courtesy of Jeff Jacques

The right winger moved with the Toros to Birmingham, Alabama, in 1976, but he retired after being traded to Edmonton in 1977.

If you are visiting Niagara-on-the-Lake, you can find Jeff at the Davy House, a bed and breakfast he owns and operates with his wife Florence Vint.

JIM PETTIE

Toronto native Jim Pettie played one season for the St. Catharines Black Hawks in 1972-73. After being drafted by the Boston Bruins in 1973, he turned pro with the IHL Dayton Gems.

Although the goalie nicknamed "Seaweed" put up some good numbers in the minors, he saw action in only 21 regular-season games with the Bruins.

Jim Pettie with the IHL Dayton Gems
Ernie Fitzsimmons Collection

He won the IHL championship with the Dayton Gems in 1976 after posting a 2.86 goals-against average with five shutouts in the regular season.

Today Pettie resides in Rochester, New York.

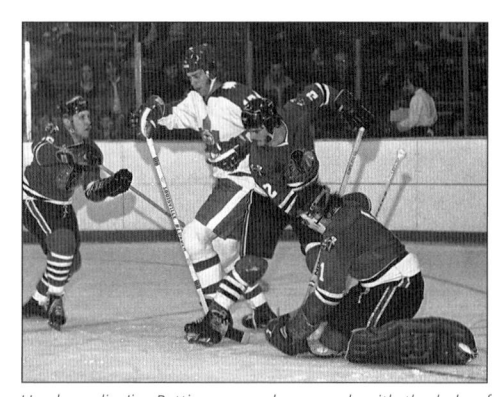

Hawk goalie Jim Pettie snags a loose puck with the help of defenceman Ron Serafini (2) in a 6-1 loss to the Toronto Marlies on March 23, 1973.
St. Catharines Standard photo

DENNIS OWCHAR

Rearguard Dennis Owchar spent part of the 1972-73 season with the Black Hawks before being drafted by Pittsburgh in the 1973 Amateur Draft.

In his rookie pro year he won the Calder Cup with the AHL Hershey Bears in 1974.

After three years with the Penguins, he played with Colorado from 1977 to 1979. The Dryden native retired in 1981 from the AHL New Haven Nighthawks.

Dennis Owchar with the Hershey Bears
Ernie Fitzsimmons Collection

Today he lives in Unionville, Ontario.

BLACK HAWKS 1973-1974

HAWKS CAPTURE FOURTH OHA TITLE

Black Hawks Wilf Paiement (left), Dave Gorman (centre), and Rick Adduono pose for a picture at the 1973 training, September 12, 1973.
St. Catharines Standard photo

A RECORD-BREAKING TEAM

The 1973-74 St. Catharines Black Hawks were one of the most successful and exciting teams ever to play in the Garden City. It's easy to see why. The Hawks finished the 70-game regular schedule with 88 points, the highest number ever attained by any St. Catharines Junior A team in its 31-year existence. The 358 goals scored by the team during the season was a record for Junior A hockey in the Garden City.

At home the club had an unbelievable record of 35 straight home games (27 regular-season and eight playoff contests) without a defeat. The Hawks lost only three home games all season. The team tied the record for most games without a defeat, 14 (1953-54 Teepees), and then broke it on December 11, 1973, with number 15.

The GAS line, comprised of Dave Gorman, Rick Adduono, and Dave Salvian, amassed 361 points in the regular season, more than any other line in the league, reminding Garden City fans of the scoring feats of the CBC line (Brian Cullen, Hugh Barlow, and Barry Cullen) that established a league record of 389 points in 1953-54.

Rick Adduono shared the OHA Junior A scoring title with Soo Greyhound Jack Valiquette and was the eighth local player to win the Eddie Powers Trophy.

Continued on page 169

ATTENDANCE FIGURES
Average per regular-season game: 1,923
Season's largest crowd: 3,427
Season's smallest crowd: 1,000

PLAYOFF ROUNDS: 3
Eliminated Oshawa 4-0-1, Toronto Marlboros 4-0, and Peterborough 4-0-1
Eliminated from Memorial Cup round robin series with 1-2 record

1973-1974

GAMES PLAYED	WON	LOST	TIED	FOR	AGAINST	POINTS	FINISH
70	41	23	6	358	278	88	2/11

Leading Scorers

PLAYER	GOALS	ASSISTS	POINTS
Rick Adduono	51	84	135
Dave Gorman	53	76	129
Wilf Paiement	50	74	124
Dave Salvian	36	61	97
Gary McAdam	30	37	67

Leading Goaltenders

PLAYER	GP	GA	SO	GAA
Bill Cheropita	47.66	188	0	3.89
Larry McIntyre	10.66	38	0	3.53

Back Row: Dave Salvian, Don Labreche, Greg Craig, Wilf Paiement, Terry Casey, Ken Breitenbach, Larry Finck, Ron Phillips, Bill Hamilton; Second Row: Trainer Bob Hill, Gary McAdam, Mark Edwards, Dr. Andy Donnelly, Dr. Al Gold, CKTB Bill Bird, Dr. H. Dyck, CHSC Karl Edmands, Director Marty Swick, Mark Dumesnil, Kevin Kennery, Trainer Vince Walker; Front Row: Larry McIntyre, Garry Lariviere, Rick Adduono, Director Walt McCollum, Owner L.A. Hap Emms, Captain Rick Hampton, Coach Paul Emms, Sportswriter Jack Gatecliff, Dave Gorman, Dave Syvret, Bill Cheropita

St. Catharines Museum - Gorman Collection, C10,630

BLACK HAWKS 1973-1974

RICK HAMPTON

Rick Hampton, the Hawks captain in 1973-74, played with the St. Catharines Black Hawks from 1972 to 1974. The 17-year-old was California Golden Seals first choice in the 1974 Amateur Draft.

St. Catharines Standard photo

The King City native spent two years playing defence with the financially-challenged Seals and two years with Cleveland after the Seals became the Barons. He ended his NHL career with the Los Angeles Kings in 1979-80.

He played in Switzerland for two seasons before ending his career with the AHL Rochester Americans in 1983. Hampton represented Canada in world tournaments in 1977 and 1978.

His pro hockey career was managed by Al Eagleson and it turned out to be a bitter and devastating financial experience. After he received his personal records from Eagleson, he turned them over to Ross Conway who was writing a book on Eagleson's misuse of NHL players' money. Eagleson was subsequently charged in both the United States and Canada, resulting in a conviction of three charges of theft in both countries. He was fined one million dollars and sentenced to 18 months in jail in Canada.

Today Hampton manages an arena in his hometown and owns a patent for Quikblade, a replaceable skate blade.

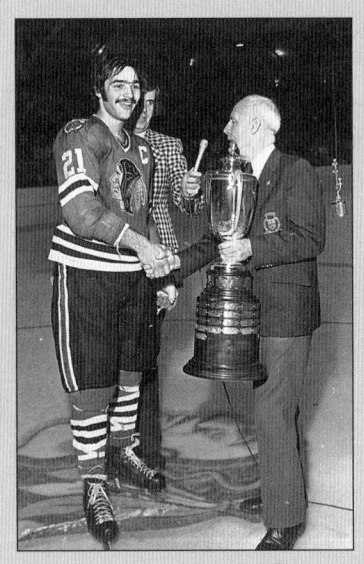

Hawks captain Rick Hampton (left) receives the J. Ross Robertson Cup from OHA executive Frank Doherty. CKTB sports announcer Bill Bird is standing behind Hampton.
St. Catharines Standard photo

Candidates for captain and assistant captain on September 25, 1973. From the left: Wilf Paiement, Larry Jacques, Dave Gorman, Garry Lariviere, Rick Adduono, Rick Hampton, and coach Paul Emms.
St. Catharines Standard photo

Hawk rookie Kevin Kennery (11) and Peterborough Petes goalie Frank Salive watch the puck roll past the net in a game which ended in a 4-4 tie on November 18, 1973.
St. Catharines Standard photo

Former NHLPA head Al Eagleson lands in St. Catharines on November 26, 1974.
St. Catharines Standard photo

Rookie Kevin Kennery *Courtesy of Kevin Kennery*

168

BLACK HAWKS 1973-1974

Continued from page 167

Three players, Rick Adduono, Dave Gorman, and Wilf Paiement, were members of the 50-goal club. Right winger Paiement made the OHA First All-Star Team and Gorman was on the Second Team. Gorman won the Jim Mahon Memorial Trophy as top scorer among all right wingers in the league with 129 points.

Bill Cheropita was the Hawks leading goalie, playing in 47 games, winning 30, and achieving a 3.89 goals-against average during the season.

In the playoffs, the Hawks

Hawk Rick Adduono (left) accepts the Eddie Powers Trophy from OHA executive Frank Doherty on March 21, 1974.
St. Catharines Standard photo

OHA executive Frank Doherty presents the Jim Mahon Trophy to the league's highest-scoring right winter, Dave Gorman, on April 28, 1974.
St. Catharines Standard photo

Bill Cheropita Courtesy of Bill Cheropita

Hawk goalie Bill Cheropita clutches the puck as London player Dennis Maruk (9) drives to the net in a 7-2 loss to the Knights on September 30, 1973.
St. Catharines Standard photo

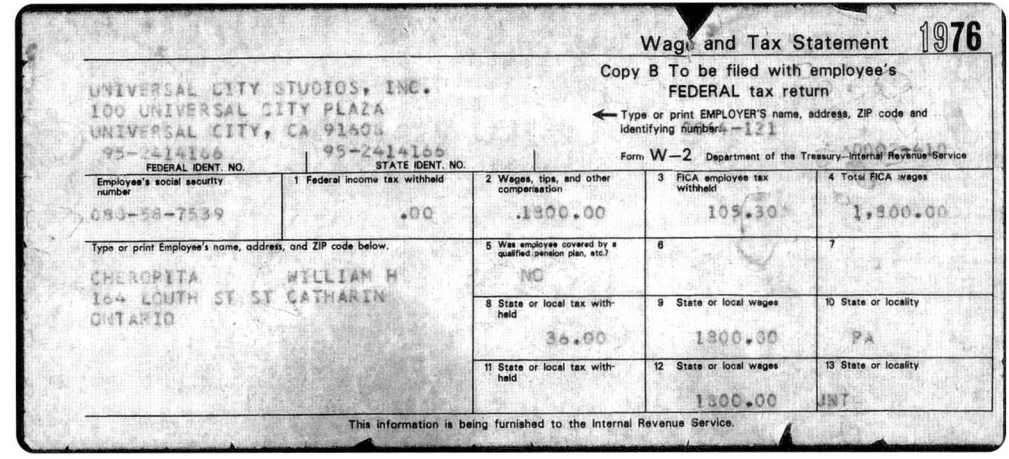

Bill Cheropita's pay stub for his work as a netminder in the film Slap Shot
Courtesy of Bill Cheropita

WILF PAIEMENT

Six-foot-1, 210-pound Wilf Paiement spent two years with the Black Hawks, 1972 to 1974. He scored 50 goals and was a First Team OHA All-Star in 1973-74.

St. Catharines Standard photo

The Earlton native was Kansas City's first draft choice, second overall in 1974. After two years in Kansas City, the right winger was relocated to Colorado and later dealt to the Toronto Maple Leafs. After the Leafs, it was on to Quebec, then New York Rangers, Buffalo, and finally Pittsburgh.

He had his best year with Toronto in 1980-81 when he scored 40 goals and collected 97 points. In 946 regular-season NHL games he scored 814 points, including 356 goals.

Paiement played in three NHL all-star games and represented Canada at three world championships. He was named the best forward (tied with Sergei Makarov) at the 1979 World and European Championships.

Today he manages his real estate holdings and lives in Mississauga.

Wilf Paiement (9) scores one of his three goals in an 11-8 Hawks victory over the Toronto Marlies on October 3, 1973.
St. Catharines Standard photo

BILL HAMILTON

Bill Hamilton played with the IHL Muskegon Mohawks. He was a stickhandling smoothie and one of Jack Gatecliff's favourite players of all-time.

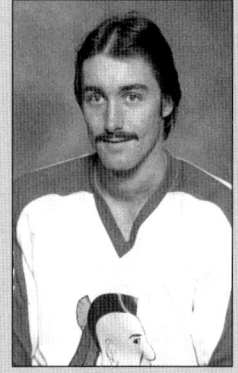

Ernie Fitzsimmons Collection

DAVE GORMAN

At 15, Dave Gorman saw action in a few junior A games, and at 16 was a regular with the St. Catharines Black Hawks. In two of his three years with the club, 1971 to 1974, he scored over 100 points, and ranks fourth in career points (329) in the 34-year history of Junior A hockey in the Garden City. In 1974 he was the winner of the Jim Mahon Memorial Trophy as the league's top-scoring right winger.

In 1974 he opted to turn pro with the WHA Phoenix Roadrunners who traded him to the Birmingham Bulls in 1976. In 1979 the Atlanta Flames inherited his contract with the dissolution of the WHA and he played three games with the Flames. In 1980 he was traded to the Montreal Canadiens who sent him to the AHL Nova Scotia Voyageurs where he had his best season as a pro, collecting 90 points, including 43 goals. He finished third in AHL scoring and was a First Team All-Star.

In 1982 he moved to Europe and played in Switzerland, where once again he was an offensive force, scoring 50 goals in his third season. In 1985 he was a member of the Canadian team that won the Spengler Cup.

After retiring in 1985 he owned and operated a fast food restaurant and today he is a property consultant in Niagara Falls.

St. Catharines Standard photo

Hawk Dave Gorman, with both hands in the air, celebrates his 100th point in a Black Hawk 11-3 victory over the Kingston Canadians on February 17, 1974. Gorman scored four more goals in the game.
St. Catharines Standard photo

BLACK HAWKS 1973-1974

Dave Gorman pots his 50th goal of the season against Oshawa goalie Paul Harrison in a 9-5 win on March 17, 1974.
St. Catharines Standard photo

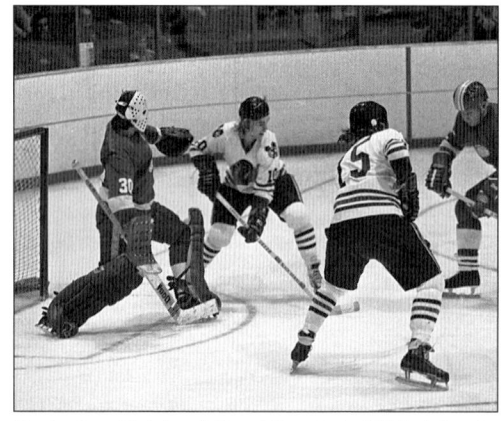

Hawks Gary McAdam (15) and Greg Craig (10) look for the puck in front of Hamilton Red Wings goalie Greg Redquest in a 9-5 victory December 9, 1973. The win tied the St. Catharines Junior A record of 14 games without a defeat.
St. Catharines Standard photo

steamrolled over the opposition, taking only 14 games (12 wins and two ties) to eliminate the Oshawa Generals, Toronto Marlies, and Peterborough Petes en route to the OHA Junior A championship. It was the fourth and last J. Ross Robertson Cup won by a St. Catharines team, and the Hawks are the only St. Catharines team to win the championship without losing a game in the playoffs.

Despite the long list of achievements during the season, fans did not rush to see the team in action. As of January 1, 1974, the Hawks were tied for second place in the league, but stood tenth in the 11-team league in attendance, attracting only 31,407 fans. Kingston, a new club, which was tenth in the standings, was first in attendance with 58,429 customers. Unlike the days of Marcel Dionne (1968 to 1971), when sellouts were the order of the day, average attendance for home games during the season was 1,923 in an arena that had seating for 3,090. It's

Hawk Don Labreche (14) deflects the puck past Ottawa goalie Jim Fraser in a 5-1 win on December 2, 1973.
St. Catharines Standard photo

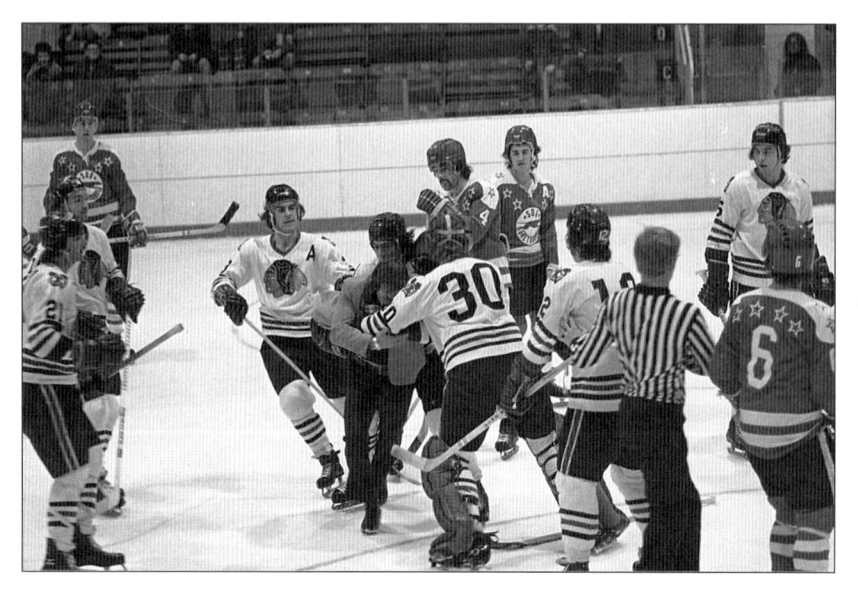

Hawks coach Paul Emms is restrained by goalie Larry McIntyre (30) as he tries to get at referee Ken Bondenistel. When the play resumed, the Hawks went on to defeat the Soo Greyhounds 5-3 on December 23, 1973.
St. Catharines Standard photo

difficult to understand why fans didn't turn out to see the team.

Standard Sports editor Jack Gatecliff couldn't understand the lack of fan support especially when the city had "one of the best-balanced, most pleasing teams we've had in a good many years."

Owner Hap Emms was criticized for not promoting the club like previous owner Fred Muller. "If it's [poor attendance] something we've done, [the Emms family] then I'd like to hear about it," Hap Emms told Gatecliff. There were, however, other factors at work as well. Garden City Arena was not a modern facility and there was plenty of hockey available on TV and in Niagara district arenas.

NIGHTMARE IN CALGARY

Whatever the reasons were for poor attendance, the Hawks concentrated on only one thing in May of 1974 and that was traveling to Calgary and winning the Memorial Cup. For the third year in a row, the Memorial Cup was to be decided by a round-robin series played in Calgary by the winning teams from the Ontario, Quebec and Western Canada junior leagues.

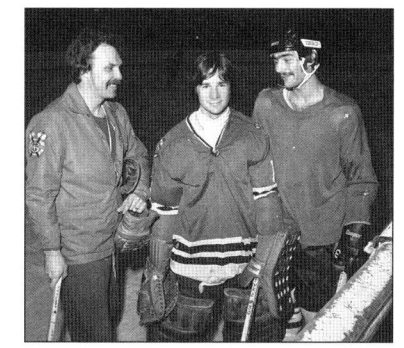

For the first time since 1919, the Memorial Cup tournament had a sponsor, CCM, which presented each player with a ten speed bicycle. The company also provided all the hockey sticks for the series.

Hawks coach Paul Emms (left) and captain Rick Hampton (right) welcome Peterborough goalie Frank Salive to the team on May 1, 1974.
St. Catharines Standard photo

The round-robin series started well for the Hawks with a 4-1 win over the Quebec Remparts, but the team lost the next game 4-0 to the Regina Pats. Before a crucial game with Quebec to see who would enter the sudden-death final, Hap Emms sent goaltender Bill Cheropita home for breaking team rules. The Black Hawks were devastated, not so much because Emms sent their goalie home, but because he had become involved in an off-ice controversy that was the talk of the series.

Without the club's star netminder, the team seemed to fall apart. The Remparts whipped the Hawks 11-3 and eliminated them from the tournament. It was a bitter pill for the team to swallow, and 33 years later, the controversy over Cheropita, and Emms' decision to send him home, continues to be a topic of discussion. What might have happened if Cheropita had played is still a question which haunts many of the 1973-74 Black Hawks.

After 17 playoff games, Dave Gorman led the club with 32 points followed by Wilf Paiement with 29 and Rick Adduono with 27.

In the 1974 NHL draft, Paiement was chosen second by Kansas City Scouts, and Rick Hampton was chosen third overall by the California Golden Seals. At the time NHL clubs could only select two underage players from each junior club.

Dave Gorman was the number one pick of the WHA Phoenix Road Runners in the second round of the amateur draft. Although he had one more year of junior eligibility, Gorman had no intention of playing another year under the Emms regime.

1973-74 Black Hawks Award Winners, May 18, 1974
St. Catharines Standard photo

Front row: Wilf Paiement, most improved (SC); Dave Salvian, most popular (SC); Gladys Crowe; Peter Hookings, St. Catharines Central Midget Lions MVP (SC); Greg Craig, most gentlemanly and most colourful (SC); Back row: Dave Gorman, most popular (BH); Kevin Kennery, top rookie (BH); Ken Breitenbach, most under-rated (SC); Terry Casey, best attitude (SC); Dave Syvret, outstanding defenceman (BH)
Supporters' Club Awards (SC)
Black Hawks Executive Awards (BH)

GARRY LARIVIERE

St. Catharines Standard photo

Garry Lariviere patrolled the St. Catharines Black Hawks blueline from 1971 to 1974.

The St. Catharines native was drafted by the Buffalo Sabres and the WHA Chicago Cougars in 1974, but turned pro with the Phoenix Roadrunners who had obtained him in a trade from Chicago. Playing with the CHL Tulsa Oilers in his rookie year, he made the First All-Star Team, and the next year he suited up with Phoenix.

In 1977 he was traded to the Quebec Nordiques who won the Avco Cup. He stayed with the team when it entered the NHL in 1979. In 1981 he was dealt to Edmonton Oilers where he played until 1983.

From 1983 to 1986 he was with the AHL St. Catharines Saints, and in 1984 he was named the AHL MVP, won the Eddie Shore Award as the league's outstanding defenceman, and was selected to the First All-Star Team.

He was an assistant coach with the Saints for two years before joining the Toronto Maple Leafs as assistant coach from 1986 to 1990.

Off the ice, Lariviere and player agent Frank Milne ran the Blueliner Stables, which enjoyed a great deal of success with its trotting star, Twin B Playboy.

Today he is the co-owner/operator of Servicemaster in St. Catharines, his present home. In 2006-07 he was the head coach of the St. Catharines Junior B Falcons.

In 2008-2009 he is the Falcons' general manager.

Hawk defenceman Garry Lariviere (4) crashes into Hamilton goalie Steve Miskiewicz in a 4-4 draw on February 11, 1973.
St. Catharines Standard photo

HAP EMMS — HE KNEW HOW TO WIN

St. Catharines Standard photo

They called him "Hap" because he seldom smiled, but Leighton Emms had plenty of reasons to be happy during the 1973-74 OHA Junior A season. The St. Catharines Black Hawks team that he had purchased in 1972 from Fred Muller was one of the Garden City's most exciting and successful clubs.

Success in junior A hockey was nothing new for Emms. Before coming to the Garden City, eight of his junior clubs had won OHA Junior A championships and four of those clubs (two in Barrie and two in Niagara Falls) went on to win Memorial Cups. It looked like a fifth Memorial Cup in 1974 was a real possibility.

Before owning, coaching and managing junior teams, Emms had spent ten years playing in the NHL with Montreal Maroons, New York Americans, Detroit Red Wings, and Boston Bruins. In the 1930s, he established an electrical contracting and appliance business in Barrie where his junior coaching career began in 1945 with the Barrie Flyers. Fifteen years later he moved the team to Niagara Falls. In 1972 he sold the Flyers to Sudbury and then bought the Black Hawks.

In addition to his junior experience, Emms also spent two seasons (1965 to 1967) as the Boston Bruins GM and he signed Bobby Orr to his first pro contract. He found dealing with pro hockey players was much different than working with juniors.

Over the years Emms sent more than 100 players to the NHL, including Derek Sanderson, Bernie Parent, Doug Favell, Tom Webster, Rick Ley, and Brad Selwood.

Many players believe that Emms not only prepared them for hockey, but for life as well. Other players respected his hockey knowledge, but chafed under his strict code of discipline and unforgiving nature.

In the OHA, Emms had a reputation as an owner who was tight with the buck. Former Hawks captain Rick Hampton recalled an incident in the 1974 Memorial Cup playoffs which showed how far Hap would go to control expenses. With a game to go in the round-robin series, teammate Dave Salvian's skate blade came unhinged from the boot. He clearly needed a new skate, but Emms told him to tape the blade to the boot, which Salvian did. After Emms checked the tape work, he chastised Salvian for using white tape. Black tape was cheaper and that's what players were told to use.

Emms also tried to cut costs by having his wife Mabel make sandwiches on road trips, and they were often stale by the time they were eaten. Players usually got a dollar for meal money on the road and McDonald's became a favourite place to eat. One player actually burned his dollar bill on one of the road trips to show what he thought of the meal allowance.

During the 1974 Memorial Cup playoffs the club's regular goalie, Bill Cheropita, broke team rules, and Emms had a tough decision to make before a crucial game. Should Cheropita be punished then and there or be allowed to play? Emms, who at one time refused to attend his team's Sunday games, sent Cheropita home, and the Hawks lost the game and the chance to win a Memorial Cup.

For the next two seasons, the Hawks were not contenders; they were ousted from the playoffs in the first round of each year. Attendance declined to the point where Emms moved the club to Niagara Falls in 1976. Some criticized Emms for not promoting the club as Fred Muller had done. In fairness to Emms, there were other factors at work, including the presence of several hockey teams in the area competing for fan attention.

In 1978 Emms sold the Flyers and retired from hockey. He died at 83 in 1988, but his name and reputation are not forgotten. The Emms Trophy is awarded each year to the OHL Central Division winner and the Hap Emms Memorial Trophy goes to the top goaltender in the Memorial Cup. The OHL top rookie receives the Emms Family Award.

Mention Hap Emms' name today, and opinions may range from benevolent tyrant to hockey innovator. However, there are two things on which all critics and supporters can agree: Emms knew hockey, and he knew how to win.

Hawks owner Hap Emms takes to the ice at Garden City Arena, November 5, 1974. Emms played with five different NHL clubs from 1926-1938.
St. Catharines Standard photo

BLACK HAWKS 1974-1975

ST. CATHARINES FANS LOSE INTEREST IN THE BLACK HAWKS

ATTENDANCE FIGURES
Average per regular-season game: 1,359 (for 32/35 games)
Season's largest crowd: 2,205
Season's smallest crowd: 681

PLAYOFF ROUNDS: 1
Eliminated by Hamilton 4-0

Interim Hawks coach Bob Craig (left) watches the game action with his son Greg (10). The London Knights won 6-4 on December 15, 1974.
St. Catharines Standard photo

1974-1975

GAMES PLAYED	WON	LOST	TIED	FOR	AGAINST	POINTS	FINISH
70	30	33	7	284	300	67	6/11

Leading Scorers

PLAYER	GOALS	ASSISTS	POINTS
Dave Salvian	44	51	95
Greg Craig	47	41	88
Gary McAdam	25	53	78
Bill Hamilton	30	40	70
Rick Adduono	27	40	67

Leading Goaltenders

PLAYER	GP	GA	SO	GAA
Bill Cheropita	37	137	1	3.83
Kevin Walton	17	75	0	4.39

Despite losing 14 players from the previous year, the Hawks opened the 1974-75 season with a 5-3 road victory over Kitchener Rangers. It was the first time a St. Catharines team had won an opening game since October 5, 1967. Starting in goal for the home opener, a 7-6 loss to Hamilton Fincups, was 17-year-old, 6-foot-6 George Scott. His dad, George Scott Sr., had been in goal for the Teepees 26 years earlier. It was the team's first home loss since November 4, 1973.

The low attendance at the first three Hawks games in the season indicated that Junior A hockey in St. Catharines could be on the way out. Small crowds were unexpected, especially when the team shared first place in the league. Heating problems in the arena and a lack of promotion for the club didn't help matters. As the season progressed, there was more and more talk about losing junior hockey because of poor

Front row: Bob Froese, Ken Breitenbach, Rick Adduono, Hap Emms (owner and president), Bill Cheropita, Paul Emms (coach and manager), Greg Craig, Dave Salvian, Kevin Walton; Middle row: Dale Ambridge (bus driver), Bill Hamilton, Bob Manno, Karl Edmands (CHSC Radio), Marty Swick (director), Bob Craig (interim coach), Jack Gatecliff (sports director, Standard), Brian Iggulden (CKTB Radio), Willi Plett, Joe Grant, Kevin Kennery, Vince Walker (trainer); Back row: Mark Fiorentino, Wayne Briscall, Ken Martyn, Gary McAdam, Don Wilson, Steve Cupolo, Andy Edur, Doug Caines, Ted Lis, Gary Sobchak. Absent: Bill Hill (trainer)

Courtesy of Bob Mann

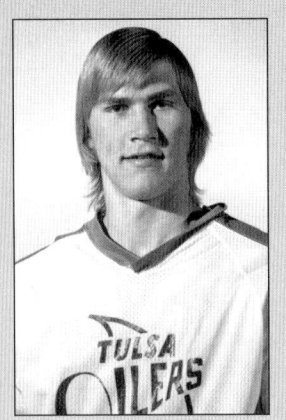

BLACK HAWKS 1974-1975

WILLI PLETT

Willi Plett was born in Paraguay, South America, but played his minor hockey in the Niagara district. He was with the Black Hawks for part of the 1974-75 season before turning pro with the Atlanta Flames in 1975.

After one year in the minors, he joined the Flames and won the Calder Trophy as the NHL's top rookie in 1977 with 56 points, including 33 goals. From Atlanta, he transferred to Calgary, and then moved on to the Minnesota North Stars. He ended his NHL career after one year with the Boston Bruins.

In 834 regular-season NHL games, the 6-foot-3, 205-pound right winger collected 437 points, including 222 goals.

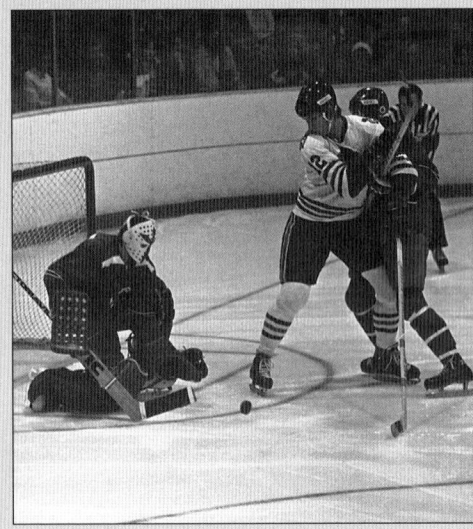

Ernie Fitzsimmons Collection

Hawk Willi Plett is unable to get to the puck in front of Oshawa goalie Rick St. Croix in a 6-2 loss on November 3, 1974.
St. Catharines Standard photo

support in the city. The team ended the regular season averaging 1,359 fans per game.

On the ice Rick Adduono struggled with injuries, as did several other players, including Kevin Kennery, Doug Caines, and Bill Hamilton. The total number of games missed due to injuries was 141. Not one player participated in every regular-season game.

In November the Hawks executive allowed the players to vote for a captain and Rick Adduono won the honour. It is believed he was the only married captain in the history of the team.

In January of 1975, relations between reporters and broadcasters with Black Hawks officials had broken down. *Standard* sports editor Jack Gatecliff noted that the media was not being kept up to date about team injuries. Two injured players, Kevin Kennery and Dave Salvian, re-appeared in the Hawks lineup with no notice from the team.

Earlier in the season, goalie Bill Cheropita had been suspended for two months for breaking training rules. Gatecliff called him "The Prodigal Son of St. Catharines hockey." On January 10, 1975, Gatecliff wrote that he had talked to Cheropita who told him that everything was settled and that he would be back in the net after a few workouts. Owner Hap Emms denied anything was settled and scolded the press.

Bill Cheropita December 13, 1973
St. Catharines Standard photo

"The news media is making reports without checking the facts with the Hawks management," Emms said.

HAP EMMS GIVES A BLACK EYE TO JUNIOR HOCKEY

It has been said that Hap Emms never met a controversy that he didn't like and a good example of that assertion was evident when he became involved in a protest on February 28, 1975.

In late February, the WHA Toronto Toros co-owner John Bassett Jr. signed Toronto Marlboros under-age player Mark Napier to a three-year pro contract.

Bassett made the deal despite the fact that the Canadian Amateur Hockey Association and the WHA had an agreement that no under-age juniors would be signed at least for the 1974-75 season. Bassett also ignored his own league rule, which stipulated that any junior player had to go through a WHA draft before a contract was sanctioned.

Hap Emms was determined to make a point about the indiscriminate stealing of players from junior hockey by the WHA and getting no money in return. The Hawks were scheduled to play Napier and the Marlies on February 28, 1975, in Brantford.

Hawk goalie Bill Cheropita gloves a shot from Toronto Marlie and future NHLer John Tonelli (22) in a 5-3 loss on March 23, 1975.
St. Catharines Standard photo

BLACK HAWKS 1974-1975

At first, Emms said the Hawks wouldn't play the game if Mark Napier was in the lineup because he was now a pro. Then he changed his mind and said his team would play the game under protest. A possible law suit from Napier's agent helped to change Emms' mind. Emms said he did it as a favour to OHA Major Junior Commissioner Clarence (Tubby) Schmalz.

What happened next made a farce of the game and gave junior hockey a black eye. Paul Emms refused to coach the Hawks, so injured goalie Bill Cheropita stepped behind the bench. Cheropita wanted to coach in a serious manner, but he never had a chance. The game was delayed 37 minutes and when it did begin, Hap Emms made a mockery of it.

Former Hawk defenceman Bob Manno hasn't forgotten Emms' instructions in the dressing room before the game. "I always remember them making us turn our shirts around [inside out]," he said, 31 years later. "The only guy [who didn't] was Ken Martyn. He wore number 14 [Mark Napier's number]".

One faceoff was taken with the butt-end of a Hawks stick instead of the blade, and icing the puck was encouraged. For the first half of the first period, Hawks goalies were alternated at every stoppage of play. The 2,276 Brantford fans at the game watched the Marlies outshoot the hapless Hawks 69-16 and humiliate them on the scoreboard 14-0. "How ironic was it that 14 was up," Manno said in reference to Napier's sweater number.

Some of the Hawks players were in their draft year and didn't agree with what happened, but Emms was the boss. Ken Breitenbach was one of those players hoping to be drafted, and he remembered what happened during the game. "Breitenbach, the scouts are in the crowd," some of the Toronto players shouted from their bench. "The scouts are watching."

It was an embarrassing situation for the Hawks. After the league reviewed the situation, both Hap and Paul Emms were penalized. Hap was suspended for

Hawk Dave Salvian (7) deposits the puck behind Peterborough goalie Frank Salive in a 5-5 draw on December 1, 1974.
St. Catharines Standard photo

Ace Hawk stickhandler Bill Hamilton (16) puts one past Peterborough netminder Frank Salive in an 8-2 victory on February 23, 1975.
St. Catharines Standard photo

Hawk Gary McAdam (15) scores against Oshawa Generals during a 6-2 win on January 12 1975. McAdam finished the contest with 2 goals and 2 assists.
St. Catharines Standard photo

DAVE SALVIAN

Left winger Dave Salvian played for the Black Hawks from 1972 to 1975 and scored more than 90 points in each of his last two seasons.

The Toronto native was the second choice of the New York Islanders in the 1975 Amateur Draft, but he only suited up with the team for one game. His best year as a pro was in 1976-77 when he scored 60 points with the CHL Fort Worth Texans. In 1978 he was with Fort Worth when it won the Adams Cup.

After five seasons, mainly in the CHL, he retired in 1980. Since that time he has been involved in car sales. Today Salvian lives in Oakville.

St. Catharines Standard photo

KEN BREITENBACH

Ken Breitenbach patrolled the blueline for the St. Catharines Black Hawks from 1972 to 1975 and was a Second Team OHA All-Star in his last year.

He turned pro with the Buffalo Sabres in 1975, but from 1975 to 1979, the Welland native played mostly with the AHL Hershey Bears.

A broken leg in 1977 hampered his career and he retired in 1979 at age 24.

He now resides in Fonthill, Ontario.

St. Catharines Standard photo

GARY McADAM

Gary McAdam played two years for the St. Catharines Black Hawks before being drafted by the Buffalo Sabres in 1975.

In 534 regular-season games from 1975 to 1986, the Smith Falls native saw action with Buffalo, Pittsburgh, Detroit, Calgary, Washington, New Jersey and Toronto.

The left winger's most productive pro season came in 1982-83 when he collected 69 points with the AHL champion Rochester Americans. He scored 228 points, including 96 goals, during his NHL career.

Today McAdam is a surgical technician who resides in Portland, Maine.

Ernie Fitzsimmons Collection

the balance of the season and Paul was gone for six games.

Napier, who had three assists in the game, joined the Toros the next season and scored 43 goals in his rookie year. He jumped to the Montreal Canadiens in 1978 and stayed in the NHL for 11 years.

The Hawks finished in sixth place in the 11-team league. Dave Salvian was the Hawks scoring leader with 95 points. Greg Craig, who collected 88 points behind Savian, lead the team in goals with 47. Over the course of the season, Niagara Falls native Bob Manno became a key player, both offensively and defensively. He was the team's highest-scoring defenceman in 1974-75 and 1975-76. "I realized I had to play aggressively if I wanted to be drafted," Manno said in 2006.

In the first round of the playoffs the team met the powerful Hamilton Fincups who won the series in four straight games. Gary McAdam tallied four goals in four games to lead the Hawks in playoff scoring.

Three Hawks made the OHA Second All-Star Team: Bill Cheropita, Ken Breitenbach, and Dave Salvian. Seven members of the team were graduating, including four of the team's top point-getters during the regular season. ∎

1974-75 Black Hawks Award Winners
Supporters' Club Awards (SC) and Black Hawks Executive Awards (BH)
Left to right: Doug Caines, top rookie (BH); Gary McAdam, playoff most valuable player (SC) and most colourful (BH); Roy Kerling, Central Lions Midgets, Gordon Crowe Memorial Award (SC); Ken Breitenbach, Gordon Crowe Memorial Award (SC); Dave Salvian, most popular (SC) and (BH)
St. Catharines Standard photo

Left to right: Rick Adduono, captain's award (SC) and most gentlemanly (BH); Greg Craig, most valuable player (SC) and (BH); Bill Hamilton, Gordon Crowe Memorial Award (SC); Andy Edur, most under-rated (SC) and most improved (BH); Joe Grant, most under-rated (SC)
St. Catharines Standard photo

BLACK HAWKS 1975-1976

THE HAWKS FLY AWAY

Despite the rumours of junior hockey moving out of St. Catharines for 1975-76, Hap Emms stayed put. For the first time, the Ontario Major Junior Hockey League was divided into two divisions: The Emms Division with six teams, including St. Catharines, and the Leyden Division that also had six teams. Windsor was back in the league after an absence of more than 20 years.

The league introduced a new rule which allowed each team to dress three over-age players. Former Oshawa General Andy Whitby was signed as one over-age player with the Hawks and then was released during the year.

In the season's opening game at Kitchener the Hawks lost 6-3, but followed up with a home victory over the London Knights 7-2. Greg Craig paced the home team with three goals and three assists.

Peterborough Petes goalie Greg Millen (21) watches Kevin Kennery's shot enter his net on December 14, 1975. The Hawks won 6-2.
St. Catharines Standard photo

Front row: Bob Froese, Bob Manno, Kevin Kennery, Paul Emms (coach and general manager), Greg Craig, Hap Emms (owner and president), Doug Caines, Bill Stewart, Kevin Walton. Middle row: Brian Patafie (trainer), Kevin Osmars, Bill Hamilton, Jack Gatecliff (sportswriter), John Larocque (public relations director), Dr. Gordon Powell (team physician), Dave Honsberger (statistician), Karl Edmands (CHSC sports director), Brian Iggulden (CKTB sports), Tim Stortini, Barry Callahan, Vince Walker (trainer). Back row: Mark Fiorentino, Andy Edur, Peter Hookings, Marc Thiel, Don Wilson, Kevin McCloskey, Ken Campbell, Ron Wilson, Steve Cupolo, Andy Whitby

ATTENDANCE FIGURES
Average per regular-season game: 931
Season's largest crowd: 1,538
Season's smallest crowd: 472

PLAYOFF ROUNDS: 1
Eliminated by Kitchener Rangers 3-1

1975-1976

GAMES PLAYED	WON	LOST	TIED	FOR	AGAINST	POINTS	FINISH
66	16	40	10	283	366	42	5/16 EMMS DIV.

Leading Scorers

PLAYER	GOALS	ASSISTS	POINTS
Ron Wilson	37	60	97
Doug Caines	38	56	94
Greg Craig	41	38	79
Bill Hamilton	29	37	66
Kevin Osmars	25	37	62

Leading Goaltenders

PLAYER	GP	GA	SO	GAA
Bob Froese	32.04	187		5.84
Rick Szabo	17.93	99		5.52

Courtesy of Bob Manno

RON WILSON

The scoring leader for the last Black Hawks team was centre Ron Wilson with 97 points. The Toronto native spent one year with the Hawks before turning pro with the Montreal Canadiens who had drafted him in 1976.

After three seasons with the AHL Nova Scotia Voyageurs, with whom he won a Calder Cup in 1977, he was traded to the Winnipeg Jets, and for the next 15 years saw action with the Jets, St. Louis Blues, and finally the Montreal Canadiens. In 832 NHL regular-season contests he earned 326 points.

After his playing days were over Wilson turned to coaching, and in 2001 helped guide the St. John Flames to a Calder Cup. From 2005 to 2007, he was the assistant coach of the Hamilton Bulldogs who won the Calder Cup in 2007.

Ernie Fitzsimmons Collection

Peterborough Petes goalie Howie Murney can't stop the Hawks Ron Wilson (7) during the January 25, 1976 game. The Hawks won 5-3.
St. Catharines Standard photo

LAST OF THE BLACK HAWKS

For the first time in 33 years of St. Catharines Junior A hockey, the opening game was not on radio. This was mutually agreed on by radio station CHSC and the Hawks management. It was a sign of things to come. Tommy Garriock was not the emcee at the opening game ceremonies for the first time in 20 years. His place was taken by radio personality John Larocque.

Soon after the season began, attendance at home games hit new lows. "Even if there was a slight increase we'd know we were heading in the right direction," Paul Emms said on October 21, 1975, after 586 fans showed up for a 5-5 tie with London. "But so far that hasn't happened."

On December 18, just 472 fans showed up at Garden City Arena. It was the smallest audience to watch a major junior game since December 14, 1943, when 439 fans watched the Falcons shut out the Toronto Young Rangers 6-0. By January, the club was averaging only 1,000 a game. Hap Emms said he needed 2,400 a game to break even. The writing was on the wall. By the end of the season, after 35 home games, the club had attracted a total of 33,306 fans, an average of 952 a game.

"It seemed like hockey was dying in our area through the seventies," former Hawk Bob Manno said in Niagara Falls in February of 2006.

Even promotions, like admitting high school students for one of the games for a quarter and welcoming senior citizens free of charge on another night, didn't change the downward trend.

Jack Gatecliff suggested the team change its name back to Teepees; Thompson Products, now known as TRW Canada, would have allowed the change, but nothing came of the idea.

Reports circulated that Emms wanted to sell the club for $300,000. He had paid $230,000 to Fred Muller for the team in 1972.

Before the season began, NHL and WHA teams paid junior clubs when they drafted their players, but now the funds had dried up because there was no written agreement between the pros and the amateurs. It was predicted that Emms would lose at least $50,000 in 1975-76, especially after the club had a paid average attendance of only 973 after 25 home games.

At age 74, long-time junior supporter Gladys Crowe was still behind the Hawks, but membership in her group had dropped from 220 to 47. Twenty members came from her own family.

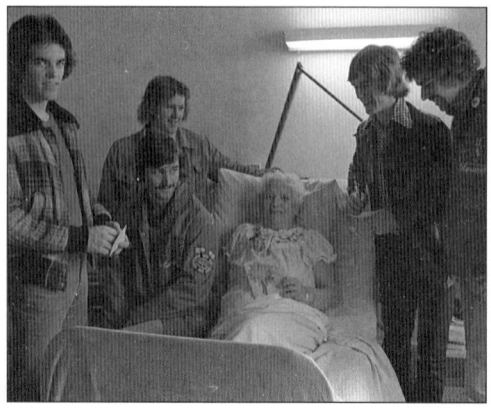

St. Catharines Black Hawks visit Supporters' Club President Gladys Crowe in the hospital on December 31, 1975. Left to right: Bill Stewart, Bill Hamilton, Kevin Kennery, Gladys Crowe, Greg Craig and Don Wilson.
St. Catharines Standard photo

In March of 1976 there was no definite decision as to whether Emms would move the Black Hawks out of St. Catharines. At one time it appeared that local businessmen Archie Katzman and Brian Cullen might take over the team, but it didn't happen.

"About three weeks ago we offered Mr. Emms $150,000 for the Hawk franchise," Katzman told Gatecliff. "He [Emms] told me it was no use discussing it any further because he was asking much more than that." ($300,000 was said to be the asking price.) Even if the two men were able to buy the club, they were too busy with their business interests to run it themselves. "The major problem was getting someone capable to run it for us," Brian Cullen said at the time. Rudy Pilous was contacted, but he had two years to go on his contract with the WHA Winnipeg Jets and he wasn't available.

During the season there were at least three other offers to buy the Hawks, but none of them panned out. One potential buyer wanted to move the club to the Toronto area, but to do that he needed a suitable arena (which he didn't have) and approval from area teams who had territorial rights covering a 50-mile radius of the cities in which they played. Nothing happened.

The Hawks finished the season in fifth place in the Emms division with 42 points and were defeated in the first round of the playoffs by Kitchener, 3-1. The

Hawk Doug Caines, with hands in the air, celebrates after scoring in a 5-5 tie with the Soo Greyhounds on February 1, 1976.
St. Catharines Standard photo

leading scorer in the regular season and playoffs was former Toronto Marlie Ron Wilson with 97 and eight points respectively. Doug Caines was second to Wilson during the regular season with 94 points. Caines and Wilson were co-winners of the club's MVP award.

On April 20, 1976, Paul Emms announced what everyone had expected: Major Junior hockey in St. Catharines was finished. The sign hanging outside Rex Stimers Arena was taken down after Hap Emms decided to move the team to Niagara Falls. "Couldn't they have waited until the body was cold," Gatecliff wrote. "There is no person more upset over the Hawks leaving than yours truly."

The loss of the Hawks ended the longest continuous association with the Ontario Major Junior A League enjoyed by any community, 33 years. ∎

Hawk rearguard Bob Manno (3) is taken out of the play in front of the Windsor Spitfire goalie after Greg Craig (not shown) scored. 821 fans watched the Hawks win 10-6.
St. Catharines Standard photo

Greg Craig
St. Catharines Standard photo

Hawk forward Greg Craig (10) falls behind the Soo Greyhound net during a 6-2 loss on December 7, 1975.
St. Catharines Standard photo

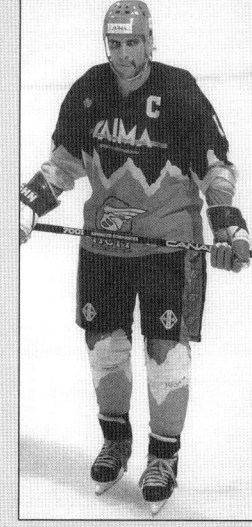

Bob Manno was captain of the Italian League Champion Hockey Club Milano in 1990-91.
Courtesy of Bob Manno

BOB MANNO

Niagara Falls native Bob Manno spent his junior A career with the Hamilton Red Wings (1973-74) and two years with the St. Catharines Black Hawks (1974 to 1976).

The talented rearguard was Vancouver's first choice in the 1976 Amateur Draft and played for the club for parts of five seasons before moving on to the Toronto Maple Leafs and then the Detroit Red Wings.

In 371 NHL regular-season games, he collected 172 points. He had his most productive NHL year in 1981-82 with the Toronto Maple Leafs with 50 points, including nine goals and he played in the 1982 All-Star Game.

From 1985 to 1994, he saw action in Italy where he earned a reputation as one of Europe's premier players. "It was a little more relaxing lifestyle. I had a little bit more free time," he said.

He represented Italy in seven world championship tournaments and the 1992 Olympics In Albertville, France. He was named to three all-star teams and was voted the best defenceman in the World and European Championships Pool B in 1989.

After retiring in 1994, he coached in Italy, winning two Italian league titles with Bolzano. Before returning to Canada in 2001, he coached for three years in Germany.

In 2004 he was inducted into the Niagara Falls Sports Wall of Fame. Today Manno lives in Niagara Falls, Ontario, and spends his time managing his investments.

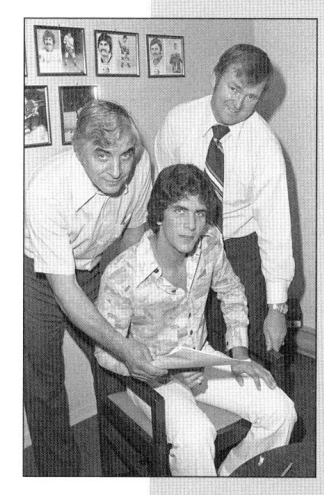

Ex-Black Hawk Bob Manno, seated, signs an NHL contract with the Vancouver Canucks on September 3, 1976. Looking on are his dad Bruno (left) and his agent Frank Milne (right).
St. Catharines Standard photo

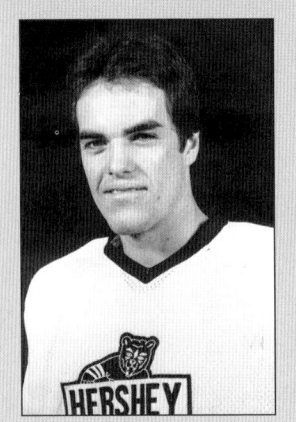

BLACK HAWKS 1975-1976

BILL STEWART

Bill Stewart spent the 1975-76 season with the Black Hawks. The defenceman was drafted by the Buffalo Sabres in 1977 and from 1977 to 1986 saw action in 261 regular-season NHL games with the Sabres, St. Louis, Toronto and Minnesota.

Bill Stewart with the AHL Hershey Bears   Ernie Fitzsimmons Collection

From 1986 to 1995, he played in Italy.

After his playing career ended, the Toronto native turned to coaching in the OHL and reached the NHL as head coach of the New York Islanders for part of the 1998-99 season.

BOB FROESE

Goaltender Bob Froese played for the Black Hawks from 1974 to 1976 before moving on to the Oshawa Generals and then the Niagara Falls Flyers.

He was drafted by St. Louis Blues in 1978 and started his pro career with the IHL Saginaw Gears and the Milwaukee Admirals. In 1981 he was with Saginaw when it won the IHL championship. He won 12 of 13 playoff games with a 2.16 goals-against average.

Bob Froese with the AHL Maine Mariners   Ernie Fitzsimmons Collection

The St. Catharines native made it to the NHL with the Philadelphia Flyers in the 1982-83 season and remained with this team until 1986 when he was traded to the New York Rangers. In 1986 he shared the William M. Jennings Trophy with Darren Jensen and played in the 1986 NHL All-Star game.

When he retired from the Rangers in 1990, he had played in 242 regular-season NHL games, winning 128 and posting a 3.10 goals-against average.

Today Froese is a pastor in the Buffalo, New York area.

Lou Franceschetti in an AHL Binghamton Whalers uniform   Ernie Fitzsimmons Collection

LOU FRANCESCHETTI

Toronto native Lou Franceschetti was called up to the St. Catharines Black Hawks from the Toronto Nationals of the Provincial Junior League for a game in March of 1976. The right winger's next two junior years were spent with the Niagara Falls Flyers.

Drafted by the Washington Capitals in the 1978 Amateur Draft, Franceschetti, very popular wherever he played, saw action in 459 regular-season NHL games with the Capitals, Toronto Maple Leafs, and Buffalo Sabres, earning 140 points.

His best NHL year came with the Leafs in 1989-90 when he scored 21 goals and collected 36 points.

Franceschetti, who won a Calder Cup with the Hershey Bears in 1980, retired from pro hockey in 1996.

Black Hawks ready for 1975 training camp. Left to right: Tim Stortini, Steve Cupolo, Kevin Kennery, Greg Craig, and Doug Caines, September 5, 1975   St. Catharines Standard photo

St. Catharines Standard photo

LARRY LANDON

Niagara Falls native Larry Landon, who had played a few games with the Hawks in 1975-76, played hockey and earned a college scholarship with Rensselaer Polytechnic Institute in 1977. He finished with a bachelor of science degree in business management in 1981.

After turning pro in the AHL with the Nova Scotia Voyageurs, he played a few NHL games with Montreal and Toronto before retiring in 1985. His best pro season was 1984-85 when he collected 57 points in 44 games with the AHL St. Catharines Saints.

Since 1993 he has been the executive director of the Professional Hockey Players' Association that represents 1,400 players on 54 teams in the AHL and ECHL. The PHPA has its headquarters in St. Catharines.

Landon resides in Burlington, Ontario.

BLACK HAWKS 1975-1976

Winners of Black Hawk Trophies 1975-76, March 18, 1976
Front row: Kevin Kennery, most colourful; Greg Craig, most gentlemanly; Bill Stewart, most improved; Bob Manno, outstanding defenceman. Back row: Ron Wilson, most valuable player (tied); Kevin Osmars, top rookie; Doug Caines, most valuable player (tied); Bill Hamilton, most popular
St. Catharines Standard photo

Winners of the Supporters' Club Awards 1975-76, March 26, 1976
Front row: Andy Edur, Gordon Crowe Award; Bill Hamilton, Thank You Award and the Donald Grant Memorial Award; Doug Caines, most gentlemanly; Bob Cullen, most valuable player (St. Catharines Lions Midgets) Back row: Greg Craig, most popular; Bob Froese, most under-rated; Don Wilson, most under-rated
St. Catharines Standard photo

MIKE GARTNER

Mike Gartner was called up from the Toronto Young Nats to the St. Catharines Black Hawks for seven games in 1976, but spent the rest of his junior career with Niagara Falls Flyers from 1976 to 1978.

The right winger was the Washington Capitals first choice in the 1979 Entry Draft and he spent the next 19 years in the NHL with the Capitals, Minnesota, the New York Rangers, Toronto and Phoenix, amassing 1,335 points, including 708 goals in 1,432 regular-season games.

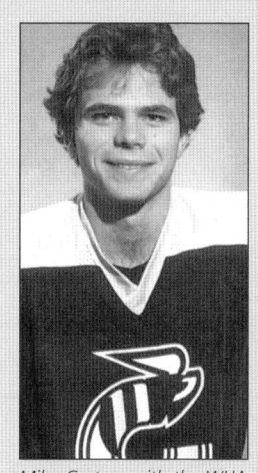

Mike Gartner with the WHA Cincinnati Stingers
Ernie Fitzsimmons Collection

He played in seven NHL all-star games and represented Canada in five world tournaments and two Canada Cups. The Ottawa native was inducted into the Hockey Hall of Fame in 2001.

After working for the NHL Players' Association for several years, he resigned in March of 2007.

Hawk defenceman Peter Hookings (left) is held by Kitchener Ranger Don Maloney while future NHL Hall of Famer Mike Gartner (17) follows the play during a 6-3 loss to the Rangers on March 18, 1976.
St. Catharines Standard photo

ARCHIE KATZMAN - The Kat Came Back

If there is one person in St. Catharines who needs no introduction, it's lifelong resident Archie Katzman. He's a volunteer and fundraiser extraordinaire who has served the Niagara community for many years – and he keeps on giving.

But there's another not so well-known side to the man they call "The Kat." Growing up on Water Street in the Garden City, Katzman, a Central Public School student, was a rink rat at Garden City Arena. "Vic Teal was our mentor," Katzman recalled.

At 13 he was a member of the St. Catharines bantam minor hockey team that won the 1943-44 Ontario championship. "I don't recall us ever losing a bantam game," Katzman said. In 1945-46 his Wethy's Midget team won another Ontario championship. The club, coached by Ashton Morrison, played 27 games without a loss and scored 181 goals while allowing just 27. It was one of the best records ever set in Ontario Minor Hockey Association annals. Katzman played right wing on a line with close friends Connie Switzer and Archie Meloni. *St. Catharines Standard* sports editor Clayton Browne named the trio the SMAK line.

In 1946-47 Katzman and his teammates, including Ellard (Obie) O'Brien, George (Porky) Douglas, Bill Buschlen, and Tom Buck, captured the All-Ontario juvenile championship. He ended his city minor league career with a second All-Ontario juvenile title in 1947-48.

His buddies, O'Brien and Douglas, joined the St. Catharines Teepees in 1948, but Katzman traveled to Belleville to try out with the AHL Philadelphia Rockets coached by Max Kaminsky, who would lead the St. Catharines Teepees to a Memorial Cup in 1960. He didn't make the team, but he was invited to join the OHA Junior A Stratford Kroehlers. The 18-year-old made the club and scored a goal in his first game.

Two of Katzman's teammates at the Stratford training camp were future NHLers Danny Lewicki and George Armstrong. Armstrong moved on to the Toronto Marlboros before the season began, but Lewicki stayed with the Kroehlers for the 1948-49 season.

When he wasn't playing hockey, Katzman attended a business college and worked as a bellhop at the Queen's Hotel in Stratford.

After a one-sided loss to the Oshawa Generals early in the season, he was traded to the Galt Black Hawks. In Galt, he met a recruiter for Scottish hockey teams and it changed his life. "I convinced my parents that this is what I wanted to do [play in Scotland], but it was a tough sell," Katzman said. "It was the best thing that ever happened to me. What I learned abroad, I always treated as my college education: Meeting people, knowing people, traveling, playing."

Katzman signed with the Perth Panthers, but during the season he was traded to Falkirk Lions. It was a fortunate move because Falkirk won the 1949 Scottish National League championship and Katzman, who collected 51 points in 34 games, was the league's top rookie.

In his second season, he had 50 points, including 32 goals in 59 games, and the Lions won their second consecutive championship. "I had two great years," he said. "We played to sellout crowds and were treated like royalty."

After his second year in Scotland, he returned to St. Catharines and drove a cab for his dad who owned Central Taxi. But he wasn't finished with hockey. He joined the Senior B Stamford Kerrios for one season and then the Port Colborne Sailors who won an Ontario Senior B championship. After three years of senior hockey, he joined Floyd's Falcons of the Factory League in the Garden City. Then, at 25, he left the game. "If they didn't have corners, I'd still be playing today," Katzman said with a big smile.

After Katzman and Len Herzog built the Parkway Lanes on Ontario Street in 1958, it became a sports meeting centre, especially for hockey players, coaches, managers and owners. Punch Imlach and the Toronto Maple Leafs were frequent guests. "When the Black Hawks were in town I used to let them bowl," he said.

There are few people in hockey who don't know the Kat, a longtime supporter of St. Catharines Junior A hockey. "It was the networking," said Katzman who introduced hockey agent Al Eagleson to Marcel Dionne.

In 1976 Katzman and former Teepees star Brian Cullen offered to buy the St. Catharines Black Hawks from Hap Emms for $150,000, but their offer was rejected. One year later, the Garden City was without a junior A team.

Today Katzman is the general manager of the St. Catharines Club and once again networking has paid off. The Ontario Street business is the fastest-growing private club in Ontario. He is also the honorary co-chair of the Community Leaders Invitational Golf Tournament which over the last 35 years has raised more than $4.5 million for the betterment of health care in Niagara.

The citizens of St. Catharines and the Niagara region are thankful that The Kat came back.

Photo by Denis Cahill

Archie Katzman in Perth Panthers uniform in Scotland
St. Catharines Museum - *Hyndman Collection 2004.127.21*

FINCUPS 1976-1977

HAMILTON FINCUPS FIND A HOME IN ST. CATHARINES

Fans line up at Garden City Arena to buy tickets to see the Moscow Selects play the Fincups on December 10, 1976.
St. Catharines Standard photo

These St. Catharines Fincups can't wait for the 1976-77 season to begin. From left to right: Dale McCourt, Bob Cullen, Joe Contini and Mark Plantery. Cullen and Plantery were both born in St. Catharines.
St. Catharines Standard photo, September 2, 1976

Fincups coach Bert Templeton watches Moscow Selects defeat his club 11-2 in an exhibition game on December 10, 1976.
St. Catharines Standard photo

183

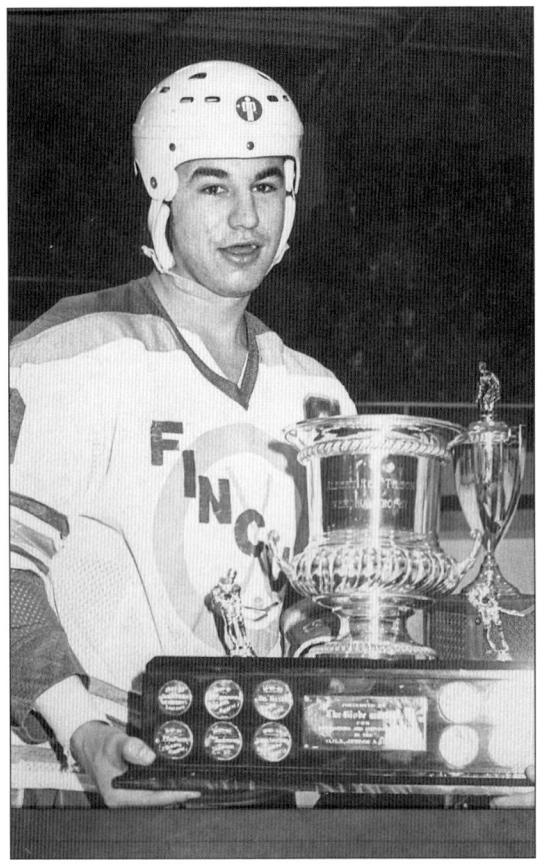

DALE McCOURT

Fincups Captain Dale McCourt finished the 1976-77 season as the highest scorer in OMJHL history, surpassing Ottawa 67's Peter Lee who had accumulated 444 points. The nephew of former Toronto Maple Leafs captain George Armstrong won the Hanley Trophy as the most gentlemanly player in the league for the second year in a row and the Red Tilson Trophy as the league's MVP. To cap off his five-year junior career, the OHA First Team All-Star centre was named the Canadian Major Junior Player of 1977.

It came as no surprise that the Falconbridge native was picked first overall in the 1977 Amateur Draft by Detroit Red Wings. He played 532 regular-season NHL games with Detroit, Buffalo and Toronto, scoring 194 goals and accumulating 478 points. His best pro season came in 1980-81 with the Red Wings when he collected 86 points in 80 regular-season games.

After his NHL career ended, he spent seven years playing in Switzerland. He turned to coaching after he retired and was on the coaching staff of the Italian national team in the 1994 Olympics.

Today McCourt drives a truck across Western Canada and resides in Garson, Ontario.

Dale McCourt with Red Tilson Trophy
St. Catharines Museum - Standard Collection N 5698

St. Catharines Mayor Roy Adams (left) congratulates Fincups captain Dale McCourt in a ceremony honouring the team for winning a silver medal at the World Junior Championships, January 4, 1977.
St. Catharines Standard photo

Captain Dale McCourt is honoured in the Mount Hamilton Arena on "Dale McCourt Day" on March 11, 1977. Making the presentation is Ron Cupido (right) and radio sports broadcaster Norm Marshall.
St. Catharines Standard photo

OHA President Hugh McLean presents Fincups captain Dale McCourt with the William Hanley Trophy on April 1, 1977.
St. Catharines Standard photo

Supporters' Club head Gladys Crowe presents a trophy to Dale McCourt on February 19, 1977, for breaking the OMJHL career points record. McCourt accumulated 477 points during his junior career.
St. Catharines Standard photo

FINCUPS 1976-1977

FINCUPS MOVE INTO GARDEN CITY ARENA

ATTENDANCE FIGURES
Average per regular-season game: 1,635*
Season's largest crowd: 3,246
Season's smallest crowd: 943

PLAYOFF ROUNDS: 2
Eliminated Windsor 4-2
Lost to London 4-3-1

In the spring of 1976, junior A hockey, which had been a fixture on the St. Catharines sports scene for 33 years, seemed to be finished. The situation changed when Hamilton Fincups, the 1976 Memorial Cup champions, became a team without a place to play. The breakdown of ice-making equipment in the old Hamilton Forum and the failure of several plans to build a new arena in Hamilton forced Fincups owners, Ron and Mario Cupido and Joe Finochio, to look for a new venue for the 1976-77 season.

In the summer of 1976 the Fincups owners decided that St. Catharines would be the ideal location for their team, but there were a number of approvals needed to pave the way for their move to the Garden City.

Regular-season attendance figure is for 31/33 games. One game was played in Hamilton and one game had no attendance record.

Joe Finochio (left) and Mario Cupido pictured here in 2004
St. Catharines Museum - Photo Collection 2004 AA-21

1976-1977

GAMES PLAYED	WON	LOST	TIED	FOR	AGAINST	POINTS	FINISH
66	50	11	5	438	242	105	1/6

Leading Scorers

PLAYER	GOALS	ASSISTS	POINTS
Dale McCourt	60	79	139
Mike Keating	52	61	113
Ric Seiling	50	61	111
Steve Hazlett	42	58	100
Denis Houle	43	41	84

Leading Goaltenders

PLAYER	GP	GA	SO	GAA
Al Jensen	44	168	2	3.69
Rick Wamsley	11	36	0	3.34

Ron Cupido
St. Catharines Standard photo

Front row: Al Jensen, Tim Coulis, Bert Templeton, Joe Contini, Dale McCourt, Danny Shearer, Dave Draper, Brian Ostroski, Rick Wamsley; Second row: Bud Mountain, Bill Dynes, Dr. Gold, Dr. Park, Mario Cupido, Ron Cupido, Joe Finochio, Joe Rolo, Dr. Manoian, Andy Alway, Nino Picone; Third row: Scott Vanderburg, Denis Houle, Rob Mierkalns, Al Secord, Mike Boyd, Mike Forbes, Geoff Shaw, Jody Gage, Steve Hazlett; Back row: Brian Anderson, Jay Johnston, Ric Seiling, Willie Huber, Mark Plantery, Mike Keating, Rob Street

Courtesy of Mario Cupido

FINCUPS 1976-1977

BERT TEMPLETON

Bert Templeton, who was born in Scotland, came to St. Catharines with a very impressive resume and a hard, uncompromising style of coaching that had produced outstanding results.

St. Catharines Standard photo, November 13, 1976

In 1975 he was the Ontario Major Junior Hockey League coach-of-the-year and in 1976 led the Hamilton Fincups to the Memorial Cup. After leaving the Fincups, he coached the North Bay Centennials, Barrie Colts, and then the Sudbury Wolves, winning several more honours along the way.

At the time of his death in December of 2003, the veteran of 26 OHL seasons had an amazing record of 907-678-148, second only to Ottawa's Brian Kilrea who has won more than 1000 junior games.

DAVE DRAPER

Former St. Catharines Fincups GM Dave Draper has a resume filled with success from playing, coaching, managing and scouting over the last 50 years.

St. Catharines Standard photo, November 13, 1976

After winning a junior B championship and a Memorial Cup with St. Michael's College Majors, he played college hockey for the Division 1 Michigan Tech Huskies.

Although he graduated with a business degree in 1965, he decided to follow a coaching career, eventually becoming the bench boss for the Loyola University hockey club in Montreal. After winning three Quebec championships, he became the coach of the OHA Junior A Hamilton Red Wings in 1972. When the team was sold and re-named the Fincups in 1974, Draper was the team GM and manager of the Hamilton Forum.

"I worked for that franchise, different teams, different locations for 17 years and you never felt you had a home," he said.

In 1986 he joined the Canadian Amateur Hockey Association's Program of Excellence and scouted for the Canadian junior team. He has gold medals from Team Canada's world junior championships in 1988 and 1990.

In 1991 he was a pro scout for the NHL Quebec Nordiques and was with the club when it won a Stanley Cup in 1996 in Colorado.

Today, the Burlington Ontario resident scouts for the Washington Capitals.

The Junior B St. Catharines Stewart-Hinan Falcons had the right to block the Fincups transfer if they wanted to do so. Instead, the Falcons executive, led by Ted Fauteux, welcomed the club and cleared the way for the next hurdle, the St. Catharines city council. No problem. The mayor and council cut through red tape and signed a two-year contract with the team's owners.

There was one more potential obstacle. Niagara Falls Flyers held territorial rights within a 50-mile radius of the Honeymoon Capital and could stop the entry of a second major junior hockey team into the Niagara district. It was no big surprise that Hap Emms gave his okay. He knew the renewal of a rivalry with a St. Catharines team would be good for his hockey club.

The Fincups, coached by Bert Templeton and managed by Dave Draper, would turn out to be one of the strongest, most successful, and entertaining teams to ever play in the Garden City.

The big question in the fall of 1976 was whether or not St. Catharines fans would support the 1976 Memorial Cup team from Hamilton. It didn't take long to find an answer. In the opening home game on September 24, Captain Dale McCourt scored a goal and added four assists in a 9-3 win over the Windsor Spitfires before only 1,331 fans. It was Grape and Wine weekend, so perhaps attendance would pick up when fans saw just how good this team was.

Soon after the season started, the scoring power and success of the Fincups were the talk of the league, but not in the Garden City. From October 10 to November 5, 1976, the team won 12 straight games, setting a new team record. It had 17 consecutive home victories before leaving for Europe on December 20, 1976, but as of January 11, 1977, the average home attendance was only 1,800 in an arena seating 3,090.

The team had scheduled 20 Tuesdays, one Wednesday, two Fridays, five Saturdays and five Sundays for its home dates, hoping to attract more fans. "Most teams found Sundays just don't work any more," Fincups GM Dave Draper said at the season's start. Another factor taken into consideration was that Buffalo Sabres played many of their home games on Sunday nights.

The largest crowd before Christmas was 2,432 and the smallest 943. Who was it who said all a team has to do is win games and the fans will turn out?

FINCUPS WIN SILVER AT WORLD JUNIOR CHAMPIONSHIPS

(Players picked up from other organizations are noted) Back row: Jay Johnston, Mike Keating, Mark Plantery, Brad Marsh (London Knights), Willie Huber, Dave Simpson, Ron Duguay (Sudbury Wolves), Mike Boyd, Brian Anderson. Third row: Brian Ostroski, Steve Hazlett, John Anderson (Toronto Marlies), Al Secord, Ric Seiling, Mike Forbes, Geoff Shaw, Trevor Johansson (Toronto Marlies), Jody Gage, Denis Houle. Second row: Bob Daly (Ottawa 67s), Bill Dynes, Bert Templeton, Mario Cupido, Ron Cupido, Joe Finochio, Dave Draper, Andy Alway, Rob Street. Front row: Al Jensen, Dwight Foster (Kitchener Rangers), Craig Hartsburg (Soo Greyhounds), Joe Contini, Dale McCourt, Danny Shearer, Rob Ramage (London Knights), Dave Hunter (Sudbury Wolves), Rick Wamsley   St. Catharines Standard photo

FINCUPS 1976-1977

In December of 1976, the Fincups were chosen to represent Canada in the first sanctioned World Junior Hockey tournament, played at Banska Bystrica and Zvolen near Bratslava, Czechoslovakia. The Fincups won the right to represent Canada by putting together the best record of any Ontario Major Junior Hockey League team in the first ten games of the season with nine wins and one loss.

After the team arrived in Europe, it was announced the Fincups had to go into the tournament with a set 20-man roster. The Fincups had been bolstered by eight players from other OMJHL teams, including future NHLers Rob Ramage, Dave Hunter, Craig Hartsburg, and Ron Duguay. Templeton and Draper thought they would be able to juggle their lineup during the tournament, but found they couldn't do that. This meant eight Fincups players wouldn't be playing. It was a huge disappointment for those players, and Hartsburg was one of the imports who didn't play. The parents of one of the players cut from the team had already spent $5,000 to take their family on the trip.

The team ended the tournament with a 5-1-1 record, losing only to Russia in the final game, 6-4. Moscow Dynamo was up 6-0 in the first period; the Fincups, however, regained their composure and scored four goals in the third period, but it wasn't enough.

"First of all, we met a good team," Fincups coach Bert Templeton said after winning the silver medal in the final game. "Secondly, we were under a lot of pressure with a generally hostile crowd while playing six time zones away from home."

Dale McCourt was the leading scorer in the tournament with 20 points and the all-star centre was named the outstanding forward in the series.

The Fincups were welcomed home by a crowd of 400 at Garden City Arena where they were congratulated by Mayor Roy Adams and members of city council during a civic reception on January 4, 1977.

After the Fincups came home in January of 1977, they continued their strong play and ended up first overall in the league with 105 points, winning the Hamilton Spectator Trophy for earning the most points in the OMJHL and the Emms Trophy for being the top club in the Emms Division. The 105 points tied the league

Fincups goalies Rick Wamsley (front left) and Al Jensen (right) carry their gear to the team bus which is headed for the airport and a trip to the 1977 World Junior Championships in Czechoslovakia. Following behind are Joe Contini (left) and Mike Forbes. December 19, 1976.
St. Catharines Standard photo

Fincups coach Bert Templeton relaxes with players (left to right) Danny Shearer, Joe Contini and Willie Huber before the team's first playoff series with Windsor Spitfires on March 23, 1977.
St. Catharines Standard photo

RIC SEILING

One of the offensive forces on the 1976-77 Fincups was right wing/centre Ric Seiling who had won a Memorial Cup in 1976 with the Hamilton Fincups. The Elmira native scored his 50th goal in the last regular-season game, giving him 111 points in 62 games.

Seiling was Buffalo Sabres first pick, 14th overall in the 1977 Amateur Draft. During his nine years with Buffalo and one with Detroit Red Wings, he scored 387 points, including 179 goals in 738 regular-season games.

After retiring in 1988, he got his driving licence for harness racing and drove on Standardbred tracks in Buffalo and Ontario until 1992.

Today he lives and works in Rochester, New York.

Courtesy of M.J. Wilks

TIM COULIS

Kenora native Tim Coulis split the 1976-77 season between the Soo Greyhounds and the St. Catharines Fincups. The fearless left winger spent the next season with the Hamilton Fincups before becoming a first round pick of the Washington Capitals in 1978.

He saw limited NHL action with Washington and Minnesota North Stars before retiring in 1988. Most of his pro career was spent in the AHL, CHL and IHL with the exception of 1982-83 when he was suspended for the season for assaulting a referee. His best pro season was in 1983-84 with the CHL Salt Lake Golden Eagles when he collected 60 points in 63 regular-season contests.

Coulis now lives in Kenora, Ontario.

St. Catharines Standard photo

FINCUPS 1976-1977

MIKE FORBES

Brampton native Mike Forbes played two seasons with the Kingston Can-adians before joining the St. Catharines Fincups in 1976.

Forbes was Boston Bruins third choice in the 1977 Amateur Draft. In his ten-year pro career, the rearguard spent time in the AHL, CHL, IHL and saw NHL action with the Bruins and Edmonton Oilers before he retired in 1987.

In 1986 and 1989, he earned IHL Turner Cup rings. He also has a Stanley Cup ring as a reward for developing Muskegon Lumberjacks players who contributed to the Pittsburgh Penguins Stanley Cups in 1991 and 1992.

Today he lives in Grand Haven, Michigan.

St. Catharines Standard photo

RICK WAMSLEY

Netminder Rick Wamsley played one junior season in St. Catharines with the 1976-77 Fincups. In 1977-78 he shared the Pinkney Trophy with Hamilton Fincups teammate Al Jensen.

He was drafted by the Montreal Canadiens in 1979. After one season with the AHL Nova Scotia Voyageurs, the Simcoe native made his NHL debut with the Canadiens in 1980-81. He shared the 1981-82 Jennings Trophy with Montreal teammate Denis Herron.

Four seasons later, he was traded to St. Louis where he stayed for four years before being traded to the Calgary Flames with whom he won the Stanley Cup in 1989.

On January 2, 1992, he was part of the ten-player trade that saw him join the Toronto Maple Leafs.

His NHL career, which ended in 1992-93, showed 407 regular-season NHL games played with 204 victories, 12 shutouts, and a goals-against average of 3.34.

In 2006-07 he was the assistant coach and goaltending coach of the St. Louis Blues.

He lives in Oakville, Ontario.

Courtesy of M.J. Wilks

A civic reception for the Silver Medalist St. Catharines Fincups was held at Garden City Arena on January 4, 1977.
St. Catharines Standard photo

Fincups co-owner Mario Cupido shakes hands with his players after capturing the league pennant with 105 points on March 15, 1977.
St. Catharines Standard photo

record set by the 1974-75 Toronto Marlboros. The 438 goals scored in the regular season placed the club second to the Marlies 1974-75 record of 469.

On February 15, 1977, Dale McCourt scored five points and became the all-time leading scorer in the Major Junior Hockey League with 448, passing Peter Lee who had earned 444. McCourt ended his career with 477.

In 33 home games, the Fincups were beaten only twice with an outstanding record of 29-2-2. On January 18, 1977, the Fincups won their 20th straight home game, the longest home winning streak in the history of Junior A hockey in St. Catharines.

It was the first pennant for a St. Catharines team in 18 years, but St. Catharines hockey fans hadn't bought the product. The team's attendance record was no better than tenth out of 12 teams in the league, averaging 1,722 for regular-season and playoff games. Ironically, the club was a big draw on the road.

"The attendance has been not only discouraging but a downright disgrace if you want to put it bluntly," Jack Gatecliff wrote in January of 1977.

In the playoffs, the Fincups eliminated the Windsor Spitfires in six games, but in the second round, the London Knights won the eight games series 4-3-1. London, which had finished one point behind the Fincups in the regular schedule, won the deciding game 3-2. For the seventh game in St. Catharines, the attendance was only 2,168.

Continued on page 190

FINCUPS 1976-1977

Dan Shearer scored the last goal for a St. Catharines Ontario Major Junior Hockey League team in a playoff game against the London Knights in London on April 20, 1977.
Courtesy of M.J. Wilks

Fincups captain Dale McCourt (10) chases the puck during a 6-1 win over the London Knights on December 14, 1976.
St. Catharines Standard photo

Hap Emms (left) and Fincups assistant captain Danny Shearer pose with the Emms Division Trophy on April 1, 1977.
St. Catharines Standard photo

Fincup Al Secord (20) shoots at Sudbury goalie Jack Shaw in an 8-5 win on February 19, 1977. It was the Fincups 25th victory in 27 home games.
Courtesy of M.J. Wilks

STEVE HAZLETT

Sarnia native Steve Hazlett played junior hockey with the St. Catharines Fincups and the Hamilton Fincups from 1976 to 1978. He was with the 1976 Memorial Cup Champion Fincups and was the tournament's top goal scorer.

Ernie Fitzsimmons Collection

The left winger turned pro with the Vancouver Canucks, but saw action in only one NHL game. His pro career, which lasted from 1978 to 1983, was spent in the CHL and the IHL. His best pro season came in 1978-79 when he collected 76 points, including 44 goals, in 76 games with the CHL champion Dallas Black Hawks.

Hazlett resides in Frisco, Texas, where he is a manufacturer's agent.

AL SECORD

Sudbury native Al Secord played three years of major junior hockey, two with Hamilton Fincups with whom he won a Memorial Cup in 1976, and one with St. Catharines Fincups.

Courtesy of M.J. Wilks

He was Boston's first choice, 16th overall in the 1978 Amateur Draft. From 1978 to 1990, the left winger played 766 regular-season NHL games with the Bruins, Chicago Blackhawks, Toronto Maple Leafs, and Philadelphia Flyers. In 12 NHL seasons, he recorded 495 points, including 273 goals. His best NHL season was with the Blackhawks in 1982-83 when he scored 54 goals and had 86 points.

In 1994 he ended four years of retirement to play two seasons with the IHL Chicago Wolves.

Secord, who played in two NHL all-star games and represented Canada twice in international tournaments, is a commercial pilot and lives in Southlake, Texas.

FINCUPS 1976-1977

JODY GAGE

From 1976 to 1979, Jody Gage played junior hockey for St. Catharines, Hamilton and Kitchener before turning pro with the Detroit Red Wings in 1979.

The right winger's 17-year pro career was mainly in the AHL where he had an outstanding record, scoring 504 goals and 1,048 points with the Adirondack Red Wings and Rochester Americans. He is the third highest all-time points leader in the AHL.

Gage in an AHL Rochester Americans uniform
Ernie Fitzsimmons photo

Gage also set several scoring records in Adirondack, Rochester, and the AHL during his career.

From 1980-81 to 1991-92, he was called up to the Detroit Red Wings and Buffalo Sabres six times, playing in 68 NHL games.

In addition to making the AHL first all-star team three times, the Toronto native was the league's MVP in 1988 and has three Calder Cup rings from 1981 (Adirondack), 1987 (Rochester) and 1996 (Rochester).

After retiring in 1996, he became the assistant Rochester GM and was the GM the following season. In 1998-99 he was voted the AHL's outstanding executive. In 2006 he was named to the Rochester Americans dream team and to the inaugural class of the AHL Hall of Fame. His number 9 hangs from the rafters of Rochester's War Memorial Arena and he is known as "Mr. Amerk."

Today Gage is still the GM of the Rochester Americans and the NLL Rochester Knighthawks. He resides in Chili, New York.

High-scoring forward Denis Houle
Courtesy of M.J. Wilks

Continued from page 188

"It was a brutal series," recalled former Fincup Mark Plantery in August of 2005. He recalled that Templeton instructed some of the Fincup players to go on the ice and fight specific London players in a game before the playoffs. According to Plantery, Templeton wanted to intimidate the London players before the playoffs, but it didn't work. Plantery didn't want to fight just because he was ordered to do so, but like his teammates, he knew that Templeton was the boss. If he refused to follow orders, the coach could ruin his career.

Although the Fincups had signed a two-year contract with the city in 1976, there was no way the club was going to stay in St. Catharines and lose more money. Some estimated the Fincups owners had lost $100,000 in 1976-77. Fincup owner Mario Cupido confirmed it was at least that much.

In July of 1977, the owners announced that the team was moving back to Hamilton and playing its home games at the Hamilton Mountain Arena.

The St. Catharines Black Hawks, who had moved to Niagara Falls in 1976, were sold by Hap Emms to businessman Reg Quinn in 1978. In 1982 the Flyers were moved to North Bay and stayed as the Centennials until the club was relocated to Saginaw, Michigan, in 2002, for $3,000,000. The team is now known as the Saginaw Spirit.

As of 1977, St. Catharines hockey fans had wonderful memories of 34 years of junior hockey in the old Garden City Arena, including:

- Two Memorial Cups (1954, 1960)
- Four OHA Junior A championships (1954, 1960, 1971, 1974)
- Thirteen NHL scoring championships won by three former Teepees, Phil Esposito (five), Stan Mikita (four), Bobby Hull (three), and one by ex-Black Hawk Marcel Dionne
- Every major NHL trophy won by former St. Catharines players at least once
- One or more former juniors on the NHL all-star teams for 16 straight years

"St. Catharines has no place where we can go and pat ourselves on the back," St. Catharines booster Terry O'Malley said in 2004. ∎

1976-77 St. Catharines Fincups Trophy Winners April 27, 1977
Left to right: Bill Muirhead, most valuable player with St. Catharines Lions Midgets; Jay Johnston, top rookie; Ric Seiling, most colourful; Willie Huber, attitude winner; Mike Forbes, best defenceman; Dale McCourt, most valuable player, most gentlemanly, most popular; Rick Wamsley and Al Jensen, goaltending award.
St. Catharines Standard photo

FINCUPS 1976-1977

WILLIE HUBER

Willie Huber was born in Strasskirchen, Germany, but played his major junior hockey with the Hamilton and St. Catharines Fincups from 1975 to 1978. He participated in two world junior tournaments, earning a silver and a bronze medal, and the World and European championship series in 1981.

Courtesy of M.J. Wilks

The 6-foot-5, 228-pound defenceman, who has a 1976 Memorial Cup ring, was drafted by the Detroit Red Wings and played for that club from 1978 to 1983. He was Detroit's top rookie in 1978-79.

In 1983 he was traded to the New York Rangers and after four years with the Rangers, he ended his career with Vancouver and Philadelphia in 1988. He accumulated 321 points in 655 regular-season NHL games.

Today he lives in Hamilton.

MARK PLANTERY

One of the Fincups steadiest performers on the blueline in 1976-77 was St. Catharines-born and Thorold-raised Mark Plantery.

After two seasons with the Thorold Paper Bees, he was the first draft choice of the Fincups in 1976.

Plantery was also a baseball prospect who had been signed by the New York Yankees when he was only 15.

Courtesy of M.J. Wilks

He was the youngest player ever signed by the Yankees.

After catching in Class A ball for a couple of summers, he concentrated on hockey, playing two more seasons of major junior before turning pro in 1979 with the CHL Tulsa Oilers, a farm team of the Winnipeg Jets.

With the exception of 25 games with the Jets in 1980-81, most of his pro career, which ended in 1985, was spent in the CHL, AHL and IHL. He also spent one season in Italy with HC Gardena-groden.

Plantery is now a commodity trader in Chicago, Illinois.

MIKE KEATING

Left winger Mike Keating ended his junior A career with the St. Catharines Fincups, scoring 51 goals and collecting 113 points in 1976-77, after two years with the Hamilton Fincups.

The 1976 Memorial Cup winner was the New York Rangers third choice in the 1977 Amateur Draft, but only suited up with the Rangers for one game.

Courtesy of M.J. Wilks

After spending time in the AHL and IHL, the Toronto native retired in 1980. His best pro season was with the IHL Toledo Goaldiggers in 1979-80 when he earned 60 points in 63 regular-season games.

Keating lives in Toronto.

AL JENSEN

Hamilton native Al Jensen played three years of junior hockey, two with the Hamilton Fincups and one with the St. Catharines Fincups in 1976-77. He earned a Memorial Cup ring in 1976 and participated in two world junior tournaments, winning a silver medal in 1977 and a bronze in 1978. In 1978, he was an OMJHL First All-Star Team selection and he and Rick Wamsley shared the Dave Pinkney Trophy for having the lowest goals-against average in the league.

Courtesy of M.J. Wilks

Detroit Red Wings drafted him in 1978 and he started his pro career with the IHL Kalamazoo Wings with whom he won a Turner Cup in 1979. After playing one game with Detroit in 1980 and winning the AHL Calder Cup with Adirondack Red Wings in 1981, he was traded to Washington where he played 174 games until 1987 when he was traded to Los Angeles.

In addition to setting several netminding records for the Capitals, in 1984 he shared the William M. Jennings Trophy with Pat Riggin. He played 179 regular-season NHL games, winning 95 with a goals-against average of 3.35.

Jensen lives in Grimsby, Ontario, and is a hockey scout for the NHL's Central Scouting Service.

JOE CONTINI

Galt native Joe Contini played two years of junior in Hamilton and finished his career with St. Catharines Fincups in 1977.

As a member of the 1976 Memorial Cup champion Hamilton Fincups, Contini set three different single game records in an 8-4 victory over the New Westminster Bruins on May 12, 1976

Courtesy of M.J. Wilks

MOST POINTS: 6 (three goals and three assists)

FASTEST TWO GOALS: (scored eight seconds apart in the first period)

FASTEST THREE GOALS: (scored in one minute and twelve seconds in the first period)

The points' record is now shared, but the two fastest goals' records have yet to be broken.

The centre/left wing saw limited NHL action with the Colorado Rockies and Minnesota North Stars after turning pro in 1977. He had his best pro year in 1980-81 with the CHL Oklahoma City Stars when he earned 95 points in 77 regular-season games.

He currently lives in Arthur, Ontario, and has a drycleaning business in Guelph.

JAY JOHNSTON

Rearguard Jay Johnston spent two years with the Fincups, 1976 to 1978 in St. Catharines, and the next year with Hamilton.

The Steel City native was drafted by the Washington Capitals in 1978, but only saw action with the Capitals for a handful of games between 1980 and 1982.

Courtesy of M.J. Wilks

He spent the majority of his career with the AHL Hershey Bears, with whom he won a Calder Cup in 1980, and the IHL Fort Wayne Komets. He retired in 1987.

After one year of coaching the OHL Dukes of Hamilton, he worked for United Rentals in West Lafayette, Indiana, before returning to Hamilton in 2006.

EPILOGUE

In the spring of 2004 I was writing a series of articles for the St. Catharines Standard on the 1953-54 Teepees and their first Memorial Cup victory. I thought it was time to honour the team and everyone I talked to agreed, but I wondered if there was anyone who would help me do something about it.

That's when St. Catharines Museum Curator of Collections, Arden Phair, stepped up and pledged his support. The Museum staff and a committee of dedicated volunteers worked countless hours to help the St. Catharines Museum host a 50th anniversary celebration for the 1953-54 team. Eight former 1953-54 Teepees, including Captain Brian Cullen, Ian Cushenan, Marv Edwards, Peter Koval, Jack Higgins, Cec Hoekstra, Reg Truax, and Chester Warchol showed up at the Museum on May 16, 2004, 50 years to the day that they had won the Memorial Cup.

Special guest, former NHL great, Dick Duff, presented the original Memorial Cup to Brian Cullen. It was a memorable moment, as Duff had not forgotten that the Teepees had defeated his team, the St. Michael's College Majors, on their road to the 1954 Memorial Cup victory. Duff was assisted by Jeremy Stunt and Trace Hanlon, grandsons of former Teepees coach Rudy Pilous. More than 400 witnessed the event, which was emceed by well-known St. Catharines businessman and former Stratford Junior A hockey player, Archie Katzman.

SEPTEMBER 25, 2004

When we started to talk about a May celebration in the fall of 2003, Arden Phair kept insisting that we should have a reunion of all former St. Catharines Junior A players as well. Having been involved in a few high school reunions, I knew it would be a lot of work and doubted if we had enough time — but his persistence won out. The task was daunting.

We had no money and certainly little credibility, so I decided to approach a person whom I felt might like the idea: former Harvard hockey star and internationally renowned advertising executive, Terry O'Malley. O'Malley loves his hometown and if anybody could help us, it was he.

I contacted O'Malley on the pretext that I wanted to interview him, which I honestly did want to do. However, my mission on the day I met him in his office above the old Bissonnette, Joy and Company building in downtown St. Catharines was to see what he thought about our idea to have two hockey celebrations in 2004. To my delight, he warmed to the idea immediately. He pledged financial help and challenged us to raise more money, and if we did, he would raise the ante.

Arden and I had found an angel in disguise. From that moment on – it was near Christmas 2003 – we had money in the bank and credibility. By using Terry's name we were able to raise more money, and more importantly, gain the support of some high-profile people in the community, including Archie Katzman, Walt Marsh, Obie O'Brien, and Doug Smith of the Wise Guys, who helped make both events a huge success.

We spent a year preparing for the big event, and it all came together because of the efforts of our Junior Hockey Committee, sponsors, volunteers and staff at the St. Catharines Museum: Rosemary, Grace, Karen, Megan, Anthony, Martin, Brent, Nancy, Pat and Randy. They spent many hours getting ready for the hockey reunion of all former St. Catharines Junior A hockey players on Saturday, September 25, 2004.

The Niagara Wine Festival made St. Catharines Junior A hockey the theme of the 2004 Grape and Wine Grande Parade: "Hockey Homecoming, The Pride is Back". Terry O'Malley came up with the idea that it was time to bring the pride in junior hockey back to the city.

Serving as parade marshals on September 25 were ex-Falcon Doug McMurdy, the first recipient of the Red Tilson Trophy, two-time Stanley Cup winner Fred Stanfield, Hockey Hall of Fame member Marcel Dionne, and the 1977 Canadian Major Junior Player of the Year, Dale McCourt.

Riding in a separate car with the Memorial Cup were 1954 Memorial Cup champions: Captain Brian Cullen, Ian Cushenan, Marv Edwards, and Cec Hoekstra. Three-time Norris Trophy winner Pierre Pilote rode in the parade in a vintage red Corvette driven by former Black Hawks dentist Bob McKay. Riding in a special float sponsored by the *St. Catharines Standard* were several former Falcons, Teepees, Black Hawks, and Fincups. They were having a ball! From 2 to 5 p.m., the public met and greeted former junior players at the St. Catharines Museum located at Lock 3 of the Welland Canal. On a sunny, warm afternoon, more than 120 former junior players and their fans exchanged hugs, handshakes and the occasional tear. It was a sight to behold. Some Falcons players hadn't seen each other for 60 years.

After supper, which was served in three tents and in the old restaurant upstairs in the Museum, the evening ended with a hilarious hour of entertainment by local entertainers, Malton and Hamilton. The comedy duo at one time had a singer, Eilleen, in their act in Deerhurst, Ontario. She later changed her name to Shania Twain.

By midnight, only the cleanup crew was present at the site. The players had left and many, perhaps, were never to see each other again. As I stood looking at the scene of so much fun and laughter, a Peggy Lee song came to mind. You remember the lyrics don't you? "Is that all there is…?"

Not quite.

On January 30, 2006, Ernie Coetzee, president of JDS Delcor Inc., made a proposal to the St. Catharines City Council to retrofit Jack Gatecliff Arena and bring an OHL franchise to the Garden City. Backing the plan were former NHL player and coach Steve Ludzik, (projected coach and GM of the new OHL team), St. Catharines native and advertising guru Terry O'Malley, and Hockey Night in Canada star Don Cherry, who would be the director of scouting for the new franchise.

During the presentation some councillors were more interested in getting Cherry's autograph than paying attention to the various speakers outlining the proposal.

"Thank you for a wonderful presentation," Mayor Tim Rigby said. "With the amount of private money you have proposed to put into a downtown project, we really have a wonderful opportunity."

The project, which was estimated to cost about 30 million dollars (the city would put up 1/3 of that), would see Jack Gatecliff Arena transformed into a 5,800-seat venue not only for an OHL team, but for a variety of sports and entertainment events. For many, it was the answer to revitalizing the downtown area that was, and still is, suffering from a number of problems.

After the slide show, which took viewers on a tour of the proposed building, Coetzee asked for a decision as soon as possible so work could begin and be completed in time for the 2007-08 OHL season.

"I am excited by this," Councillor Charles Gervais said. "You are no doubt able to assemble a great team and deliver a great product."

After several weeks of studying the pros and cons of the proposal, St. Catharines Parks and Recreation director Ron Zizman made his recommendation to council.

"It was a good opportunity and we had a really hard look at it," Zizman said. "I brought forward the best proposal I thought we could achieve. We had the essence of an agreement."

The councillors, many of whom had welcomed the proposal in January, voted not to present Zizman's offer to JDS. The deal was dead, much to the dismay of Mayor Rigby and Deputy Mayor Sue Erskine, who had both supported it.

"They [councillors] were looking at all the things [projects costs] on the table," Zizman said.

Opportunity knocked and city councillors, facing a November 2006 election, didn't answer the door. ....

Pierre Pilote enjoys his parade ride in a vintage Corvette. — Arden Phair

Former St. Catharines captains Marcel Dionne (left) and Dale McCourt greet the parade-day crowd. — Arden Phair

Former Garden City Junior A players on their own float — Arden Phair

Former Teepees travel with the Memorial Cup. — Stan Lapinski

Fred Stanfield in the back and Doug McMurdy in the front travel in style during the parade. — Stan Lapinski

THE NIAGARA ICEDOGS

On Tuesday, April 17, 2007, another door opened. The city of St. Catharines received an offer to host an OHL team when the prospective owner of the Mississauga IceDogs, Bill Burke, met with Mayor Brian McMullan and the city's chief administrative officer. Burke wanted renovations made to the existing dressing rooms in Jack Gatecliff Arena and was really interested in moving the IceDogs here for three seasons.

On April 23, 2007, a deal was made, and Burke signed a five-year lease with the city in return for $250,000 for a new dressing room and renovation of the dressing room used by the St. Catharines Junior B Falcons.

The new owner of the IceDogs wanted the city to build a new arena but only after he had established the team's fan base. "I want to have it sold out every night so people will want to get into it and then we'll get a new arena," Burke told the *St. Catharines Standard*.

Burke, a 50 year-old printing executive from Newmarket, is a graduate of Ridley College (class of 1977). He and his wife Denise, president of the IceDogs, fell in love with the OHL when their son Bill Jr. played one season with the Barrie Colts.

As of 2008, Denise was the only female president in the Canadian Hockey League, which is made up of the Ontario, Quebec Major Junior, and Western hockey leagues.

"I want to give St. Catharines and Niagara a chance to experience something they haven't had in the past...the ability to see the greatest amateur hockey in the world," Bill Burke said.

On March 2, 2008, Niagara Falls businessman Bob Gale, the owner and operator of a chain of gas bars, tried to kick-start plans to build a new arena for the IceDogs. He offered $100,000 to fund youth activities if the city of St. Catharines could satisfy him that plans were in place to build a new arena within a year. Stay tuned for the results of his offer.

Denise and Bill Burke — Stan Lapinski

Bob Gale — Stan Lapinski

The last Ontario Major Junior Hockey League (OHL) game played in Jack Gatecliff Arena (Garden City Arena then) took place on Tuesday, April 19, 1977, when the St. Catharines Fincups beat the London Knights in playoff action with only 2,168 fans in attendance.

The Niagara IceDogs played their first regular-season OHL game in the Garden City on Friday, September 21, 2007, in front of a sellout crowd of 3,145.

After the 68-game schedule was completed, the IceDogs finished fourth in the final standings of the Eastern Conference of the OHL with 85 points, and met St. Michael's College Majors in the first round of the playoffs. The IceDogs swept the Majors in four straight games. The team was eliminated from the playoffs in six games by their next opponent, the Oshawa Generals, who were led by junior superstar John Tavares.

Every playoff game at Garden City Arena was a sellout.

With such a successful first season of OHL hockey, the Burkes and Bob Gale could be the driving forces behind a new golden age of hockey in St. Catharines and the Niagara region.

Go Dogs Go!!!

— *John Charles Hewitt*

Jack Andrews
Former Teepee defenceman Jack Andrews (1949-50) is the grandfather of Niagara IceDog forward Johnson Andrews. Johnson's father, John, played for the Peterborough Petes.

St. Catharines Museum
- Frank Martin Collection, C10780

2 0 0 7 - 2 0 0 8   N I A G A R A   I C E D O G S

Back Row: Ivan Bokanovic - Athletic Therapist, Andrew Agozzino, Matt Sisca, Jason Bergeron, Alex Friesen, Jordan Foreman, Chris DeSousa, Matt Maione, Barry Sanderson, Garry Buxton - Equipment Manager

Middle Row: Ron Mays - Goalie Coach, Michael MacIsaac, Dylan MacEachern, Reggie Traccitto, Josh Day, Scott Fletcher, Andrew Merrett, Drew Schiestel, Johnson Andrews, Adrian Volpe, Peter Dobbin - Trainer

Front Row: Lucas Lobsinger, Dave Brown - General Manager, Mario Cicchillo - Head Coach, Alex Pietrangelo, Matt Corrente, Michael Swift, Denise Burke - President, Bill Burke - Owner, Stefan Legein, Luca Caputi, Mike McCourt - Assistant Coach, Paul Simpson - CFO, Sebastian Dahm

Photo by Rick Denham

MEMORIAL CUP CHAMPIONSHIP
50TH ANNIVERSARY COMMEMORATION — MAY 16, 2004

Hockey celebration committee members (left to right) Bob Cornelius, John Hewitt, and St. Catharines Museum Curator of Collections Arden Phair, admire the Memorial Cup.
— Stan Lapinski

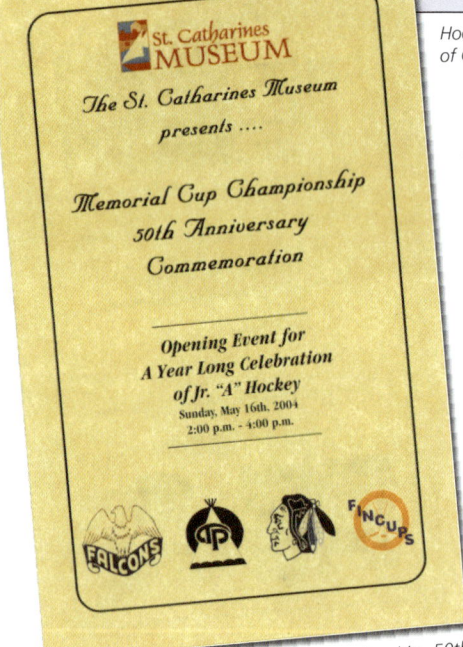

Cover of the Memorial Cup Championship 50th Anniversary Commemoration

Holding the Memorial Cup are (left to right) Trace Hanlon, Jeremy Stunt (grandsons of Rudy Plous), Dick Duff, and Brian Cullen
— Stan Lapinski

Photos for the St. Catharines Musueum taken by Stan Lapinski and Arden Phair

GARDEN CITY HOCKEY HEROES

Special guests at the celebration. Left to right: artist George Upper and Teepees Brian Cullen, Ian Cushenan, Marv Edwards, Jack Higgins, Reg Truax, Cec Hoekstra, Peter Koval, and Chester Warchol
— Arden Phair

Emcee Archie Katzman (left) with special guest former NHL great Dick Duff, May 16, 2004
— Stan Lapinski

Former Black Hawk coach John (Peanuts) O'Flaherty (left) attended the homecoming on September 25, 2004 with Val DeLory (centre) and his son John O'Flaherty Jr.
— Stan Lapinski

Sporting their St. Catharines Black Hawk jackets, Mel Burtnik and daughter Sheila Kennedy enjoy the festivities on May 16, 2004. The jackets were a gift to Mel from the Black Hawks, after being "called up" from the "B" team to drive the "A" bus when needed.

Sheila Kennedy, who did the layout design and pre-press production for this book, has been involved with other pictorial history projects. She collaborated with Stan Lapinski on "Denis Morris: A Rowing Tradition Since 1959" (2001), "The St. Catharines Rowing Club: 100 Years in a Row" (2003), and "Brock University Athletics: 40 Exciting Seasons of Generals and Badgers" (2006). She also did the design and layout for "Images of a Century: The City of Niagara Falls, Canada, 1904-2004" (2004).
— Stan Lapinski

The Bell Ringers, Helen and John Brown, lead the procession for the 50th anniversary celebration of the 1954 Teepees Memorial Cup victory on May 16, 2004.
— Stan Lapinski

Members of the first St. Catharines Junior A team 1943-44. Left to right: Laurie Peterson, Tom Smelle (1944-1946), Frank Long, Neal Jackson, Harvey Jessiman, Doug McMurdy, Nick Phillips, and Stan Welsh
— Stan Lapinski

Nick Phillips (left) and Frank Long. Original Falcons, 1943-44
— Stan Lapinski

St. Catharines Falcons (1943-47) who attended the homecoming
— Stan Lapinski

Former St. Catharines Junior A captains. Left to right: Harvey Jessiman, Laurie Peterson, Eric Unger, Red Sullivan, Wayne (Weiner) Brown, Brian Cullen, John Brenneman, Fred Stanfield, Ross Eichler, Tom Reid, Skeeter Teal, Marcel Dionne, Jeff Jacques, Greg Craig, and Dale McCourt

— Stan Lapinski

1976-77 Fincups get together. Left to right: Gary Sobchak, Bob Cullen, Mike Forbes, Geoff Shaw, Rob Street, Denis Houle, Dale McCourt, and Ric Seiling

— Stan Lapinski

Red Tilson Trophy winners. Left to right: Doug McMurdy (1945), Brian Cullen (1954), and Dale McCourt (1977), September 25, 2004

— Stan Lapinski

Former St. Catharines Teepees, 1947-1962, pose for a picture. — Stan Lapinski

Former St. Catharines Black Hawks, 1962-1976, face the camera. — Stan Lapinski

Homecoming attendees, September 25, 2004 — Stan Lapinski

ST. CATHARINES JUNIOR A HOCKEY HONOUR ROLL

ST. CATHARINES JUNIOR A HOCKEY ROLL OF HONOUR

DECEASED TEAM MEMBERS	YEARS AFFILIATED	DECEASED TEAM MEMBERS	YEARS AFFILIATED	DECEASED TEAM MEMBERS	YEARS AFFILIATED
George Aitken	1946-47	Dr. David Houston	1947-48	Wilf Roberts	1951-55
Jack Andrews	1949-50	Arthur Jackson	1947-51	Robert Schnurr	1951-52
Harry Argent	1962-72	Jimmy Joy	1943-65	Gilbert Service	1947-48
Jack Armstrong	1953-54	Winston Juckes	1943-44	Brian Shaw	1968-70
Vic Auger	1945-46	Vic Kafun	1946-47	Carl Smelle	1944-46
Bruce Beaupit	1965-69	Max Kaminsky	1959-61	Miles Smith	1950-52
Jerry Binns	1962-63	Joe Krahulec	1947-48	Larry Smith	1956-59
Carl Boone	1949-52	Ken Laidlaw	1962-66	Bill Speer	1959-62
Edgar Brenchley	1964-66	Edward Lancaster	1958-69	George Stauffer	1947-61
Tommy Buck	1946-50	Jack Leach	1943-61	Jim Steele	1969-70
Gord Byers	1948-50	Peter Long	1943-44	Jack Steele	1952-60
Tony Cammaretta	1968-71	Jay MacDonald	1943-61	Bill Stewart	1944-45
Ken Campbell	1961-66	Matthew MacIntosh	1944-45	Rex Stimers	1947-65
Henry Ciesla	1950-55	Garry MacMillan	1964-66	Stan Stocker	1947-48
Marcel Clements	1948-49	Wayne Maki	1964-65	Connie Switzer	1948-50
Brian Cousineau	1971-73	Frank Martin	1949-52	Bob Taylor	1950-51
Gladys Crowe	1966-77	Ken Mann	1946-47	Allan (Skip) Teal	1950-51
Roger Crozier	1959-62	Edward Mateka	1952-53	Vic Teal	1946-47, 1960-61
Ron Cupido	1976-77	Bob Maxwell	1951-54		
Jimmy Dawdy	1944-46	Dean McBride	1943-45	Thomas Teather	1960-61, 1962-63
Dr. Frank Dawe		Walt McCollum	1971-76		
Rodger Day	1954-56	Don McComb	1950-51	Ronald Telford	1948-49
Armand Delmonte	1943-45	John McIntyre	1947-50	Bert Templeton	1976-77
Bill Dynes	1976-77	John McKenzie	1959-60	Maitland Thompson	1954-56
Roy Edwards	1955-57	Frank Milne	1970-73	Bob Thompson	1969-70
Leighton Emms	1972-76	Stan Milne	1947-48	Robert Thorpe	1943-44
Jack Gatecliff	1944-45	Ray Milner	1956-58	Zellio Toppazzini	1947-48
Fiori Goegan	1946-48	John Mongeon	1958-59	Franklin Toyota	1949-51
Pete Grammar	1943-45	Ashton Morrison	1943-60	Frank Vanderhart	1972-73
Oswin Graves	1943-45	Fred Muller	1964-72	Elmer Vasko	1953-56
Ted Graves	1943-51	Ron Murphy	1952-53	Phil Vitale	1960-61
Ben Greco	1959-60	Gord Myles	1951-52	Stan Warecki	1943-44
Roy Greenen	1954-56	Don O'Donoghue	1967-69	Harry Watson	1958-59
Dr. Alan Greenwood	1944-48	Albert O'Hearn	1950-51	Dennis White	1944-46
Cec Gruhl	1947-48	Rudy Pilous	1943-46, 1950-61	Daniel Wilbur	1944-45
Doran Hallett	1947-50			Bill Young	1950-52
Thomas Heit	1943-45	Tom Pollock	1943-44	Dr. Michael Zaritsky	1956-66
Ozzie Hill	1960-76	Emerson Reynolds	1945-46		
Wayne Hillman	1955-59	Bob Richmond	1951-52		
Bob Hookings	1944-45	Rino Robazza	1956-58		

Compiled by the St. Catharines Museum

ONTARIO HOCKEY LEAGUE

OHA Major Junior "A" logo (1972-1981)

ONTARIO HOCKEY ASSOCIATION (OHA) JUNIOR (1896-1934)

Junior hockey was first played at the turn of the century and quickly grew in popularity. In 1919 the Memorial Cup was first presented in commemoration of the many great hockey players who sacrificed their lives in World War I. It was originally the symbol of junior hockey supremacy in Canada.

OHA JUNIOR "A" (1934-1972)

In 1934 junior hockey in Ontario was split into "A" and "B" divisions with the "A" teams competing for the Memorial Cup and the "B" teams for the Sutherland Cup. The 1930s saw the birth of such notable "A" teams as the Oshawa Generals, St. Michael's Majors, and Toronto Marlboros. New entries in the 1940s included the St. Catharines Teepees, Barrie Flyers, and Guelph Biltmores. In the 1950s, Kitchener and Hamilton entered the league.

For two years in the 1960s, the league split into a Metro Toronto league and a league for the rest of the province. Then a new unified league emerged without St. Michael's, but with new clubs from Niagara Falls, Montreal, London and Ottawa.

OHA MAJOR JUNIOR "A" (1972-1981)

In the 1970s, Junior "A" split into Tier I and Tier II. The only Tier I league in Ontario became known as OHA Major Junior "A". In 1972 its winner represented Ontario in a round-robin Memorial Cup playoff with a team from the West and another team from Quebec.

ONTARIO HOCKEY LEAGUE (1981-PRESENT)

In 1981 the league was renamed the Ontario Hockey League (OHL). New teams from Belleville and Cornwall were added. In the 1990s, the League expanded into the USA with teams from Detroit and Erie. Some teams relocated and there was more expansion with the addition of Barrie, Brampton and Mississauga.

Today, the OHL has 20 teams organized into four divisions and two conferences.

The items to the right were on display at the St. Catharines Museum in the fall of 2004. Photos for the St. Catharines Museum by Stan Lapinski.

Left to right: Original Falcons sweater and jacket. Teepees sweater with "Pee Wee" on the logo

Left to right: Teepees team blazer, St. Catharines Fincups jersey, Team Canada sweater from 1977 World Junior Championships

Left to right: Sweater from first OHA Junior A All-Star game in 1958. Black Hawks jersey and team jacket

ONTARIO HOCKEY LEAGUE

JUNIOR A TROPHIES

THE HAMILTON SPECTATOR TROPHY
– First Place Regular Season

The Hamilton Spectator Trophy goes to the Ontario Hockey League team which finishes in first place overall at the end of the regular season. The Trophy was presented to the OHL by the *Hamilton Spectator* in 1957. The St. Catharines Teepees were the first winners of the Trophy in 1957-58 and 1958-59. Since 1958, the Peterborough Petes have won the Trophy seven times, more than any other team in the OHL. The Toronto Marlboros won the Trophy five times. Guelph captured the Trophy four times, including three times in four years from 1995 to 1998. The winner of the Hamilton Spectator Trophy has gone on to win the OHL Championship 15 times, and the Memorial Cup seven times.

St. Catharines Teams Which Have Won the Hamilton Spectator Trophy:

SEASON	WINNER	GP	W	L	T	PTS
1957-58	St. Catharines Teepees	52	32	14	6	70
1958-59	St. Catharines Teepees	54	40	11	3	83
1976-77	St. Catharines Fincups	66	50	11	5	105

Prior to the awarding of the Hamilton Spectator Trophy in 1957, other St. Catharines teams which finished in first place included:

1943-44 (group 2)	St. Catharines Falcons
1953-54	St. Catharines Teepees
1954-55	St. Catharines Teepees
1955-56	St. Catharines Teepees

J. ROSS ROBERTSON CUP
– OHA/OHL Champions

The J. Ross Robertson Cup is presented annually to the winner of the Ontario Hockey League's playoff championship. The Cup was named in honour of J. Ross Robertson, president of the Ontario Hockey Association from 1901 to 1905.

Since its inception in 1934, the Cup has been won by several different teams, led by Oshawa Generals with 11 championships, including seven consecutive titles

Trophy photos taken for the St. Catharines Museum by Stan Lapinski

Eddie Powers Memorial Trophy

Red Tilson Trophy

Memorial Cup

between 1938 and 1944. The Toronto Marlboros have the most final appearances with 15.

St. Catharines Teams Which Competed for The J. Ross Robertson Cup:

YEAR	CHAMPIONS / RUNNER-UP	WINNING COACH	GAMES
1952	Guelph/St. Catharines	Alf Pike	4-1
1954	St. Catharines/Toronto Marlboros	Rudy Pilous	4-3
1955	Toronto Marlboros/St. Catharines	Turk Broda	4-2
1957	Guelph/St. Catharines	Ed Bush	4-2
1960	St. Catharines/St. Michael's College	Max Kaminsky	4-1 (1 tie)
1969	Montreal/St. Catharines	Roger Bedard	4-0 (2 ties)
1971	St. Catharines/Toronto Marlboros	Frank Milne	4-0
1974	St. Catharines/Peterborough	Paul Emms	4-0 (1 tie)

GEORGE T. RICHARDSON MEMORIAL TROPHY
– Eastern Canada Championship

The George T. Richardson Memorial Trophy was presented annually to the junior hockey champions of Eastern Canada (Ontario and Quebec). The Trophy was named in honour of George T. Richardson, an Allan Cup winner with Queen's University in 1909. He was killed in action in World War I on February 9, 1916.

The Trophy was first presented in 1932 and until 1972 it was awarded to the winner of the Ontario and Quebec junior series. In 1972 the format for the Memorial Cup was changed to a round-robin series involving the winners of the Ontario, Quebec, and Western major junior leagues. As a result, the OHL no longer plays in the Eastern Canada Final.

St. Catharines Teams Which Competed For The George T. Richardson Trophy:

YEAR	CHAMPIONS / RUNNER-UP	WINNING COACH	GAMES
1953-54	Teepees/Quebec Frontenacs	Rudy Pilous	4-2
1959-60	Teepees/Montreal Junior Canadiens	Max Kaminsky	4-3 (1 tie)
1970-71	Black Hawks defaulted to Quebec Remparts with Quebec leading the series 3-2		

THE MEMORIAL CUP

The Memorial Cup, which was first presented in 1919, was dedicated to the many great Canadian hockey players who sacrificed their lives in defence of their country in the First World War. At first, the Cup was the symbol of the national junior championship. In 1934, the Cup signified Junior "A" supremacy, and then Major Junior supremacy in 1972. Today, the Western Hockey League, the Quebec Major Junior Hockey League, and the Ontario Hockey League, along with the host club, compete for junior hockey's top trophy in a round-robin series.

St. Catharines Junior "A" Teams which Won The Memorial Cup In 1954 And 1960:

YEAR	CHAMPIONS / RUNNER-UP	WINNING COACH	GAMES
1954	St. Catharines Teepees/Edmonton Oil Kings	Rudy Pilous	4-0 (1 tie)
1960	St. Catharines Teepees/Edmonton Oil Kings	Max Kaminsky	4-2

THE EDDIE POWERS MEMORIAL TROPHY

The Eddie Powers Memorial Trophy was donated by the Toronto Marlboro Athletic Club in memory of Edward Powers. It goes to the top scorer in the Ontario Hockey League. The trophy was first presented to St. Michael's College star Tod Sloan at the conclusion of the 1945-46 OHA Junior A season.

St. Catharines Winners:

SEASON	WINNER	GP	G	A	PTS
1953-54	Brian Cullen	59	68	93	161
1954-55	Hank Ciesla	45	57	49	106
1957-58	John McKenzie	52	48	51	99
1958-59	Stan Mikita	45	38	59	97
1959-60	Chico Maki	47	39	53	92
1964-65	Ken Hodge	55	63	60	123
1969-70	Marcel Dionne	54	55	77	132
1970-71	Marcel Dionne	54	62	81	143
1973-74	Rick Adduono (co-winner)	70	51	84	135

THE RED TILSON TROPHY

When the Red Tilson Trophy was first presented by *The Globe and Mail* in 1945, it was to go to the player best combining outstanding play and gentlemanly conduct.

Today the Red Tilson Trophy is the most prestigious award presented by the Ontario Hockey League. Each year it goes to the player voted the most outstanding during the regular season by OHL writers and broadcasters.

The award was named in honour of former Oshawa Generals Junior player Albert "Red" Tilson, who was killed in action in Europe in World War II. He played the game by the book and was rarely penalized. The first winner of this award was St. Catharines Falcons defenceman Doug McMurdy.

St. Catharines Junior Players Who Have Won The Red Tilson Trophy Include:

SEASON	WINNER	TEAM
1944-45	Doug McMurdy	St. Catharines Falcons
1953-54	Brian Cullen	St. Catharines Teepees
1954-55	Hank Ciesla	St. Catharines Teepees
1958-59	Stan Mikita	St. Catharines Teepees
1976-77	Dale McCourt	St. Catharines Fincups

Some of the players from other teams who have received this prestigious award read like a who's who of hockey and include:

- Tod Sloan
- Glenn Hall
- Frank Mahovlich
- Gilbert Perreault
- Doug Gilmour
- Eric Lindros
- Alyn McCauley

ST. CATHARINES JUNIOR A HOCKEY – RECORDS AND STATISTICS

ST. CATHARINES JUNIOR "A" TEAM STATISTICS
Percentages rounded off to the nearest whole number

NUMBER OF JUNIOR "A" SEASONS: 34 (1943-77)
- Winning Seasons   19 (56%)
- Losing Seasons   13 (38%)
- Even Seasons   2   (6%)

REGULAR-SEASON FINISHES

First	7 (21%)	Falcons (1)	TPs (5)	Fincups (1)	
Second	5 (15%)	Falcons (1)	TPs (1)	Hawks (3)	
Third	5 (15%)	TPs (3)	Hawks (2)		
Fourth	3 (9%)	Falcons (1)	TPs (2)		
Fifth	5 (15%)	TPs (1)	Hawks (4)		
Sixth	6 (18%)	TPs (3)	Hawks (3)		
Seventh	1 (3%)	Hawks (1)			
Eighth	2 (6%)	Falcons (1)	Hawks (1)		

REGULAR-SEASON GAMES PLAYED: WON, LOST, TIED

TEAM		GP	WON	LOST	TIED
Falcons	1943-47	112	50 (45%)	56 (50%)	6 (5%)
Teepees	1947-62	756	416 (55%)	284 (38%)	56 (7%)
Hawks	1962-76	814	355 (44%)	349 (43%)	110 (14%)
Fincups	1976-77	66	50 (76%)	11 (17%)	5 (8%)
Total		1748	871 (50%)	700 (40%)	177 (10%)

ATTENDANCE FOR REGULAR-SEASON HOME GAMES 1947-77

TEAM	HOME GAMES	ATTENDANCE	AVG. PER HOME GAME
Falcons	53	78,233	1,476
Teepees	379	837,768	2,210
Hawks	406	837,406	2,078 *
Fincups	32	50,690	1,635 **
Total	**870**	**1,804,097**	**2,083**

(avg. based on available attendance figures for 866 games)   * 3 games missing
** 33 home games, but one game was played in Hamilton, and one game had no announced attendance figure)

ATTENDANCE FOR PLAYOFF GAMES 1943-77

TEAM	HOME GAMES	ATTENDANCE	AVG. PER HOME GAME
Falcons	7	19,779	2,826
Teepees	68	236,149	3,473
Hawks	56	163,252	2,915
Fincups	7	18,173	2,596
Total	138	437,353	3,169

Total attendance for all 1,004 home games for which figures are available:
2,241,440 for an average of 2,232.

ST. CATHARINES JUNIOR "A" TEAM RECORDS 1943-1977

SEASON	TEAM	GP	W	L	T	GF	GA	PTS	FINISH	PLAYOFF ROUNDS
1943-44	Falcons	26	15	9	2	125	103	32	1/5	1
1944-45	Falcons	22	14	8	0	115	98	28	2/6	1
1945-46	Falcons	28	14	14	0	134	123	28	4/8	1
1946-47	Falcons	36 (30)	7	25	4	101	219	18	8/10	0
1947-48	Teepees	36	19	17	0	137	155	38	6/10	1
1948-49	Teepees	48	25	20	3	191	198	53	4/9	2

SEASON	TEAM	GP	W	L	T	GF	GA	PTS	FINISH	PLAYOFF ROUNDS
1949-50	Teepees	48	27	17	4	269	211	58	3/9	1
1950-51	Teepees	54	23	24	7	200	192	53	6/10	2
1951-52	Teepees	54	30	23	1	249	229	61	6/10	3
1952-53	Teepees	56	31	20	5	219	204	67	4/9	1
1953-54	Teepees	59	42	15	2	328	211	86	1/8	4

OHA CHAMPS, EASTERN CANADA CHAMPS, MEMORIAL CUP

1954-55	Teepees	49	32	15	2	260	176	66	1/8	2
1955-56	Teepees	48	28	17	3	219	197	59	1/8	1
1956-57	Teepees	52	25	25	2	184	193	52	3/8	3
1957-58	Teepees	52	32	14	6	246	174	70	1/8	1
1958-59	Teepees	54	40	11	3	257	175	83	1/7	1
1959-60	Teepees	48	25	19	4	209	191	54	2/7 TIED	5

OHA CHAMPS, EASTERN CANADA CHAMPS, MEMORIAL CUP

1960-61	Teepees	48	18	24	6	167	204	42	5/7	1
1961-62	Teepees	50	19	23	8	194	206	46	3/6	1
1962-63	Hawks	50	15	24	11	172	224	41	5/6	0
1963-64	Hawks	56	29	20	7	244	215	65	3/8	2
1964-65	Hawks	56	19	28	9	236	253	47	6/8	1
1965-66	Hawks	48	15	26	7	182	231	37	8/9	1
1966-67	Hawks	48	19	20	9	175	155	47	5/9	1
1967-68	Hawks	54	21	30	3	200	210	45	6/10	1
1968-69	Hawks	54	31	11	12	297	206	74	2/10	3
1969-70	Hawks	54	30	18	6	268	210	66	3/10	2
1970-71	Hawks	62	40	17	5	343	236	85	2/10	4

OHA CHAMPS

1971-72	Hawks	63	25	31	7	253	308	57	7/10	1
1972-73	Hawks	63	24	28	11	280	319	59	5/10	1
1973-74	Hawks	70	41	23	6	358	278	88	2/11	4

OHA CHAMPS

1974-75	Hawks	70	30	33	7	284	300	67	6/11	1
1975-76	Hawks	66	16	40	10	283	366	42	5/6	1

IN EMMS DIVISION

1976-77	Fincups	66	50	11	5	438	242	105	1/6	2

ST. CATHARINES JUNIOR "A" HOME ATTENDANCE 1943-1977

FALCONS

SEASON	GP	HOME GAMES	ATTEND	AVG.	PLAYOFF GAMES	PLAYOFF ATTEND	TOTAL ATTEND	AVG.	MOST	LEAST
1943-44	26	13	11,489	884	3	7,124	18,613	1,163	2,760	439
1944-45	22	11	18,244	1,659	2	7,266	25,510	1,962	3,797	674
1945-46	28	14	30,714	2,194	2	5,389	36,103	2,256	4,244	658
1946-47	36	15	17,786	1,186	0	0	17,786	1,186	1,649	732
TOTALS	**112**	**53**	**78,233**	**1,476**	**7**	**19,779**	**98,012**	**1,634**		

TEEPEES

SEASON	GP	HOME GAMES	ATTEND	AVG.	PLAYOFF GAMES	PLAYOFF ATTEND	TOTAL ATTEND	AVG.	MOST	LEAST
1947-48	36	18	44,250	2,458	1	3,744	47,994	2,526	3,744	1,175
1948-49	48	23*	79,797	3,469	3	11,998	91,795	3,531	4,097	2,429
1949-50	48	23**	57,871	2,516	3	9,875	67,746	2,606	3,803	1,533
1950-51	54	27	53,485	1,981	4	13,605	67,090	2,164	3,972	1,295

TEEPEES cont'd

SEASON	GP	HOME GAMES	ATTEND	AVG.	P-OFF GAMES	P-OFF ATTEND	TOTAL ATTEND	AVG.	MOST	LEAST
1951-52	54	27	61,093	2,263	6	23,142	84,235	2,553	4,089	712
1952-53	56	28	63,616	2,272	1	3,332	66,948	2,309	4,113	1,385
1953-54	59	32	72,868	2,277	9	35,873	108,741	2,652	4,264	1,356
1954-55	49	25	60,067	2,403	6	22,474	82,541	2,663	3,997	1,579
1955-56	48	24	59,405	2,475	3	10,378	69,783	2,585	3,672	1,585
1956-57	52	26	51,983	1,999	7	24,069	76,052	2,305	4,132	1,207
1957-58	52	26	60,266	2,318	4	13,517	73,783	2,459	3,717	1,399
1958-59	54	27	59,142	2,190	4	14,104	73,246	2,363	3,773	1,339
1959-60	48	24	40,262	1,678	11	33,387	73,649	2,104	3,673	835
1960-61	48	24	35,779	1,491	3	6,766	42,545	1,576	2,481	1,002
1961-62	50	25	37,884	1,515	3	9,885	47,769	1,706	3,464	722
Totals	756	379	837,768	2,210	68	236,149	1,073,917	/ 2,402		

* recorded ** 1 game played in Niagara Falls

BLACK HAWKS

SEASON	GP	HOME GAMES	ATTEND	AVG.	P-OFF GAMES	P-OFF ATTEND	TOTAL ATTEND	AVG.	MOST	LEAST
1962-63	50	25	35,506	1,420	0	0	35,506	1,420	2,779	624
1963-64	56	28	41,159	1,470	6	17,243	58,402	1,718	3,637	678
1964-65	56	28	45,140	1,612	2	4,665	49,805	1,660	2,809	821
1965-66	48	24	41,616	1,734	3	6,955	48,571	1,799	2,979	1,089
1966-67	48	24	67,563	2,815	3	9,292	76,855	2,846	3,852	1,946
1967-68	54	27	58,376	2,162	2	5,076	63,452	2,188	3,080	1,332
1968-69	54	27	89,257	3,306	9	32,749	122,006	3,389	4,117	2,506
1969-70	54	27	91,683	3,396	5	15,060	106,743	3,336	4,038	2,721
1970-71	62	31	92,712	2,991	10	32,440	125,152	3,052	3,361	1,970
1971-72	63	31	68,944	2,224	2	5,045	73,989	2,242	2,839	1,752
1972-73	63	31	63,944	2,063	2	5,009	68,953	2,089	3,099	1,331
1973-74	70	35	67,292	1,923	8	23,129	90,421	2,103	3,427	1,000
1974-75	70	35	43,481	1,359*	2	4,016	47,497	1,397	2,205	681
1975-76	66	33	30,733	931	2	2,573	33,306	952	1,538	472
Totals	814	406	837,406	2,078	56	163,252	1,000,658	/ 2,180		

* based on 32 games

FINCUPS

SEASON	GP	HOME GAMES	ATTEND	AVG.	P-OFF GAMES	P-OFF ATTEND	TOTAL ATTEND	AVG.	MOST	LEAST
1976-77	66	32	50,690	1,635 *	7	18,173	68,863	1,722	3,246	943

*for 31 games

GRAND TOTALS

SEASON	GP	HOME GAMES	ATTEND	AVG.	P-OFF GAMES	P-OFF ATTEND	TOTAL ATTEND	AVG.
1943-77	1,748	870	1,804,097	2,083*	138	437,353	2,241,440	2,232

* based on 866 games **based on 1,004 games

ST. CATHARINES JUNIOR "A" TEAM AND INDIVIDUAL RECORDS (Unofficial)

TEAM RECORDS – REGULAR SEASON AND PLAYOFFS
Most Wins In A Season: 50 / 66 - 1976-77 Fincups
Most Home Wins In A Season: 29 / 33 - 1976-77 Fincups
Most Losses In A Season: 40 / 66 - 1975-76 Black Hawks
Most Home Losses In A Season: 15 / 33 - 1975-76 Black Hawks
Fewest Losses In A Season: 8 / 22 - 1944-45 Falcons
Fewest Home Losses In A Season: 2 / 27 - 1968-69 Black Hawks And 2 / 33 - 1976-77 Fincups
Most points in a season: 105 - 1976-77 Fincups
Least points in a season: 18 - 1946-47 Falcons

Most goals scored in a season: 438 - 1976-77 Fincups
Fewest goals scored in a season: 101 - 1946-47 Falcons
Most goals scored against in a season: 366 - 1975-76 Black Hawks
Most consecutive games without a loss: 15 (12 wins and 3 ties) - 1973-74 Black Hawks
Most consecutive road game victories: 8 - 1973-74 Black Hawks
Longest winning streak in a season: 12 (from Oct. 10 to Nov. 5, 1976) - 1976-77 Fincups
Most consecutive home games without a loss: 35 (27 regular season and 8 playoff games) from Nov. 11, 1973 to Apr. 28, 1974 - 1973-74 Black Hawks
Best playoff record: 12 wins, 0 losses, 2 ties - 1973-74 Black Hawks, OHA Champions
Longest home winning streak: 20 games (Sept. 24, 1976 to Jan. 18, 1977) - 1976-77 Fincups
Widest margin of victory in a league game: 19-0 (Tom Smelle had 5 goals and 3 assists, Laurie Peterson scored 4, Chick Zamick had 3) - Falcons vs. Hamilton Lloyds in St. Catharines, Nov. 16, 1945
Worst defeat in a league game: 1-18 - Falcons vs. Galt Red Wings, Jan. 4, 1947 at Galt
Largest turnout for a single Junior "A" game at Garden City Arena: 4,264 - Apr. 2, 1954, St. Michael's College Majors lost to the Teepees 7-3
The single game record for attendance at a hockey game at Garden City Arena: 4,412 - Playoff contest between the Senior "A" St. Catharines Saints and Niagara Falls, Feb. 27, 1942
Lowest turnout for a game in Garden City Arena: 439 - Dec. 14, 1943, Falcons beat the Toronto Young Rangers 6-0
Largest attendance record at Garden City Arena for a season: 125,152 - 1970-71 Black Hawks
Most points scored by a line in a single game: 22 (10 goals and 12 assists) - The CBC line (Brian Cullen, Hugh Barlow, Barry Cullen) against Jonquieres Marquis in a 16-1 win, Jan. 5, 1954, Garden City Arena

INDIVIDUAL RECORDS – REGULAR SEASON
Most goals in a regular season game:
6 - Brian Cullen, Jan. 5, 1954 in a 16-1 win against Jonquieres QC
6 - Matt Ravlich, Jan. 4, 1958 against Guelph (8-3 victory). Bruce Gamble was the goalie for the Biltmores. Jan. 18, 1958 in 15-4 win against Barrie. Russ Brooks was the Barrie goalie.
Most goals in one season: 68 - Brian Cullen, 1953-54 Teepees
Most assists in one season: 93 - Brian Cullen, 1953-54 Teepees
Most points in one season: 161 - Brian Cullen, 1953-54 Teepees
Most penalties in a regular season: 231 - Pierre Pilote, 1950-51 Teepees
Best goals against average in one season, for the team and the league: 2.93, Peter McDuffe, 1966-67 Black Hawks. He was the recipient of the Dave Pinkney Trophy, the only St. Catharines netminder to win it.

INDIVIDUAL RECORDS – PLAYOFFS
Most goals in one season: 33 - Marcel Dionne, 1970-71 Black Hawks
Most assists in one season: 33 - Brian Cullen, 1953-54 Teepees
Most points in one season: 64 - Marcel Dionne, 1970-71 Black Hawks

LEADING CAREER RECORDS

REGULAR SEASON

PLAYER	GP	GOALS	ASSISTS	POINTS
Marcel Dionne	150	154	221	375
Rick Adduono	180	123	188	311
Brian Cullen	169	135	155	290
Dave Gorman	190	130	157	287
Ken Hodge	181	127	138	265

PLAYOFFS

PLAYER	GP	GOALS	ASSISTS	POINTS
Marcel Dionne	48	60	72	132
Chico Maki	62	26	44	70
Brian Cullen	43	32	37	69
Ray Cullen	53	35	32	67
Hank Ciesla	51	23	38	61

REGULAR SEASONS AND PLAYOFFS

PLAYER	GP	GOALS	ASSISTS	POINTS
Marcel Dionne	198	214	293	507
Brian Cullen	212	167	192	359
Rick Adduono	205	135	208	343
Dave Gorman	216	144	185	329
Ray Cullen	253	162	167	329
Chico Maki	252	133	175	308

On February 15, 1977, St. Catharines Fincup Dale McCourt scored 5 points and broke Peter Lee's OHA Major Junior "A" regular-season career points record of 444 points with his 452 points. He finished the season with a new record of 477 points. He also broke Marcel Dionne's St. Catharines record of 154 regular-season career goals, but most of his 194 goals were scored with Hamilton.

TOP TEN SINGLE SEASON LEADERS

GOALS

	NAME	GOALS	SEASON	TEAM
1.	Brian Cullen	68	1953-54	Teepees
2.	Ken Hodge	63	1964-65	Black Hawks
3.	Barry Cullen	62	1953-54	Teepees
	Marcel Dionne	62	1970-71	Black Hawks
4.	Dale McCourt	60	1976-77	Fincups
5.	Obie O'Brien	58	1949-50	Teepees
6.	Hank Ciesla	57	1954-55	Teepees
7.	Marcel Dionne	55	1969-70	Black Hawks
8.	Dave Gorman	53	1973-74	Black Hawks
9.	Mike Keating	52	1976-77	Fincups
10.	Rick Adduono	51	1973-74	Black Hawks

ASSISTS

	NAME	ASSISTS	SEASON	TEAM
1.	Brian Cullen	93	1953-54	Teepees
2.	Brian McKenzie	85	1970-71	Black Hawks
3.	Rick Adduono	84	1973-74	Black Hawks
4.	Marcel Dionne	81	1970-71	Black Hawks
5.	Dale McCourt	79	1976-77	Fincups
6.	Connie Switzer	77	1949-50	Teepees
	Marcel Dionne	77	1969-70	Black Hawks
7.	Dave Gorman	76	1973-74	Black Hawks
8.	Fred Stanfield	75	1963-64	Black Hawks
9.	Wilf Paiement	74	1973-74	Black Hawks
10.	Hugh Barlow	73	1953-54	Teepees

POINTS

	NAME	POINTS	SEASON	TEAM
1.	Brian Cullen	161	1953-54	Teepees
2.	Marcel Dionne	143	1970-71	Black Hawks
3.	Dale McCourt	139	1976-77	Fincups
4.	Rick Adduono	135	1973-74	Black Hawks
5.	Marcel Dionne	132	1969-70	Black Hawks
6.	Ken Hodge	124	1964-65	Black Hawks
7.	Connie Switzer	112	1949-50	Teepees
8.	Rick Adduono	109	1972-73	Black Hawks
	Fred Stanfield	109	1963-64	Black Hawks
9.	Hank Ciesla	106	1954-55	Teepees
10.	Marcel Dionne	100	1968-69	Black Hawks

ST. CATHARINES JUNIOR "A" COACHES 1943-1977

ST. CATHARINES FALCONS 1943-47
1943-1945	Rudy Pilous
1945-1946	Red Reynolds, Rudy Pilous
1946-1947	Vic Teal

ST. CATHARINES TEEPEES 1947-62
1947-1950	Art Jackson
1950-1957	Rudy Pilous
1957-1958	Rudy Pilous, Glen Sonmor
1958-1959	Harry Watson
1959-1960	Max Kaminsky
1960-1961	Max Kaminsky, Vic Teal, Phil Vitale, Gus Bodnar
1961-1962	Ken Campbell

ST. CATHARINES BLACK HAWKS 1962-76
1962-1964	Ken Campbell
1964-1965	Chirp Brenchley
1965-1966	Chirp Brenchley, Obie O'Brien, Johnny (Peanuts) O'Flaherty
1966-1968	Peanuts O'Flaherty
1968-1970	Brian Shaw
1970-1973	Frank Milne
1973-1976	Paul Emms

ST. CATHARINES FINCUPS 1976-77
1976-77	Bert Templeton

ST. CATHARINES JUNIOR "A" CAPTAINS 1943-1977

1943-1945	Harvey Jessiman
1945-1946	Laurie Peterson
1946-1947	Eric Unger
1947-1948	Fiori Goegan
1948-1949	Jack McIntyre, George (Red) Sullivan (shared)
1949-1950	Red Sullivan, Gord Byers
	(Byers became Captain when the Bruins called up Sullivan in 1949)
1950-1951	Wayne Brown
1951-1952	Frank Martin
1952-1954	Brian Cullen
1954-1955	Hank Ciesla
1955-1956	Elmer Vasko
1956-1958	Ed Hoekstra
1958-1959	Wayne Hillman
1959-1960	Chico Maki
1960-1962	Ray Cullen
1962-1963	John Brenneman
1963-1964	Fred Stanfield
1964-1965	Ross Eichler
1965-1966	
1966-1967	
1967-1968	Barry Salovaara
1968-1969	Skeeter Teal
1969-1970	Al McDonough
1970-1971	Marcel Dionne
1971-1972	Bob MacMillan
1972-1973	Jeff Jacques
1973-1974	Rick Hampton
1974-1975	Rick Adduono
1975-1976	Greg Craig
1976-1977	Dale McCourt

ST. CATHARINES JUNIOR "A" PLAYERS
WHO MADE IT TO THE NHL

Total Number Of Forwards And Defencemen Who Played at Least One NHL Game:

Falcons	3
Teepees	42
Teepees and Black Hawks	6
Black Hawks	46
Fincups	12
Total	**109**

Number of Goaltenders Who Played in the NHL:

Falcons	0
Teepees	7
Black Hawks	6
Fincups	2
Total	**15**

Grand Total of St. Catharines Juniors Who Played in the NHL – 124

FORWARDS AND DEFENCEMEN
WHO PLAYED IN THE NHL
(prepared from Total Hockey and Jack Gatecliff's columns)

PLAYER	YEAR(S) / ST. CATHARINES TEAM	NHL TEAM(S)
Adduono, Rick	1972-75 Black Hawks	Boston, Atlanta
Bloom, Mike	1969-72 Black Hawks	Washington, Detroit
Boone, Buddy	1949-52 Teepees	Boston
Breitenbach, Ken	1972-75 Black Hawks	Buffalo
Brenneman, John	1959-62 Teepees	
	1962-63 Black Hawks	Chicago, New York Rangers, Toronto, Detroit, Oakland
Brown, Wayne	1948-51 Teepees	Boston
Burrows, Dave	1967-69 Black Hawks	Pittsburgh, Toronto
Byers, Gord	1948-50 Teepees	Boston
Ciesla, Hank	1951-55 Teepees	Chicago, New York Rangers
Contini, Joe	1976-77 Fincups	Colorado Rockies, Minnesota North Stars
Corcoran, Norm	1949-50 Teepees	Boston, Detroit, Chicago
Coulis, Tim	1976-77 Fincups	Washington, Minnesota North Stars
Cullen, Barry	1953-55 Teepees	Toronto, Detroit
Cullen, Brian	1951-54 Teepees	Toronto, New York Rangers
Cullen, Ray	1958-62 Teepees	New York Rangers, Detroit, Minnesota North Stars, Vancouver
Cushenan, Ian	1952-54 Teepees	Chicago, Montreal, New York Rangers, Detroit
Delory, Val	1945-46 Falcons	New York Rangers
Delmonte, Armand	1943-45 Falcons	Boston
Delparte, Guy	1968-69 Black Hawks	Colorado Rockies
Dionne, Marcel	1968-71 Black Hawks	Detroit, Los Angeles, New York Rangers
Dudley, Rick	1968-69 Black Hawks	Buffalo, Winnipeg
Esposito, Phil	1961-62 Teepees	Chicago, Boston, New York Rangers
Foley, Gerry	1951-52 Teepees	Toronto, New York Rangers, Los Angeles
Forbes, Mike	1976-77 Fincups	Boston, Edmonton
Fortier, Dave	1970-71 Black Hawks	Toronto, New York Islanders, Vancouver
Franceschetti, Lou	1975-76 Black Hawks	Washington, Toronto, Buffalo
Gage, Jody	1976-77 Fincups	Detroit, Buffalo
Gartner, Mike	1975-76 Black Hawks	Washington, Minnesota North Stars, New York Rangers, Toronto, Phoenix
Gorman, Dave	1971-74 Black Hawks	Atlanta

Forwards and Defencemen Who Played In The NHL - cont'd

PLAYER	YEAR(S) / ST. CATHARINES TEAM	NHL TEAM(S)
Hadfield, Vic	1958-60 Teepees	New York Rangers, Pittsburgh
Hall, Murray	1959-61 Teepees	Chicago, Detroit, Minnesota North Stars, Vancouver
Hampton, Rick	1972-74 Black Hawks	California, Cleveland, Los Angeles
Harris, George (Duke)	1958-61 Teepees	Minnesota North Stars, Toronto
Hazlett, Steve	1976-77 Fincups	Vancouver
Hillman, Wayne	1955-59 Teepees	Chicago, New York Rangers, Minnesota North Stars, Philadelphia
Hodge, Ken	1961-62 Teepees	
	1962-65 Black Hawks	Chicago, Boston, New York Rangers
Hoekstra, Cec	1953-55 Teepees	Montreal
Hoekstra, Ed	1954-58 Teepees	Philadelphia
Huber, Willie	1976-77 Fincups	Detroit, New York Rangers, Vancouver, Philadelphia
Hughes, Brent	1961-63 Teepees	Los Angeles, Philadelphia, St. Louis, Detroit, Kansas City
Hull, Bobby	1955-57 Teepees	Chicago, Winnipeg, Hartford
Hull, Dennis	1960-62 Teepees	
	1962-64 Black Hawks	Chicago, Detroit
Jacobs, Tim	1969-72 Black Hawks	California
Jarrett, Doug	1960-62 Teepees	
	1962-64 Black Hawks	Chicago, New York Rangers
Jarry, Pierre	1967-68 Black Hawks	New York Rangers, Toronto, Detroit, Minnesota North Stars
Johnston, Jay	1976-77 Fincups	Washington
Juckes, Winston (Bing)	1943-44 Falcons	New York Rangers
Keating, Mike	1976-77 Fincups	New York Rangers
Korab, Jerry	1966-68 Black Hawks	Chicago, Vancouver, Buffalo, Los Angeles
Landon, Larry	1975-76 Black Hawks	Montreal, Toronto
Lariviere, Garry	1972-74 Black Hawks	Quebec, Edmonton
LeBlanc, Jean-Paul	1965-67 Black Hawks	Chicago, Detroit
MacMillan, Bob	1970-72 Black Hawks	New York Rangers, St. Louis, Atlanta Flames, Calgary, Colorado Rockies, New Jersey, Chicago
Maki, Ron (Chico)	1956-60 Teepees	Chicago
Maki, Wayne	1964-65 Black Hawks	Chicago, St. Louis, Vancouver
Manno, Bob	1974-76 Black Hawks	Vancouver, Toronto, Detroit
Martin, Frank	1949-52 Teepees	Boston, Chicago
McAdam, Gary	1973-75 Black Hawks	Buffalo, Pittsburgh, Detroit, Calgary, Washington, New Jersey, Toronto
McCourt, Dale	1976-77 Fincups	Detroit, Buffalo, Toronto
McDonald, Ab	1954-56 Teepees	Montreal, Chicago, Boston, Detroit, Pittsburgh, St. Louis
McDonald, Brian	1963-65 Black Hawks	Chicago, Buffalo
McDonough, Al	1967-70 Black Hawks	Los Angeles, Pittsburgh, Atlanta, Detroit
McIntyre, Jack	1947-50 Teepees	Boston, Chicago, Detroit
McKenzie, Brian	1968-71 Black Hawks	Pittsburgh
McKenzie, Johnny	1956-58 Teepees	Chicago, Detroit, New York Rangers, Detroit, Boston
Mikita, Stan	1956-59 Teepees	Chicago
O'Brien, Dennis	1968-69 Black Hawks	Minnesota North Stars, Colorado Rockies, Cleveland, Boston
O'Brien, Ellard (Obie)	1948-50 Teepees	Boston
O'Donoghue, Don	1967-69 Black Hawks	Oakland, California
Owchar, Dennis	1972-73 Black Hawks	Pittsburgh, Colorado Rockies
Paiement, Wilf	1972-74 Black Hawks	Kansas City, Colorado Rockies, Toronto, Quebec, New York Rangers, Buffalo, Pittsburgh

Forwards and Defencemen Who Played In The NHL - cont'd

PLAYER	YEAR(S) / ST. CATHARINES TEAM	NHL TEAM(S)
Pilote, Pierre	1950-52 Teepees	Chicago, Toronto
Plantery, Mark	1976-77 Fincups	Winnipeg
Plett, Willi	1974-75 Black Hawks	Atlanta Flames, Calgary, Minnesota North Stars, Boston
Poliziani, Dan	1952-54 Teepees	Boston
Popiel, Poul	1960-62 Teepees	
	1962-63 Black Hawks	Boston, Los Angeles, Detroit, Vancouver, Edmonton
Ravlich, Matt	1955-58 Teepees	Boston, Chicago, Detroit, Los Angeles
Redmond, Dick	1968-69 Black Hawks	Minnesota North Stars, California, Chicago, Atlanta Flames, Boston
Reid, Tom	1964-67 Black Hawks	Chicago, Minnesota North Stars
Robinson, Doug	1958-61 Teepees	Chicago, New York Rangers, Los Angeles
Rombough, Doug	1968-70 Black Hawks	Buffalo, New York Islanders, Minnesota North Stars
Ronson, Len	1955-56 Teepees	New York Rangers, Oakland
Salovarra, Barry	1965-68 Black Hawks	Detroit
Salvian, Dave	1972-75 Black Hawks	New York Islanders
Schinkel, Ken	1952-53 Teepees	New York Rangers, Pittsburgh
Secord, Al	1976-77 Fincups	Boston, Chicago, Toronto, Philadelphia
Seiling, Ric	1976-77 Fincups	Buffalo, Detroit
Serafini, Ron	1971-73 Black Hawks	California
Shakes, Paul	1969-72 Black Hawks	California
Sheehan, Bob	1968-69 Black Hawks	Montreal, California, Chicago, Detroit, New York Rangers, Colorado Rockies, Los Angeles
Shelton, Doug	1963-66 Black Hawks	Chicago
Speer, Bill	1959-62 Teepees	Pittsburgh, Boston
Standing, George	1961-62 Teepees	Minnesota North Stars
Stanfield, Fred	1961-62 Teepees	
	1962-64 Black Hawks	Chicago, Boston, Minnesota North Stars, Buffalo
Stanfield, Jack	1961-62 Teepees	Chicago
Stanfield, Jim	1964-66 Black Hawks	Los Angeles
Stapleton, Pat	1958-60 Teepees	Boston, Chicago
Stewart, Bill	1975-76 Black Hawks	Buffalo, St. Louis, Toronto, Minnesota North Stars
Stratton, Art	1955-56 Teepees	New York Rangers, Detroit, Chicago, Pittsburgh, Philadelphia
Sullivan, George (Red)	1947-49 Teepees	Boston, Chicago, New York Rangers
Teal, Allan (Skip)	1950-51 Teepees	Boston
Teal, Victor (Skeeter)	1966-69 Black Hawks	New York Islanders
Terbenche, Paul	1964-66 Black Hawks	Chicago, Buffalo
Toppazzini, Jerry	1948-49 Teepees	Boston, Chicago, Detroit
Toppazzini, Zellio	1947-48 Teepees	Boston, New York Rangers, Chicago
Vasko, Elmer	1953-56 Teepees	Chicago, Minnesota North Stars
Ververagret, Dennis	1970-71 Black Hawks	Vancouver, Philadelphia, Washington
Wilson, Ron	1975-76 Black Hawks	Winnipeg, St. Louis, Montreal
Wylie, Duane	1969-70 Black Hawks	Chicago

GOALTENDERS WHO PLAYED IN THE NHL

PLAYER	YEAR(S) / ST. CATHARINES TEAM	NHL TEAM(S)
Crozier, Roger	1959-62 Teepees	Detroit, Buffalo, Washington
Defelice, Norm	1952-53 Teepees	Boston,
DeJordy, Denis	1957-59 Teepees	Chicago, Los Angeles, Montreal, Detroit
Edwards, Marv	1950-55 Teepees	Pittsburgh, Toronto, California
Edwards, Roy	1955-57 Teepees	Detroit, Pittsburgh
Favell, Doug	1962-63 Black Hawks	Philadelphia, Toronto, Colorado Rockies
Froese, Bob	1974-76 Black Hawks	Philadelphia, New York Rangers
Jensen, Al	1976-77 Fincups	Detroit, Washington, Los Angeles
McDuffe, Peter	1965-68 Black Hawks	St. Louis, New York Rangers, Kansas City, Detroit
Pettie, Jim	1972-73 Black Hawks	Boston
Riggin, Dennis	1954-55 Teepees	Detroit
Simmons, Don	1950-51 Teepees	Boston, Toronto, New York Rangers
Sneddon, Bob	1963-64 Black Hawks	California
Taylor, Bobby	1964-65 Black Hawks	Philadelphia, Pittsburgh
Wamsley, Rick	1976-77 Fincups	Montreal, St. Louis, Calgary, Toronto

PLAYERS AND COACHES WHO COACHED IN THE NHL
REGULAR-SEASON RECORDS

PLAYER / COACH	GAMES COACHED	WON	LOST	TIED	WINNING %
Crozier, Roger, Washington	1	0	1		.000
Dudley, Rick, Buffalo	188	85	72	31	.535
Esposito, Phil, New York Rangers	45	24	21	0	.533
Kelly, Pat, Colorado	101	22	54	25	.342
Pilous, Rudy, Chicago	387	162	151	74	.514
Schinkel, Ken, Pittsburgh	203	83	92	28	.478
Sonmor, Glen, Minnesota	417	174	161	82	.516
Stewart, Bill, New York Islanders	37	11	19	7	.392
Sullivan, George (Red), New York Rangers, Pittsburgh, Washington	364	107	198	59	.375

PLAYERS WHO PLAYED ON NHL ALL-STAR TEAMS

PLAYER	JUNIOR TEAM	FIRST	SECOND
Crozier, Roger	Teepees	1	
Dionne, Marcel	Black Hawks	2	2
Esposito, Phil	Teepees	6	2
Froese, Bob	Black Hawks		1
Hadfield, Vic	Teepees		1
Hodge, Ken	Teepees / Black Hawks	2	
Hull, Bobby	Teepees	10	2
Hull, Dennis	Teepees / Black Hawks		1
McKenzie, Johnny	Teepees		1
Mikita, Stan	Teepees	6	2
Pilote, Pierre	Teepees	5	3
Stapleton, Pat	Teepees		3

PLAYERS WHO WON MAJOR NHL AWARDS

	PLAYER	ST. CATHARINES TEAM
ART ROSS TROPHY		
Most Points	Dionne, Marcel	Black Hawks
	Esposito, Phil (5)	Teepees
	Hull, Bobby (3)	Teepees
	Mikita, Stan (4)	Teepees
CALDER TROPHY		
Outstanding Rookie	Crozier, Roger	Teepees
	Plett, Willi	Black Hawks
CONN SMYTHE TROPHY		
Outstanding Player in the Playoffs	Crozier, Roger	Teepees
HART TROPHY		
Most Valuable	Esposito, Phil (2)	Teepees
	Hull, Bobby (2)	Teepees
	Mikita, Stan (2)	Teepees
JAMES NORRIS TROPHY		
Outstanding Defenceman	Pilote, Pierre (3)	Teepees
LADY BYNG TROPHY		
Most Gentlemanly	Dionne, Marcel (2)	Black Hawks
	Hull, Bobby	Teepees
	MacMillan, Bob	Black Hawks
	Mikita, Stan (2)	Teepees
LESTER PATRICK TROPHY		
contributions to hockey	Esposito, Phil	Teepees
in the USA	Hull, Bobby	Teepees
	Mikita, Stan	Teepees
VEZINA TROPHY		
Outstanding Goaltender	DeJordy, Denis (Glenn Hall)	Teepees
WILLIAM JENNINGS TROPHY		
goalie with team with best GAA	Froese, Bob (Darren Jensen)	Black Hawks
	Jensen, Al (Pat Riggin)	Fincups
	Wamsley, Rick (Denis Herron)	Fincups
LESTER B. PEARSON TROPHY		
Outstanding Player	Dionne, Marcel (2)	Black Hawks
Chosen NHLPA	Esposito, Phil	Teepees

ST. CATHARINES JUNIOR "A" PLAYERS AND COACHES INDUCTED INTO THE HOCKEY HALL OF FAME

PLAYER / COACH	JUNIOR TEAM	YEAR INDUCTED
Dionne, Marcel	Black Hawks	1992
Esposito, Phil	Teepees	1984
Hull, Bobby	Teepees	1983
Mikita, Stan	Teepees	1983
Pilote, Pierre	Teepees	1975
Pilous, Rudy	Falcons (coach)	
	Teepees (coach)	1985

OTHER ST. CATHARINES PEOPLE INDUCTED INTO THE HOCKEY HALL OF FAME

Cheevers, Gerry	St. Mike's Majors	1985
Gatecliff, Jack	Media	1995

ST. CATHARINES JUNIOR "A" PLAYERS WHO PLAYED IN THE WORLD HOCKEY ASSOCIATION

compiled by Mike Smith

PLAYER	YEAR	TEAM
Adduono, Rick	1978-79	Birmingham
Anderson, Ron	1972-74	Chicago; 1974-75 Cleveland
Bond, Kerry	1974-76	Indianapolis
Burgess, Don	1972-73	Philadelphia; 1973-75 Vancouver;
	1975-77	San Diego; 1977-79 Indianapolis
Dudley, Rick	1975-78	Cincinnati
Golembrosky, Frank	1972-73	Philadelphia; 1972-73 Quebec
Gorman, Dave	1974-76	Phoenix; 1976-79 Birmingham
Guite, Pierre	1972-75, 1976-78 Quebec; 1974-75 Michigan/Baltimore
	1975-77	Cincinnati; 1977-79 Edmonton
Hall, Murray	1972-76	Houston
Harris, George (Duke)	1972-73	Houston; 1973-75 Chicago
Hillman, Wayne	1973-75	Cleveland
Hoekstra, Ed	1972-74	Houston
Hughes, Brent	1975-77	San Diego; 1977-79 Birmingham
Hull, Bobby	1972-79	Winnipeg
Irwin, Glen	1974-78	Houston; 1977-79 Indianapolis
Jacques, Jeff	1974-76	Toronto; 1976-77 Birmingham
Lariviere, Gary	1974-76	Phoenix; 1976-79 Quebec
Leblanc, J.P.	1972-74	Los Angeles; 1975-75 Michigan/Baltimore
MacMillan, Bob	1972-74	Minnesota
Mara, Peter	1974-75	Chicago; 1975-76 Denver/Ottawa
Mavety, Larry	1972-73	Philadelphia; 1972-75 Chicago
	1974-75 Toronto; 1975-76 Denver/Ottawa
	1976-77	Indianapolis
McCulloch, Don	1974-75	Vancouver
McDonald, Ab	1972-74	Winnipeg
McDonald, Brian	1972-73	Houston; 1973-74 Los Angeles
	1974	Michigan
	1974-77	Indianapolis
McDonough, Al	1974-76	Cleveland; 1976-77 Minnesota
McDuffe, Peter	1977-78	Indianapolis
McKenzie, Brian	1973-74	Edmonton; 1974-75 Indianapolis
McKenzie, John	1972-73	Philadelphia; 1973-75 Vancouver;
	1975-76	Minnesota; 1975-76 Cincinnati;
	1976-79	New England
O'Donoghue, Don	1972-73	Philadelphia; 1973-75 Vancouver;
	1975-76	Cincinnati
Popiel, Jan	1972-75	Chicago; 1975-76 Denver/Ottawa;
	1975-76	Houston; 1976-77 Phoenix
Popiel, Poul	1972-78	Houston
Sheehan, Bob	1972-73	New York; 1973 New Jersey; 1973-75 Edmonton
Sicinski, Bob	1972-74	Chicago; 1974-77 Indianapolis;
	1977-78	San Diego
Speer, Bill	1972-73	New York; 1973-74 New Jersey
Stanfield, Jack	1972-74	Houston
Stapleton, Pat	1973-75	Chicago; 1975-77 Indianapolis;
	1977-78	Cincinnati
Terbenche, Paul	1974-75	Vancouver; 1975-77 Calgary;
	1977	Birmingham; 1977-78 Houston; 1978-79 Winnipeg
Titcomb, Gord	1974-75	Toronto
Young, Bill	1972-74	Los Angeles; 1972-73 Minnesota;
	1973-74	Cleveland

ST. CATHARINES JUNIOR A HOCKEY FIRSTS AND LASTS

First Coach: Rudy Pilous
First Manager: Ed Graves
First Trainer: Jimmy Joy
First President: J. C. (Cal) Wilson
First Vice-President: Ed Graves
First Secretary-Treasurer: J. A. MacDonald
First Directors: J.R. Leach, O.T. Graves, Thos Heit, Pete Grammar
First Physician: Dr. A. Greenwood
First Property Managers: M. McIntosh, D. Wilbur
First Mascot: Connie Switzer
First Captain: Harvey Jessiman

The first goal scored by a St. Catharines Junior A player came in the Falcons first-ever regularly-scheduled game against Brantford Lions on Saturday, November 13, 1943, in Brantford. The player taking the honour was Nick Phillips of Niagara Falls. Linemate Pete Long, also from the Falls, drew an assist at 7:54 of the first period. The Falcons added four more goals and won their first-ever game 5-1.

The first St. Catharines Junior A goal scored at Garden City Arena was by Frank Long of Niagara Falls on Friday, November 19, 1943. Long was assisted by his brother Pete and defenceman Doug McMurdy at 3:45 of the first period. The Falcons added 10 more goals and came away with their first-ever win at home, 11-4. Port Dalhousie native Bobby Thorpe had a hat trick, the first-ever by a St. Catharines Junior A player.

The first St. Catharines Junior A player to play in the NHL was Falcon right winger, Armand "Dutch" Delmonte. He made his NHL debut with the Boston Bruins in the 1945-46 season.

One other Falcon from the 1943-44 team made it to the NHL and that was Winston "Bing" Juckes. While with the AHL New Haven Ramblers in 1947-48, Juckes saw action with the New York Rangers in two games. In 1948-49 he got a second shot with the Rangers and this time dressed for 14 games.

The first winner of the Red Tilson Trophy in 1945 was Falcon defenceman Doug McMurdy.

Frank Martin was born in Cayuga, but he was the first St. Catharines minor hockey system grad to play in the NHL. In February of 1953 he was called up from the AHL Hershey Bears to the Bruins to replace injured rearguard Bob Armstrong.

The first St. Catharines native to play in the NHL was Hank Ciesla in 1955; he played with the Chicago Black Hawks.

The first St. Catharines goaltender to register a shutout was Harvey Jessiman on December 14, 1943, vs Toronto Young Rangers (6-0).

The first St. Catharines native to lead a St. Catharines Junior A team in scoring was Bob Twaddle who had 16 goals and 29 points in the 1946-47 season.

The first player to score 50 or more goals in a season was Teepee Ellard "Obie" O'Brien with 58 in 1949-50.

The first two players to score more than 100 points in a regular season were Connie Switzer with 112 and linemate Obie O'Brien with 101 in 1949-50.

The first team to win the Hamilton Spectator Trophy was the 1957-58 St. Catharines Teepees.

The first St. Catharines defenceman to lead the team in total points (68) during the regular season was Paul Shakes in 1971-72.

The first St. Catharines player to win an OHA Junior A scoring championship was Brian Cullen in 1953-54 with 68 goals and 93 assists for 161 points.

The first St. Catharines team to have three 50-goal scorers was the 1973-74 St. Catharines Black Hawks: Rick Adduono (51), Dave Gorman (53), and Wilf Paiement (50).

The first St. Catharines team to have five 40-goal or more scorers was the 1976-77 St. Catharines Fincups: Dale McCourt (60), Mike Keating (52), Ric Seiling (50), Steve Hazlett (42), and Denis Houle (43).

The first St. Catharines junior to score more than 300 career points was Brian Cullen. His brother Ray became the second on January 20, 1962.

The first and only St. Catharines Junior A player to be selected first in the NHL entry draft was Dale McCourt, taken by Detroit Red Wings in 1977.

The first Japanese-Canadian to play junior A hockey was British Columbia native Frank Toyota. He played his minor hockey in St.Catharines and suited up with the Teepees in 1950-51.

The St. Catharines Junior A hockey club wore Black Hawks sweaters for the first time on December 3, 1961, in an exhibition game against St. Michael's College Majors at Toronto.

The first team, and only St. Catharines team, to win the OHA Junior A Championship without a defeat (12 wins and 2 ties) was the 1973-74 Black Hawks.

The last regular-season goal scored by a St. Catharines Junior A player was by Fincup Ric Seiling at Garden City Arena on Tuesday, March 15, 1977, at 10:32 of the third period. It was Seiling's 50th goal. Assists went to Steve Hazlett and Mike Forbes. The Fincups defeated the Peterborough Petes 5-1 and the win gave the overall points championship to the club by a one-point margin over London Knights. The 105 points tied the overall record for points set by the 1974-75 Toronto Marlboros.

The St. Catharines Standard, Dec. 21, 1938 - St. Catharines Museum - *The Standard Collection* - S1938.69.1.1

The opening ceremonies at the first hockey game played at Garden City Arena on December 20, 1938.

The St. Catharines Standard, Dec. 21, 1938 - St. Catharines Museum - *The Standard Collection* - S1938.69.1.2

The last junior A goal scored at Garden City Arena came off the stick of St. Catharines Fincup Dale McCourt at 13:49 of the third period of the seventh playoff game against London Knights on April 19, 1977. Mike Keating and Denis Houle assisted on the goal.

The last goal ever scored by a St. Catharines Junior A player came from Dan Shearer in London on Wednesday, April 20, 1977, in the eighth playoff game with the London Knights. Assists went to Mike Forbes and Joe Contini at 4:34 of the second period. The Fincups lost the game 3-2 in overtime and as a result they were eliminated from the playoffs. It was the last game played by a St. Catharines major junior hockey club.

The attendance at the last junior A game at Garden City Arena was 2,168. The crowd watched the St. Catharines Fincups defeat the London Knights 4-3 in the seventh playoff match on April 19, 1977.

The first junior A game played in the afternoon at Garden City Arena took place on Saturday, December 26, 1953. The Teepees defeated Hamiton 6-1 in front of 3,000 fans.

The first junior A game played on a Sunday took place on December 30, 1962, at 2 p.m. The Hawks defeated the Montreal Junior Canadiens 6-4 in front of 1,498 fans.

On Wednesday, February 24, 1954, a big T.C.A. plane landed at the St. Catharines Airport for the first time, and transported the St. Catharines Teepees to Dorval Airport, Montreal, to play the Montreal Royals. It was the beginning of a five-game trip in Quebec.

The first St. Catharines Junior A team to wear helmets was the Black Hawks who started this practice on Friday, October 24, 1969, in a game in Kitchener. The entire league required all teams to be wearing helmets by January 1, 1970.

The first Danish-born player to play in the NHL was former Teepee/Black Hawk Poul Popiel. He made it to the NHL with the Boston Bruins in 1965-66.

Toronto Maple Leafs owner Conn Smythe (left) defenceman Bucko McDonald and coach Dick Irvin pose for a picture in Garden City Arena, Tuesday December 20, 1938.

St. Catharines Museum - *The Standard Collection* - S1938.69.1.3

Teepees Captain Brian Cullen and broadcaster Rex Stimers at Garden City Arena Memorial Cup celebration on May 16, 1954
St. Catharines Museum - *Jimmy Simpson Collection N 5801*

ST. CATHARINES JUNIOR A HOCKEY TRIVIA

This section of the book is dedicated to my long-time friend and master of trivia, Bob (Rocket) Cornelius.

Did You Know…?

From 1943 to 1977 there were 34 opening Junior A games at Garden City Arena with the following results: wins - 19 (56%), losses - 11 (32%), ties - 4 (12%)

In 1969, Guy Lafleur almost signed with the St. Catharines Black Hawks after a visit by Marcel Dionne, Hawks owner Fred Muller, and Hawks GM Ken Campbell. Unfortunately for St. Catharines, Lafleur was coaxed into staying with the Quebec Remparts.

Teepee-to-be Connie Switzer (1948-50) scored 27 goals and added an assist as St. Nicholas School won the 1942 St. Catharines elementary school championship game, beating Robertson School 28-0. The contest was played in one hour and thirty minutes, straight time.

Jack Gatecliff's favourite interviewee was Stan Mikita.

Gatecliff's first job for the *St. Catharines Standard* was translating the report of a cricket match into story form. There was an instant response, said Gatecliff: "Bad".

Gatecliff wrote at least 59 columns on Rudy Pilous.

Former NHL star and now senator, Frank Mahovlich, almost joined the St. Catharines Teepees when Teepee owner George Stauffer offered to buy a farm in Niagara for Mahovlich's family. Mahovlich's parents decided to send him to St. Mike's where he could combine hockey and schooling.

Two-time Memorial Cup winner (1953 and 1954) Marv Edwards was the goaltending coach of the Peterborough Petes. They went on to the 1996 Memorial Cup finals.

The first two St. Catharines-born men to play junior A hockey were Harold Crooker and goalie Mert Prophet, who suited up with the newly-formed Hamilton Whizzers in 1942-43. Crooker scored the winning goal in his and the team's first game, a 3-2 win over Toronto Marlboros at the Barton Street Arena in front of 4,000 fans. Prophet defeated Stratford 7-2 in his debut.

In 1982, former St. Catharines Black Hawk Marcel Dionne became the first NHL player to get his 500th goal with an expansion team, the Los Angeles Kings.

The Gyr Falcon is the national bird of Iceland.

While *Standard* sports reporter Jack Gatecliff was watching the Teepees being eliminated by the Guelph Biltmores in the fifth game on March 31, 1952, his wife Alice gave birth to their son John.

The Eddie Powers Memorial Trophy awarded to the OHA's top points-getter was first presented in 1946. The initial recipient was St. Michael's College Majors player Tod Sloan.

The J. Ross Robertson Cup awarded to the OHA Junior A (OHL) champions was first presented in 1934 to the St. Michael's College Majors. Former Teepees coach (1947-1950) Art Jackson was a member of that team.

St. Catharines Black Hawk Mickey Cherevaty scored the first junior A goal in the new Oshawa Civic Auditorium at the official opening on December 19, 1964. The Oshawa Generals won 6-4.

In 1976-77, the seating capacity of Garden City Arena was 3,090.

When Dale McCourt came to Hamilton to play junior hockey he asked for and received sweater #10, the number worn by his uncle, George Armstrong, former Maple Leaf great.

Ex-St. Catharines Teepee (1961-62) Phil Esposito was the first player in the NHL to score more than 100 points (126 in 1968-69) in a season.

In 1970-71 Espo set the record for most goals in a season (76), breaking ex-Teepee Bobby Hull's record of 58 scored in 1968-69. Esposito's total points, 152 in 1970-71, broke the NHL record for total points in a season. He was an NHL all-star eight years in a row.

"Jesus Saves, But Esposito Scores On The Rebound" was a popular bumper sticker in the Boston area in 1970-71.

There was at least one former St. Catharines Junior A player on the first or second NHL all-star team for 16 consecutive seasons: 1959-60 to 1974-75.

Between 1960 and 1974, former St. Catharines Junior A players won 12 Art Ross Trophies (Esposito, five, Mikita, four, Hull, three).

Stan Mikita was the first player in NHL history to win three major awards in one year (Art Ross, Hart and Lady Byng) and he did it twice, in 1967 and 1968.

The fewest games played in a St. Catharines Junior A regular season were 22 in 1944-45.

The most games played in a St. Catharines Junior A regular season were 70 in 1973-74 and 1974-75.

The most tie games played in a St. Catharines Junior A regular season were 12 in 1968-69.

GARDEN CITY HOCKEY HEROES

Teepees Secretary Jay MacDonald goes over train and airline tickets for a Quebec trip during the 1955-56 season. November 12, 1955

St. Catharines Standard Photo

There were no tied games in 1944-45, 1945-46, and 1947-48.

Former Memorial and Minto Cup winner Doug Favell was the starting goalie in the first NHL game played in five different arenas. Can you name the teams and the arenas?

Favell was also the only player to be claimed in both the 1967 and 1979 NHL Expansion Drafts.

On Sunday, February 6, 1972, referee Tom Brown called a tripping penalty to Hawk defenceman Larry Jacques. It was the only penalty called in the 6-2 home win over the Niagara Falls Flyers.

The first regularly-scheduled home game on a Thursday for a St. Catharines Junior A team took place on November 1, 1973, against the Oshawa Generals.

On Friday, December 16, 1960, St. Mike's netminder and future NHL star Gerry Cheevers played right wing in a game against the Barrie Flyers while Dave Dryden took his place in the St. Mike's net.

Helmets became mandatory for all OHA officials in the 1975-76 season.

Before the advent of the curved stick, former Teepees Frank Martin and Brian Cullen were among only a few NHL players who could shoot either left or right-handed. Martin's switch-shooting ability led to this headline in the 1953 *Hockey News*: "Martin Joins Howe As The Only Other NHL Ambidextrous Shot." Cullen, who set an OHA Junior A record for goals in 1953-54 with 68, recalled that 35 of them were "wronghanded".

From 1943-1977 there were 12 players who scored 50 or more goals in a single season: four Teepees (Barry and Brian Cullen, Hank Ciesla, and Obie O'Brien), five Black Hawks (Ken Hodge, Marcel Dionne (twice), Rick Adduono, Dave Gorman, and Wilf Paiement), and three Fincups (Mike Keating, Dale McCourt, and Ric Seiling).

Former Black Hawk Bob Manno assisted on Steve Yzerman's first NHL goal during Detroit Red Wings October 5, 1983 game at Winnipeg.

Rex Stimers ran away from home when he was 16 and sailed from Montreal on a boat named the Ursula for Salonica. On December 12, the Ursula was sunk by an Austrian submarine. After being adrift for one day, the survivors, including Stimers, were picked up by a British cruiser. The story came from *The Mail and Empire* April 13, p.2, col. 7.

Ex-Teepee Bobby Hull scored his first NHL goal for the Chicago Black Hawks on former Teepee netminder Don Simmons who was the Boston Bruins netminder on October 22, 1957.

The second German-born player to play in the NHL was ex-St. Catharines Fincup defenceman Willie Huber. The first player was former New York Ranger Walter Tkaczuk.

Former Teepee goalie Norm Defelice (1950-51) can thank Boyd Prentice for starting his netminding career in Schumacher, Ontario. Boyd, who owned his brother Dean's goalie equipment, didn't want Dean to be a goalie, so Dean gave the gear to his childhood friend, Defelice. "I said, 'Normie, you go in and I'll go out' ," Prentice told the *Hockey News* (December 26/06 edition). Dean Prentice went on to play 1,378 NHL games, scoring 20 or more goals 10 times. Defelice had an outstanding minor pro career and 10 games with the Boston Bruins in 1956-57.

Ex-Teepee John Brenneman played 41 regular-season games with the Stanley Cup Toronto Maple Leafs in 1966-67, but didn't appear in the playoffs and is not named on the Cup.

The last player to wear jersey number 99 in the NHL, other than Gretzky, was ex- St. Catharines Black Hawk Wilf Paiement.

It may surprise some people to learn that the term "hat trick" as it relates to sports actually originated in British cricket. A bowler who retired three batsmen with three consecutive balls was entitled to a new hat, at the expense of the club, to commemorate this feat.

According to the Society for International Hockey Research, it must have driven the Boston Bruin's trainer crazy in the 1970s when he had to outfit former Teepee Johnny McKenzie with skates. McKenzie wore size 7½ on his right foot, but size 6 on his left!

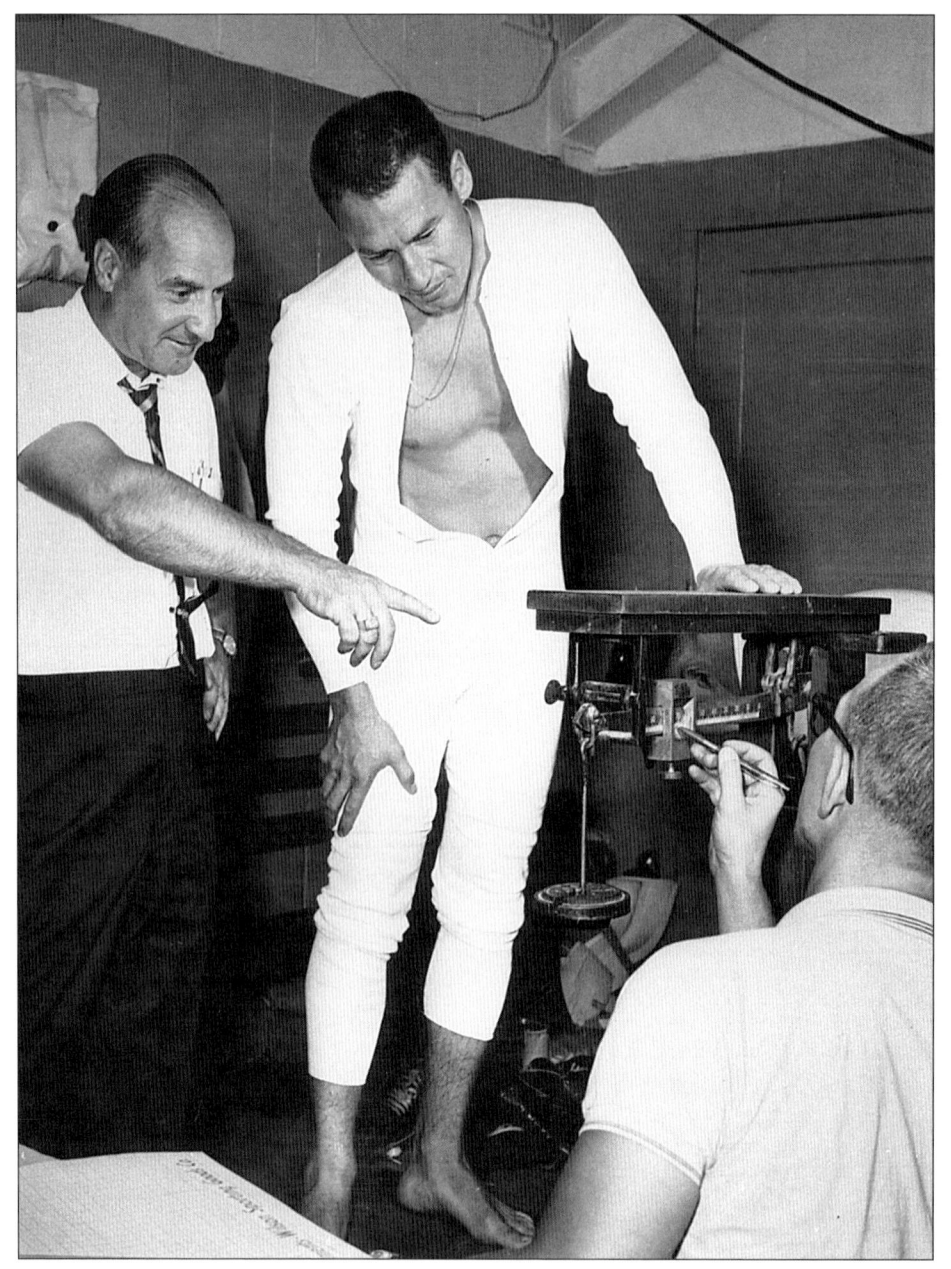

Ex-Teepee Pierre Pilote steps on the scales for Chicago Black Hawks coach Billy Reay (left) in September of 1964.

St. Catharines Museum - *Standard Collection N 5703*

ERRORS AND OMISSIONS

Truth can be a tentative thing. Although every effort has been made to make sure that names, facts and figures in this book are complete and accurate, there are bound to be mistakes and omissions.

Identifying players and spelling names correctly after many years have passed has been a challenging job. I apologize in advance to anyone whose name has been misspelled. Some scans of old programs and papers contain spelling and grammar errors that have been left in their original form.

It is important to note that there is no one official source of statistics for the 34 junior teams covered in this book.

Several photos in the book are not of the highest quality because they were very old or in poor condition. We decided to include them because they helped to identify individuals and various aspects of the history of Junior A hockey in the Garden City.

From 1943 to 1947, when the St. Catharines Falcons played in the Garden City, detailed records were not always available. For example, every game summary in the *St. Catharines Standard* for the 1943-44 Falcons had to be examined on microfilm in order to find the season's wins, losses and ties, along with the scoring totals for each player on the team. To make it even more frustrating, sometimes the summaries were not complete, and different sources like *the Globe and Mail* didn't always agree on statistical information from the *Standard*. The only official OHA Junior A stats in the Falcons era could be found in Jack Gatecliff's records for 1945-46. Gatecliff had written to the OHA for detailed info on this time period and what he got was some information on 1946-47; he was told there were no official records.

From 1947 to 1977, there was statistical information available, mainly from the *St. Catharines Standard* and Gord Jennings who is known as Mr. Teepee. *St. Catharines Standard* stats were used whenever they were available over any other sources. The calculation of some of the goals-against averages for some St. Catharines netminders is in question.

A great deal of information on stats, players and team personnel came from *St. Catharines Standard* columns written by Clayton Browne and Jack Gatecliff. Gatecliff's records were donated to the St. Catharines Museum.

After Gatecliff was hired by the *Standard* in 1947, he pasted every St. Catharines Junior A game summary for the regular-season and playoff games into a small notebook. He did this for every year from 1947-48 to 1976-77. Unfortunately, the scoring and goalie records for some of these seasons were not available. The St. Catharines Museum has these notebooks.

The OHA Major Junior A League didn't produce detailed records until it started to publish its annual yearbook in the 1974-75 season.

NHL statistics for former St. Catharines Junior A players came from *Total Hockey: The Official Encyclopedia of the NHL,* and *Players*, a book written by Andrew Podnieks. St. Catharines Museum volunteer Mike Smith prepared a list of former St. Catharines Junior A players who made it to the World Hockey Association from 1972 to 1979.

Paid attendance figures for 1943 to 1973 were taken from the actual attendance record book that was kept at Garden City Arena. The book also detailed revenue earned from each home game and how it was divided between the arena and the team. There were some differences and omissions in this book when compared to newspaper game dates and summaries.

After 1973 the attendance figures were taken from game summaries in the *St. Catharines Standard* and it was assumed these were gross attendance numbers and not paid figures because several games allowed free entry for specific groups and individuals, especially on promotional evenings. The bottom line is that theses attendance figures are probably as close to the exact numbers as we will ever get.

Every effort has been made to credit material which is used in this book. If you find any errors or omissions, please forward your information to jchewitt@sympatico.ca. Corrections and new information will be included in subsequent editions of this book.

Thank you in advance for helping to put together what we hope will be the most accurate record of major junior hockey in St. Catharines up to 1977.

THANK YOU

The publication of this book would not have been possible without the generous help and co-operation of many people. I have tried to include everyone to whom I am indebted, but if I have missed anyone, I apologize in advance.

First of all, I thank St. Catharines Museum Curator of Collections, Arden Phair, for planting the idea of a book on junior hockey in my head and then reminding me regularly that I should get started. On September 3, 2003, I began my research and Arden became a strong supporter. The Museum archives provided the foundation of my research material.

I first met Stan Lapinski at the St. Catharines Museum where we were both volunteers in the Collections department. After I began writing the book, I started to come to Stan with questions on just about everything. I could never have started or finished this project without Stan's assistance. He was always there with wise advice that only an experienced author and editor could supply. One of the most thoughtful things Stan did was to introduce me to Sheila Kennedy.

Sheila Kennedy is the talented graphic artist who is responsible for the design of *Garden City Hockey Heroes*. Sheila has the extraordinary ability to take raw data and present it in an attractive and appealing manner. She showed me that anything is possible. All I had to do was ask. Thank you Sheila for everything.

One of the kindest things Sheila Kennedy did for me was to introduce me to her friend Candy Hillier. Candy agreed to be my proofreader and I am indebted to her for helping to correct and polish the text.

I am deeply indebted to Andrea Kriluck, the managing editor of the *St. Catharines Standard,* for granting permission to use *Standard* pictures and 267 negatives that were scanned for the book.

Special thanks goes out to former *St. Catharines Standard* sports editors Clayton Browne and Jack Gatecliff.

Many photographs and documents in the book came from the archives of former Hawks owner Fred Muller. Janine Muller, Fred's widow, donated his hockey material to the St. Catharines Museum. Thank you Janine for your support and generosity.

I would also like to express my gratitude to:
St. Catharines Standard Photographers, Don Sinclair, Mike Conley and Denis Cahill (former keeper of the negs). Special thanks to Denis who guided me to the various locations of the *Standard* negatives.

Other Photograpers:
Don Foley, Stan Lapinski, Arden Phair, Jimmy Simpson, Bert Titley, Ron Roels

Scanner and technical expert: Dennis Munn

St. Catharines Museum staff and volunteers:
Arden Phair, Anthony Percival, Brent Smith, Grace Ostrihon, Karen Cockerham, Megan Gilchrist, Rosemary Harper, Mike Smith, Stan Lapinski, Rosetta Bishop, Margaret Ferguson, Cathy Teshima

Terry O'Malley's support for the 2004 Junior A reunion and this book have helped to make a dream come true.

The painting, *The Pride is Back!* by George Upper is included in the book. The painting, another one of George's masterpieces, became the focal point of the reunion, and sales of the prints helped to finance two special St. Catharines Junior A events in 2004. The original piece of art now has a home at the St. Catharines Museum at Lock 3 of the Welland Canal.

To help raise funds to finance the graphic design of this book I am indebted to Walt Marsh, who used his charm to convince friends and local businesses to support this project. Everybody who knows Walt realizes how much he has contributed in helping to raise funds for many projects in the Garden City.

Special thanks goes out to Archie Katzman who introduced me to Bob Gale. Bob's financial and moral support are greatly appreciated.

Marcel Dionne wrote the foreward for this book and for that I will be eternally grateful. He's a Hockey Hall of Famer with a big heart.

The following people, organizations and companies have given permission to use copyrighted material and/or donated (or loaned) photos, scrapbooks and memorabilia to the St. Catharines Museum or to me personally:

Shirley Angood
Bill Argent
Eddie Barber
The Barrie Examiner
Joan Bigger
John and Helen Brown
Larry Brooks
Wayne Brown
Wilma Brown
Mrs. William Brown
Bill Buschlen
Pete Cameron
Bill Cheropita
Bob Cornelius
Bob Corupe
Don Cosburn
Mario Cupido
Brian Cullen
Norm Defelice
Lino Delmonte

Val DeLory
E.A. Donegan
Porky Douglas
Al Dunn
East Coast Hockey League
Marv Edwards
Lillian Elvins
Bob Ewer
Doug Favell Jr.
Mary Frado
Whitey Frick
David Fujiwara
Kay Fujiwara
Bill Gallaway
Tommy Garriock
Alice Gatecliff
Jack Gatecliff
Dave Gorman
Nick Grammar
Max Hansen

THANK YOU

Brian Heit	Don MacLean	Laurie Peterson	Jim Stirrett
Marcella Heit	Bob Manno	Mark Plantery	Wanda Swan
Gordon Helmkay	Frank Martin	Lou Polgrabia	Skeeter Teal
Jack Higgins	Betty Maxwell	Ron Quenneville	Cathy Teshima
The Hockey News	Dean McBride	David Reppen	TRW Canada
Bob Hookings	Dale McCourt	Lorraine Robazza	Thompson Products-Friendly Forum
George Hulme	Brian McDonald	Stu Roberts	Jim Thorpe
Wendy Hyndman	Randy McIntyre	Jim and Shirley Robertson	Jerry Toppazzini
Neal Jackson	Rick McIntyre	Marion Romanowsky	Bob Twaddle
Jeff Jacques	Helen McKenna	Bonnie Saveall	Eric Unger
Edith Joy	Don McLean	Doris Smelle	Harry and Myrna Watson
Jimmy Joy Jr.	Doug McMurdy	Tom Smelle	Ralph Willis
Jon Jouppien	McSloy Estate	Bill Smith	Mary Jane Wilks
Bill Kadotsky	Lionel Middleton	Monica Smith	
Joe Kastelic	Frank Milne	Ron Smith	
Archie Katzman	Paul Moore	Society for International Hockey Research	Computer and typing help:
Al Kellogg	Ashton Morrison Estate	Donna Speer	Erin Hewitt
Pat Kelly	Betty Myles	Fred Stanfield	Lee Hewitt
Kevin Kennery	Henry Nicowski	George Stauffer	Carole Hewitt
Frank Long	Ellard Obie O'Brien	Cheryl Steele	Karen Cockerham
Ted Lott	John O'Flaherty	Rex Stimers	
Fred MacKenzie	Terry O'Malley		

Through good and sometimes trying times, my wife Carole was always there. When my computer acted up and whenever I needed copies of the manuscript in a hurry, she always came to my rescue.

Thank you Carole.

THE END

INDEX

Adair, Pat 83, 84

Adams, Mayor Roy 184, 187

Adams, Weston 46, 48, 57

Adduono, Rick 165-169, 171, 173, 174, 176, 204, 206, 207, 211, 217

Aitken, George 201

Aldcorn, Gary 76

Altoft, Bill 45, 47, 126

Alway, Andy 185, 186

Ambridge, Dale 173

Anderson, Brian 185, 186

Anderson, Ron 137, 139

Andreatta, Jerry 155

Andrews, Jack 201

Argent, Harry 137, 145, 146, 149, 151, 155, 201

Armstrong, Jack 67, 69, 70, 201

Auger, Vic 25, 27, 201

Black, Gord 162

Bald, Mayor Wilfred 103

Balfour, Murray 107, 108

Ballanger, Mike 155

Ballard, Harold 14

Banich, Frankie 67

Barber, Eddie 18

Barlow, Hugh 63, 67, 68, 70, 76, 167, 207

Bassett, John Jr. 174

Bauer, Father David 108, 109

Bayes, Ritchie 131, 133-135

Bayne, Dean 145

Beaupit, Bruce 131, 201

Beaupit, Howie 145, 151, 155

Bell Ringers, Helen And John Brown 121, 197

Bennett, Billy 83

Berge, Peter 99

Berish, Dennis 109

Best, Bill 160

Binns, Jerry 201

Bird, Bill 134, 167, 168

Bird, George 127

Blair, Danny 162

Blake, Toe 13

Bloom, Mike 116, 151, 155, 158, 159, 161-163

Bodnar, Ernie 51

Bodnar, Gus 105, 131

Bond, Kerry 131, 133, 134

Boone, Carl (Buddy) 49, 53, 54, 56, 59-62, 201

Boyd, Mike 185, 186

Breitenbach, Ken 167, 171, 173, 175, 176

Brenchley, Edgar (Chirp) 128, 131, 132, 201, 207

Brenneman, John 99, 106, 107, 109, 113, 119, 120, 199, 207, 217

Briscall, Wayne 173

Brown, Wayne (Weiner) 45, 47, 49-54, 56, 57, 199, 207

Browne, Clayton 15, 22, 29, 37, 50, 59, 182, 219

Brunshaw, Carl 45

Buck, Tom 36-38, 45, 126, 182, 201

Bulloch, Nelson 67, 75

Burgess, Don 137

Burke, Bill 194

Burke, Denise 194

Burnett, Bill 59, 99

Burns, Larry 99

Burrows, Dave 8, 145, 146

Burtnik, Mel 197

Bury, Ed 27

Buschlen, Bill 29, 33, 36-39, 45, 47, 84, 126, 182

Bush, Eddie 78

Butler, Rob (Bob) 75, 79

Byers, Gord 45, 46, 201, 207

Caines, Doug 173, 174, 176, 177, 179-181

Callahan, Barry 177

Cammarata, Tony 137, 201

Campbell, Brian 158

Campbell, Don 33, 45, 46, 49

Campbell, Gary 140

Campbell, Greg 140

Campbell, Ken 6, 7, 109, 110, 112, 113, 116, 117, 119, 120, 122, 123, 126, 127, 129, 131-133, 137, 139, 141, 146, 147, 161, 177, 201, 207, 215

Carpenter, Rick 145

Carr, Donnie 85

Carson, Bill 128

Carter, Don 79, 82, 84

Casey, Terry 163, 167, 171

Channell, Bob 148

Cheevers, Gerry 32, 101, 107, 108, 217

Cheevers, Joe 122

Cherevaty, Mickey 127

Cheropita, Bill 147, 162, 163, 165, 167, 169, 171-176

Cherry, Don 57, 62, 192

Chown, Mayor Mac 154, 161

Choyce, John 7, 126

Chrysler, Wayne 165

Cibik, Bernie 142, 143

Cibik, Brian 99

Cibik, Ricky 99

Cickello, Glenn 155

Ciesla, Henry (Hank) 23, 32, 59, 61, 63, 67, 68, 75-78, 201, 204, 206, 207, 211, 217

Clements, Marcel 45, 47, 201

Coetzee, Ernie 192

Conacher, Charlie 22

Contini, Joe 183, 185-187, 191, 213

Conway, Ross 168

Cooke, Lorne 93

Corcoran, Norm 49, 50, 51

Cornelius, Bob 4, 196

Corupe, Bob 83, 84, 86, 88, 94

Cosburn, Don 83, 87

Cotton, Harold (Baldy) 48, 57

Coulis, Tim 185, 187

Cousineau, Brian 161, 162, 165, 201

Craig, Bob 173

Craig, Greg 164, 167, 170, 171, 173, 176-181, 199, 207

Crichton, Glen 151

Croft, Ken 126

INDEX

Crooks, Art 121

Crosbie, Peter 155, 162

Crowe, Gladys 116, 142, 143, 163, 171, 178, 184, 201

Crozier, Roger 34, 99, 100, 105, 109-111, 119, 122, 201

Cullen, Barry 67-70, 75-78, 167, 198, 206, 207

Cullen, Bob 183, 198

Cullen, Brian 4, 7, 23, 34, 58-61, 63-65, 67-70, 72-74, 77, 92, 103, 112, 156, 166, 167, 178, 182, 192, 196, 197, 199, 204, 206, 207, 211, 217

Cullen, Ray 94, 97, 99-102, 105-107, 109, 111-113, 206, 207

Culligan, Andy 131

Cunningham, Garry 145, 146, 151

Cupido, Mario 185, 186, 188, 190

Cupido, Ron 184-186, 201

Cupolo, Steve 173, 177, 180

Currie, C. 29

Cushenan, Ian 63, 67, 70, 192, 197, 198

Davidson, Bill 36

Davison, Jack 132, 133, 140

Dawdy, Jim 21, 25-27, 126, 201

Dawe, Dr. Frank 201

Day, Rodger 75, 79, 201

Dearing, Rhoda (Ma) 20

Defelice, Norm 13, 63, 65, 217

DeJordy, Denis 89, 92, 95-97, 100

Delmonte, Armand (Dutch) 15, 18, 21-24, 201

DeLory, Val 26, 27, 197

Desbiens, Brian 118

Devine, Jack 149

Dionne, Marcel 5, 8, 28, 116, 144-146, 148, 149, 151, 153-159, 166, 170, 182, 190, 192, 193, 199, 204, 206-210, 215, 217

Dionne, Ron 155

Diotte, Gene 83

Doherty, Frank 153, 168, 169

Donnelly, Dr. Andy 167

Douglas, George (Porky) 33, 45, 46, 49, 126, 182

Douglas, Jim 141

Draper, Dave 185, 186

Dudley, Rick 8, 145, 150

Duff, Dick 68, 192, 196, 197

Dumesnil, Mark 167

Dyck, Dr. H. 145, 151, 155, 167

Dynes, Bill 185, 186, 201

Eagleson, Al 168, 182

Eatough, Gary 79

Edmands, Karl 147, 167, 173, 177

Edur, Andy 173, 176, 177, 181

Edwards, Mark 167

Edwards, Marv 10, 11, 34, 53, 57, 59-61, 63-68, 70, 74-76, 78, 84, 192, 197, 215,

Edwards, Roy 79, 83, 87, 201

Egerter, Ken 162

Ego, Wayne 145

Eichler, Ross 128, 129, 199, 207

Elliott, Stan 51

Ellis, Bill 151

Emms, Leighton (Hap) 57, 62, 65, 96, 113, 117, 122, 150, 163, 165, 167, 171-175, 177-179, 182, 186, 189, 190

Emms, Paul 165-168, 170, 171, 173, 175, 177-179, 204, 207

Emms, Suzanne 166

Esposito, Phil 7, 34, 50, 101, 109-111, 113, 190, 208-210, 215

Evans, Walter (Buddy) 36, 45, 47

Ewer, Bobby 83

Ezinicki, Bill 19

Farenzena, Chi-Chi 109, 113

Fauteux, Ted 186

Favell, Doug 108, 118, 119, 122, 172, 217

Favell, Doug Sr. 122

Feasby, Hugh 112, 113, 119

Fegan, Art 109

Ferguson, John 14

Finck, Larry 167

Finochio, Joe 185, 186

Fiorentino, Mark 173, 177

Fisher, John 137, 141, 142, 143

Foley, Gerry 59, 61, 62

Forbes, Mike 185-188, 190, 199, 211, 213

Ford, Peter 109

Forester, Bob 137

Fortier, Dave 155, 156, 158

Franceschetti, Lou 180

Franklin, Mayor John 61

Frick, Bill (Whitey) 29, 30

Froese, Bob 173, 177, 180, 181

Gage, Jody 185, 186, 190

Gagne, Pierre 99

Gale, Bob 4, 194

Garriock, Tommy 5, 7, 42, 43, 134, 178

Gartner, Mike 181

Gatecliff, Jack 3, 5, 7, 14, 15-17, 21, 22, 26, 28, 33, 34, 42, 43, 46, 50, 53, 61, 95, 97, 98, 103, 116, 120, 126, 134, 142, 143, 149, 156, 167, 169, 171, 173, 174, 177, 178, 188, 192-194, 201, 208, 215, 219

Gendron, Guy 83

Gervais, Councillor Charles 193

Giannini, Dennis 145, 148, 149, 151, 152

Gibbons, Larry 137, 143

Gibbons, Wayne 95

Goegan, Fiori (Fiery) 29, 38, 40, 201, 207

Gold, Dr. Al 167, 185

Goldham, Bob 90

Gorman, Dave 106, 160-165, 167-171, 206-208, 210, 211, 217

Goss, Bob 145

Gottselig, Johnny 81

Gould, Orrin 53, 54, 59, 61

Graham, Art 118

Grammar, Pete 15, 16, 201, 211

Grant, Joe 173, 176

Graves, E.J. (Ted) 15, 16, 21, 31, 201, 211

Graves, Oswin 15, 16, 201

Greco, Ben 99, 201

Green, Dave 123

Greenen, Roy 75, 79, 201

Greenwood, Dr. Alan 201

Groh, Bob 122-124, 127, 128

Grosso, Don 83, 95, 96, 99

INDEX

Gruhl, Cecil 36, 37, 38, 201

Guite, Pierre 8, 116, 151, 153, 155, 161, 210

Haas, Willard (Bill) 59, 61, 63, 64, 65, 66

Hadfield, Vic 99-101

Hall, Dennis 119

Hall, Murray 99, 105-107

Hallett, Doran 201

Hamilton, Bill 167, 169, 173-178, 181

Hamilton Forum 97

Hampton, Rick 165, 167, 168, 171, 172, 207

Hanlon, Trace 192, 196

Hannah, Dr. Bob 155

Hansen, Max 155, 160, 164

Harris, Duke 99, 102, 105, 110, 112

Haunn, Max 25, 27, 29

Hazlett, Steve 185, 186, 189, 211

Heit, Thomas 15, 16, 201, 211

Hendrick, Larry 156

Henry, Bill 109, 110, 112, 113, 116, 119, 120, 125, 127

Hewitt, John 196

Higgins, Jack 34, 67, 73, 74, 192, 197

Hildebrand, Fred 36, 37, 39, 45, 47

Hilderbrand, Ike 26

Hill, Bob 167

Hill, Ozzie 142, 143, 201

Hillman, Wayne 79, 83, 89, 93, 95, 96, 100, 107, 201, 207

Hilts, Fred 95-97

Hockey Hall Of Fame 3, 14, 23, 27, 28, 95, 97, 108, 113, 150, 157, 159, 181

Hockey Homecoming, The Pride Is Back 192

Hodge, Charlie 65

Hodge, Ken 109, 110, 119, 123-125, 127-129, 204, 206, 207, 217

Hoekstra, Cec 67, 68, 74, 75, 78, 92, 192, 197

Hoekstra, Ed 75, 79, 82, 83, 86, 88, 89, 92, 93, 207

Hoffman, Abigail 81

Holmes, Larry 131, 135, 137

Honsberger, Dave 177

Hookings, Bob 18, 21, 201

Hookings, Peter 171, 177, 181

Horton, Jim 119, 122

Houle, Denis 185, 186, 190, 199, 211, 213

Houston, Doug 36

Houston, Dr. David 201

Hubbard, Pete 75

Huber, Willie 185-187, 190, 191, 217

Hughes, Brent 109-111

Hull, Bobby 5, 7, 34, 47, 50, 79, 80, 83-87, 89, 106, 107, 121, 149, 190, 208-210, 215, 217

Hull, Dennis 28, 106, 109, 119, 123, 125

Hulme, George 11, 145, 147, 151, 153, 155-158

Iggulden, Brian 173, 177

Irvin, Dick 213

Irwin, Glen 152

Ivan, Tommy 75, 79, 89, 105, 113, 140

Ives, Bill 99, 102, 107, 109

Jackson, Art 33, 36, 37, 45, 49, 52, 53, 55, 201, 207, 215

Jackson, Neal 17-19, 198

Jacobs, Tim 151, 155, 161-163

Jacques, Jeff 155, 161-163, 165, 166, 199, 207

Jacques, Larry 217

Jarrett, Doug 109, 111, 113, 123-125

Jarry, Pierre 142

Jensen, Al 185-188, 190, 191

Jessiman, Harvey 15, 17, 18, 20-21, 22, 24, 198, 199, 207, 211

Johnston, Jay 185, 186, 190, 191

Joy, Jimmy 17, 50, 53, 59, 63, 67, 73, 74, 79, 83, 99, 102, 114, 118, 126, 201, 211

Juckes, Winston (Bing) 15, 18-20, 201

Kafun, Vic 201

Kamin, Howard 112, 113

Kaminsky, Max (Teepee coach) 98-103, 105, 106, 112, 124, 182

Kaminsky, Max (Black Hawk owner) 113

Kamula, Peter 63

Kastelic, Joe 63-65

Katzman, Archie 28, 50, 126, 178, 182, 192, 197

Keating, Mike 185, 186, 191, 207, 211, 213, 217

Kellogg, Al 33, 59, 63, 76, 79, 126

Kellough, Howard 105, 106

Kelly, Chuck 124

Kelly, Pat 11, 64, 75-77, 79, 81, 84, 147

Kelly, Red 23

Kennedy, Sheila A. 197

Kennery, Kevin 167, 168, 171, 173, 174, 177, 178, 180, 181

Keough, Jim 119, 122, 128

Knowles, Bob 45

Kodatsky, Bill 36, 39, 40, 41

Korab, Jerry 137, 138, 141-143

Kostandoff, Jerry 34

Koval, Peter 67, 192, 197

Krahulec, Joe 36, 38, 40, 201

L'Abbe, Maurice (Moe) 131, 137, 139, 141, 142, 143

Labreche, Don 167, 170

Lachowich, Rick 109

Lafleur, Guy 8, 124, 157, 159

Lafontaine, Richard 79

Laidlaw, Ken 119, 131, 133-135, 201

Lamourie, Ken 75

Lancaster, Edward 201

Landon, Larry 180

Lariviere, Garry 162, 163, 165, 167, 168, 171

Larocque, John 177, 178

Latinovich, Steve 131, 137, 139, 140

Leach, Jack 15, 16, 22, 50, 112, 201

LeBlanc, Jean-Paul 137-139

Lepp, Linda 146

Leslie, Alex 63, 64

Lever, Norm 112, 113

Linder, Cec 43

Lindros, Carl 129

Lindsay, Anne 121

Lis, Ted 173

Litzen, Fred 155

Lomer, Gord 53

Long, Bill 122

Long, Frank 17, 18, 20, 198, 211

INDEX

Long, Peter 17, 18, 19, 201, 211

Longarini, Carlo 99, 100, 102

Lott, Ted 48

Ludzik, Steve 192

MacDonald, Francis 29

MacDonald, Jay 9, 13, 15, 17, 43, 63, 67, 79, 80, 81, 99, 201, 216

Macdonald, Mayor Dr. W.J. 19, 25

MacGuigan, Bob 160, 164, 165

MacIntosh, Matthew 201

MacMillan, Bob 8, 116, 155, 158, 159, 161, 162, 207

MacMillan, Garry 127, 128, 131, 135, 201

Mahovlich, Frank 204, 215

Maki, Bob 99, 103

Maki, Ron (Chico) 34, 50, 83, 89, 95, 97, 99, 100, 101, 102, 107, 113, 204, 206, 207

Maki, Wayne 127, 128, 129, 201

Malton And Hamilton 192

Mann, Ken (Chic) 29, 32, 201

Manno, Bob 173, 175-179, 181, 217

Manoian, Dr. Archie 116, 137, 143, 145, 146, 147, 151, 185

Mara, Peter 137, 138, 141, 142

Markarian, Ralph 51

Marsh, Walt 102, 192

Marshall, Charlie 53, 54, 55, 59, 61, 63, 64

Martin, Frank 11, 17, 32, 51, 53, 54, 56, 59-62, 207, 211, 217

Martyn, Ken 173, 175

Mateka, Edward 63, 201

Matthews, Jim 117

Maxwell, Bob 63, 74, 78, 201

Maxwell, Jim 36-38

Maybee, Archie 84

McAdam, Gary 167, 170, 173, 175, 176

McBratney, Brian 155

McBride, Dean 18, 20-23, 25, 32, 126, 201

McClelland, Ivan 36

McCloskey, Kevin 177

McCollum, Walt 167, 201

McComb, Don 201

McCourt, Dale 23, 183-190, 192, 193, 199, 204, 207, 211, 213, 215, 217

McCulloch, Don 145, 146, 151

McDermott, Gary 83

McDonald, Alvin (Ab) 75, 79-81, 107, 198

McDonald, Brian 116, 123-125, 127-129

McDonald, Wilfred (Bucko) 213

McDonough, Al 142, 143, 145, 148, 151-153, 207

McDowall, Dave 141, 143, 145, 146

McDuffe, Peter 131, 133, 137-139, 141, 142, 206

McGuire, Terry 89, 99, 100

McIntyre, John (Jack) 36, 38, 41, 45, 49, 51, 201, 207

McIntyre, Larry 167, 170

McKay, Dr. Bob 192

McKenny, Brian 133, 207

McKenzie, Brian 145, 151, 154-157

McKenzie, Johnny 83, 86, 87, 89-93, 99, 204, 217, 201

McKey, Fran 151, 152

McLean, Don 69, 74, 84

McLelland, Ivan 37, 40

McMahon, Bob 145, 146, 151, 155-158

McMullan, Mayor Brian 194

McMurdy, Doug 15, 17, 18, 21-23, 192, 193, 198, 199, 204, 211

McNamara, Gerry 67, 68

McNeil, Al 75, 76, 78, 81

McOustra, Bill 30

McTaggart, John 134

Meloni, Archie 182

Mierkalns, Rob 185

Mikita, Stan 5, 7, 23, 28, 32, 34, 43, 50, 54, 80, 82, 83-89, 92, 94, 95, 97, 100, 102, 106, 107, 121, 190, 204, 215

Miller, Red 59, 63

Milne, Andy 37, 39

Milne, Frank 7, 116, 155-157, 161, 163, 165, 166, 171, 179, 201, 204, 207

Milne, Stan 201

Milner, Ray 201

Mongeon, John 201

Moore, Francis W. (Dinty) 15

Morrison, Ashton 17, 83, 85, 142, 201

Morton, Grant 83

Mountain, Bud 185

Mullens, Doug 36, 37, 39

Muller, Fred 5-8, 34, 112, 116, 117, 125, 127, 131, 133, 134, 137, 139, 141-143, 145, 150-152, 155-159, 161, 163, 171, 172, 178, 201, 215

Mundrick, Paul 15

Murphy, Ron 201

Myles, Gord 59, 61, 201

Napier, Mark 174, 175

Newman, Jim 112, 113

Niagara IceDogs 194, 195

Nicowski, Henry 18, 20

Norris, Jim 120

O'Brien, Dennis 8, 145, 146, 149

O'Brien, Ellard (Obie) 45, 49, 50, 116, 126, 131-133, 137, 182, 192, 207, 211, 217

O'Brien, Jim 118, 119

O'Donoghue, Don 142, 145, 148, 150, 201

O'Flaherty, John (Peanuts) 131, 132, 133, 137, 139, 141, 147, 197, 207

O'Hearn, Albert 201

O'Hearn, Bibber 46, 53, 126

O'Hearn, Don (Nip) 25, 26, 29, 126

O'Malley, Terry 34, 48, 71, 190, 192

Oliver, Bill 34

Ormston, Alex 70

Orr, Bobby 123, 132, 134, 172

Orr, Dr. Robert 145, 151

Osmars, Kevin 177, 181

Ostroski, Brian 185, 186

Owchar, Dennis 166

Paiement, Wilf 164, 165, 167-169, 171, 207, 211, 217

Pallett, Keith 145, 154

Parent, Bernie 122

Park, Dr. 185

Patafie, Brian 177

INDEX

Paul, Charlie 145, 151

Pay, Dave 155, 158

Pearson, Jim 151, 153

Peppler, Bob 155, 158

Peterson, Laurie 15, 18, 20-22, 24-27, 198, 199, 206, 207

Pettie, Jim 165, 166

Phair, Arden 3, 192, 193, 196

Phillips, Nick 17-20, 198, 211

Phillips, Ron 167

Picone, Nino 185

Pilote, Pierre 7, 34, 53-55, 59, 60, 61, 64, 82, 106, 107, 121, 192, 193, 198, 206, 209, 210, 218

Pilous, Rudy 5, 9, 13-17, 19, 20, 23-25, 31, 33, 34, 47, 50, 53, 56, 57, 59, 61-63, 65, 67, 68, 70, 73, 75, 78, 79, 81, 83, 85, 87, 89, 90, 91, 98-100, 103, 105-107, 109, 112, 113, 116, 120, 121, 131, 146, 178, 192, 201, 204, 207, 211, 215

Plantery, Mark 183, 185, 186, 190, 191

Plata, Matthew (Mitch) 75, 79

Plett, Willi 173, 174

Polgrabia, Lou 133, 137, 138

Poliziani, Dan 64

Pollock, Tom 18, 20, 25, 201

Popiel, Jan 131, 132, 137

Popiel, Poul 109, 111, 119, 120, 213

Powell, Dr. Gordon 177

Power, Dale 141, 146

Power, Ted 53, 55

Predovich, Rich 99

Purser, Tom 118, 122, 124

Quenneville, Ronnie 83

Ralph, Mike 161, 162

Ramsay, Don 79

Ravlich, Matt 79, 83, 86, 88, 89, 91-93, 206

Reay, Billy 14, 120, 122, 140

Redmond, Dick 8, 145, 146, 149

Reid, Tom 131, 134, 137, 138, 198, 199

Reynolds, Emerson (Red) 13, 25, 201, 207

Richmond, Bob 201

Riddle, Pete 99

Rigby, Mayor Tim 192

Riggin, Dennis 65, 76

Robazza, Rino 83, 88, 201

Roberts, Stu 94, 119, 129, 137, 139, 140

Roberts, Wilfred (Wimpy) 64, 65, 67, 78, 201

Robertson, Bobby 27

Robertson, J. Ross 203

Robertson, Jim 51, 53-55, 62, 65

Robinson, Doug 92, 94, 99, 100, 102, 105, 107

Rolo, Joe 185

Romanowsky, Marian 20

Rombough, Doug 145, 151, 153

Ronson, Len 79, 80, 82

Ross, Art 29, 37, 46, 48, 80

Roxburgh, Jack 97, 102

Rubic, Ron 45

Running, Gary 155

Salovaara, Barry 131, 133, 135, 137, 141-143, 207

Salvian, Dave 164, 165, 167, 171-176

Sanko, Jim 109

Schinkel, Ken 63, 64

Schmalz, Clarence (Tubby) 175

Schnurr, Robert (Joe) 59, 62, 201

Scott, Bob 151

Scott, George 45, 173

Secord, Al 185, 186, 189

Seiling, Ric 185-187, 190, 199, 211, 217

Serafini, Ron 163, 166

Service, Gilbert (Wayne) 36, 37, 39, 40, 201

Shakes, Paul 151, 153, 155, 156, 158, 161-163

Shaw, Brian 6, 7, 145, 146, 147, 150, 151, 152, 154, 155, 201, 207

Shaw, Geoff 185, 186, 199

Shearer, Danny 185-187, 189, 213

Sheehan, Bobby 8, 145-150, 156

Shelton, Doug 123, 131, 132, 134, 135

Sherwood, Glen 131, 137

Shore, Eddie 19, 22, 23, 26, 41, 55, 57

Sicinski, Bob 127-129, 131, 133, 137

Simmons, Don 47, 53-55, 217

Simon, Clyde 151-155

Sinclair, Don 134

Slap Shot, The Movie 117, 169

Smelle, Carl 21, 22, 27, 32, 114, 126, 201

Smelle, Tom 21, 23-25, 27, 114, 126, 198, 206

Smith, Bob 83

Smith, Bud 51, 53, 59

Smith, Doug 192

Smith, Larry 201

Smith, Miles 201

Smith, Pat 54

Smythe, Conn 9, 29, 213

Smythe, Stafford 76, 81

Smythe, Tommy 152

Sneddon, Bob 123, 124

Snider, Don 118, 120

Sobchak, Gary 173, 199

Soloman, Les 83

Sonmor, Glen 91, 95

Speer, Bill 99, 109, 110, 112, 201

Standing, George 109-111

Stanfield, Fred 96, 109, 110, 113, 119, 120, 123-125, 192, 193, 199, 207

Stanfield, Jack 109, 110

Stanfield, Jim 131, 133, 137

Stapleton, Pat 34, 97, 99-102

Stauffer, George 13, 14, 30, 33, 34, 37, 48, 50, 55, 65, 70, 71, 73, 79, 81, 91, 92, 120, 201, 215

Steele, Jack (Pop) 63, 67, 79, 83, 99, 201

Steele, Jim 151, 201

Stevens, Gary 155, 156, 162

Stewart, Bill 177, 178, 180, 181, 201

Stewart, Brian 94

Stewart, John 152

Stimers, Rex 3, 5, 7, 30, 33, 42, 43, 46, 49, 53, 54, 61, 63, 67, 68, 69, 70, 73, 77, 78, 90, 134, 201, 214, 217

Stirrett, Jimmy 15, 16

Stocker, Stan 36, 37, 201

Stortini, Tim 177, 180

Stratton, Art 79, 80, 82

INDEX

Street, Rob 185, 186, 199

Stunt, Jeremy 192, 196

Sullivan, George (Red) 34, 36, 38, 40, 45, 46-51, 62, 199, 207

Swain, Jim 51

Swayze, Craig 70, 97, 134

Swick, Marty 167, 173

Switzer, Connie 45, 47, 49, 50, 51, 126, 182, 201, 207, 211, 215

Syvret, Dave 167, 171

Szabo, Rick 177

Taylor, Bob 53, 54, 127, 130, 131, 201

Teal, Allan (Skip) 51, 53, 57, 126, 201

Teal, Victor (Skeeter) 32, 137, 138, 140-143, 145, 147, 148, 150, 156, 199, 207

Teal, Vic 18, 29, 32, 51, 54, 57, 84, 105, 126, 182, 201, 207

Teather, Thomas 201

Telford, Ron 45, 201

Templeton, Bert 183, 185-187, 201, 207

Terbenche, Paul 128, 130, 131, 134, 135

Terry, Willie 131, 134, 135, 137

Thiel, Marc 177

Thompson, Bob 201

Thompson, Maitland 64, 75, 79, 201

Thomson, Andy 30

Thorne, Brian 151

Thorpe, Bobby 1-20, 201

Tilson, Albert (Red) 23, 204

Toppazzini, Jerry 34, 45, 47, 48

Toppazzini, Zellio 36, 37, 39, 40, 45, 201

Toyota, Frank 51, 53, 56, 201

Trojan, Bill 53

Truax, Reg 67, 70, 74, 75, 192, 197

Twaddle, Bob 26, 29, 30, 33

Udvari, Frank 54

Unger, Eric 21, 29, 31, 199, 207

Upper, George 197

Vanderburg, Scott 185

Vanderhart, Frank 201

Vasko, Elmer (Moose) 32, 43, 55, 64, 67, 74, 75, 79, 80, 82, 106, 107, 121, 201, 207

Ververgaert, Dennis 158

Viskalis, Alex 75

Vitale, Phil 105, 106, 201, 207

Walker, Vince 167, 173, 177

Walters, Hap 146

Walton, Kevin 173, 177

Wamsley, Rick 185-188, 190, 191

Warchol, Chester 67-70, 74, 75, 84, 92, 192, 197

Warecki, Stan 15, 17, 18, 19, 201

Watson, Harry 94-96, 201, 207

Welsh, Stan 18, 20, 198

Whelan, George 37

Whitby, Andy 177

White, Dennis 21, 201

White, Denny 126

White, Jack 49

Wilbur, Dan 36, 201

Willis, Ralph 43, 57

Wilson, Bob 80, 96, 105, 110, 113

Wilson, Don 173, 177, 178, 181

Wilson, J.C. (Cal) 15, 16, 21

Wilson, Ron 177-179, 181

Wilson, Ross 109, 111, 112

Woodhouse, Ron 151

Woods, Bob 29

Wright, Ted 100

Wylie, Duane 151, 152, 153

Young, Alan 145

Young, Bill 53, 54, 59, 119, 137-139, 201

Zamick, Victor (Chick) 25, 26

Zaritsky, Dr. Michael 67, 99, 201

Zaroda, Pete 151

Zizman, Ron 193

Zupan, Bob 100

AWARDS AND TROPHIES

Adams Cup 175

Allan Cup 57, 61, 65, 78, 120, 166

Art Ross Trophy 97, 159, 210

Avco Cup 14, 80, 130, 153

Calder Cup 23, 40, 51, 62, 69, 96, 70, 76, 78, 81, 107, 108, 132, 133, 138, 148, 150, 152, 153, 156, 162, 166, 178, 180, 181, 190, 191

Calder Trophy 100, 105, 107, 174, 210

Conn Smythe Trophy 100, 210

Dave Pinkney Trophy 188, 191

Eddie Powers Memorial Trophy 67, 69, 77, 85, 97, 102, 153, 159, 167, 169, 203, 204, 215

Eddie Shore Award 171

Emms Family Award 172, 187, 189

George T. Richardson Memorial Trophy 69, 101, 102, 204

Hamilton Spectator Trophy 187, 203, 211

Hap Emms Memorial Trophy 172

Hart Trophy 97, 209

J. Ross Robertson Cup 8, 69, 101, 168, 170, 203, 204, 215

Jim Mahon Memorial Trophy 169, 170

Kelly Cup 81, 166

Lady Byng Trophy 92, 97, 159, 209

Lester B. Pearson Award 113, 159, 209

Lester Patrick Trophy 97, 113, 209

Mann Cup 15, 19, 22, 26, 28, 29

Max Kaminsky Trophy 108, 110, 123, 124

Memorial Cup 13, 15, 18, 19, 22, 23, 32, 34, 37, 42, 47, 53, 57, 62, 65, 67-70, 72-78, 81, 82, 85, 88, 97, 99-103, 105, 107, 108, 110-112, 114, 117, 118, 121, 122, 128, 132, 139, 150, 155, 157, 158, 165-167, 171, 172, 182, 185-187, 189, 191-193, 196, 197, 202-205, 214, 215

Red Tilson Trophy 21, 23, 51, 69, 75, 77, 78, 85, 95, 97, 99, 102, 153, 157, 184, 192, 199, 203, 204, 211

Roger Crozier MBNA Saving Grace Award 100

Spengler Cup 170

Stanley Cup 14, 37, 55, 57, 60, 70, 78, 80, 81, 91, 92, 95-97, 100, 102, 107, 112, 113, 120, 129, 150, 186, 188, 192

Sutherland Cup 46, 202

Turner Cup 65, 82, 147, 188, 191

William Hanley Trophy 124, 184